LATE BRONZE PALESTINIAN PENDANTS

JSOT/ASOR MONOGRAPH SERIES

edited by

Eric M. Myers

Number 1

LATE BRONZE PALESTINIAN PENDANTS
Innovation in a Cosmopolitan Age

by

Patrick E. McGovern

LATE BRONZE
PALESTINIAN
PENDANTS

innovation in a cosmopolitan age

Patrick E. McGovern

Published by
JSOT Press
Department of Biblical Studies
The University of Sheffield
Sheffield S10 2TN
England

for The American Schools of Oriental Research

Printed in Great Britain
by Redwood Burn Limited
Trowbridge, Wiltshire

British Library Cataloguing in Publication Data

McGovern, P. E.
   Late bronze Palestinian pendants innovation in
   a cosmopolitan age.—(JSOT/ASOR monographs,
   ISSN 0267–5684; no. 1)
   1. Pendants (Jewellry)   2. Bronze age—
   Palestine
   I. Title   II. Series
   739.27   NK7307

   ISBN 0–905774–90–6

CONTENTS

LIST OF CHARTS

LIST OF MAPS

LIST OF FIGURES

(All shown at scale 1:1 except where specified in the text)

LIST OF PLATES

PREFACE

This study is the revised version of my doctoral dissertation, written for the Oriental Studies Department of the University of Pennsylvania. Its genesis was a detailed investigation of the pendants and beads from levels IX–VII at Beth Shan, most of which are unpublished and comprise an unparalleled collection of Late Bronze Age Palestinian jewelry. Since the Beth Shan investigation was carried out in conjunction with Dr. Frances James's thorough re-examination and publication of the site, I especially thank her for her indispensable help and encouragement. Without the innumerable discussions concerning the intricacies and often frustrating intractability of Beth Shan stratigraphy, the present study would never have been possible.

An Albright Fellowship from the American Schools of Oriental Research and a Penn-Israel Exchange Fellowship provided me with an extended period of research in the Middle East to study the important collections of jewelry in Jerusalem and Amman.

Since the approximately 350 Late Bronze Age pendants in Jerusalem's Rockefeller Museum from Tell el-'Ajjul, Megiddo, Lachish, Tell Abu Hawam, and other Palestinian sites constitute the most representative collection of excavated Late Bronze Age jewelry available, I am particularly grateful to the staff of the museum and the Department of Antiquities: A. Eitan (Director), L. Y. Rahmani, I. Pommerantz, S. Ben-Arieh, M. Dayagi, and J. Zias, who often went out of their way in helping me to locate and examine various specimens. They also enabled me to examine the equally representative collections of pendants from other archaeological periods for comparative purposes.

S. Ben-Arieh also directed my attention to a large number of other, mostly unpublished, Late Bronze Age sites with important material, including jewelry, which I was able to review at the Annex of the Department of Antiquities through the assistance of its curator, V. Sussman.

Pendants from other excavations, some quite recent and still unpublished, were also made available to me for comparative study, e.g., E. Stern (Tel Mevorakh), E. Eisenberg (Tel Kittan), G. Van Beek (Tell Jemmeh), A. Glock (Ta'anach), and the Ecole Biblique (Tell el-Far'ah North). M. Tadmor, curator of the Bronze Age collections at the Israel Museum, provided me with information on a group of unprovenanced Late Bronze Age pendants, probably from the Gaza region, now on exhibit in the museum.

Even where an excavation had produced no pendants, I was still interested in studying the pottery and small objects for dating purposes. Besides the excellent museum collection, this was especially true of the finds from two recent salvage excavations of very rich Late Bronze Age burial caves, one in the vicinity of Shechem and the other near Hebron, which C. Clamer and S. Ben-Arieh showed me at the Rockefeller Museum.

Although Transjordan has produced nowhere near the number of pendants found in Cisjordan, the Jordanian Department of Antiquities and its director, Dr. Adnan Hadidi, as well as the staffs of the Jordanian Museum and the Archaeological Museum of the University of Jordan, kindly allowed me to examine the available material, including excellent Late Bronze Age pottery collections.

A three-week period of study at the Institute of Archaeology, the British Museum, the Petrie Museum of University College, the Ashmolean, and the Fitzwilliam Museum in England enabled me to round out my firsthand examination of Late Bronze Palestinian pendants. It also gave me the opportunity to discuss various problems with J. Samson, O. Tufnell, R. Maxwell-Hyslop, and V. Hankey.

Of the many individuals who offered advice and help on various aspects of my research, Dr. Stuart Fleming, Scientific Director of the Museum Applied Science Center for Archaeology (MASCA), should be singled out for his editorial assistance and his general support of this study and the Baq'ah Valley Project. The latter site produced much-needed evidence for jewelry production and use in Transjordan. In addition to MASCA and the University Museum, the Baq'ah Valley Project has been supported by the National Geographic Society, the American Center of Oriental Research (ACOR) in Amman, the Jordanian Department of Antiquities, and the Kyle-Kelso and Jerome Levy Funds.

Other individuals who made valuable suggestions include T. Dothan, A. Ben-Tor, D. O'Connor, J. Pritchard, J. Sauer, J. Tigay, P. Vandiver, and J. Weinstein. I am very much indebted to B. Hopkins. H. Schenck, and M. Hayman for the line drawings; N. Olague E., M. Harmelin, K. Ryan, L. Reynolds, and C. West for the statistical charts; and N. Hartmann for the photographs of several Level IX pendants from Beth Shan (Pls. 3:50, 8:96, 10:135, 12:196, 15:233, 21:310–313).

I am also most grateful to Eric Meyers, First Vice President for Publications of the American Schools of Oriental Research and Editor of the recently inaugurated JSOT-ASOR Monograph Series, for accepting and expediting the publication of this study. The copy editing was capably done by M. Zeiger; and other members of Dr. Meyers' staff were most helpful.

I owe an extraordinary debt of gratitude to my wife Doris, who has helped out in many ways, not the least of which was her unflagging encouragement.

ACKNOWLEDGEMENTS

The permission to reproduce photographs and line drawings was kindly granted through the courtesy of the following:

The Oriental Institute, University of Chicago: Pls. 2:43; 5:63, 69; 8:90,95; 9:114; 18:274, 275; 22:324, 327; 23:335, 340; 25:354.

Israel Department of Antiquities and Museums: Pls. 1:3, 9, 12; 2:38; 4:61; 5:65, 66, 68, 70; 6:71, 76, 79, 82, 83; 8:93, 94, 97; 9:104, 112; 10:136, 142; 11:155; 13:209, 215; 15:244, 249, 250; 17:260–262, 265, 266; 18:270, 278, 287; 19:290, 291, 296; 20:301–303; 21:305, 306, 308; 23:337, 338; 24:351, 352; 25:356.

Miriam Tadmor, Jerusalem: Figs. 41:139; 46:189; 66:271, 272; 75:334.

Edward F. Campbell, McCormick Theological Seminary: Pl. 24:345.

Western Asiatic Section, British Museum: Figs. 6:15, 17; 12:23; 14:40; 22:61; 28:80, 81; 58:243; 61:249; 66:273; 72:309. Pls. 1:13, 16; 3:45–47, 8:91, 93; 9:98, 101, 106, 107, 109, 113; 10:141; 11:170; 12:191, 207; 13:212, 213, 217; 15:246; 16:257; 24:347, 348.

THE SYSTEM OF CLASSIFICATION AND ITS USE

The discussion of a particular pendant type can be most efficiently located in this volume by referring to the System of Classification below. There are six main classes of Late Bronze Age Palestinian pendant types: Egyptian Deities, Human Forms, Fauna, Flora, Egyptian Hieroglyphs, and Geometric Forms. Within each class, types are arranged alphabetically.

Although the main discussion of a type will be found on the pages indicated, specifics of individual specimens are given in the Catalogue. The significance of a type for the class as a whole is discussed in the Summary for each class. General historical, cultural, and technological implications are broached in Chapter 8.

When faced with the task of classifying an unpublished or newly discovered pendant, a perusal of the plates at the end of volume may help to delimit the type.

SYSTEM OF CLASSIFICATION

V. EGYPTIAN HIEROGLYPHS

VI. GEOMETRIC FORMS

Chapter 1

INTRODUCTION

Late Bronze Age Palestine[1] witnesses a remarkable *floruit* of ornamental and amuletic jewelry pendants. In marked contrast to the preceding Middle Bronze Age – and for the first time in the history and archaeology of Palestine – pendants appear in an enormous array of materials and styles; and their numbers, while not as great as those of neighboring Egypt, are considerable. As this study shows, the profusion of pendants has its basis in a series of historical events that had a profound effect on the art, technologies, religion or magic, and socioeconomic structure of Late Bronze Age Palestine.

Since pendants remain an important element of Palestinian material culture throughout the first millennium B.C., the dramatic upsurge in pendant popularity in Late Bronze Age Palestine needs to be explained. Also, as the major land bridge between Syria and Egypt, Palestine benefited from the best that both major cultures had to offer. Consequently, an assessment of the Palestinian jewelry evidence, besides being valuable in its own right, is necessary for an overall understanding of Late Bronze Age civilization and serves as a touchstone for developments in neighboring countries, such as the emergence of new stylistic motifs and technologies.

Whereas it is not unreasonable to assume that jewelry pendants were used for adornment in Late Bronze Age Palestine, their symbolic and possibly amuletic import is much more difficult to establish because of the paucity of textual evidence from Palestine itself. Even amuletic pendant types that were standard in Egypt or Syria may have been worn purely for adornment in Palestine; or, if they did serve a magical/religious function, their meaning may have been reinterpreted in a 'Palestinian sense' (see Chapter 8).

A. Present State of Pendant Scholarship

A study of Late Bronze Age Palestinian pendants[2] is justified by the lack of any comprehensive, adequately argued, and up-to-date survey of the evidence, which would provide the basis and general context for the solution of specific problems. Almost all scholarly discussion of Late Bronze Palestinian pendants to date has been confined to site reports and museum catalogues (e.g., Rowe 1936; Tufnell, Inge, and Harding 1940: 75–76), which by their very nature deal with a restricted body of material in summary fashion, furnishing a photograph and/or a drawing of the pendant and some notes on the provenience, dating, and material of the specimen. At best, additional remarks about parallel examples, manufacturing technique, religious or magical import, etc. may be included. Some of these studies are also vitiated by inadequate archaeological methodology, both typological and chronological (e.g., Macalister 1912: 449–53). Although the generally impoverished state of scholarship in this field has occasionally been relieved by a more critical study (e.g., Negbi 1970), it is fair to say that the present study is long overdue.

Other small artifacts, apart from scarabs and cylinder seals suffer from similar neglect, no doubt due to excavators' preoccupation with pottery chronology and with architecture. However, now that a sizable corpus of material has accumulated from numerous excavations, studies of some small artifacts promise to shed light on other cultural aspects that pottery and architectural studies cannot (e.g., other technologies, magic or religion). R. Maxwell-Hyslop's call (1971: 224) for a major study of Iron Age Syro-Palestinian gold and silver jewelry should be extended to other periods, artifacts, and materials.[3]

B. Methodology and Goals

Late Bronze Age Palestine is unusual for the efflorescence of jewelry pendants over a relatively short time. Indeed, although the wealth of examples might be thought to be an excavator's boon, too often it has turned into the archaeologist's nightmare when he is faced with classifying the many materials, shapes, sizes, and colors of the pendants and beads generally.[4]

Poor publication has too frequently been the inevitable outcome of this mental impasse. The extent of this problem can only be appreciated by one who has actually struggled with the excavation reports, attempting to use the often inadequate drawings, blurred photographs, and general descriptions with their confused and inconsistent terminology. Sometimes the excavator spares the student some aggravation by merely reporting that 'beads and pendants were also found.'

However, the very wealth of the material invites a sounder and more rewarding approach. Like pottery, most pendant types were mass-produced (Petrie 1898: 28–30; Samson 1972: 16, 77–84; Bruyère 1953: 52–54), and correspondingly they could pass in and out of style fairly easily. Large quantities of similar pendants should thus provide a good statistical base for typological and chronological distinctions.

On the other hand, considerable caution is demanded on the part of the researcher who is interested in establishing the archaeological and historical significance of pendants. Pendants often become treasured heirlooms or the focus of religious sentiments,[5] especially in their more durable and beautiful varieties.

Since pendants can be made in uniform, countable, recognizable, and limited numbers, they can readily be used as trading items. Their light weight and easy handling, coupled with their high value, make them a desirable form of booty from an invasion. Thus, a pendant's lifespan can be enormously lengthened and its distribution can even become world-wide. The modern museum's and collector's acquisition and 'hoarding' of beads, albeit for scientific purposes, are only the most recent examples of this ages-long activity of man.

The lasting value of pendants over large areas and timespans would appear to diminish, if not eliminate, their typological and chronological usefulness. Indeed, some rare pendant types are inadequate chronological indicators, and can only provide an approximate *terminus ante quem* for a particular locus. In the case of Late Bronze Age Palestine, however, the mass-production argument should carry the greater weight.

1. *Typology*

A major objective of this study has been to construct a chronologically-ordered typology of the major jewelry pendant classes and types for Late Bronze Age Palestine, which can be useful for archaeological dating and which can form the basis from which sound cultural conclusions may be drawn.

Various typologies have been used by previous researchers of pendants, dependent upon the culture area; historical period; and perhaps most importantly, the researcher's interpretive system. Often, the scholar's imputation of magical or religious significance to types of pendants has dictated his typology. For example, Petrie (1914: 1–4), following an out-dated theory of magic (cf. Evans-Pritchard 1965: 27–29), assigns pendants to five classes of doubtful validity: (1) similars, (2) powers, (3) property, (4) protection, and (5) gods.

Other scholars have not straight-jacketed their data quite to the extent that Petrie has done; they attempt to sort out basic classes and types of pendants with greater attention to the material itself. Thus, Bonner (1950), concentrating on a group of Egyptian pendants mainly of Hellenistic date, settles upon the following system: (1) natural objects, (2) knots, (3) demons and gods, (4) animals and parts of animals, (5) parts of the human body, (6) symbols, (7) crowns and signs of rule, and (8) funerary ornaments and furniture.

From the Mesopotamian side, Van Buren's excellent synoptic study (1945b), which combines textual and iconographic evidence with only an occasional reference to excavated pendants, divides her body of material into the following categories: (1) agricultural, (2) animals, (3) architectural, (4) bodily parts, (5) celestial bodies, (6) dress, (7) Egyptian symbols, (8) geometric designs, (9) household utensils, (10) scepters, (11) symbols of power, (12) weapons, and (13) unidentified symbols.

Further afield, it is instructive to review the typologies proposed for several detailed studies of Carthaginian pendants, dated from the seventh through the third centuries B.C. For the Punic pendants proper, Cintas (1946: 82–96) follows a tripartite schema: (1) divinities, (2) animals, and (3) miscellaneous. For both imported and local pendants, Vercoutter (1945: 266) divides his material under the headings of (1) those of a royal character (e.g., uraeus), (2) those of a divine character (e.g., the gods represented either in anthropomorphic or theriomorphic form), and (3) hieroglyphic symbols.

The categories that each researcher finally settles upon are obviously a blend of his knowledge of a wide range of topics (materials, stylistic designs, fauna, flora, religion/magic, etc.) as applied to his specific culture area.

For Late Bronze Age Palestine, the question of the precise religious or amuletic significance of jewelry pendants generally poses an insurmountable problem. Not having documentary evidence for Palestine as for Egypt and Mesopotamia, how can one determine the meaning attached to a specific pendant type by the average Palestinian peasant or his overlord? Even when the Egyptian derivation of a pendant type seems clear, there is no way to know whether the object was not 'reinterpreted' by its owner.

The el-Amarna correspondence (cf. Knudtzon 1907–1914: Letters 21, 22, and 25), the Ras Shamra texts (Pritchard 1955: 133; Driver 1956: 91), the Qatna inventories (Bottéro 1949), and the Hebrew Scriptures (especially, Exod. 13:16, 28:17–21, 39:10–14; Judg. 8:24; Ezek. 16:10–13; Isa. 3:18–24) provide a certain amount of information about jewelry and pendant types, but often the interpretation of specific terminology is in question (Maxwell-Hyslop 1971: 137; Platt 1979). Moreover, the Ras Shamra and Qatna texts can be argued to be from a different cultural sphere with limited applicability to Palestine, and the relevant biblical texts date to a later period (Fohrer 1968, *passim*). Under these circumstances, the pendant classification proposed here (see System of Classification) follows a minimalist course, avoiding 'amuletic' classes and concentrating on 'natural' forms (flora, fauna, etc.) as much as possible. However, two classes (I and V) are so obviously Egyptian-related and depictive of the same figures and symbols as those found in Egypt that the best course has been to call the object by its obvious name. Whether the latter necessarily implies some magical/religious meaning for the specific pendant type is moot.

The detailed justification for the typology proposed here is to be found in the chapters devoted to each class of pendants. As will be seen, this has been arrived at by a judicious appraisal of the textual, iconographic, and archaeological evidence from both a local Palestinian and a cross-cultural perspective. Fully three-quarters (more than 642 examples) of Late Bronze Age jewelry pendants were examined first-hand. Of these, 36 percent are unpublished (35 percent from Beth Shan) and are discussed and illustrated here for the first time. Where a personal examination was not possible, well-published drawings and photographs have been relied upon. The opportunity to examine pendants from peripheral areas in museums in Egypt, Syria, Iraq, Turkey, Cyprus, Greece, Europe, and the United States, has been important in determining the foreign relations of manufacturing techniques and stylistic conventions.

2. Chronological Criteria

The pendant typology is based on a full evaluation of the archaeological context of each specimen. This has necessitated critically examining and independently dating the associated pottery and artifacts of the loci from which the pendants come. If inadequate data

were available to date a pendant to a specific phase of the Late Bronze Age or even to the Late Bronze Age generally, it has been left out of the catalogue. This particular stricture applies to the pioneering excavations in Palestine by Macalister (1912), Bliss (1894), Petrie (1891b), and others, where because the excavations were not adequately controlled, it is nearly impossible to reconstruct the stratigraphy or the integrity of given loci (Wheeler 1954: 32; Kenyon 1979: 14). Similarly, unstratified surface finds and specimens bought on the antiquities' market, which are now in museums and private collections, together with un-published examples, generally have been excluded from the catalogue.

The logic for this procedure should be obvious: a solidly based, chronologically ordered typology must be based on reasonably well-stratified, well-excavated, and well-published loci, to provide a reliable framework for less well-controlled examples and future finds.

The various phases and subphases of the Late Bronze Age in Palestine can be approximately dated to within ±50 years, and, if the synchronisms of specific destruction levels with specific Egyptian military campaigns is correct, perhaps to within ±20 years. Possible time lags owing to regional variation in the material culture between the coast and the hill country and between Cisjordan and Transjordan must also be kept in mind.[6]

Of those Late Bronze (LB) Palestinian sites that produced pendants (Map 1), Tell el-'Ajjul and Megiddo are the most important in defining the cultural assemblages for LB I (Charts 1–3).

The start of the Late Bronze Age in Palestine is usually correlated with the campaign in which Ahmose drove out the 'Hyksos' from Egypt at the beginning of the 18th Dynasty and with a series of destruction levels at Palestinian sites (Jericho; Megiddo, Stratum X; Tell Beit Mirsim, Stratum D; Tell el-'Ajjul, Town III/Palace I; Hazor, Stratum XVI; Tell el-Far'ah North, Niveau 5; and Beth Zur; also see Wright 1965: 110–12; Yadin 1967: 260; Albright 1961: 87; Kenyon 1970–75: 528; Seger 1974: 117–30; 1975: 44*–45*).

Depending upon whether one uses a higher, middle, or lower chronology for the start of Thutmose III's reign, this event can be dated between ca. 1580 and 1545 B.C. (Hankey and Warren 1974). Moreover, because of the cultural continuum from MB III into LB I (Kenyon 1966: 76; Weinstein 1981: 6–7) and the similar artifactual assemblages for the two periods, some of the destruction layers listed above might be argued to be the result of later Egyptian campaigns (Amenhotep I, Thutmose I, or Thutmose II) or of

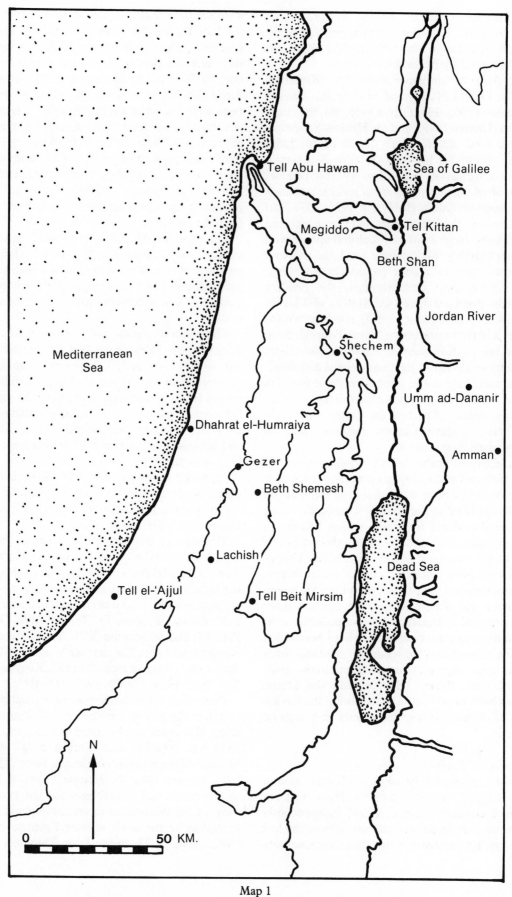

Map 1
Palestine: Distribution of Late Bronze Age Sites with Pendants

local city-state hostilities, particularly with the return of the 'Hyksos' to Palestine.

Tell el-'Ajjul provides the best evidence for destruction by Ahmose, followed by a distinct LB IA phase (Negbi 1970; Weinstein 1981: 4). Above the massive burn layer of City III/Palace I, which may constitute the 'Hyksos' bastion of Sharuhen destroyed by Ahmose after a three-year siege, a somewhat different pottery repertoire predominates in City II/Palace II. The corpus includes 'Ajjul Bichrome and Chocolate-on-White types, Cypriot Black Lustrous and White-Slipped I wares, and modified MB III forms (such as the truncated juglet), which can be used to delimit LB IA phases at other Palestinian sites. The ceramic sequences for these sites cannot be as well correlated if the higher MB III dating for City II/Palace II is followed (Kempinski 1974: 147–50; Stewart 1974: 62–63).

Megiddo presents many stratigraphic problems (Kenyon 1969: 49–50; 1979: 193–94). Foremost is the attribution of tell tombs to the stratum in which they were found rather than from which they were dug. Additionally, there was a major uprooting of parts of the temple area of Strata IX and VIII in Area BB. However, four loci and tombs in Level IX, which contained pendants, can be dated to LB IA on the basis of the associated pottery.

The dating for Stratum III of the Tel Kittan 'temple' is based on a personal examination of the pottery in the Rockefeller Museum, Jerusalem, which has been only partially published (Eisenberg 1977). A number of other tombs and loci at Megiddo, Tell el-'Ajjul, Lachish, and Umm ad-Dananir, which had pendants belonging to this phase, had to be assigned to LB I generally because of admixture with LB IB material. Some contexts had to be omitted altogether because of the impossibility of segregating MB III and LB I deposits.

Many other Palestinian sites have produced LB IA material (for example, Beth Shan, Ta'anach, Hazor, Tel Mor, Tel Nagila, Tell Zeror, Yavneh Yam, Jebel el-Jofeh el-Gharbi, Pella, Dominus Flevit in Jerusalem, Irbid). However, apparently no pendants were discovered in the LB IA contexts.

Chart 1
Site Loci and Tombs with Pendants
Dated to Late Bronze IA

Megiddo, Stratum IX
  Tomb 2009, Area CC
  Locus 2134, Area AA
  Locus 4004, Area AA
  Locus 5029, Area BB

Tel Kittan
  'Temple,' Stratum 3

Tell el-'Ajjul
  Area AN?, Town II
  Area AN 748, Town II
  Area AT 659–760, Town II
  Area EAD 877, Town II
  Area ECE 785, Town II
  Area LH⁴ 976, Palace II
  Area LK 1002, Palace II
  Area NB 995, Palace II or IIIA
  Hoard 277, Area GDF 921, Town II
  Hoard 1299, Area EAA?, Town II
  Hoard 1312, Area TV (above 910), Town II
  Hoard 1313, Area TV, Town II
  Tomb 1203, Town II
  Tomb 1740, Town II
  Tomb 1998, Town II
  Tomb 2070, Town II

Chart 2
Site Loci and Tombs with Pendants
Dated to Late Bronze I

Lachish
  Fosse Temple I, Room D

Megiddo
  Tomb 1145 B

Tell el-'Ajjul
  Area TDK 885, Town II
  Tomb 447
  Tomb 1502, '18th Dynasty' Cemetery

Umm ad-Dananir
  Burial Cave A2, Layer 2a, Locus 3

Chart 3
Site Loci and Tombs with Pendants
Dated to Late Bronze IB–IIA

Megiddo, Stratum VIII
  Locus S=2048, Area BB
  Square O 14, Area BB
  Tomb 2094, Area BB
  Tomb 3016, Area BB
  Tomb 3100, Area AA
  Tomb 5020, Area DD

Tell el-'Ajjul
  Tomb 425

The Late Bronze I period can be divided into LB IA and LB IB, on the basis of a correlation of the first campaign of Thutmose III in regnal year 23 and the destruction layer of Level IX at Megiddo (Albright 1937: 22–23; Wright 1965: 112–13, Charts 6–7; Kenyon 1979: 183), which is dated to 1482 B.C. (following Wente and Van Siclen 1976: 218, Table 1).

Again, correlations are possible with another Egyptian campaign (Thutmose III returned to Palestine 13 more times between regnal years 23 and 43) or with a local attack. In Thutmose's account of the Battle of Megiddo, no mention is made of actually destroying the town (Shea 1979), although he may well have done this in view of the serious challenge he faced from as many as 350 Asiatic princes.

Ta'anach, the one site that has a well-defined LB IB assemblage, is still largely unpublished. However, several tombs and loci at Megiddo and Tell el-'Ajjul with pendants (Chart 3) appear to have an admixture of LB IB and IIA pottery. The pottery types that can be said to characterize LB IB are less elaborate bichrome vessels, lamps with slightly inturned spouts, the earliest form of the pilgrim flask, etc.

Much more archaeological research is needed to define this phase more exactly. However, the hypothesis that Thutmose III's campaigns, together with Ahmose's invasions a century earlier, virtually depopulated Palestine is improbable (contra Kenyon 1979: 189). It would not be in Egypt's best interests to decimate a population from which it hoped to exact tribute. Since a large ethnically mixed population certainly existed in the country by LB IIA (cf. the el-Amarna correspondence), it must have arrived earlier (Kenyon 1966: 76). Certainly, the rich tomb deposits at Shechem, Gezer, Umm ad-Dananir, Qweilbeh, and Qatarat es-Samra are not what one would expect from an impoverished people. Rather, limited archaeological investigation and major architectual projects in LB II, which uprooted earlier structures, are more probably responsible for the small body of data presently available for both LB IA and IB. In addition, there may have been a population movement away from the large urban centers.

LB IIA (the 'Amarna Age,' ca. 1400–1300 B.C.) evidences a flourishing culture in Palestine. It is marked by the probable expansion of some LB I settlements (e.g., Lachish), the rebuilding of towns following destruction (Hazor), and the resettlement of previously abandoned sites (Tell Beit Mirsim) or the establishment of new sites (Tell Abu Hawam).

Trade relations among Palestine, North Syria, and Egypt were excellent throughout this period (Sasson 1966; Drower 1970–75: 506–519; Merrillees 1968:

197–202; Astour 1970; Schaeffer 1952: 141–42; Bass 1973: 29–38; Knudtzon 1907–1914: Amarna Letters 8, 226, 255, 264, 287, 295, and 316); and, despite the occasional obstruction to trade and the inevitable bickering of local Palestinian dynasts, the 'Amarna Age' was generally a very prosperous period (Several 1972; Weippert 1971: 71–74; contra Breasted 1933: 319). Perhaps their economies were spurred by the intense rivalry and competition among Palestinian city-states, along with the stimulus of new ideas and techniques introduced by the occupying forces.

The prosperity of the period is reflected in the material culture. Mycenaean IIIA: 1–2, White-Slipped II, Base-Ring II, and local Palestinian types (imitation Base-Ring, ring-based bowls, lamps with more inturned spouts than those in LB IB) clearly mark this phase.

Fosse Temple II and Tomb 216 at Lachish, which produced an excellent collection of pendants, provide representative cultural assemblages (Chart 4). Pendants also were found in loci and tombs at Dhahrat el-Humraiya, Lachish, Megiddo, Shechem, and Tell el-'Ajjul.

Chart 4
Site Loci and Tombs with Pendants Dated to Late Bronze IIA

Dhahrat el-Humraiya
  Grave 8

Lachish
  Fosse Temple II, Rooms D and E
  Pit 199, Fosse Temple II
  Pit 248, Fosse Temple II
  Pit 4019
  Tomb 216
  Tomb 502

Megiddo
  Tomb 36 B

Shechem
  Cellar under Room G, Stratum 14

Tell el-'Ajjul
  Area M0 1040, Palace IIIB
  Tomb 1037, '18th Dynasty' Cemetery
  Tomb 1064, '18th Dynasty' Cemetery
  Tomb 1073, '18th Dynasty' Cemetery
  Tomb 1080, '18th Dynasty' Cemetery
  Tomb 1085, '18th Dynasty' Cemetery
  Tomb 1663, Lower Cemetery

Other LB IIA sites, which were unsuccessfully culled for pendants, include Tell Beit Mirsim, Tell Abu Hawam, Ashdod, Tell Zeror, Dominus Flevit and Nahalat Ahim tombs (Jerusalem), Jericho, Tel Mor, Hazor, Tell el-Far'ah North, Beth Shemesh, and Tell Jerishe.

Level IX at Beth Shan, which was originally dated to Thutmose III and then later assigned to the 14th century B.C. as part of the general lowering in date of the other major strata (Albright 1938b: 76–77), is a very mixed stratum with material covering the entire Late Bronze Age (see Section C, below).

The transition to LB IIB (ca. 1300–1200 B.C.) is correlated with the campaigns of Seti I (1291–1279 B.C.) in his first three years. As before, correlations of Egyptian military expeditions (including those of Ramesses II, 1279–1212 B.C.) with specific archaeological strata can be questioned (Franken 1970–75: 333; Faulkner 1970–75: 219–20, 228–29). In general there seems little reason to question the approximate dates bracketing **the period.**

Cultural life in **Palestine continues** to flourish in this period, as reflected by the large number of pendants found at Beth Shan, Beth Shemesh, Gezer, Lachish, Megiddo, Tell Abu Hawam, Tell el-'Ajjul, and Tell Beit Mirsim (Chart 5). Fosse Temple III and Beth Shan Levels VIII–VII are typical assemblages for the period; the local and imported pottery types are comparable to those for LB IIA, but are more carelessly made. LB IIB sites, which did not produce pendants, should also be noted: 'Afula, Ashdod, Tell el-Far'ah North, Tel Mor, Tel Sippor, Tell Zeror, and Hazor.

Mixed LB II contexts with pendants (Chart 6) include the Amman Airport, Beth Shemesh, Dhahrat el-Humraiya, Lachish, Tell Abu Hawam, and Tell el-'Ajjul. Besides Level IX at Beth Shan, several contexts at Lachish, Megiddo, and Tell Beit Mirsim produced pendants, which could only be dated to the Late Bronze Age generally (Chart 7).

The transition from the Late Bronze to the Iron Age is complex, and it is often difficult to decide whether to assign a locus or tomb group to the end of Late Bronze Age or the beginning of the Iron Age.

The 'incursions' of the Sea Peoples, the Israelites, and others, coupled with the attempts of the Egyptians to maintain their sphere of influence in Palestine, obviously had serious cultural repercussions. This is reflected in the archaeological record where many sites show evidence of destruction (Lapp 1967a; Wright 1965: 114–15, Charts 7–8) and by the advent of new pottery and artifact types (e.g., the collar-rimmed storage jar, Ibrahim 1978: 117–26). However, the fact that many 'LB' types continue into the Iron Age and the probability that there are regional variants make it difficult to isolate definitive Iron IA assemblages for all of Palestine (McClellan 1979; Kenyon 1979: 207).

Chart 5
Site Loci and Tombs with Pendants
Dated to Late Bronze IIB

Beth Shan
Level VIII, Loci 1062A (below south wall), 1068C (below floor), 1068D (below steps), 1068E (below east wall), 1072C (below steps), 1092, 1108, 1287, 1292, 1300, 1301

Level VII, Loci 1068, 1068A (near steps), 1068B (north of steps), 1070, 1072, 1072A (west side), 1072B (near northwest magazine), 1085, 1086, 1087, 1089, 1104, 1107, 1251, 1255, 1262, 1263, 1284, 1359, 1362, 1365, 1366, 1382A (near wall)

Beth Shemesh
Room 73, Stratum IV

Gezer
Locus 2009.1, Field I, Stratum 5B/5A
Locus 3012.1, Field I, Stratum 5B/5A

Lachish
Fosse Temple III, Rooms D and E
Pit 118, Fosse Temple III
Pit 172, Fosse Temple III
Pit 176, Fosse Temple III
Pit 246, Fosse Temple III
Burial Cave 4004
Burial Pit 556
Burial Pit 4013
Tomb 4011

Megiddo
Locus 1834, Area CC, Stratum VII B
Locus 2039, Area AA, Stratum VII B
Locus E=2041, Area AA, Stratum VII B
Lucus 2064, Area BB, Stratum VII B
Locus 3187, Area AA, Stratum VII B
Tomb 877 A 1
Tomb 877 B 1
Tomb 912 B
Tomb 989 C 1

Tell Abu Hawam
Square C 6, Stratum V
Square D 6, Stratum V

Tell el-'Ajjul
Tomb 1095, '18th Dynasty' Cemetery

Tell Beit Mirsim
Square SE 22 C–8, Stratum C

Chart 6
Site Loci and Tombs with Pendants
Dated to Late Bronze II

Amman Airport Building
Dedicatory fill

Beth Shemesh
Near Square V 26, Stratum IVb

Dhahrat el-Humraiya
Grave 57

Lachish
100 Houses, Fosse Temple Area
Burial Cave 4002
Burial Pit 542
Tomb 216

Tell Abu Hawam
Square D 5, Stratum V
Building 53, Stratum IV

Tell el-'Ajjul
Area G 950, Town I
Tomb 1166, Northeast Fosse
Tomb 1514

Umm ad-Dananir
Burial Cave B3, Locus 3

Chart 7
Site Loci and Tombs with Pendants
Dated to Late Bronze Age

Beth Shan
Level IX, Loci 1092A (below threshold), 1092B (below floor), 1232, 1233, 1234, 1234A (east side), 1234B (south of temple), 1235, 1238, 1240, 1241, 1322, 1326, 1330, 1332, 1339, 1397, 1403

Lachish
Burial Pit 555
Fosse Temple Area

Megiddo
Square M 13, Area BB, Stratum IX or later

Tell Beit Mirsim
Square SE 23 C, Stratum C

Glueck (1951: 423) argues that the Iron Age may have arrived a full century earlier on the East Bank than in Cisjordan, thus compressing LB II to ca. 1400–1300

B.C. However, this reconstruction relies heavily upon putative biblical records for the arrival of Transjordanian peoples (Edomites, Moabites, Ammonites) prior to that of the Israelites (cf. the modified position of Lapp 1967a: 285–86).

In researching Late Bronze Age pendants, this writer has compiled an extensive catalogue of Iron I types, which shows that by the end of Iron I (approximately contemporary with the beginning of the 22nd Dynasty in Egypt), a major change in pendant types had obviously occurred. This change appears to have taken place over the preceding years (cf. Petrie 1891a: 26). It would require a separate study to document and account for these changes. However, so as not to obscure the Late Bronze Age evidence, only pendants from definite LB IIB contexts are included in the catalogue. If there is any question about a context having Iron Age material (e.g., Deir el-Balah, Deir 'Alla, Tell el-Far'ah South, 900-series tombs), pendants from that context have been omitted from the catalogue.

Parallels for Palestinian Late Bronze Age pendants have been drawn from all over the then-civilized world; but, since Egyptian parallels provide the largest body of *comparanda*, several cautionary remarks about Egyptian dating are in order, which *mutatis mutandis* apply to other culture areas as well.

Since this writer cannot claim to be equally competent in ascertaining the date of Egyptian archaeological contexts as the excavators or other specialists who have carried out detailed analyses of that material, it was often necessary to rely on their dating. All too often, even if one wanted to form an independent judgment, the necessary stratigraphic and artifactual data were lacking. Many of the Egyptian tomb groups, which furnish numerous pendant parallels, suffer from this insufficiency; and the reader should correspondingly adopt a critical stance vis-à-vis the Egyptian dates in this study.

El-Amarna, which produced the majority of parallels for Late Bronze Age Palestinian pendants, is closely dated to an approximately 20-year period toward the end of the 18th Dynasty (ca. 1350–1330 B.C.). However, a limited post-Amarna–Age occupation of the site – not well defined by the excavators – has introduced later pendant types. These can be screened out by comparisons with pendants from other 18th to 20th Dynasty sites.

The very broad dating for many of the Egyptian parallels (e.g., 18th Dynasty), apart from Amarna, detracts from any advantage that might have been gained from the fairly tight Egyptian dynastic chronology for the New Kingdom (Wente and Van Siclen 1976).

3. *Cultural Import*

Once a chronologically ordered typology has been constructed, the historical, technological, artistic, religious/magical, and socioeconomic ramifications of Late Bronze Age jewelry pendants can be meaningfully explored (Chapter 8). Since this is primarily an archaeological study, the main emphasis here has been on an analysis of the geographical, contextual, chronological, and material distributions of the pendant classes and types, and on how such distributions compare with the evidence from neighboring countries, particularly Egypt and Syria.

For example, can a specific contextual distribution of a pendant type in time and space be correlated with certain aspects of Palestinian culture: a religious or magical significance if found primarily in temples; a mark of class rank if found mainly in residential contexts; or a funereal purpose if concentrated in tombs? Since the efflorescence of pendants in the Late Bronze Age especially needs to be explained, attention is directed toward determining whether the pendants are of logical or foreign manufacture. If the latter, what are the implications for the presence of foreign artisans in Palestine, trade relations, or possibly more indirect foreign connections? If some Egyptian-related or northern-related pendants are found in Palestine, why only those and not others that are known to occur contemporaneously in those countries?

The materials from which Late Bronze Age Palestinian pendants were made have been approached with the same questions in view. Mass-production techniques using glass and faience are of particular importance here, since these industries, requiring advanced technical knowledge, were greatly expanded during the Late Bronze Age in neighboring countries. Evidence from Palestine, lying between the major industrial centers in Egypt and Syria, may help to clear up some of the problems of the origin(s), development, and foreign connections of the glass and faience industries. Other materials, such as precious metals and semiprecious stones, also suggest geographical sources and places of manufacture.

Finally, the inferences that can be drawn from the pendant evidence per se are related to ancient Near Eastern texts, which provide essential information on the historical and cultural significance of the pendants. In keeping with the archaeological character of this study, such discussion is kept to a minimum, since fundamental studies of jewelry terms are still lacking (Maxwell-Hyslop 1971: xliii). The pendant data are also related to evidence that can be gleaned from other archaeological materials (cylinder seals, scarabs, reliefs, frescos, etc.).

C. Beth Shan

Since the pendants from Beth Shan comprise 51 percent of the Late Bronze corpus, of which 69 percent are unpublished, clarification of the site's dating criteria used in this study are obviously important, pending the publication of James's Late Bronze Age volume.[7]

Beth Shan was dug during 1921–1934, when stratigraphic methods were still in their formative stages; and the excavators relied greatly upon associated Egyptian-related artifacts, especially scarabs and inscriptional evidence, in deriving the chronology of the site. However, scarabs have since been shown to be notoriously poor criteria for dating, since they were often kept as heirlooms, probably served an amuletic function, and were sometimes made many years after the reign of the particular pharaoh whom they celebrate (Horn 1962: 13, n. 86). Statuary, stelae, and other inscribed objects can also be reused in later periods, as Rowe was belatedly forced to recognize in his redating of Level V (cf. the discussion in Rowe 1930: 31–38 with 1940: 22). Although Rowe recognized his error in dating Level V, he continued to base his chronology of the site exclusively upon inscriptional evidence. The reassessment of the Iron Age levels at Beth Shan by F. James suggests that Level V was built soon after Level VI (ca. 1075 B.C.) and was finally destroyed ca. 800 B.C. (1966: 151–53).

Publication of the excavation results was also haphazard and selective. Although the temple sequence was rather fully discussed, surrounding structures, extending over the entire area of the tell, were only briefly touched upon. James (1966: 2–3) estimates that probably about half of the excavated material was published, excluding the cemetery (see Oren 1973). The pottery was partially published (FitzGerald 1930, 1935), omitting Level IX altogether, so that until recent efforts to publish the rest of the evidence were begun, Palestinian archaeologists could only make educated guesses about the approximate chronology of the Late Bronze Age sequence at Beth Shan.

This writer has been privileged to examine the unpublished pottery and artifacts from Beth Shan in the Palestinian storeroom of the University Museum, in conjunction with the original field records and diaries. A careful examination of the material – particularly the pottery – has led to the conclusion that Levels VII (Map 2) and VIII (Map 3) should be dated to LB IIB.

The Level VII dating is supported by V. Hankey's studies of the Mycenaean pottery. A preliminary examination of the Level VII Mycenaean ware has revealed that 17 out of the 19 pieces are Mycenaean IIIB/nondescript Simple Style, while another two pieces appear to be IIIA:2 (Hankey and Warren 1974).

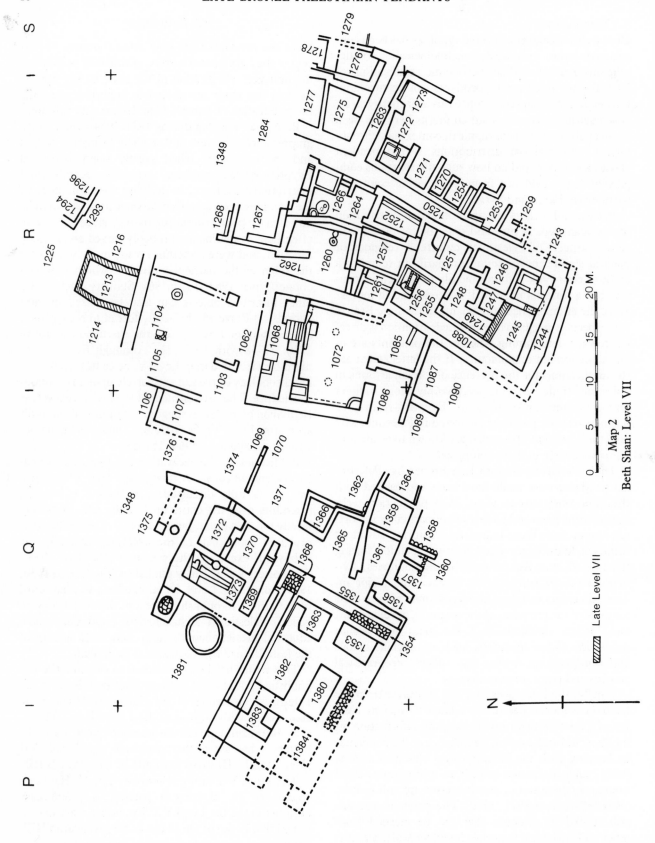

Map 2
Beth Shan: Level VII

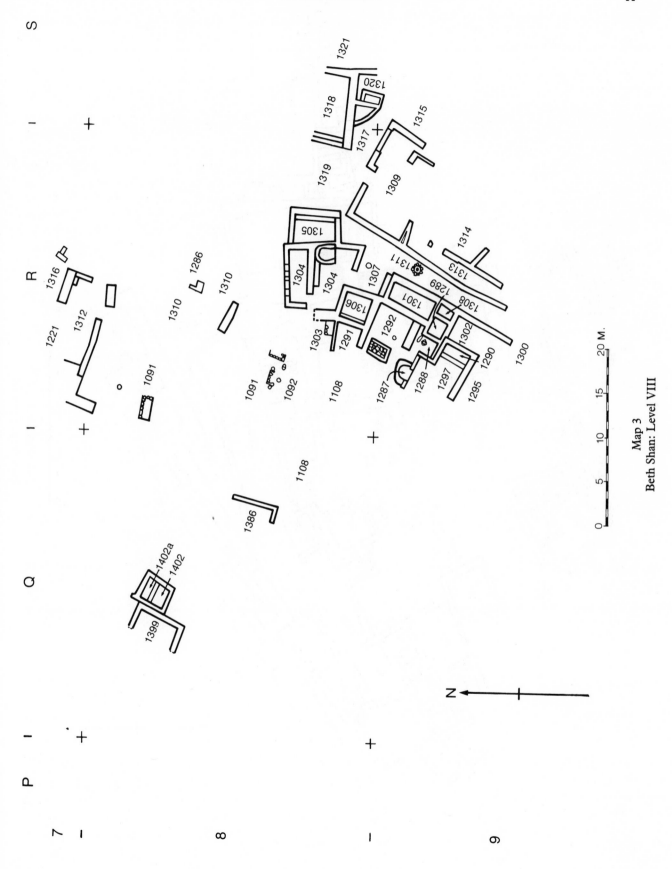

Map 3
Beth Shan: Level VIII

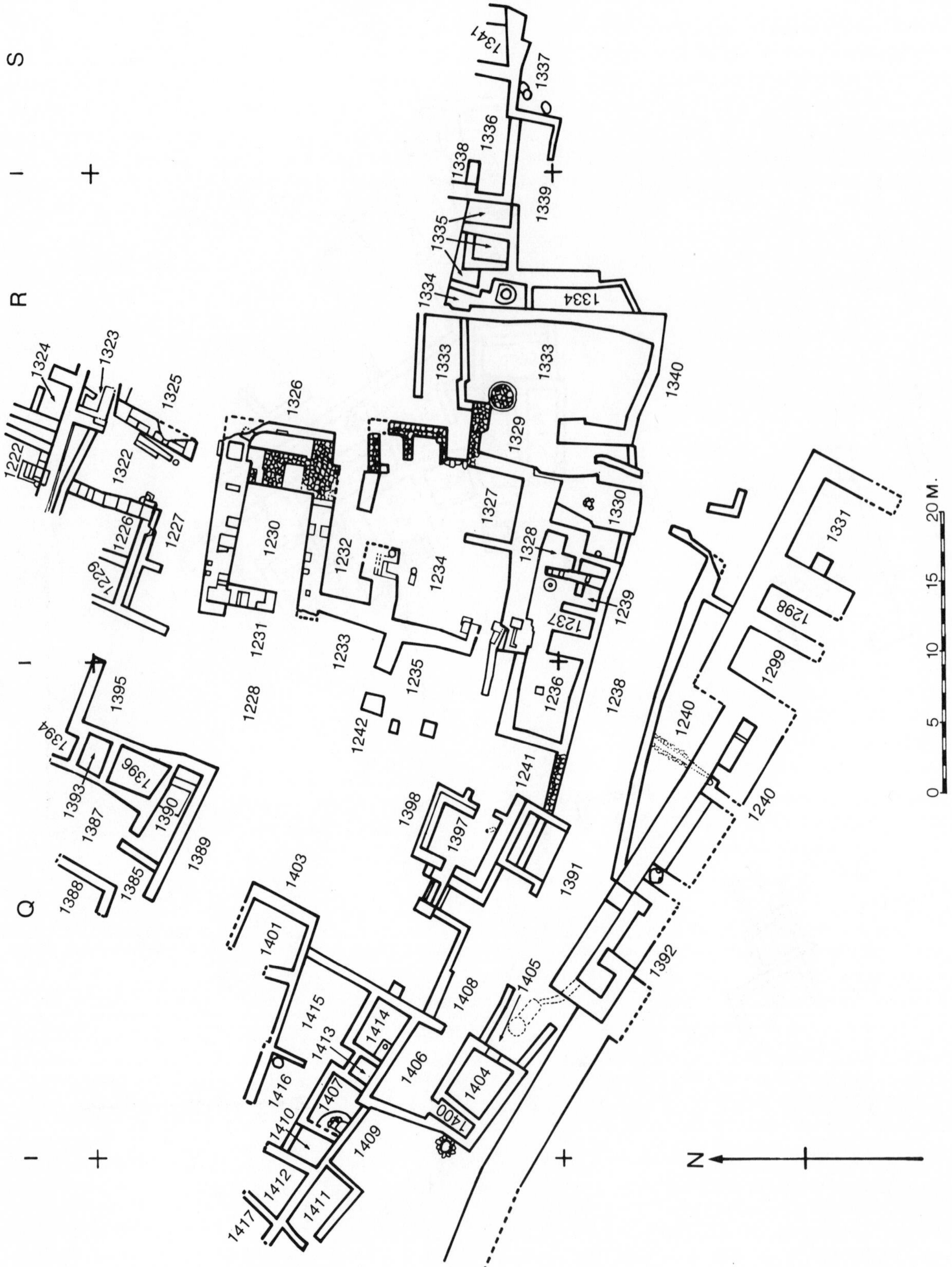

Map 4
Beth Shan: Level IX

Further confirmation of the dating is provided by Albright's critical reappraisal of the material (1938b: 77). Albright argues that the paucity of Base-Ring II ware and the presence of LB IIB painted sherds support a dating for Level VII to the reign of either Seti I or Ramesses II.[8] The latter now appears more acceptable, as a result of James's stratigraphic reworking of the material.

Level VIII, although it was preserved only in part and very little of it could be recovered, probably had the same architectural layout as Level VII. Only the southeast residential areas of the two levels are directly comparable. James argues convincingly that the empty region in the middle of the Level VIII plan, where only remnants of walls and thresholds are seen, contained earlier phases of the same structures recorded on the Level VII plan. These included the temple, the 'migdal,' and the 'commandant's house'. Thus, rather than positing a destruction of Level VIII and a subsequent rebuilding of Level VII along similar lines, she accounts for the slight architectural differences between the two levels by limited alterations and repairs. These differences are particularly evident in the southeastern residential area.

The pottery repertoires of the two levels are so close that one should be wary about placing Level VIII very much earlier than VII. In fact, if the two stelae of Seti I (Albright 1952; Rowe 1930: 29–30, pls. 42–44, fig. 6) are considered, it is clear that this pharaoh was very active in the vicinity of Beth Shan. As James contends, the initial founding of the Levels VIII/VII complex of buildings should probably be attributed to Seti I, who may have used Beth Shan as his base of operations against the highly independent and aggressive city–states nearby as well as the increasingly active tribes in the hill country. In more general chronological terms, the Level VIII phase of the temple area and the associated residential area can be dated to early LB IIB and the Level VII phase to later LB IIB.

Level IX (Map 4) presents virtually insurmountable problems as to dating. As mentioned above, pottery coming from all phases of the Late Bronze Age have been found throughout Level IX. Until now, it has been impossible to segregate closed deposits or rooms having a corpus of pottery that would provide a closer dating (James, personal communication). The scarab evidence, including four Thutmose III scarabs and one of Thutmose IV may suggest an LB IB date, as Rowe originally argued (1928: 145; independently confirmed by J. Weinstein, who is preparing the Late Bronze Age scarabs from Beth Shan for publication). W. F. Albright (1938b: 76–77) argued for an LB IIA dating for the level, but it is unclear what pottery he used to arrive at this conclusion.

Because more definitive evidence is unavailable at this time, in this study the pendants from Level IX will be dated to the Late Bronze Age generally. The pendants are found primarily in the area of the Levels VIII/VII temple; since some are identical to types found in the Level VII temple, a good case can be made for a continuity of occupation from Level IX through Level VII. Almost all of the Level IX pendants are unpublished, and some represent types rare not only for Beth Shan but for Late Bronze Age Palestine. For these reasons, it was decided to include them, with hopes that closer dating will be possible in the future.

Notes

1 The geographical limits for Palestine are difficult to establish for any historical period. Here, its boundaries are defined to include present-day Israel and the West Bank (Cisjordan), and Jordan excluding the Syrian desert (Transjordan). The available archaeological evidence for the Late Bronze Age indicates that this region should be treated as a single cultural sphere, separate from the areas of modern Lebanon, Syria, and the Sinai.

2 In this study, a pendant is understood in its etymological sense as something that hangs down. Specifically, ornamental and amuletic jewelry pendants are specialized beads of distinctive style and workmanship, perforated to be suspended from a necklace, earring, or other composite jewelry piece. In contrast to beads, pendants are typically perforated away from their center of gravity, providing greater stability when suspended. Admittedly, it is sometimes difficult to know where to draw the line between a pendant and a bead (Beck 1973: 1; Brunton and Engelbach 1927: 5), or, for that matter, between a jewelry pendant and a pendant that might have been used for some other purpose (e.g., a wall plaque).

3 Maxwell-Hyslop's survey (1971) of the vast field of gold and silver jewelry from Greater Mesopotamia and beyond has provided an excellent context in which to pursue studies of Palestinian jewelry. Tufnell and Ward's study (1966) of the Montet Jar collection well illustrates how archaeological, textual, and iconographical data can be combined to elucidate the historical setting and significance of a jewelry corpus. Other areas are poorly covered by comparison. Even the wealth of material from Egypt (Aldred 1971: 115) has not guaranteed reliable results. As Martin points out in his introduction to a recent reprinting of Petrie's corpus of Egyptian amulets (1972: xi), this unique compendium lacks a 'reasoned argument from a chronological point of view.'

4 Macalister 1912: 104. See also the remarks by Myres following Beck's definitive paper on the classification and nomenclature of beads and pendants (1973; reprint of the 1927 article).

5 Budge (1970; reprint of 1930 edition) gives a broad overview of amuletic pendants throughout history, although he heartily endorses the debatable hypothesis of the amuletic origin of the bead.

6 Cf. Merrillees' (1971) discussion of the origins of Late Cypriot IA pottery types in western Cyprus, which spread to the rest of the island during LC IB.

7 Cf. the Iron Age study (1966). Since her death, this writer has assumed responsibility for the publication of the Late Bronze Age levels (IX–VII). The memorial volume, to appear in the University Museum monograph series, will represent a final tribute to Frances James's labor of love, the 're-excavation' of Beth Shan.

8 A stela of Ramesses II for year 18, discovered in Lower Level V, describes an operation against the city–states of Hamath and Pella in the Jordan Valley (Černý 1958; Rowe 1930: 33–36, pl. 46).

Chapter 2
CLASS *I* JEWELRY PENDANTS EGYPTIAN DEITIES

A. Typology and Dating

As explained in Chapter 1, Class *I* pendants are so similar to their Egyptian counterparts of the New Kingdom that the best procedure is to classify them by their standard Egyptian names without necessarily implying Egyptian importation or religious significance (see Chapter 8). Twenty-six types of pendants can be distinguished, of which 12 are classified as uncertain. Seventy-eight pendants – 9 percent of the total for Late Bronze Age Palestine – are distributed among these types.

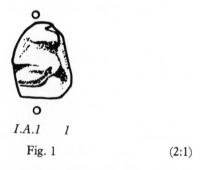

I.A.1   1

Fig. 1   (2:1)

Type I.A.1–2 Baboon of Thoth (1–4; pl. 1)
The sacred animal of Thoth (Bonnet 1952: 7–8; Helck and Otto 1975: 83–85) is represented by two types. Type *I.A.1 (1–2, pl. 1)* shows the animal in profile in a crouching position. Although the only example (*1*) available for examination was badly worn, its head is well-delineated and an eye is marked out. A mane of hair hangs down over the shoulders and appears to be incised with vertical lines. The tail is clear, but the legs are worn away at the front. The animal sits on a plinth. The two examples (*2*) from Beth Shan could not be located in Jerusalem (possibly J. 36.1701, no provenance); but since they are typed to *1* and are of the same material and approximate dimensions, there is little doubt that they belong to this type. *1* is flat-backed and has a vertical perforation. All the examples are relatively small (10 mm high) and mold-made of white glazed faience.

The three specimens of *I.A.1* are all from Locus 1068, the upper altar room of the Level VII temple at Beth Shan, which dates to a late phase of LB IIB. A very close parallel occurs at el-Amarna both as a mold and as a blue-green glazed pendant,[1] which is of a comparable size and is perforated vertically. However, the Amarna specimens have better definition of head, mane, and legs. Petrie also cites a very similar example in his corpus (1914: 43, pl. 37:206g), which he assigns to the 18th Dynasty. Middle Kingdom and earlier examples[2] are very schematic and probably include examples of other species of apes besides the baboon. Less schematic are the transitional Late Bronze–Iron Age examples from both Palestine and Egypt.[3] Thus, the type appears to be confined to LB II for both Egypt and Palestine.

I.A.2   4

Fig. 2

The baboon also occurs in a frontal position and crowned with a crescent and disc (*I.A.2, 3–4; pl. 1*). The modeling of this pendant type is much better than that of Type *I.A.1*. The typical dog-like face of the baboon stands out 15 mm from the flat base and shows well-defined eyes, nose, mouth, and shrunken cheeks. The mane on either side of the face has incised horizontal lines. The animal is probably depicted in a crouching position, since the legs are bent slightly outward. A short tail is shown between the lower half of the legs, nearly reaching the plinth upon which the animal sits. *3* and *4* are identical in regard to these stylistic features. However, several minor differences should be noted:

1. The horizontal perforation on *3* is positioned closer to the head than on *4*.
2. The base of *3* curves upward in the back, which could be due to either wear or manufacture;
3. *4* is 7 mm shorter than *3* and appears more stocky as a result;
4. *3* is of faded blue-green glazed faience, and *4* of white glazed faience, possibly leached out and faded.

These differences indicate that the pendants were made in similar but not identical molds.

As with Type *I.A.1*, the baboon crowned with crescent and disc occurs only at Beth Shan in Loci 1068 and 1072, the upper altar room and the court of the Level VII temple, dated to late LB IIB. The closest parallel is again from el-Amarna,[4] and is virtually identical to *3*. *4* is close to a transitional Late Bronze–Iron Age example from Tomb 934 at Tell el-Far'ah South.[5] Another white glazed faience example from Tomb 934[6] shows the crowned baboon in profile, facing right (the reverse of Type *I.A.1*), and is about half the size of *3–4*.[7] Other transitional LB–Iron Age examples from Far'ah South are three dimensional and have good detail of the mane and facial features.[8] However, highly stylized modeling reaches its peak by the 22nd Dynasty.[9] An LB II period of manufacture for Type *I.A.2* seems assured.

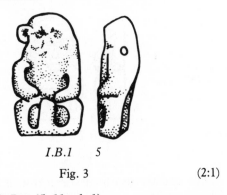

I.B.1   5

Fig. 3   (2:1)

Type I.B.1–2 Bes (5–11; pl. 1)
Bes, known as the god of merriment and dance and the protector of the mother and her newborn in Egypt (Wilson 1975; Bonnet 1952: 101–9), is depicted on two types of Late Bronze Age Palestinian pendants. In the so-called standard form (*I.B.1*, 5–9, pl. 1), which is the most common type in Palestine and Egypt, Bes is shown bandy-legged in frontal view and with a leering face and a lion's mane. The arms are bent inward, so that the hands rest on the hips and sometimes touch the stomach. Below the stomach an ape's tail or part of a lion's mane extends between the legs. Facial features (ears, eyes, nose, mouth, and mane) are barely visible

on the badly worn examples. Hands appear as knobs, and the stomach is occasionally enlarged (*6*) but not to the extent of the Ptah-Sokar pendants (*16*, pl. 1). All the examples are flat-backed, of blue-green glazed faience, and perforated behind the head, except *6*, which has a double suspension ring at the top. Two of the Megiddo examples (*8–9*; pl. 1) may well have been made from the same mold; *7*, also from Megiddo, is slightly larger. The Beth Shan (*5*, pl. 1) and Lachish (*6*) examples, of which the latter appears to have better delineation of the facial features, were probably made from separate molds.

Every *I.B.1* pendant is from an LB IIB context:

1. The single Beth Shan example (*5*) comes from Locus 1072, the court of the Level VII temple, dated to late LB IIB;
2. The Lachish example (*6*) was found in Room E of Fosse Temple III (Tufnell, Inge, and Harding 1940: 42, 74–76, pl. 8:4);
3. The three examples from Megiddo (*7–9*) come from different parts of Tomb 877 (Guy 1938: 33–36):
   7 from 877A 1, a homogeneous LB IIB locus;[10]
   8 and 9 from 877 B 1, a probable LB IIB context.[11]

The closest parallels for this type are from Amarna in blue, blue-green, red, and yellow glazed faience.[12] Other parallels come from New Kingdom Gurob[13] and Buhen.[14] *Comparanda* without provenance occur in Egypt,[15] and at Gezer[16] and Megiddo.[17] Four Lachish examples from Tomb 4002[18] are similar to *I.B.1*, but the context has LB II and Iron I material mixed. Transitional Late Bronze–Iron Age examples can also be cited from Tell Far'ah South[19] and Deir el-Balah.[20] Iron I examples[21] are already beginning to develop in the direction of the more elaborately rendered Iron II types with high feather headdresses.[22] The same trend can be observed in Egypt.[23] The period of manufacture of Type *I.B.1* is LB II, with a probable overlap into Iron Age I.

I.B.2   10

Fig. 4   (2:1)

Type *I.B.2* (*10–11*) shows Bes dancing in profile with what is most likely a tambourine (Wilson 1975: 80). Unfortunately, no personal examination was possible. The lion's mane, some facial features, and a tail can be made out on the line drawing. It is probable that both examples were made in the same mold, since they come from the same locus and are of the same material (blue-green glazed faience) and of approximately the same size.

10–11 were found in the jewelry hoard near the steps of the upper altar room (Locus 1068) of the Level VII temple at Beth Shan, dated to late LB IIB. El-Amarna again provides the closest parallels.[24] Other Egyptian parallels can be cited from Saft el-Henneh,[25] Buhen,[26] and Thebes.[27] A more schematic specimen in carnelian with a high headdress comes from Iron Age Beth Shan.[28] Type *I.B.2* is an LB II type.

Type I.C.1–3 Hathor (12–14; pl. 1)

Hathor, the popular Egyptian goddess of love and joy (Bonnet 1952: 277–82; Bleeker 1973), is represented by three pendant types in Late Bronze Age Palestine. Type *I.C.1* (*12*; pl. 1) shows the head or face of Hathor projecting from a flat-backed plaque, with a single suspension ring at the top. Hairline, eyes, nose, mouth, and characteristic cow's ears are indicated, and as on sistra, Hathor does not wear a wig. The seven examples under this entry exhibit the same stylistic features and are of the same size and material (faded blue-green glazed faience), so that they must have been made from the same mold or molds derived from a common original.

The seven examples of *12* were found together in the deposit of beads and pendants near the west wall of Room E of Fosse Temple III at Lachish (Tufnell, Inge, and Harding 1940: 42, 74–76, pl. 8:4). This is definitely an LB IIB context, but the necklaces of which the plain Hathor head or face was a part could well have been heirlooms (Tufnell, Inge, and Harding 1940: 75, pl. 14). There are no exact parallels from either Egypt or Palestine, but several sistrum-mounted types with more detail from el-Amarna are close.[29] More elaborate Hathor head or face pendants occur in transitional Late Bronze–Iron Age contexts at Deir el-Balah,[30] Tell el-Far'ah South,[31] Buhen,[32] and Gurob,[33] and continue into Iron II.[34] The simpler head or face without wig and not part of a sistrum is probably confined to LB II.

Type *I.C.2* (*13*, pl. 1) shows Hathor wearing the horned crescent and disc above the standard Egyptian wig (note particularly how the horns of the crescent project above and curve away from the disc). A very elaborate collar (sometimes incorrectly referred to as

an aegis) is well-delineated with two rows of pendants and beads. The lower half of the face is badly worn but, judging from the eyes, the head or face as a whole was well-formed. The example is flat-backed, mold-made of blue-green glazed faience, and has a horizontal perforation between the wig and the horned crescent.

The single example of the type comes from Pit 246 to the east of the Fosse Temple at Lachish, and is assigned to Structure III, dated to LB IIB (Tufnell, Inge, and Harding 1940: 90). Oddly enough, the only comparable examples are from Iron Age contexts at Lachish[35] and Megiddo.[36] Without additional data, all that can be said at present is that either the type has a very long time-range or the single specimen is an Iron Age intrusion, despite the homogeneous LB IIB pottery context of Pit 246.

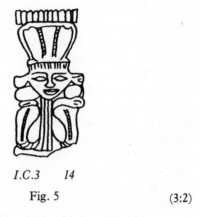

I.C.3   14

Fig. 5   (3:2)

Type *I.C.3* (*14*) is also a unique specimen, which unfortunately could not be located by the writer for a first-hand examination. The head or face of Hathor is shown in frontal view as part of a sistrum, and with well-defined hair (vertical lines), nose, mouth, and cow's ears. The head or face is flanked by two coiled uraeus snakes crowned with solar discs, whose heads are raised to show the partially hatched throats. A ribbed suspension cylinder is attached above the top of the sistrum. The pendant is reported to be of gold, but no details are provided about manufacturing technique.

The Type *I.C.3* pendant is from Tomb 1514, located in a cemetery north of Tell el-'Ajjul (Petrie 1932: 15–16, pl. 52), which can be assigned an LB II date.[37] The flanking uraei are an unusual feature, paralleled at Late Bronze Age Beth Shan[38] and New Kingdom Thebes.[39] The motif also occurs as a Late Bronze Age plaque and scarab design.[40] The detailed rendition in gold compares closely with transitional LB–Iron Age examples of Type *I.C.1*.[41] A LB II–Iron I dating fits the available evidence.

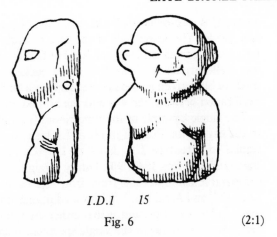

I.D.1   15

Fig. 6   (2:1)

Type I.D.1–2 Ptah-Sokar (15–16; pl. 1)

Ptah-Sokar, combining Ptah, the creator god of Memphis, with Sokar, the god of the dead at Saqqara (cf. Petrie 1914: 38), appears in a common, standard form, which is often confused with Type *I.B.1*. However, the standard Ptah-Sokar is of a smooth-faced young child with a somewhat bulbous head, in contrast to the bearded, grotesque face of Bes. In other respects, Types *I.B.1* and *I.D.1* are virtually identical, viz., arms bent in, with hands on the hips or over the stomach (more protruding for Ptah-Sokar), and bandy-legged (more corpulent for Ptah-Sokar). Except for the occasional ithyphallic example, nothing appears between the legs of the standard Ptah-Sokar. Although *15* is broken at the waist, most of these details are clear. The eyes, protruding ears, nose, mouth, and breast are well-modeled on this example, which is flat-backed, mold-made of green glazed faience, and horizontally perforated at the back of the neck.

The single example of Type *I.D.1* comes from Tomb 502 at Lachish, which is a homogeneous LB IIB context (Tufnell 1958: 288). The type apparently does not occur at el-Amarna, and even well-dated New Kingdom parallels from Egypt generally are lacking.[42] However, it is clear that by the end of the Late Bronze Age and in Iron I, the type was well-established in Palestine at Tell Far'ah South,[43] Tell Abu Hawam,[44] and Megiddo,[45] as well as in Egypt.[46] Although the type begins in LB IIB,[47] it also occurs in Iron I, thus diminishing its chronological usefulness.

Type *I.D.2* (*16*; pl. 1) is very similar to the standard form of Ptah-Sokar. Apart from the unusual black 'tonsure,' an open circular disc of black glazed faience impressed into a 'mat of hair' of blue-glazed faience on top of the head and which may represent a scarab (Petrie 1914: 38; Budge 1972: 216), there are only slight differences from Type *I.D.1*.

The *I.D.2* pendant is from the area of the LB II '100

Houses,' northwest of the Fosse Temple at Lachish (Tufnell, Inge, and Harding 1940: 43).[48] Parallels for the black open disc, the main distinguishing feature of *I.D.2*, occur in Iron II contexts at Lachish[49] and Megiddo.[50] The 'mat of hair' appears on Iron Age I examples.[51] Possibly, the black disc, whether open or closed, is a peculiarity of Palestinian pendants.[52]

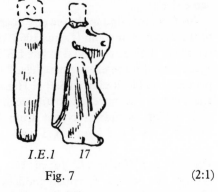

I.E.1   17

Fig. 7   (2:1)

Type I.E.1–2 Taurt (17–18)

Type *I.E.1* (*17*) depicts Taurt, the Egyptian goddess of pregnancy (Bonnet 1952: 530–35) in her standard form of a hippopotamus in profile, standing upright on her hind legs. The eyes, snout, wig, legs, and long tail (crocodile's?) are rather schematically indicated on *17*, which shows Taurt facing left. The four examples of *17* are from the same family of mold(s) and of the same material (faded blue-green glazed faience). A suspension ring is variously attached at the top of each pendant.

The four examples of *I.E.1* were associated with LB II burials in Cave 4004 at Lachish (Tufnell 158: 89, 281–85).[53] A more detailed rendition of the type occurs at el-Amarna, which has a greater resemblance to *I.E.2* than *I.E.1*, except that it faces left.[54] Petrie (1914)[55] illustrates a more schematic variant in his corpus, which also occurs at New Kingdom Buhen.[56] Beginning in Iron II, a very rigid, detailed type appears.[57] Despite the lack of close parallels, an LB II date of manufacture for this type is most probable.

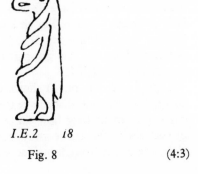

I.E.2   18

Fig. 8   (4:3)

Type *I.E.2* (*18*) exhibits greater detail. The standing hippopotamus is shown in profile facing right; and the back legs, front legs over an enlarged belly, breast, wig, and tail are very clearly indicated. *18* is more than twice the height of *17*, and is recorded as being of violet glazed faience.

The one example of *I.E.2* is from Tomb 1663 in the Lower Cemetery to the northeast of Tell el-'Ajjul (Petrie 1934: 11, pl. 58), which most likely dates to LB IIA.[58] Except that it faces right, the form and detail are closest to an Amarna type.[59] The type is apparently confined to LB II.

I.F.1   20

Fig. 9

Type I.F.1–2 Uraeus (19–22; pl. 1)
The standard uraeus pendant type (*I.F.1.a*, *19–20*, pl. 1) shows the snake, the guardian deity of the pharaoh, coiled in profile on a platform base. The throat has the characteristic cross-hatching, and the eye is marked. The six examples of *19–20* are of the same material (faded blue-green glazed faience) and of approximately the same size (despite the slight variation in dimensions cited in the Catalogue, owing to the variable attachment of the top suspension ring). The examples were probably all made in the same or affiliated molds.

19 and *20* were found together in a group of jewelry below the steps leading to the upper altar room (Locus 1068) of the Level VII temple at Beth Shan, dated to early LB IIB. A very close parallel was found at el-Amarna.[60] Petrie includes an example of this type in his corpus (1914: 18–19, pl. 4:58o, assigned to 18th Dynasty).[61] The type does not continue into the Iron Age, and has a date of manufacture restricted to LB II.

I.F.2.a   21   I.F.2.b.   22
Fig. 10   Fig. 11

I.F.2.a (*21*) and *I.F.2.b* (*22*; pl. 1) are almost indistinguishable from each other, except that for the former the uraeus faces to the left and for the latter to

the right. Both types are also similar to *I.F.1.a*, which is otherwise different in having a wigged human head. The glaze color for *21* is not given in the field register, but was most likely blue-green glazed faience, in accord with the other uraeus types.

Types *I.F.2.a–b* are attested only at Beth Shan in Loci 1070 (central part of the outer courtyard) and 1068D (below the steps of the upper altar room), dated to late and early phases of LB IIB, respectively. A comparable example comes from New Kingdom Gurob.[62] The types were manufactured only in LB II.

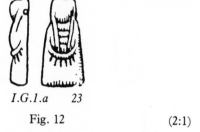

I.G.1.a   23

Fig. 12   (2:1)

Type I.G.1.a–b Bastet or Sekhmet (23–26; pl. 1)
Type *I.G.1.a* (*23*) could represent either Bastet or Sekhmet, cat goddesses often identified with each other (Bonnet 1952: 80–82). The three examples of *23*, possibly all from the same or affiliated molds, show the head or face in frontal view, with a five-rowed collar of beads very roughly delineated below. Long strands of hair, probably part of a wig, fall down over the collar on either side of the face; other facial features are worn away. The pendants are flat-backed, of faded blue-green glazed faience, and have a horizontal perforation at the back of the head.

The three examples of *23* are from Tomb 216 at Lachish (Tufnell 1958: 232–34), which probably dates to LB IIA.[63] The closest parallel is from el-Amarna.[64] Several other types with wider collars appear in Iron I and reach their peak in popularity in Iron II.[65] Type *I.G.1.a* is apparently limited to LB II.

24–26 (*I.G.1.b*, pl. 1) were not examined by the writer; and it is difficult to make out details on the published photographs, which show the three specimens from different perspectives. It appears that Bastet or Sekhmet is depicted in a very schematic way. With her right arm at her side, she is shown standing and holding a scepter before her with the left hand. Facial features are roughly indicated, and there may be a disc on her head (Petrie 1914: pl. 35:195a–b). The examples are flat-backed, of faience (glaze color not given), of about the same size, with a horizontal perforation at the back of the head. They are most likely identical and made from the same mold.

The three examples of Type *I.G.1.b* are from

adjoining sections of the Stratum VII B palace in Area AA at Megiddo (Loud 1948: 158). *24* and *25* were found in a room (Locus 2039) to the north of the central courtyard of the palace for which no floor is shown on the plan. *26* is from the east side of the palace courtyard where only remnants of walls and floors remained. Despite the questionable stratigraphy, the published pottery supports an LB IIB dating. Assuming that the description above is correct, possible parallels can be cited from New Kingdom Egypt.[66] The Iron Age types of Sekhmet, Bastet, or Mut are larger and more detailed.[67] Thus, Type *I.G.1.b* is most likely limited to LB II.

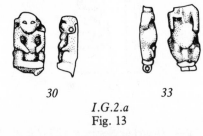

30   *33*

I.G.2.a
Fig. 13

Type I.G.2.a–b Bes or Ptah-Sokar (27–40; pl. 2)
The difficulty of distinguishing between standard Bes and Ptah-Sokar pendants has been discussed above under Types *I.B.1* and *I.D.1*. Types *I.G.2.a–b* bring all the questionable specimens together. The problem of identification arises for three main reasons:

1. The head and sometimes the torso are missing (*27, 33, 34, 36,* and *37*);
2. Features are excessively worn away (*30, 32, 38,* and *40*);
3. The examples are inadequately published or are unpublished, and unavailable for first-hand examination (*28, 31, 35, 39*).

27–36 (*I.G.1.a*) are classified as small (average dimensions of 14 × 7 × 5 mm), whereas *37–40* (*I.G.2.b*) are approximately twice as large. Although the glaze color is not always recorded and some examples are said to be white glazed (perhaps leached out and faded) or 'blue' glazed (*34*), most of the examples are of faded blue-green glazed faience. *33* should be noted for its misshapen appearance, which may have resulted from overfiring.

The small type of Bes or Ptah-Sokar (*I.G.2.a*) was found in each LB level at Beth Shan:

1. Level IX (Late Bronze Age):
   Locus 1238, a street south of the temple area (*27*);
2. Level VIII (early LB IIB):
   Locus 1092, an area below the steps of the

Level VII temple (*28*);
Locus 1068D, below the steps of the upper altar room (*29*);
Locus 1072C, below the steps of the temple court (*30*);
3. Level VII (late LB IIB):
   Locus 1068, the upper altar room of the temple (*31*);
   Locus 1072, the temple court (*32–33*);
   Locus 1086, the anteroom of the temple (*34*).

The Megiddo example (*35*) comes from Square M 13 in Area BB, where stratigraphic problems necessitate a general Late Bronze Age dating.[68] *36* is from Square SE 23 C (Stratum C) at Tell Beit Mirsim, another uncertain context that may date to LB II.[69] The same dating considerations apply to this type as to those outlined for Type *I.B.1* (see above). In addition, a small standard Ptah-Sokar, unrepresented in Late Bronze Palestine, occurs in 18th to 20th Dynasty contexts in Egypt,[70] and extends into Iron I in both Palestine[71] and Egypt.[72] However, while the most distinctive part of the Bes or Ptah-Sokar pendants is the head, which undergoes its most dramatic changes in Iron II (especially the headdress and facial features), the transitional Late Bronze–Iron Age form of the lower torso and legs continues into Iron II, together with some variant forms.[73] Thus, the torso and legs of this type can be highly unspecific for chronological purposes. Head and facial features are determinative for an LB II–Iron I dating.

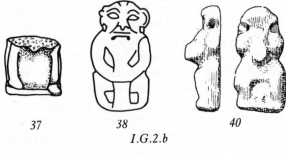

37   *38*   *40*

I.G.2.b

Fig. 14

The large type, *I.G.2.b*, is represented by two examples from Beth Shan: (1) *37* from below the floor of Locus 1068, the upper altar room of the Level VII temple, probably belonging to an early phase of LB IIB, and (2) *38* from Locus 1068 proper, dated to a late phase of LB IIB. The Beth Shemesh example (*39*) comes from near Square V 26,[74] which can probably be assigned to Stratum IVb and dated to LB II. *40* was found in LB II Burial Pit 542 at Lachish (Tufnell 1958: 242).[75] The larger version of the standard Bes or Ptah-Sokar presents the same problems of chronological control as Type *I.G.2.a*, since the legs again are highly nonspecific and occur from LB II to Iron II.[76] If a relatively plain upper torso and head with no headdress is present, the presumption must be that the pendant dates to either LB II or Iron I.

I.G.3   41

Fig. 15

Type I.G.3 Horus? (41)

This type is represented by a single example, which Petrie (1934: 9) suggests should be identified with Horus (cf. Petrie 1914: pl. 26:145f, k, etc., for a similar posture). However, the pendant, which was not available for examination, appears from the photograph (Petrie 1934: pls. 19:152, 20:152) to be so badly worn that it is impossible to confirm Petrie's judgment. The pendant is said to be of gray lazuli and is set in a gold mounting with a granulated border.

The Type *I.G.3* pendant (*41*) comes from Tomb 447, an LB I child's jar burial in an open space west of building LA at Tell el-'Ajjul (Petrie 1934: 8–9, pl. 61).[77] The pendant has such obscure features that it would be presumptuous to cite parallels and suggest a period of manufacture.[78]

I.G.4   42

Fig. 16

Type I.G.4 Horus the Child or Ptah (42–43; pl. 2)

The two examples of Type *I.G.4* (*42–43*) show a figure standing upright and facing forward, and holding a staff in front of the body with both hands. Resemblances with typical Ptah pendants end there (cf. Petrie 1914: pl. 31:177). Moreover, it is not clear that either example is mummiform as Ptah is usually depicted. *43* (pl. 2) appears to be crowned with crescent and disc, and has a sidelock of youth, which falls upon the right shoulder. Both features are highly atypical of Ptah. Possibly, Sekhmet (Guy 1938: legend for pl. 95) or another deity (e.g., Bastet or Hathor) is portrayed, but a more likely possibility is Horus the Child. Since

42 has no head, this example is especially problematic. Both specimens are of blue-green glazed faience, flat-backed, of approximately the same size, and with horizontal perforations at the back of the head. *42* comes from Locus 1108, Level VIII at Beth Shan, which is a large open area with no building remains beneath the southern half of the Level VII temple, which probably dates to early LB IIB. *43* was found in Tomb 877 B 1 at Megiddo, and probably also dates to LB IIB (Guy 1938: 36). Virtually identical Iron Age parallels for *43* occur at Lachish[79] and Megiddo.[80] Since there is no conclusive evidence for Iron Age intrusion in the Late Bronze contexts or vice versa, the type must be broadly dated to LB II–Iron II.[81]

Type I.G.5 Taurt? (44–49; pl. 3)

44–48 are probably schematic renderings of Taurt in profile (cf. *17*, Type *I.E.1*, for an initial trend towards schematization). *45* (pl. 3; shown upside down in Tufnell, Inge, and Harding 1940: pl. 35:83) faces left, and has legs, mouth, eye, and tail indicated with incised lines. *44*, *46–48* (pl. 3) are even more schematic, with notched edges producing a figure that suggests Taurt, who faces right. All five examples of *45*, probably from the same mold or affiliated molds, are of faded blue-green glazed faience and are horizontally perforated through the middle of the head. In contrast, *44*, *46–48* are perforated vertically and said to be of gray 'paste,' possibly faience; *44* and *47* are identical, as are *46* and *48*. *49* is included under this questionable type, because it is so badly worn that precise identification is impossible. However, it is similar to *18* (*I.E.2*) in style, with a long tail (incised with hatching; cf. Petrie 1914: pl. 40:235j), hands over belly, and well-marked legs. It is of yellow glazed faience, and has a suspension ring at the top.

Except for *49*, all the examples of Type *I.G.5* are from Lachish:

1. *44* comes from LB IIA Pit 199, located to the east of the Fosse Temple;[82]
2. *45–47* were found together in the deposit of beads and pendants near the west wall of Room E of Fosse Temple III, dated to LB IIB (Tufnell, Inge, and Harding 1940: 42, 74–76, pl. 8:4);
3. *48* is from LB IIB Pit 172, east of the Fosse Temple and over Pit 199.[83]

The example (*49*) from Tell el-'Ajjûl comes from Tomb 1064 of the '18th Dynasty' Cemetery (Petrie 1932: 14–15, pl. 52), and dates to LB II.[84] *45* is comparable to Egyptian New Kingdom examples from Gurob,[85] Buhen,[86] and el-Amarna.[87] The parallels cited in Petrie's corpus (1914: pl. 40:236e, f, j) date to the 18th Dynasty, suggesting that the type does not continue into the Iron Age. Although no close parallels for *44, 46–48* could be found, the further schematization of the Taurt form is in keeping with an LB II dating; the form of Old Kingdom and First Intermediate degraded Taurt pendants in Egypt[88] are easily distinguishable from the LB II types.

Type I.G.6.a–c Standing Figure (50–56; pls. 3–4)
All the examples of this group are definitely Egyptian in inspiration and most likely are deities. However, they lack heads and sometimes upper torsos, so that precise identification is not possible.

I.G.6.a   50

Fig. 17

Type *I.G.6.a* (female) is represented by a single example (*50*, pl. 3), which shows a figure standing upright with arms straight down at the sides of the body. The distinct breasts and the suggestion of a long dress favor identifying the figure with a female, but what deity it actually is cannot be determined; Isis, Nebhat, Sekhmet or Bastet, Mut, or even Horus the Child are all possibilities (Petrie 1914: 34–37, pls. 26:145, 149, 27:154, 30:164). The example is flat-backed, of faded blue-green glazed faience; it would probably have been perforated at the back of the head.

The Type *I.G.6.a* pendant comes from below the altar steps of Locus 1072, the court of the Level VII temple at Beth Shan, dated to early LB IIB. Even with head and upper torso, the type is highly unspecific chronologically, with parallels from LB II to Iron II.[89]

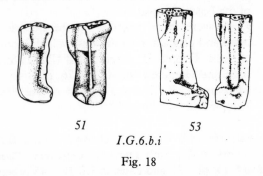

51   53

I.G.6.b.i

Fig. 18

Type *I.G.6.b.i* (*51–54*, pl. 3) is characterized by figures that are standing upright in frontal position with the right arm straight down at the side and the left holding a scepter positioned at the center of the body (*51–53*) or to the left of the body (*54*). Two of the figures (*51* and *52*) wear short skirts, and are so similar in other respects that they may have been made in the same mold. The sex of the figures is uncertain, because both sexes are depicted wearing skirts (e.g., Sekhmet, Bastet, Mahes, and Khnum; Petrie 1914: 40–41, pls. 33:187, 34:192, 35:194). *53*, on the other hand, shows a figure possibly wearing a long dress, which suggests a female; it is somewhat larger than *51* and *52*, and the scepter forms a thick ridge on the left side of the pendant. Although *54* was not available for examination, the inadequate register drawing shows the scepter (lotus or *was*?) to the left of the body.

Type *I.G.6.b.i.* examples (*51–54*) are from various loci of Level VII at Beth Shan, dating to late LB IIB:

1. Locus 1087, a partially defined room to the south of the temple and possibly associated with it (*51*);
2. Locus 1263, a road running toward the east in the southeastern residential sector (*52*);
3. Locus 1284, a problematical locus east of Fitz-Gerald's deep sounding, above Level IX (*53* and *54*).

As these pendants again lack a distinctive head, dating can be anywhere from LB II through Iron II for *51–53*.[90] *54* is possibly paralleled by an Amarna example,[91] and is probably confined to LB II.

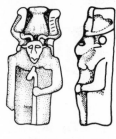

I.G.6.b.ii   55

Fig. 19

55 (pl. 4) is the only example of Type *I.G.6.b.ii.* A ram-headed figure is shown wearing the *atef* crown and a short skirt, with the right arm straight down at the side and the left hand holding a *was* scepter in front of the body. The lower half of the face is badly worn, but the eyes, nose, and ears can be distinguished. Rowe's identification (1936: 268) with the Khnum is possible, but Egyptian Khnum pendants normally have horns bending around the side of the head and projecting forward rather than straight back along the sides of the head (cf. Petrie 1914: pl. 33:187). They do not have *atef* crowns with their separate pair of horns. The *atef* crown could point to Amun-Re, but the Theban ram also has horns curving down and forward (Murray 1953: 380). A more likely possibility is Mahes, who is often shown wearing an *atef* crown (Petrie 1914: pl. 34:192). The problem of the 'horns' would be bypassed, since they could be interpreted as long, leonine ears. The example is flat-backed, of faded blue-green glazed faience, and perforated at the back of the head.

The Type *I.G.6.b.ii* example comes from Locus 1072, the court of the Level VII temple at Beth Shan, which is dated to late LB IIB. An unpublished Amarna example (Petrie Museum Amarna Cabinet, no. 1199) is virtually identical. The type extends into the Iron Age.[92]

I.G.6.c   56

Fig. 20

The Type *I.G.6.c* (56) pendant could not be examined, and only a side-view drawing from the field register was available for study. An upright standing figure with right arm straight down at the side and a face with eye and mouth indicated can be discerned. The example must have been badly worn, since Rowe's suggested identification (1940: 80, legend to pl. 34) with Taurt does not fit with the figure's profile (cf. Petrie 1914: pl. 40:236). On the basis of available information, it is impossible to determine what deity is represented or whether it is a male or female. The example is of faience (glaze color unspecified), flat-backed, and with a perforation at the back of the neck.

The one example of Type *I.G.6.c* was found together with a large group of beads and pendants below the steps of Locus 1072, the court of the Level VII temple at Beth Shan, which is dated to an early phase of LB IIB. Without additional data, this type's dating to LB II–Iron I cannot be further delimited.

Type I.G.7 Uraeus? (57; pl. 4)
The bad condition of the single example of this type, which could not be personally examined, precludes precise identification. The most likely possibility is a couchant snake with its head and neck raised in standing uraeus fashion and the rest of the body extending straight out behind. The broadening of the pendant near its base with small notches along the side is suggestive of a uraeus hatched neck. However, it is also conceivable that this example portrays a couchant animal with its head turned back over the top of its body (Petrie 1914: pl. 38:215). The example has a flat base, is of green glazed faience, and is perforated at one end.

The specimen of Type *I.G.7* was found during the sifting of soil from the Lachish Fosse Temple area; since its exact provenience is unknown, it must be assigned a general Late Bronze Age date. Although various Amarna examples can be cited that show a couchant uraeus with its head raised,[93] no exact parallels could be found and the dubious nature of the type renders even a Late Bronze Age date for the type questionable.

B. Summary

Class *I* pendants are almost evenly divided between Beth Shan and Lachish (Chart 8). Four other sites (Megiddo, Tell el-'Ajjul, Beth Shemesh, and Tell Beit Mirsim) with noticeably smaller numbers complete the picture. Class *I* pendants are thus far absent from the central Hill Country, the Galilee, Huleh Valley, Jordan Valley (apart from Beth Shan), and Transjordan.

Class *I* pendant types are all Egyptian-related by definition. Still, it is remarkable to discover that 17 of the 26 types have close parallels at el-Amarna. Even of those types apparently absent at Amarna (*I.C.2–3*, *I.D.1–2*, *I.F.2*, *I.G.3*, *I.G.4*, and *I.G.6.c*), three are represented by badly worn or poorly illustrated examples (*I.G.3*, *I.G.4*, and *I.G.6.c*), two may be Iron Age intrusions (*I.C.2* and *I.D.2*), and one may be unique (*I.C.3*). Of the remaining two types (*I.D.1* and *I.F.2*), parallels may exist but none have yet been published.

When this result is combined with the fact that most of the closely dated Class *I* pendant types come from LB IIB loci and to a much lesser extent from LB IIA contexts (Chart 9), it is difficult not to conclude that these types emerge in Egypt at least by the Amarna period and over the next century become popular in Palestine, as well. The impact of Egyptian styles is first noticeable in the south at Lachish (*I.G.1.a* and *I.G.5*) and Tell el-'Ajjul (*I.E.2* and *I.G.5*) no later than LB IIA (an example of *I.G.3* was found in an LB I burial at 'Ajjul). Egyptian influence was only felt further north at Beth Shan (*I.A.1–2*, *I.B.1–2*, *I.F.1.a–2.b*, *I.G.2.a–b*, *I.G.4*, *I.G.6.a–c*) and Megiddo (*I.B.1*, *I.G.1.b*, and *I.G.4*) in LB IIB.

Chart 8
Site Distribution of Class *I* Pendants in Late Bronze Age Palestine

Description	Type	Beth Shan	Beth Shemesh	Lachish	Megiddo	Tell el-'Ajjul	Tell Beit Mirsim	Total	%
Baboon of Thoth	*I.A.1*	3	–	–	–	–	–	3	4
Baboon of Thoth	*I.A.2*	2	–	–	–	–	–	2	3
Bes	*I.B.1.*	1	–	1	3	–	–	5	6
Bes	*I.B.2*	2	–	–	–	–	–	2	3
Hathor head or face	*I.C.1*	–	–	7	–	–	–	7	9
Hathor head or face	*I.C.2*	–	–	1	–	–	–	1	1
Hathor head or face	*I.C.3*	–	–	–	–	–	–	1	1
Ptah-Sokar	*I.D.1*	–	–	1	–	–	–	1	1
Ptah-Sokar	*I.D.2*	–	–	1	–	–	–	1	1
Taurt	*I.E.1*	–	–	4	–	1	–	4	5
Taurt	*I.E.2*	–	–	–	–	–	–	1	1
Uraeus	*I.F.1.a*	6	–	–	–	–	–	6	8
Uraeus	*I.F.2.a*	1	–	–	–	–	–	1	1
Uraeus	*I.F.2.b*	1	–	–	–	–	–	1	1
Bastet or Sekhmet	*I.G.1.a*	–	–	3	–	–	–	3	4
Bastet or Sekhmet	*I.G.1.b*	–	–	–	3	–	–	3	4
Bes or Ptah-Sokar	*I.G.2.a*	9	–	–	1	–	–	11	14
Bes or Ptah-Sokar	*I.G.2.b*	2	1	1	–	–	–	4	5
Horus?	*I.G.3*	–	–	–	–	1	–	1	1
Horus Child or Ptah	*I.G.4*	1	–	–	1	–	–	2	3
Taurt?	*I.G.5*	–	–	9	–	1	–	10	13
Standing figure	*I.G.6.a*	1	–	–	–	–	–	1	1
Standing figure	*I.G.6.b.i*	4	–	–	–	–	–	4	5
Standing figure	*I.G.6.b.ii*	1	–	–	–	–	–	1	1
Standing figure	*I.G.6.c*	1	–	–	–	–	–	1	1
Uraeus?	*I.G.7*	–	–	1	–	–	–	1	1
Total		35	2	29	8	4	1	78	98
%		45	3	37	10	5	1	101	

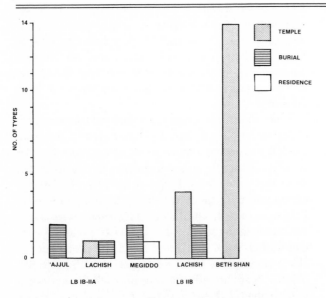

Chart 9
Contextual Distribution of Class *I* Pendant Types for Late
Bronze Age Palestinian Sites

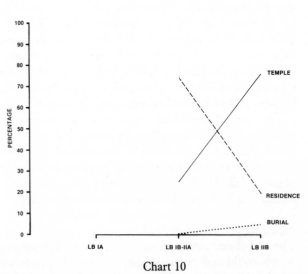

Chart 10
Comparative Importance of Contexts for Class *I* Pendant Types

Chart 11
Quantitative Analysis of Materials Used for Class *I* Pendants in Late Bronze Age Palestine

Description	Type	Faience									Au	?	Total	%
		B	B–G	B&BL	G	GR	V	W	Y	?				
Baboon of Thoth	I.A.1	–	–	–	–	–	–	3	–	–	–	–	3	4
Baboon of Thoth	I.A.2	–	1	–	–	–	–	1	–	–	–	–	2	3
Bes	I.B.1.	1	4	–	–	–	–	–	–	–	–	–	5	6
Bes	I.B.2	–	1	–	–	–	–	–	–	1	–	–	2	3
Hathor head or face	I.C.1	–	7	–	–	–	–	–	–	–	–	–	7	9
Hathor head or face	I.C.2	–	1	–	–	–	–	–	–	–	–	–	1	1
Hathor head or face	I.C.3	–	–	–	–	–	–	–	–	–	1	–	1	1
Ptah-Sokar	I.D.1	–	–	–	–	1	–	–	–	–	–	–	1	1
Ptah-Sokar	I.D.2	–	–	1	–	–	–	–	–	–	–	–	1	1
Taurt	I.E.1	–	4	–	–	–	–	–	–	–	–	–	4	5
Taurt	I.E.2	–	–	–	–	–	–	–	–	–	–	–	1	1
Uraeus	I.F.1.a	–	6	–	–	–	1	–	–	–	–	–	6	8
Uraeus	I.F.2.a	–	–	–	–	–	–	–	–	1	–	–	1	1
Uraeus	I.F.2.b	–	1	–	–	–	–	–	–	–	–	–	1	1
Bastet or Sekhmet	I.G.1.a	–	3	–	–	–	–	–	–	–	–	–	3	4
Bastet or Sekhmet	I.G.1.b	–	–	–	–	–	–	–	–	3	–	–	3	4
Bes or Ptah-Sokar	I.G.2.a	–	1	–	–	–	–	5	–	3	–	2	11	14
Bes or Ptah-Sokar	I.G.2.b	1	3	–	–	–	–	–	–	–	–	–	4	5
Horus?	I.G.3	–	–	–	–	–	–	–	–	–	–	1	1	1
Horus Child or Ptah	I.G.4	–	2	–	–	–	–	–	–	–	–	–	2	3
Taurt?	I.G.5	–	5	–	4	–	–	–	1	–	–	–	10	13
Standing figure	I.G.6.a	–	1	–	–	–	–	–	–	–	–	–	1	1
Standing figure	I.G.6.b.i	–	3	–	–	–	–	1	–	–	–	–	4	5
Standing figure	I.G.6.b.ii	–	1	–	–	–	–	–	–	–	–	–	1	1
Standing figure	I.G.6.c	–	–	–	–	–	–	–	–	1	–	–	1	1
Uraeus?	I.G.7	–	–	–	1	–	–	–	–	–	–	–	1	1
	Total	2	44	1	4	2	1	10	1	9	1	3	78	98
	%	3	56	1	5	3	1	13	1	12	1	4	100	

Au = gold GR = green
B = blue V = violet
B–G = blue-green W = white
BL = black Y = yellow
G = gray ? = Unidentified

Matching this chronological shift between northern and southern Palestine are specific repertoires for each region, which appear primarily in burial contexts in the south in LB IIA and in temple contexts in both north and south in LB IIB (Charts 9–10). Even including less well-dated specimens, there is essentially no correspondence between the Lachish and Beth Shan collections, with the exception of *I.B.1* and *I.G.2.b.* Thus, *I.B.2, I.F.1.a–2.b, I.G.4,* and *I.G.6.a–c* are found only in the north along the major inland valley of the Esdraelon (Megiddo and Beth Shan), whereas *I.C.1–3, I.D.1–2, I.E.1–2, I.G.1.a, I.G.3, I.G.5,* and *I.G.7* are restricted to the south (Lachish and Tell el-'Ajjul). This distribution is highly suggestive of different cultural milieus in Late Bronze Age Palestine.

Except for *I.C.3,* every example in this class was mold-made of faience, generally with a blue-green glaze (Chart 11). Other colors are almost invariably employed for a specific type: *I.A.1* (white), *I.D.1* (green), *I.D.2* (blue and black), *I.E.2* (violet), and

I.G.7 (green). When both white and blue-green glazes are recorded for a type (*I.A.2*, *I.G.2.a*, and *I.G.6.b.ii*), quite possibly an original blue-green has been leached out and faded to white. *I.G.5* occurs in gray, blue-green, and yellow glazed faience.

When compared with their Egyptian counterparts, especially the Amarna specimens, the Palestinian corpus is more limited in the variety and intensity of glaze colors. Since as much as a century may separate the two groups, quality may have deteriorated and standardization may already have set in for the native Palestinian industry (see Chapter 8). This trend became especially pronounced in Iron I, leading toward a repertoire of rigidly defined Iron II types (cf. Petrie 1891a: 26). The lackluster appearance of some Palestinian pendants may be due to differential leaching; the Lachish and Tell el-'Ajjul examples, which would have been better preserved in the dry, southern climate, exhibit more intense colors than those from Beth Shan.

The single pendant in gold (*I.C.3*) comes from an LB II burial at Tell el-'Ajjul, which is not surprising in view of the amount of goldwork found at this site (see Classes *II* and *VI*).

Notes

1 Petrie 1894: 29, pl. 17:294; Petrie Museum Amarna Cabinet, no. 1217.

2 Brunton 1937: pl. 56:14H (Mostagedda, 4th–11th Dynasties); Engelbach 1923: pl. 50:2D (Harageh, Middle Kingdom); Tufnell and Ward 1966: 198, fig. 5:103 (Byblos, Montet Jar, probably Middle Kingdom); Petrie and Brunton 1924: I, pl. 43:70 (Mayana, group 1262, Second Intermediate Period); Petrie 1914: 43, pl. 37:206a–d (undated); cf. Brunton and Engelbach 1927: pl. 21:32 (Gurob, Tomb 75, early 18th Dynasty).

3 Starkey and Harding 1932: pl. 70:63–64 (Tell el-Far'ah South, EF 386, uncertain context, transitional Late Bronze–Iron Age); Brunton and Engelbach 1927: pl. 42:2A, F, H, M (Gurob, Tombs 450, 418, and 490, uncertain 18th–19th Dynasty contexts), Petrie 1906a: pl. 37B: group 66 (Saft el-Henneh, uncertain date and context).

4 Petrie Museum Amarna Cabinet, no. 23677 (blue-green glazed faience, perforated horizontally, badly worn).

5 Starkey and Harding 1932: 24–25, pl. 51, bottom.

6 Starkey and Harding 1932: pl. 51, bottom.

7 Cf. Starkey and Harding 1932: pl. 73:70 (Tell el-Far'ah South, EF 386, transitional Late Bronze–Iron); Brunton and Engelbach 1927: pl. 42:2P (Gurob, Tomb 490, uncertain 18th–19th Dynasty context, facing left, blue glazed faience).

8 Starkey and Harding 1932: pl. 73:59–60 (EF 386).

9 Petrie 1891a: 25, pl. 29:42 (Illahun); Petrie 1914:pls. 37:206h, 45:206m; Engelbach 1915: pl. 19:2, bottom

(Riqqeh); Loud 1948: pl. 205:39 (Megiddo, Level VI); Bliss and Macalister 1902: 26–27, pl. 84:4 (Tell Zakariya); Macalister 1912: pl. 210:23 (Gezer, unprovenanced and undated); Guy 1938: pl. 165:13 (Megiddo, Tomb 39, Iron I).

10 30cm of sterile fill separated this context from EB IV remains.

11 This area of the tomb produced a Mycenaean IIIB stirrup-jar and a probable Ramesses II scarab (Rowe 1936: no. 712), despite some admixture with EB IV pottery.

12 Petrie 1894: pl. 17:291; Frankfort and Pendlebury 1933: 116, pl. 28(6), two examples in top row, especially the fourth one from the left; Petrie Museum Amarna Case, nos. 1135 and 2023.

13 Brunton and Engelbach 1927: pl. 42:1E (Tomb 450, an uncertain 18th–19th Dynasty context).

14 Randall-MacIver and Woolley 1911: pl. 55:10225 (Tomb J 12, 18th–19th Dynasties).

15 Petrie 1914: pl. 33:188s (assigned to 18th Dynasty).

16 Macalister 1912: pl. 210:5.

17 Lamon and Shipton 1939: pl. 74:4 (Stratum IIIB, probably an intrusion of an LB type).

18 Tufnell 1958: 89, 280–81, pl. 29:53.

19 Starkey and Harding 1932: pl. 54: group 960, bottom left.

20 Dothan 1979: 84, fig. 204.

21 E.g., Loud 1948: pl. 205:18 (Megiddo, Level VIIA); James 1966: fig. 101:9 (Beth Shan, Level VI); Hamilton 1934: 27, pl. 35:143–44 (Tell Abu Hawam, Stratum II).

22 Tufnell 1953: pls. 34:14, 36:48 (Lachish, Tombs 120 and 1002); Crowfoot, Crowfoot, and Kenyon 1957: pls. 8:9, 91:8 (Samaria); Lapp 1967c: 37, fig. 25:6 (Taanach); Rowe 1936: 269, pl. 30:A. 11; Bliss 1894: 153, pl. 33 (Tell el-Hesi); Petrie 1928: pl. 45:53 (Tell Jemmeh); Bliss and Macalister 1902: 40, pl. 83, Amulet 2 (Tell es-Safi).

23 E.g., Petrie 1914: pl. 33:188r; 1906a: pls. 19: groups 13 and 62, 19A: group 306 (Tell el-Yehudiyeh), 38:31–32 (Saft el-Henneh); 1891a: pl. 29:25, 39 (Illahun).

24 Petrie 1894: pl. 17:288; Frankfort and Pendlebury 1933: 116 (Type IV.A.10), pl. 28:7; Petrie Museum Amarna Cabinet, nos. 1138 and 1144 (multicolored and more detailed); Aldred 1968: pl. 109 (found in or near the Royal Tomb).

25 Petrie 1906a: pls. 37B:56=38:56 (similar to the more detailed Amarna variety, uncertain context and dating).

26 Randall-MacIver and Woolley 1911: pl. 55:10205 (18th–19th Dynasties).

27 Petrie 1897: 13, pl. 3:34 (foundation deposit of Merenptah).

28 James 1966: fig. 113:11 (Locus 4, Upper Level V, Iron II; probably the pendant in Rowe 1936: 269–70, pl. 30:A. 13, mistakenly said to come from Level IX).

29 Petrie 1894: pl. 17:280–81; cf. Petrie 1914: pl. 30:171d (18th Dynasty); cf. Bruyère 1953: 53–54, fig. 11, top row, middle (Deir el-Medineh, 19th–20th Dynasties).

30 Dothan 1973: 136, pl. 45 (no provenance, and not published in Dothan 1979).

31 Petrie 1930: 6–7, pl. 37 (Tomb 902).

32 Randall-MacIver and Woolley 1911: pl. 55:10207 (Tomb H 21, 18th–19th Dynasties).

33 Brunton and Engelbach 1927: pl. 42:1V, W (Tombs 490 and 609, 18th–19th Dynasties); cf. Petrie 1914: pl. 30:171 a,b,f (18th Dynasty).

34 Petrie 1891a: pls. 29:23, 45:171g (Illahun, 22nd Dynasty).

35 Tufnell 1958: 203–5, pl. 34:26 (Tomb 218, Iron II).

36 Loud 1948: pl. 206:56 (Locus E=2057, Stratum VA, Iron I).

37 The tomb had been used throughout LB II, since LB IIA and IIB pottery forms, including Base-Ring II, were mixed together, frustrating any effort for closer dating.

38 Oren 1973: 129, 217, figs. 41:32, 77:4=Rowe 1936: 271–72, pl. 31: A. 27.

39 Davis *et al.* 1908: 44, no. 34 (Tomb of Siptah).

40 E.g., Tufnell 1958: 104, pl. 37:319=38:319 (Lachish, dated to LB IB).

41 See Dothan 1973 pl. 45, and Petrie 1914: pl. 30:171a,b.

42 Cf. Randall-MacIver and Woolley 1911: pl. 55:10232 (Buhen, Tomb J 39, probably early 19th Dynasty); Brunton and Engelbach 1927: pl. 42:1C (Gurob, Tomb 450, uncertain 18th–19th Dynasty context); Petrie 1914: 38, pl. 31:176b,c (assigned to 18th Dynasty).

43 Starkey and Harding 1932: 24–26, pls. 59–60 (plans of tombs), 51 (top, left and right; Tomb 934), 49 (bottom left; Tomb 952), 48:33, 49 (Tomb 914, and an unpublished example from Tomb 960C [J. I9749]).

44 Hamilton 1934: 27, pl. 35:145 (Stratum III).

45 Lamon and Shipton 1939: pl. 74:12 (Stratum V).

46 Petrie 1914: pl. 31:176f (assigned to the 22nd Dynasty); 1906a: 32, pl. 3, fourth group from top, middle (Tell er-Retabeh).

47 Also cf. Tufnell 1958: 89, 280–81, pl. 29:54–55 (Lachish, Cave 4002, ca. 1400–900 B.C.); Loud 1948: pl. 205:13 (Megiddo, Stratum VIIA).

48 The houses were not well-stratified, having few floors and many robbed-out walls, but the presence of LB II local pottery types, together with White Slip II, Base-Ring II, and Bucchero wares, assures a general LB II dating.

49 Tufnell 1958: 380, pl. 34:11 (Tomb 120), 36:49 (Tomb 1002).

50 Lamon and Shipton 1939: pl. 74:13, 14, 16, 17 (Stratum V).

51 Cf. especially, Loud 1948: pl. 206:52 (Stratum VA); Petrie 1914: 38, pl. 31:176f (assigned to the 22nd Dynasty).

52 However, note its use on child pendants of a much earlier date in Egypt; Brunton 1937: pl. 56: type 3:D$_4$, L$_5$ (Mostagedda).

53 The cave was used for burials during earlier and later stages of the LBA with at least a century interval between the two. Tufnell suggests that *17* should be associated with the later burial period, but the assignment of the finds is not clear and her argument appears to be based solely on typological grounds.

54 Petrie 1894: pl. 17:299; Frankfort and Pendlebury 1933: 116, Type IV.A.5; Petrie Museum Amarna Cabinet, nos. 1207 and 23682; cf. Brunton and Engelbach 1927: pl. 42:9D (18th–19th Dynasties); Macalister 1912: pl. 202b:2 (possibly LB IIA, poor stratigraphic context); Petrie 1891a: pl. 18:31 (Gurob, dated to Ramesses II).

55 1914: 47, pl. 40:236e,f (assigned to 18th Dynasty).

56 Randall-MacIver and Woolley 1911: pl. 55:10221 (Tomb H 68, 18th–19th Dynasties).

57 E.g., Hamilton 1934: pl. 35:50 (Tell Abu Hawam, Stratum II); Johns 1932: 91, pl. 30:807 (top)=Rowe 1936: 274, pl. 31:A. 32 (Atlit, Persian period); Petrie 1914: pl. 40:236s,t (assigned to the 26th Dynasty).

58 Although Petrie dates it to the 18th Dynasty generally, the pottery evidence, including Base-Ring II and Bucchero wares, points to a more circumscribed dating of LB IIA.

59 Petrie 1894: pl. 17:299; also compare the somewhat different gold types from Thebes: Carnarvon and Carter 1912: 85, pl. 73:78=Hayes 1953–59: 184, fig. 101, fourth necklace from the bottom (Tomb 37, LB I).

60 Samson 1972: 80–81, fig. 46(iv), top row, second from right.

61 Cf. Petrie 1890: pl. 23:33 (Gurob, dated to Ramesses II, facing left); Starkey and Harding 1932: 30, pl. 73:61–62 (Tell el-Far'ah South, EF 386, transitional Late Bronze–Iron Age, crowned with disc); James 1966: fig. 113:8=Rowe 1936: 277–78, pl. 31: A. 46 (Beth Shan, Upper Level V, not Stratum IX as recorded by Rowe).

62 Brunton and Engelbach 1927: pl. 42:14B (Gurob, 18th–19th Dynasties).

63 The tomb contained disturbed burials which Tufnell argued were to be dated as early as ca. 1450 B.C. The local pottery and imports (Mycenaean IIIA and Base-Ring I and II), coupled with the absence of bichrome pottery, argue for a dating of LB IIA.

64 Petrie 1894: pl. 17:277; Petrie Museum Amarna Cabinet, nos. 1200, 1202.

65 Petrie 1914: 42, pl. 35:195g,j, etc. (22nd–26th Dynasties); Tufnell 1953: 379–80, pl. 34:26–27 (Lachish, Tomb 218), 36:50 (Tomb 1002); Lamon and Shipton 1939: pl. 74: 19–28 (Megiddo, Strata V–III); Petrie 1930: pl. 31:314 (Tell el-Far'ah South, Tomb 636, assigned to 20th Dynasty, but probably Iron II), 41:259 (Tomb 201, Iron II); Mackenzie 1912–13: pl. 28:9, 34, on right (Gezer, Tomb 1); Petrie 1906a: pl. 34a:Tomb 20 (Tell er-Retabeh).

66 Petrie 1914: pl. 35:194g (19th Dynasty?); Petrie 1974: 29, pl. 17:283 (el-Amarna, a mold of Mut); Frankfort and Pendlebury 1933: 116 (el-Amarna, Type IV.A.4).

67 E.g., Starkey and Harding 1932: 24–25, pl. 51 (Tell el-Far'ah South, Tomb 934); Tufnell 1953: pl. 34:18, 21 (Lachish, Tomb 208); Petrie 1906a: pl. 32, top left (Tell er-Retabeh); Hamilton 1934: pl. 35:147 (Tell Abu Hawam, Stratum III).

68 The plan of the square shows broken walls and floors. Since no associated finds are published, it must be assumed to date to the Late Bronze Age generally.

69 Since Tell Beit Mirsim appears to have had no LB I occupation, an LB II dating is likely.

70 Petrie 1914: 38, 40, pl. 38:176c (assigned to the 18th Dynasty), 34:188a,b (18th Dynasty, gold, probably Ptah-Sokar rather than Bes).

71 Tufnell 1958: 249–50, pl. 29:65 (Lachish, Tomb 571, ca. 1225–1175 B.C.); Starkey and Harding 1932: pl. 49 (Tell el-Far'ah South, Tomb 914, transitional Late Bronze–Iron Age); Petrie 1930: pl. 33:359–61 (Tell el-Far'ah South, Tomb 126, dated to Iron I).

72 E.g., Petrie 1906a: pl. 34: Tomb 4 (Tell er-Ratabeh).

73 E.g., Petrie 1906a: pl. 19A: group 306 (Tell el-Yehudiyeh, probably 22nd Dynasty); Loud 1948: pl. 206:64 (Megiddo, Stratum IV); Lapp 1967c: 37, fig. 25:5 (Taanach, Iron II context).

74 The plan of this area shows wall fragments of rooms, and no associated finds were published.

75 The pit yielded mainly LB IIB local pottery with some admixture of LB IIA local and imported forms (Mycenaean IIIA:2 and Base-Ring II). Thus, Tufnell's dating of ca. 1400–1300 B.C. must be extended to include LB IIB; there was apparently no archaeological separation of different burials belonging to the two centuries.

76 Cf. examples cited under Types *I.D.1–2* above; Petrie 1914: pls. 33:188e (assigned to the 18th Dynasty), 31:176e,f (22nd Dynasty); Tufnell 1953: pl. 34:12 (Lachish, Tomb 120).

77 The published pottery is LB I, and the granulated gold setting, common at 'Ajjul during this period, substantiates this dating.

78 However, cf. Petrie 1914: pl. 26:145c, d, f, g (undated), and Loud 1948: pl. 205:15 (Megiddo, Stratum VIIA, Iron I, gold), both with the same approximate form and posture.

79 Tufnell 1953: pl. 34:22 (Tomb 218, Iron II).

80 Loud 1948: pl. 205:35 (Stratum VI, Iron I).

81 Cf. also Macalister 1912: pl. 210:19=Rowe 1936: 268, pl. 30:A. 7 (Gezer, 'Third Semitic' Period, ca. 1400–1100 B.C.); Lapp 1967c: 37, fig. 25:4 (Taanach, mixed Iron I fill, head missing).

82 The pit was under Pit 172 and over Pit 252. It is attributed to Structure II and dated to LB IIA by Tufnell (Tufnell, Inge, and Harding 1940: 90), which accords with the LB IIA local, White-Slipped II, and Base-Ring II wares recovered.

83 The attribution (Tufnell, Inge, and Harding 1940: 65) of the pit to Structure III is borne out by the pottery evidence.

84 Although no detailed description or plan is provided, the pottery, including Base-Ring I and II, belongs to LB IIA.

85 Brunton and Engelbach 1927: pls. 26:60, 42:9L (18th–19th Dynasties).

86 Randall-MacIver and Woolley 1911: pl. 55:10221 (Tomb H 68A, probably 19th Dynasty).

87 Petrie 1894: pl. 17:297.

88 E.g., Brunton 1937: pl. 56:21M (Mostagedda, 4th–9th Dynasties); Petrie 1914: pl. 40:236a–c (6th Dynasty).

89 Petrie 1914: pls. 26:149e (assigned to the 20th Dynasty), 27:154 (22nd Dynasty); Rowe 1936: 271, pls. 30:A. 21 (Beth Shan, Level V, Iron I–II), 30:A. 3=Grant 1932: 188, no. 446 (Beth Shemesh, dated to the transitional Late Bronze–Iron Age).

90 Petrie Museum Amarna Cabinet, nos. 1211 and 1225, unpublished; Petrie 1914: 41, pl. 36:194f (19th Dynasty?); Petrie 1930: pl. 33: 358 (Tell el-Far'ah South, Tomb 127, 20th Dynasty?); Tufnell 1953: pls. 34:214 (Lachish, late Stratum IV, Iron I), 35:405 (Stratum IV, Iron I).

91 Petrie 1894: pl. 17:283 (Mut holding a lotus scepter extended away from her body); also cf. Samson 1972: 82, fig. 47(i), middle; Petrie 1914: pl. 36:201 (Sebek in profile holding *was* scepter, assigned to 18th Dynasty); Petrie 1894: pl. 19:284; Brunton and Engelbach 1927: pl. 25:14–16 (Gurob, dated to Thutmose III).

92 Petrie 1914: pl. 34:192b (undated, but Petrie begins the group as a whole with the 24th Dynasty).

93 Samson 1972: 80, fig. 46(iv), top row, left; Petrie 1894: pl. 17:252.

Chapter 3

CLASS *II* JEWELRY PENDANTS
HUMAN FORMS

A. Typology and Dating

The 18 pendants of Class *II* constitute only 2 per cent of the total number of pendants for Late Bronze Age Palestine, making it the smallest class of pendants. Two major categories and eight types are to be distinguished. Some of the types are related to Syro-Palestinian deities, but because the typological distinctions are not contingent upon such identifications, this aspect of pendant study is reserved for discussion in Chapter 8.

II.A.1   58

Fig. 21

Type II.A.1–3 Head or Face (58–61; pl. 4)
Type *II.A.1* comprises plain, even crude, head or face pendants. The sheet gold example (*58*), with its suspension ring unrolled, has eyes and nose simply indicated with punch marks. The oblong extension below may be the rest of face, neck, beard (?), or possibly the rest of the body.[1] *59* (pl. 4) has the same basic shape as *58*, with the head or face at the top and an oblong extension below. The eyes, nose, and mouth are roughly carved out of an unidentified dark stone, possibly pyramidal in shape. What may be the outline of a chin or perhaps a necklace is lightly incised with lines meeting at the middle of the pendant. The pendant is perforated through the bridge of the nose.

Of the two examples of Type *II.A.1*, one is from Locus 1322 at Beth Shan, which is a large area above Loci 1333–39 to the southeast of the Level IX temple, dated to the Late Bronze Age generally. The second example comes from Square 22 C–8 at Tell Beit

Mirsim, which was the best preserved room in the sector (Albright 1938b: 73), with pottery dating only to Late Bronze IIB. No close parallels can be cited for either specimen. However, the Beth Shan example (*58*) is similar to rectangular drop pendants in gold (Type *VI.F.2*), which occur in Level VII at Beth Shan, and to later varieties of the representational female plaque pendant (see below, under Type *II.B.2.b*). Similarly, the Tell Beit Mirsim example (*59*) fits into the same developmental stage of stylized representation.[2]

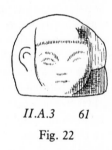

II.A.3   61

Fig. 22

Type *II.A.2* is represented by another sheet-gold example (*60*, pl. 4), a circular plaque showing a triangle-shaped face with more detail than *58*. An intact mouth, nose, the irises of the eyes, 'eyebrows' (hairline or top of head?), and possibly a stubbly beard (male?) are visible. Whereas the dots around the periphery are worked repoussé, the outlines of the eyes are incised. The suspension ring is unrolled.

The Type *II.A.2* specimen was found under the altar in Room D of Fosse Temple II, which was built during a later phase of LB IIB. The stratigraphic context implies the pendant was incorporated into the deposit during an earlier phase of LB IIB (Tufnell, Inge, and Harding 1940: 40, 65). Although unique, the repoussé technique conforms to the Syro-Palestinian workmanship of LB I–IIA (Types *II.B.2.a,b*, below). The stubbly beard may in fact represent the pubic triangle of a representational female plaque. If so, this detail would support a manufacturing date in an earlier stage of the Late Bronze Age, and should probably carry greater weight than any affinities of the type with Type *II.A.1* of LB IIB date. Schematization combined with fine workmanship prevailed in LB I–IIA, but not in LB IIB. Consequently, *60* may have been an heirloom at the time of its deposition.

The single example (*61*, pl. 4) of Type *II.A.3* is a well-modeled, wigged head or face of green glazed faience, which may have been broken away from its body. Despite its badly worn condition, eyebrows, ears, nose, and mouth are delineated. It is flat-backed and perforated at the back of the neck.

The Type *II.A.3* pendant was found in Burial Pit 4013 at Lachish, dated to LB IIB.[3] Egyptian parallels belong to the New Kingdom and the Saite Dynasty.[4] The date of manufacture is LB II and possibly as low as Iron II.

Type II.B.1.a, b Standing Figure –
Pictorial Female (62–65; pl. 5)
The division of female pendants into pictorial and representational groups follows the typological distinctions of Maxwell-Hyslop (1971: 138–39) and Negbi (1976: 95–103).

The pictorial female figurine pendant (Type *II.B.1.a*) differs from other types in this category in that it was made of a material other than gold. The Beth Shan example (*62*; pl. 5) is of badly disintegrating green glass, but enough remains to enable us to distinguish a rather clumsily formed nude female, standing upright in frontal view. She wears a wigged hair- or headdress and a schematically rendered bead or pendant necklace, has an enlarged belly, and supports her breast with her hands. There are two horizontal perforations, one at shoulder level and the other at hip level. The Megiddo example (*63*; pl. 5) is similar to the Beth Shan example, except that on the former, the headdress is marked by parallel vertical flutings and the face or head is better preserved and about twice as large. The example is of glass (misidentified as faience in Loud 1948: pl. 241:1, legend), and has a single perforation at shoulder level where the head was broken off from the now missing body. Both examples belong to the large variety as defined by Barag (1970: 188).

The Beth Shan example (*62*) comes from Locus 1390 in Level IX, a room in a residential quarter northwest of the temple area, which is dated to the Late Bronze Age generally. The Megiddo example (*63*) is from Locus 5029 in Area BB of Stratum IX, which probably dates to LB IA.[5] Barag (1970: 188–89, Appendix 2) discusses the dating and very wide geographical distribution of this type, which is found at Alalakh,[6] Hama,[7] Tell al-Rimah,[8] Boghazkale,[9] Kouklia,[10] Milia,[11] and in Egypt.[12] Additionally, poorly pro-

venanced examples were found at Megiddo,[13] Lachish,[14] Tell Mardikh,[15] Mycenae,[16] and Kakovatos.[17]

The pictorial female figurine pendant is clearly related to pottery figurine plaques that have a similar geographical and temporal distribution, extending into Iron I, throughout Mesopotamia and Syria-Palestine (Pritchard 1967: 43, nos. 62–97; Albright 1939). The majority of the figurine pendants were probably made between MB III and the beginning of LB IIA; pendants from later contexts should probably be considered heirlooms. As Barag (1970: 188–89) points out, some of the pendants may have been made in the same or nearly identical molds. Possibly all the examples share a common origin.

The one example (*65*; pl. 5) of Type *II.B.1.b* (pictorial female plaque) shows an incised nude female on a piriform gold-sheet plaque. She stands in an Egyptian pose with head and feet in profile and her body in three-quarters view. The lines of the figure and an encircling line are not continuous, but are comprised of straight, short incisions, probably made with a chisel. Wig, eye, nose, ear, mouth, breast, bracelets on both wrists, and possibly a necklace are shown. The woman holds a *was* scepter in her left hand, while the right arm is extended, possibly as a sign of benediction. There is a rolled suspension loop at the top of the plaque.

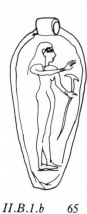

II.B.1.b   65

Fig. 23

The Type *II.B.1.b* pendant is from Locus 1403, Level IX, at Beth Shan, which is an open area on the west side of the temple courtyard, dated to the Late Bronze Age generally. No parallels could be located for this pendant, which Negbi (1970: 100) excludes from her corpus because of its Egyptian affinities. However, the manufacturing technique, the piriform-shaped plaque, and the nude female wearing jewelry and a wig, despite the Egyptianizing stance and *was* scepter, support a Syro-Palestinian origin, possibly Beth Shan (see below, Type *II.B.3*).[18] While the engraving technique by itself might be considered a late development, the piriform shape is an early feature. A date of manufacture of ca. 1300 B.C. could account for the mixed characteristics of this pendant type.

II.B.2.a   *67*

Fig. 24

Type II.B.2.a, b Standing Figure –
Representational Female (66–74; pl. 5)
The cut-out representational female plaque pendant (Type *II.B.2.a*) is represented by two sheet-gold examples (*66–67*, pl. 5). Both are dagger-shaped with heads cut out and suspension loops at the top (unrolled for *66*). *66* has eyebrows, eyes, ears, nose, mouth, necklace, breasts or nipples, and pubic triangle worked repoussé, with details of the necklace (individual beads or pendants), and pubic triangle (hair) marked by punched dots. The arms but not the legs are roughly indicated by incised lines, and the navel by a repoussé and incised circle. The pendant had been folded up in antiquity, and was broken in two pieces at the mouth. Petrie (1934: 5) claims that the pendant is of electrum with enough gold to keep it flexible, a proposal yet to be tested by composition analysis. In contrast to *66*, *67* has the hips cut out and a more elaborate, incised collar with a curious zigzag pattern below which are large pendants or vertical strings of beads. The figure is clothed in a brief tunic (incised hatched lines). Breasts or nipples and navel are just visible below the collar and above the tunic, respectively. The pendant had also been rolled up, and was found broken into five pieces of approximately the same size.

Both examples of Type *II.B.2.a* (representational female plaques) were discovered at Tell el-ʿAjjul:

1. *66* was part of Hoard 1299, which was found in a broken pottery vessel in an empty space distant from any building (Petrie 1934: 5–6, pl. 62) and which should probably be dated to the end of Town II/Palace IIIA, i.e., the end of LB IA;
2. *67* is from Hoard 1312, which overlay a wall of Town II (Petrie 1934: 8–9, pl. 62) and which should also be dated to late LB IA.[19]

The closest parallel for the types is from Ras Shamra.[20] The type may derive from earlier semi-stylized peg- and dagger-shaped figurines and pendants (Negbi 1970: 30–31; 1976: 80–82) from Byblos,[21] Nahariyah,[22] Megiddo,[23] and Gezer.[24] Later cutout dagger- and piriform-shaped figurines and pendants (Negbi 1970: 30–31; 1976: 97, nos. 1666–74) can also be cited from Hazor,[25] Megiddo,[26] Beth Shan,[27] Gezer,[28] Tell Abu Hawam,[29] and Tell Nebi Mend.[30] A class of violin-shaped pendants, which shares some of the characteristics of this type, occurs only at Ras Shamra[31] and Tell Nebi Mend.[32] The similarity of this type with the next type (*II.B.2.b*) suggests that the period of manufacture extends from MB III to the beginning of LB IIA.

The seven examples of the representational female plaque (Type *II.B.2.b*) are piriform in shape (elongated for *68*), and have rolled suspension loops at the top (unrolled for *69*). The workmanship of *68* and *69* (pl. 5) is relatively poorer than that of the other specimens. Eyes, nose, mouth, possibly ears, Hathor coiffeur, navel, and pubic triangle and vulva are worked in repoussé and by chasing (vulva only) in a rather crude fashion on *68*. *69* has eyebrows, irises, nose, cheeks, mouth, chin, breasts or nipples, hairdress (pigtails?), and navel worked repoussé; the outlines of the eyes and ears, as well as the top line of the pubic triangle, are emphasized with incised dots. Punched dots encircle the breasts or nipples, navel, and the knobs at the ends of the 'pigtails,' continuing part way up the right-hand tress. What were intended to be continuous lines are very much broken up by narrow chisel marks.

71 and *72* (pl. 6) are better made, with eyes (cross-eyed on *71*), eyebrows, ears, and cheeks, neck (with an inverted lotus flower beneath on *72*), Hathor coiffeur, and breasts/nipples well formed. *71* has a top-knob on the coiffeur, incised vertical lines on the rolled suspension loop with folded-over edges, the vulva and pubic triangle indicated by an incised vertical line and punched dots respectively, a navel marked by a larger

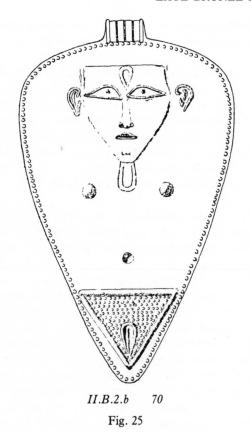

II.B.2.b   70

Fig. 25

punched dot, and a border of cross-hatched lines, which carelessly overlap with the encircling inner line in places. *72* is similar, but has no incised lines on the suspension loop. Dots worked repoussé outline the pubic hair and the periphery. A branch is engraved above the navel; no vulva is shown.

74 (pl. 6), and *70* (pl. 5) exhibit the same general characteristics, except that *70* is by far the best worked pendant in the group. The facial features (ears, eyes and irises, nose and nostrils, mouth and chin), breast or nipples, and the pubic triangle on both examples are delineated by repoussé dots. Additionally, *70* has an Egyptian-style goatee (a divine attribute), possibly a head ornament or stylized uraeus (symmetrical counterpart of the goatee?), the vulva marked in repoussé, and various details that are better defined with chasing. A unique feature of the latter is its squared-off face outlined with incised lines. Distinctive features of *74* include an incised, cross-hatched border, a line of punched dots in repoussé to mark out the hair-line (indented at the midline), and two vertically engraved lines extending down from the pubic triangle and probably representing the vulva.

Example *73* was not examined by the writer. It had been folded over and broken in antiquity, so that no distinguishable features could be made out (Petrie,

Mackay, and Murray 1952: 10). However, the plaque's piriform shape, which is a relatively uncommon attribute, argues for its inclusion in this group.

Type *II.B.2.b* is represented at three Palestinian sites. The Lachish example (*68*) was found below the altar in Room D of Fosse Temple II, an LB IIA locus (Tufnell, Inge, and Harding 1940: 65).[33] The Megiddo example (*69*) is from Square O 14, Area BB, in Stratum VIII, which was a large area with many of the walls and floors of rooms missing, presumably an LB IB–IIA context (Loud 1948: 148).[34] The six Tell el-'Ajjul examples, belonging to late LB IA, come from two jewelry hoards:

1. *72–75* from Hoard 277, which had been buried in a partially washed-away room of Town II (Petrie, Mackay, and Murray 1952: 8–9, 12, 28);
2. *70* and *71* from Hoard 1299, which was discovered in an empty space distant from any building (Petrie 1934: 5–6, pl. 62).

Excellent parallels with minor pictorial differences can be cited from Hoards *e* and *f* at Ras Shamra, which most likely belong to LB IIA.[35] Minet el-Beida, the harbor town of Ras Shamra, furnished two additional parallels, probably of the same date.[36] Further south, examples were found at Kamid el-Loz[37] and Tell Kazel.[38] A poorly made example of the same style as *69* comes from a transitional Late Bronze–Iron Age context at Megiddo,[39] and may be an heirloom. Later derivatives are the incised rectangular plaques of the Iron Age (Negbi 1970: 30, n. 133, with references). The several varieties of Type *II.B.2.b* must originate from several Syro-Palestinian centers (Ras Shamra, Tell el-'Ajjul, perhaps Gezer and Lachish), beginning in LB IA (Tell el-'Ajjul) and continuing through LB IIA.

II.B.3   75

Fig. 26

Type II.B.3 Standing Figure –
Pictorial Figure Plaque; Sex Uncertain (75–76; pl. 6)

The two examples (75–76) of Type *II.B.3* show rather clumsily executed incised figures with body in frontal view and face in profile, walking to the right (76, pl. 6) or to the left (75). The figure of 75 is masked by creases caused by folding over the plaque in antiquity. Rowe (1940: pl. 34: 7, legend on p. 80) described a winged male wearing a kilt and a Hittite-style conical crown. However, only the kilt, a raised pair of arms, and possibly an Egyptian wig could be discerned with difficulty in a reexamination of the specimen. A definite determination of sex was also impossible. The details of 76 are much clearer – Egyptian wig, left arm at the side and right arm raised, eye, nose, and mouth – but the careless rendering of the torso obscures the sex.

75 is from below the floor of Locus 1068, the upper altar room of the Level VII temple at Beth Shan, dated to the early part of LB IIB. 76 comes from Stratum V at Tell Abu Hawam, where it was found in a LB IIB dump in Square C–D 6, outside and to the west of Building 50 and above virgin sand (Hamilton 1935: 64, pls. 11, 18).[40] The development of gold plaque pendants away from a piriform shape and toward a rectangular form and the exclusive use of engraving are in accord with the LB IIB contexts in which the two examples were found (Negbi 1970: 30). Since the figure on 75 is very obscure, alleged Hittite analogues should not be stressed (cf. Negbi 1976: 45).

B. Summary

Class *II* pendants are rather evenly distributed among major Late Bronze sites along the coast, in the Shephelah, and in the main inland valley of the Esdraelon (Chart 12). Apart from the southern Hill Country site of Tell Beit Mirsim, which yielded a very crude pendant (*II.A.1*), the remainder of Palestine, including Transjordan, is conspicuous for its lack of pendants.

Although numbering only 18 specimens, the class includes some of the finest Late Bronze gold pendants (also see Class *VI*). The LB IA examples of *II.B.2.b*, in particular, make it abundantly clear that the ancient goldsmith had mastered most of the basic techniques of working in gold. Since pendants of comparable style and workmanship occur only at other Syro-Palestinian sites, in particular Ras Shamra/Minet el-Beida, there can be little doubt that these pendants were manufactured in Syria-Palestine. The fact that the *II.B.2.a* examples and the majority of the *II.B.2.b* specimens were found at Tell el-'Ajjul in jewelry hoards of LB IA houses (Chart 13) strongly suggests that workshops existed here during this period. Possibly, the LB IB–IIA examples of *II.B.2.b* from residential and temple contexts at Megiddo and Lachish, respectively, derive from 'Ajjul. A unique gold specimen (*II.B.3*) from the LB IIB temple at Beth Shan, which exhibits more Egyptianizing features and is less well made than the 'Ajjul specimens, may point to the establishment of an atelier there in late LB.

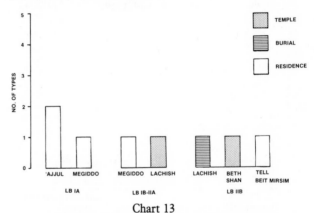

Chart 13
Contextual Distribution of Class *II* Pendant Types
for Late Bronze Age Palestinian Sites

Chart 12
Site Distribution of Class *II* Pendants in Late Bronze Age Palestine

Description	Type	Beth Shan	Lachish	Megiddo	Tell Abu Hawam	Tell el-'Ajjul	Tell Beit Mirsim	Total	%
Head or face	*II.A.1*	1	–	–	–	–	1	2	11
Head or face	*II.A.2*	–	1	–	–	–	–	1	6
Head or face	*II.A.3*	–	1	–	–	–	–	1	6
Standing figure	*II.B.1.a*	1	–	1	–	–	–	2	11
Standing figure	*II.B.1.b*	1	–	–	–	–	–	1	6
Standing figure	*II.B.2.a*	–	–	–	–	2	–	2	11
Standing figure	*II.B.2.b.*	–	1	1	–	5	–	7	39
Standing figure	*II.B.3.a*	1	–	–	1	–	–	2	11
	Total	4	3	2	1	7	1	18	101
	%	22	17	11	6	39	6	101	–

Significantly, all the closely dated pendant types were found in residential contexts at Tell el-'Ajjul (*II.B.2.a,b*) and Megiddo (*II.B.1.a*) in LB IA (Chart 13). Residences give way to burial and temple contexts from LB IB onward (Chart 14).

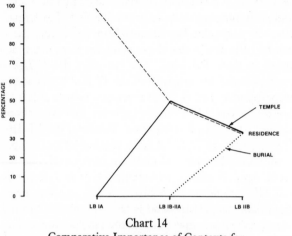

Chart 14
Comparative Importance of Contexts for
Class *II* Pendant Types

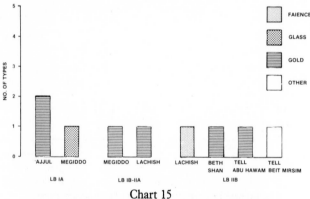

Chart 15
Material Distribution of Class *II* Pendant Types
for Late Bronze Age Palestinian Sites

Gold is the material of choice for Class *II* pendants, and was used for six of the eight types – including three well-dated types (Chart 15). The LB IIB faience example (*II.A.3*) from Lachish is of interest not only because it is the sole example in this material, but also because it is the only example from a burial context and the only Egyptian-related specimen in the group.

The two examples of *II.B.1.a* in glass from LB IA and general LB residential contexts at Megiddo and Beth Shan, respectively, also provided important results. They belong to a group of virtually identical pendants made exclusively of glass that are widely distributed throughout Syria, Mesopotamia, Anatolia, and the Mediterranean. The pendants were probably manufactured in the same or nearly identical molds be-

tween MB III and the beginning of LB IIA, perhaps at a single site in Syria-Palestine.

The several examples in glass (*II.B.1.a*), faience (*II.A.3*), and an unidentified stone (*II.A.1*) account for the minor differences in the comparative importance of gold from one LB period to the next (Chart 16).

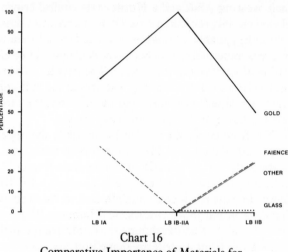

Chart 16
Comparative Importance of Materials for
Class *II* Pendant Types

Notes

1 Cf. the incised dots along its border with *66* and *70*. *68* (Type *I.B.2.b*) has a similar overall shape and the face is positioned in the same area on the plaque as for *58*.

2 Petrie 1934: 12, pls. 39:87, 10:bottom left (Tell el-'Ajjul, below wall of Town III, MB III); Lapp 1969: fig. 30, right (Taanach, EB–MB III–LB I fill).

3 In addition to a deposit of disturbed human skeletal remains, LB IIB local and imported pottery, including Base-Ring II and Bucchero wares, were found on a plaster floor.

4 Petrie 1914: 9, pl. 1:2g (assigned to the 18th Dynasty, without wig); 39–40, pl. 32:182g (Amset, undated); 35–36, pl. 43:154h (Nebhat, assigned to the 26th Dynasty).

5 A single isolated wall fragment here, which appears to be built upon a Stratum X wall, implies the continuation of the structure in Stratum IX, which must have been largely robbed out. However, all the published pottery dates to LB IA, which is therefore the most preferable date for the pendant.

6 Woolley 1955: 220, 222, 247, 302, temple, Levels VI (LB IA), V (LB IA), II/I (LB II).

7 Ingholt 1940: 105 (Level H, MB II).

8 Oates 1965: 73; 1966: 125, temple, Levels 2a (ca. 1450 B.C.) and 1b (first half of 13th century B.C.).

9 Bittel 1938: 25, fig. 26 (Level 1b, 14th–13th century B.C.)

10 Aproyi cemetery, Tomb II, mixed LC I–late LC II–LC IIIA pottery, unpublished.

11 Åström and Åstrom 1972, fig. 69 (late 16th–15th century B.C.).

12 Petrie 1914: pl. 30: 169c (unprovenanced example from Assiut).

13 Schumacher 1908: 53, fig. 79a; Watzinger 1929: 53.

14 Tufnell 1958: 83, 281–85, pl. 27:2 (Burial Cave 4004, layer 3, MB III–LB IIA).

15 Davico *et al.* 1967: pl. 66:3 (sector E).

16 Tsountas and Monatt 1887; Müller 1909: 278 (16th–13th century B.C.)

17 Müller 1909: pl. 12:6 (Tholos A, before 1450 B.C.).

18 Compare examples of the 'pictorial Qudšu' pendant and figurine plaque in Negbi 1976: 99–100, figs. 117–19, pl. 53:1701; Pritchard 1967: 32–42, nos. 1–18; Maxwell-Hyslop 1971: 139, pl. 106; Ussishkin 1978: 21, pl. 8.

19 Negbi (1970: 12–21) presents compelling arguments for an LB IA dating for all the 'Ajjul hoards (277, 1299, 1312, 1313, and 1450), which include many of the same jewelry types. Tufnell (1975: 57–59) prefers to date the hoards to the end of MB III. However, the appearance of Bichrome, White-Slip I, Black Lustrous, and Base-Ring I wares in the intermediate period between Towns III and II and Palaces I and II, with a peak in their popularity in Town II and Palaces II–IIIA, supports Negbi's position (Epstein 1966: 105, 176–79, 185; Albright 1938b: 345, 347, 356–57).

20 Negbi 1976: 96, no. 1659 (unpublished, Stratum 3, uncertain context, Late Bronze Age).

21 Dunand 1958: nos. 10633, 17789–90 (*Champs des Offrandes* and temples' area, EB IV–MB I).

22 Dothan 1956: 20, 27, pl. 5:F–I; 1957: 122–24, figs. 18–19 (Phase B of the *bamah*, MB I).

23 Loud 1948: pl. 233: 3, 9, 10 (Strata XIIIB and XII?, MB I).

24 Macalister 1912: 433, fig. 515 (foundation deposit, MB I); Seger 1976: 133–39, fig. 3:2a–c (probably MB III).

25 Yadin *et al.* 1961: pl. 339:3–4, 7–10; 1972: 82 (Area H, temples 2, 1B, and 1A, covering the entire Late Bronze Age).

26 Loud 1948: pls. 236:25, 29, 240:4 (Strata VII B and VII, LB IIB–Iron I).

27 Rowe 1940: 79, pl. 34:14 (Level VII, LB IIB).

28 Macalister 1912: 263, pl. 136:8 (silver hoard in pot, Late Bronze Age?).

29 Stratum IV, Iron I, unpublished.

30 Pézard 1931: 54, pl. 30, fig. 3 (niveau 'Syro-Hittite', Middle Bronze to Late Bronze).

31 Schaeffer 1931: 7; 1932: 22–24, pl. 16:2; 1937: 145, pl. 18; 1938: 319, fig. 48:9–11 (hoards from '*Résidence*', area of temples, and near library, LB IIA; see n. 35 below for dating.

32 Pézard 1931: 52, pl. 30, fig. 3 (niveau 'Syro-Hittite', Middle Bronze to Late Bronze).

33 The locus is properly assigned to Structure II, since it is a homogeneous LB IIA locus, which included Base-Ring II and White-Slip II wares.

34 No pottery was published for the area, but its assignment to Stratum VIII is presumptive evidence for an LB IB–IIA dating.

35 Since Hoard *f* was found in a Mycenaean IIIA jug (Schaeffer 1937: 145; 1938: 319, fig. 49:2–10; 1939a: 47, fig. 9, a *terminus ante quem* of ca. 1300 B.C. is likely, while a date after ca. 1400 B.C. is suggested by the absence of Bichrome pottery, i.e. a date in *Ugarit Récent* 2=Stratum III (1450–1365 B.C.) according to Schaeffer (1929: 87–90; 1932: 4–14; 1939a: 47) or, perhaps better, LB IIA (Negbi 1970: 34). Hoard *f*'s dating probably applies to the other Late Bronze jewelry hoards found at Ras Shamra.

36 Schaeffer 1932: 9–10, pl. 9:1; 1939a: 47, pl. 29, fig. 1 (left); Negbi 1976: 98–99 (*dépôt* 213 bis, from below the floor of what Schaeffer interpreted as a mortuary shrine [North 1973: 158]).

37 Hachmann 1970: pl. 1:3 (Level 4, probably transitional Middle Bronze to Late Bronze).

38 Dunand, Bounni, and Saliby 1964: 12, pl. 17:3 (Level V, LB IIA).

39 Loud 1948: 162, pl. 214:86.

40 The dump produced a homogeneous collection of LB IIB pottery types.

Chapter 4

CLASS *III* JEWELRY PENDANTS FAUNA

A. Typology and Dating

Class *III* is the second smallest class of LB Palestinian pendants (27 pendants, 3 percent of the total). It is comprised of eight main categories and 15 types (eight uncertain). Mammals (eight types) are best represented, followed by birds (four types), insects (one type), fish (one type), and amphibians (one type). The animal genus can only be suggested in several cases.

III.A   79

Fig. 27

ring as a pair, has wings, head, and body outlined in wire and details worked in repoussé. Additionally, triangular and circular clusters of fine granulation cover the wings; the tail feathers, body, and eye are accentuated with gold granules. Two suspension rings are soldered to the top of the wings.

All specimens of Type *III.A* are from the LB IA Hoard 277 at Tell el-'Ajjul, which had been buried within a partially washed-away room of Town II (Petrie, Mackay, and Murray 1952: 8–11, 28).[1] Although no parallels can be cited, the type was probably inspired by Egyptian pectorals of the Middle Kingdom.[2] The type occurs only in LB IA, and was most likely manufactured at 'Ajjul.

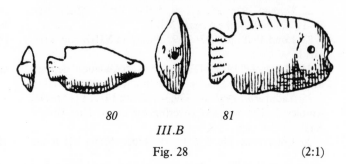

80   81

III.B

Fig. 28   (2:1)

Type III.A Falcon (78–79; pl. 6)
The two examples (*78, 79*) of this type from Tell el-'Ajjul are remarkable for their fine workmanship in gold. The falcon, the Egyptian royal and divine bird, is depicted on a crescentic plaque; it has stylized, high-arching, outstretched wings. Body and tail feathers appear in frontal view, and the head with eye and beak is turned to the right in profile. *79* (pl. 6) is about a third larger than *78*, and is unique for the amount of twisted wire work used to outline the head and eyes, talons, and body. The body, tail, and wing feathers, as well as the eye, are worked in repoussé. Since it lacks granulation, however, Petrie makes the unlikely suggestion (Petrie, Mackay, and Murray 1952: 9) that it may be incomplete. The suspension loops with incised midlines are soldered at the top of the wings. *78*, occur-

Type III.B Fish (80, 81)
The two examples (*80, 81*) of this type are both of faience (glaze color not specified) with incised eye, mouth, and fins (badly worn on *80*). *81* has a wide body, small side fin, and open mouth (cf. Petrie 1914: pl. 43:257a); it is flat-backed with a horizontal perforation. *80* is sleeker-looking (Petrie 1914: pl. 43:257c, d); it is flat-backed and the suspension ring at the top is broken off. The fish genus cannot be determined.

Both examples of Type *III.B* come from Lachish:

1. *80* from Burial Pit 4019, a homogeneous LB IIA context (Tufnell 1958: 288);
2. *81* from Pit 556, a problematical locus, probably dating to LB IIA (Tufnell 1958: 245).

Comparable broad- and slender-bodied fish pendants, sometimes with finer detailing, occur at el-Amarna[3] and Gurob.[4] Although fish pendants were popular throughout Egyptian predynastic and dynastic history, the faience varieties included under this type were probably manufactured exclusively in LB II.

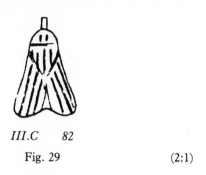

III.C   82

Fig. 29   (2:1)

Type III.C Fly (82; pl. 6)
The four virtually identical examples (82) of this type show the fly's head, body, and wings in a highly schematic fashion with incised lines, precluding assignment of genus and species. The pendants are hollow with a decorated gold sheet soldered onto a gold base (solid gold according to Negbi 1970: 32); a suspension loop is soldered to the top.

The four examples of the fly pendant type were found together in Hoard 1313 at Tell el-'Ajjul which had been deposited in a late LB IA room of Town II (Petrie 1934: 7, 11; Petrie, Mackay and Murray 1952: 13). Beginning with the Middle Kingdom, *comparanda* in gold and silver can be cited from Kahun,[5] Buhen,[6] Thebes,[7] and Qau.[8] The general popularity of the fly pendant in other materials is also attested to at el-Amarna,[9] Riqqeh,[10] Buhen,[11] Harageh,[12] Balabish,[13] and Gurob.[14] Petrie illustrates a late 18th Dynasty yellow glazed faience specimen in his corpus (1914: 12, pl. 2:19j). Although the 'Ajjul examples may well have been fabricated at this site during LB IA, the chronological span of the type is a long one – from the Middle Kingdom to the end of the New Kingdom.

Type III.D Frog or Toad (83; pl. 6)
The single example (83) of this type is very well modeled in carnelian and is shown in its typical seated position with its back legs tucked under its body. Distinguishing features of *Rana* or *Bufo* are lacking (e.g., the webbed feet of *Rana*). The pendant is pierced horizontally through the middle of the body, and is flat-based.

83 is from TDK, a room of a large building with a stone foundation, at Tell el-'Ajjul (Petrie 1934: 3, 14–15, 18, pl. 63); the published pottery points to a probable LB I dating. The frog/toad is a common pendant

type of LB Palestine and Egypt, appearing at Gurob,[15] Kahun,[16] Buhen,[17] el-Amarna,[18] and Lachish.[19] The Iron Age frog pendant type is higher-backed.[20] Because of the lack of distinguishing characteristics, 83 cannot be limited to a particular period of the Late Bronze Age.

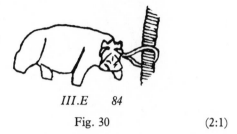

III.E   84

Fig. 30   (2:1)

Type III.E Hippopotamus (84)
The one example (84) of this type shows the body, legs, and facial features (ears, eyes, snout, and mouth) of a hippopotamus on one side of a flat-backed amethyst pendant, which has a suspension ring of gold wire.

The Type *III.E* specimen comes from Tomb 447 at Tell el-'Ajjul, which was located southwest of Building LA in an open space (Petrie 1934: 8–9, pl. 61); the published pottery dates the context to LB I. Parallels occur at Middle Bronze Mostagedda[21] and Tell Beit Mirsim.[22] The period of production for the type is MB I through LB I.

Type III.F Lion Fighting Bull or Dog (85; pl. 7)
The *III.F* example is oval-shaped and open cast in copper or bronze; it is the largest Late Bronze jewelry pendant. Although badly corroded, what is most likely a lion (note tail and paws) is shown attacking a bull or dog. This is a standard motif in ancient Near Eastern art (Hartner 1965: 1–16; Thompson 1970: 78–116, discussing the lion and dog panel from Level IX at Beth Shan). The same scene is duplicated on each side of the pendant, which has a triple-ridged suspension loop soldered to the top.

85, an unparalleled specimen, comes from Room 1235, the east side of the courtyard of the Level IX temple, which is assigned a general Late Bronze Age date.

Type III.G Ram's Head (86–89; pl. 7)
The four examples (86–89) of this type are all of glass, of approximately the same size, and except for 86, have a vertical perforation from the top of head to the base of the muzzle. 86, which has a suspension ring at the back of the head, could not be personally examined, but appears to be a schematic, flattened version of the same type. The other examples (87–89, pl. 7) are of a

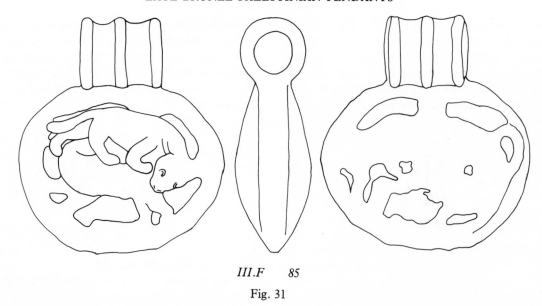

III.F   85

Fig. 31   (1:2)

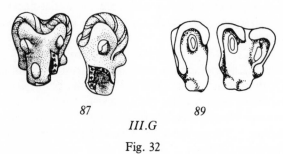

87   89

III.G

Fig. 32

three-dimensional ram's head with horns curving
down and forward, and eyes, irises, and nostrils in different colored glass than the rest of the head. The cur-
vature of the horns, as well as the use of swirled glass to
indicate their twist, more closely resembles that of a
ram's rather than a bull's horns (*contra* Åström and
Åström 1972: 591). After the basic hand-modeling of
the heads, the horns, eyes and irises, and nostrils
would have been added.

86–89 are from Beth Shan: (1) *86* and *87* are from
below the steps of Locus 1068, the upper altar room of
the Level VII temple, dated to an early phase of LB
IIB (Level VIII); and (2) *88* comes from north of the
steps of Locus 1068, and *89* from Locus 1086, the
anteroom of the temple, both dated to late LB IIB
(Level VII). Although Petrie (1914: 44, pl. 38:212a–r)
ascribes a long history to the ram's head pendant (prehistoric times to the Ptolemaic period), he does not
illustrate any New Kingdom examples comparable to
nos. 86–89. However, close parallels do occur at
Akhera,[23] Alalakh,[24] Tell el-Yehudiyeh,[25] Gezer,[26]
Megiddo,[27] and Nuzi.[28] Although the available evidence is inadequate and conflicting, Type *III.G* may
have originated in Egypt where ram's head pendants

were popular throughout predynastic and dynastic
times. The flat and rounded varieties were probably
manufactured in LB II; the Iron I examples from
Megiddo belong to a more detailed type, while the Tell
el-Yehudiyeh parallel is most likely an heirloom.

III.H.1.a–c Bird (*90–92*; pl. 8)
Three questionable types of bird pendants are included in this group. Given the numerous genera and
species of birds, the queried possibilities can only be
suggestive and not definitive (cf. Gardiner 1957: 467–
74).

90 (Type *III.H.1.a*, pl. 8) is of a small, dove-like
bird. Only the eye and beak are faintly indicated on the
white stone, and a perforation runs through the middle
of the body. *91* (Type *III.H.1.b*, pl. 8) has the general
characteristics of a goose or duck (note, especially, the
long neck). However, its highly stylized side feathers
delineated with horizontally incised lines cut by vertical lines, in addition to the badly worn head and face,
preclude precise identification (Gardiner 1957: 471, G
38, 39). It is of blue glazed faience, and has a suspension ring at the middle of the back. The proposal to
identify *92* (*III.H.1.c*; pl. 8) with an owl is tentative,
but such outstanding features as the frontal pose and
the large eyes(?) support this interpretation. The
examples were all made from the same mold or affiliated molds, are of blue-green glazed faience, and have a
suspension ring (single or double) at the top.

The single example of Type *III.H.1.a* (dove?)
comes from Tomb 3016 at Megiddo, which was presumably dug below the floor of a room in a large hous-
ing complex in Area BB (Loud 1948: 167). A
transitional LB I–IIA dating is indicated from the

III.H.1.c   92

Fig. 33

published pottery evidence. Small, rather schematic bird pendants of stone occur at Nahariyah[29] and Nuzi.[30] The period of manufacture is probably MB I through LB I.

The goose- or duck-like bird pendant (Type *III.H.1.b*) was found during the sifting of soil from the Fosse Temple area, necessitating a general Late Bronze Age date. Comparable examples can be cited from el-Amarna[31] Meydum[32] and Buhen.[33] Despite the poor context of the Lachish example, the type was probably only manufactured in LB II.

The one example of Type *III.H.1.c* (owl?) was found at Beth Shan below the steps of Locus 1068, the upper altar room of the Level VII Temple, and can be dated to early LB IIB. No parallels could be traced; the type may be confined to LB II.

Type *III.H.2 Bull?* (93; pl. 8)

The single example (*93*) of this type is very small and of worn yellow glazed faience. It depicts an animal in profile walking to the right. The pointed projections above the head are most likely the horns of a bull, and the remainder of the animal's form is in accord with this identification (Petrie 1914: pl. 37:207–9). However, it could be a cat with erect ears (Petrie 1914: pl. 39:224–27). There is a suspension ring at the middle of the back, and the pendant is flat.

93 was found in the deposit of beads and pendants near the west wall of Room E of Fosse Temple III, dated to LB IIB (Tufnell, Inge, and Harding 1940: 42, 74–76, pl. 8:4). The closest parallel that could be located is a 19th Dynasty example pictured in Petrie's corpus, which shows the bull (?) walking to the left (Petrie 1914: 44, pl. 37:208c, blue glazed faience). Another example from el-Amarna (Petrie 1894; pl. 17:303) is comparable, but the animal is crowned with a disc (Hathor?) and faces left; it is a precursor of the later *naos* plaque type (Petrie 1914; 44, pl. 37:207). Type *III.H.2* is probably limited to LB II.

Type *III.H.3 Cat?* (94; pl. 8)

The problem of identifying *94* (Type *III.H.3*) is the reverse of that for *93* (Type *III.H.2*). The couchant body and ears strongly suggest a cat (cf. Petrie 1914:

pl. 39:224). Nevertheless, the bull interpretation is still possible (Petrie 1914: pl. 37:208a). The pendant is of a green stone, and has a suspension hole bored lengthwise through its middle.

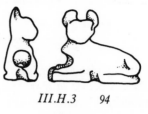

III.H.3   94

Fig. 34

The single example of *III.H.3* is from Locus 1382 of Level VII at Beth Shan, which is a room of the '*migdal*' dated to late LB IIB. Close New Kingdom parallels can be cited from el-Amarna,[34] Deir el-Medineh,[35] and Gurob.[36] Petrie also includes examples of similar 18th Dynasty bull and cat pendants in his corpus (Petrie 1914: 44, 46, pls. 37:208a, 39:224k). Type *III.H.3* was probably only manufactured in LB II.

Type *III.H.4 Dog?* (95; pl. 8)

The one example (*95*) of Type *III.H.4* could not be personally examined, and its details are obscure on the overexposed photograph. However, the posture of the animal with front legs well forward, in addition to the profile and features of the head or face, is closer to that of a dog (Petrie 1914: pl. 39:231) than to that of any other animal (e.g., a cat with much straighter posture, Petrie 1914: pl. 37:224, 227). The example is of faience (glaze color unspecified), and is probably bored through the middle of the body.

95 is from Locus 4004, Area AA, Stratum IX, at Megiddo, which was a well-defined room with the floor broken up (Loud 1948: 176). Although no associated pottery was published, Stratum IX can be assigned an LB IA date. *Comparanda* appear to be nonexistent. Indeed, the stance of the animal is suggestive of an Iron II or later date (cf. Petrie 1914: pl. 39:224b, f, 227, 231c), and the pendant may be intrusive in the Late Bronze context.

Type *III.H.5 Mouse?* (96; pl. 8)

96, with its large rounded head and small, smoothly contoured body is suggestive of a mouse. However, the couchant posture and form are in conformity with other animals such as a cat or ram (Petrie 1914: pls. 37–39). The pendant is of faded blue-green glazed faience, and has a horizontal perforation through the middle of the body.

The single example of Type *III.H.5* is from Locus 1326, Level IX, at Beth Shan, a questionable context

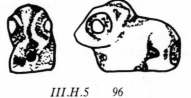

III.H.5   96

Fig. 35   (2:1)

not appearing on any plan and assigned a general Late Bronze Age date. A period of manufacture cannot be definitely established because of the identification problem and the lack of parallels; an LB II phase is most likely.

Type III.H.6 Ram? (97; pl. 8)

The one example (97) of Type *III.H.6* is of badly corroded silver; and details, especially of the head, which would help in identification are obscure. The upright stance, as well as the sagging throat and underbody, are characteristic of either a ram or sheep. However, other animals (e.g., dog, Petrie 1914: pl. 39:229) cannot be ruled out. There is a soldered suspension loop on the back.

97 is from Tomb 1037 at Tell el-'Ajjul, which was a large tomb containing a homogeneous collection of LB IIA pottery (Petrie 1932: 7–8, 10, 15–16, pl. 56). Because of the lack of parallels, assigning an LB IIA period of manufacture must remain tentative.

B. Summary

Class *III* is about evenly divided between major northern and southern sites, Beth Shan and Tell el-'Ajjul, with Lachish and Megiddo contributing several additional pendants (Chart 17). Class *III* pendants have not yet been found in the Hill Country, the Huleh or Jordan Valley (with the exception of Beth Shan), the Galilee, or Transjordan.

Although comprised of only 27 examples, closely dated faunal types are very well differentiated in terms of geographical, contextual, and material distributions. Gold types (*III.A* and *III.C*) predominate in LB IA residential contexts (jewelry hoards) at 'Ajjul (Charts 18 and 19). These exhibit the high technological standard which is characteristic of the first part of Late Bronze Palestine; they were very likely manufactured at the site (see Classes *II* and *VI*). The only other example from an LB IA context is a faience type (*III.H.4*) from Megiddo, possibly an Iron Age intrusion.

In contrast, the majority of the LB IIB types derive from temple contexts at Lachish (*III.B* and *III.H.2*) and Beth Shan (*III.G*, *III.H.1.c*, and *III.H.3*). None of these are in gold, but rather faience, glass, and semi-precious stones (Chart 20). The faience examples are mold-made; variously colored glass was used in hand-forming the specimens of *III.G*.

The LB IB–IIA period yielded only single examples

Chart 17
Site Distribution of Class *III* Pendants in Late Bronze Age Palestine

Description	Type	Beth Shan	Lachish	Megiddo	Tell el-'Ajjul	Total	%
Falcon	*III.A*	–	–	–	3	3	11
Fish	*III.B*	–	2	–	–	2	7
Fly	*III.C*	–	–	–	4	4	15
Frog or Toad	*III.D*	–	–	–	1	1	4
Hippopotamus	*III.E*	–	–	–	1	1	4
Lion, Bull or Dog	*III.F*	1	–	–	–	1	4
Ram's Head	*III.G*	4	–	–	–	4	15
Dove?	*III.H.1.a*	–	–	1	–	1	4
Goose or Duck	*III.H.1.b*	–	1	–	–	1	4
Owl?	*III.H.1.c*	4	–	–	–	4	15
Bull?	*III.H.2*	–	1	–	–	1	4
Cat?	*III.H.3*	1	–	–	–	1	4
Dog?	*III.H.4*	–	–	1	–	1	4
Mouse?	*III.H.5*	1	–	–	–	1	4
Ram?	*III.H.6*	–	–	–	1	1	4
Total		11	4	2	10	27	103
%		41	15	7	37	100	

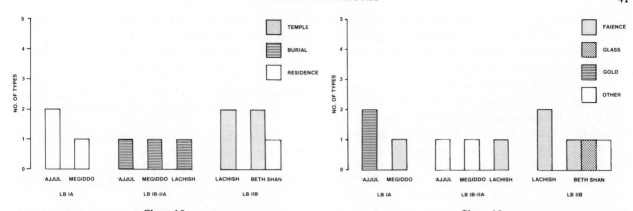

Chart 18
Contextual Distribution of Class *III* Pendant Types
for Late Bronze Age Palestinian sites

Chart 19
Material Distribution of Class *III* Pendant Types
for Late Bronze Age Palestinian Sites

Chart 20
Quantitative Analysis of Materials Used for Class *III* Pendants
in Late Bronze Age Palestine

Description	Type	Faience			Glass				Au	Ag	Cu	Stone		Total	%
		B	B–G	?	B& BR	B,BR &W	BR &W	?				SP	?		
Falcon	*III.A*	–	–	–	–	–	–	–	3	–	–	–	–	3	11
Fish	*III.B*	–	–	2	–	–	–	–	–	–	–	–	–	2	7
Fly	*III.C*	–	–	–	–	–	–	–	4	–	–	–	–	4	15
Frog or Toad	*III.D*	–	–	–	–	–	–	–	–	–	–	1	–	1	4
Hippopotamus	*III.E*	–	–	–	–	–	–	–	–	–	–	1	–	1	4
Lion, Bull or Dog	*III.F*	–	–	–	–	–	–	–	–	–	1	–	–	1	4
Ram's Head	*III.G*	–	–	–	1	1	1	1	–	–	–	–	–	4	15
Dove?	*III.H.1.a*	–	–	–	–	–	–	–	–	–	–	–	1	1	4
Goose or Duck	*III.H.1.b.*	1	–	–	–	–	–	–	–	–	–	–	–	1	4
Owl?	*III.H.1.c*	–	4	–	–	–	–	–	–	–	–	–	–	4	15
Bull?	*III.H.2*	1	–	–	–	–	–	–	–	–	–	–	–	1	4
Cat?	*III.H.3*	–	–	–	–	–	–	–	–	–	–	–	1	1	4
Dog?	*III.H.4*	–	–	1	–	–	–	–	–	–	–	–	–	1	4
Mouse?	*III.H.5*	–	1	–	–	–	–	–	–	–	–	–	–	1	4
Ram?	*III.H.6*	–	–	–	–	–	–	–	–	1	–	–	–	1	4
Total		2	5	3	1	1	1	1	7	1	1	2	2	27	103
%		7	19	11	4	4	4	4	26	4	4	7	7	100	

Ag = silver
Au = gold
Cu = copper or bronze
SP = semi-precious
? = unidentified
B = blue
B–G = blue-green
BR = brown
W = white

of *III.B*, *III.H.1.a*, and *III.H.6* from burials at Megiddo, Tell el-'Ajjul, and Lachish, respectively. Each is composed of a different material: silver, an unidentified white stone, and faience.

On the basis of this analysis, Syro-Palestinian types (see Chapter 8) are concentrated toward the beginning of the Late Bronze at Tell el-'Ajjul; the unique specimen of *III.F* from Level IX at Beth Shan, which is assigned a general Late Bronze Age dating, may also belong here. Following LB IA, a gradual penetration of Egyptian-related types (including *III.D* and *III.E*) occurs in LB IB–IIA, particularly in burials. Egyptian-related faience types reach a peak in temples of LB IIB.

Since there is no geographical overlap of types, northern and southern distributions may be defined. However, the presence of bird types (*III.A* and *III.H.1.a–c*) in both regions suggests that allowance should be made for some geographical spread.

Notes

1 See stratigraphic discussion above, Chapter 3, n. 19.

2 Hayes 1953: 233, 308, figs. 150–51; Montet 1929: 166–67, pl. 95.

3 Petrie 1894: pl. 17:330, 332; Samson 1972: 79, fig. 46(ii), bottom row, first two on the right.

4 Brunton and Engelbach 1927: pl. 42:19R, Y (Tombs 262 and 474, 18th–19th Dynasties).

5 Petrie and Brunton 1924: pl. 48:8 (dated to Amenhotep I).

6 Randall-MacIver and Woolley 1911: 215–16, pl. 89:10898 B (Tomb K 45, Second Intermediate Period).

7 Vernier 1927: 3, pls. 51, 54:C, D (18th and 19th Dynasties); Carnarvon and Carter 1912: 80, pl. 73:53 (Tomb 37, LB I); Aldred 1971: 215, pl. 86, second necklace from bottom.

8 Brunton 1930: 16, pl. 32:5 (dated to early 18th Dynasty).

9 Petrie 1894: pl. 17:337.

10 Engelbach 1915: pl. 18 (no provenience, dated to Ramesses II, carnelian).

11 Randall-MacIver and Woolley 1911: pls. 51:10347 (Tomb H 33 B, dated to 18th Dynasty), 54:10271 (Tomb H 82, dated to LB I).

12 Engelbach 1923: pl. 50: 22D (Tomb 547, Middle Kingdom, carnelian).

13 Wainwright 1920: pls. 8:1, 16, 13:7 (Pan Graves, Second Intermediate Period).

14 Brunton and Engelbach 1927: pl. 42:22A (Tomb 295, 18th–19th Dynasties, glazed steatite).

15 Petrie 1891a: pl. 22:13 (no provenience, dated to Amenhotep III, 'porcelain' [glass?]); Brunton and Engelbach 1927: pl. 42:17 (Tomb 81, 18th–19th Dynasties, blue 'paste').

16 Petrie 1891a: pl. 26:3 (Tomb of Maket, Coffin 1, probably dating to Amenhotep III, blue glass).

17 Randall-MacIver and Woolley 1911: pl. 55:10239–40 (Tomb J 50, 18th–19th Dynasties, black and white glazed and green glazed pottery?).

18 Petrie 1894: pl. 17:329 (green glazed pendant and mold).

19 Tufnell 1958: 124, pl. 39:333 (Tomb 547, LB II).

20 E.g., Petrie 1906a: pl. 18: group 307 (Tell el-Yehudiyeh, 22nd Dynasty?).

21 Brunton 1937: 125, pl. 76:1 (Burial 3143, Pan Grave culture, ca. 1900–1600 B.C.).

22 Albright 1938b: 55, pl. 30:2 (Stratum E, MB I).

23 Karageorghis 1965: 130, fig. 37:50, 70, pl. 10:4–5 (Tomb 3, dated to the beginning of LC IIC, but possibly earlier).

24 Woolley 1955: 270, pl. 68:b8 (uncertain context between Levels II and IB, ca. 1300 B.C., 'paste' [glass?]).

25 Petrie 1906a: pl. 19B (Tomb 301, Iron II, probably glass).

26 Macalister 1912: 109–11, pl. 137a:38 (Locus C, Trench 13, 'Third Semitic' Period, ca. 1400–1000 B.C., dated to Amenhotep III by Macalister, 'faience').

27 Loud 1948: pl. 205:22–23 (Stratum VIIA, Iron I, 'faience').

28 Starr 1939: 454, pl. 120: YY (Temple A, Stratum II, LB IB, schematic variety, glass).

29 Dothan 1957: 122, figs. 5, 7 (clay figurine) (Stratum C, MB III).

30 Starr 1939: 32, pl. 120: SS (Temple A, Stratum II, LB IB, glass).

31 Samson 1972: 79, fig. 46(iii), second from left (neck not as curled back and no vertical wing lines).

32 Petrie, Wainwright, and Mackay 1912: 28, pl. 22:10 (dated to 18th Dynasty).

33 Randall-MacIver and Woolley 1911: pl. 55:10206 (Area H, New Kingdom, glazed pottery?).

34 Samson 1972: 77–78, fig. 46(i), 2nd–4th examples from the left.

35 Bruyère 1953: 53–54, fig. 11, bottom row, middle.

36 Brunton and Engelbach 1927: pl. 26:19–20 (Tomb 60, 18th–19th Dynasties, seals).

Chapter 5

CLASS *IV* JEWELRY PENDANTS FLORA

A. Typology and Dating

By far the largest number of Late Bronze Palestinian pendants (490+ pendants, 58 percent of the total) belong to the floral class, which is subdivided into eight categories and 20 types (five of which are uncertain). As for Class *III* (fauna), the schematic rendering or bad condition of individual pendants usually precluded the identification of plant genera and species.

Type IV.A. Cornflower or Corn Cockle (98; pl. 9)
The 25 examples (98) of Type *IV.A* all have blue-green calyces and purple corollas in glazed faience. The form is either that of a cornflower (*Lychnis githago*) or a corn cockle (*Centaurea cyanus*). The color scheme, assuming that it is unchanged from the original (note that on some of the examples the blue-green has yellowed), is that of a cornflower (Tufnell, Inge, and Harding 1940: 76; Petrie 1894: 30, thistle; Macalister 1912: 333, lotus scepter). At least two molds must have been employed, since the cross hatchings are either uniformly and closely spaced or have an irregular placement. The pendants are flat-backed with top and bottom suspension rings attached separately.

The 25 examples were found together with the deposit of beads and pendants near the west wall of Room E in Fosse Temple III at Lachish, which is dated to LB IIB (Tufnell, Inge, and Harding 1940: 42, 74–76, pl. 8:4). A very close parallel of the same basic design and color scheme can be cited from el-Amarna.[1] LB IIA is the main period of popularity for the type, and the Lachish examples are probably heirlooms.

Type IV.B Daisy (99–101; pl. 9)
The three examples (99–101) included under Type *IV.B* exhibit the color pattern and form of a daisy, viz., a central yellow disc with radiating white petals, all in glazed faience except for 99 (frit?). 100 and 101 have sixteen petals, and the disc is marked with cross-hatched incised lines; both may have been made from the same mold. 99 has no cross hatching on the disc,

and has eight petals. All the examples are flat-backed, and have top suspension rings.

99 comes from Locus 2009.1, Area 2, Field I, at Gezer, which appears to date exclusively to LB IIB rather than extending into early Iron (cf. Dever, Lance, and Wright 1970: 23–24, 75).[2] One example (100) from Lachish was found in the southeast corner of Shrine 181 in Room D of Fosse Temple III (Tufnell, Inge, and Harding 1940: 76, pl. 7:3,4), which the local pottery evidence securely dates to LB IIB. Another two specimens (101) from Lachish come from the LB IIB deposit of beads and pendants found near the west wall of Room E of Fosse Temple III (Tufnell, Inge, and Harding 1970: 42, 74–76, pl. 8:4). This floral pendant type again has very close parallels at el-Amarna.[3] The type is also found at Serabit el-Khadem in the Sinai,[4] Qantir,[5] and Alalakh.[6] Its period of manufacture is LB II.

IV.C   103

Fig. 36

Type IV.C Date Fruit (102–103; pl. 9)
Type IV.C. is represented by 14 specimens (103) of blue-green glazed faience, with an indented line at one end of their elliptical form that justifies identifying them with dates (cf. Petrie 1894: pl. 19:449–50; Pritchard 1954: 259, pl. 73; Aldred 1971: 231, pl. 125). 102, which could not be examined, has a comparable shape and color ('light green'=blue-green?), but its smaller size indicates that it does not derive from the same family of mold(s) as the examples of 103. All the pendants are flat-backed, and have suspension rings at both ends.

The 15 examples of Type *IV.C* are from Beth Shan:

1. The one example of *102* is from below the floor of Locus 1068, the upper altar room of the Level VII temple, dated to an early phase of LB IIB;
2. The 14 examples of *103* come from the cache of jewelry near the steps of Locus 1068.

Parallels occur at New Kingdom el-Amarna,[7] Serabit el-Khadem,[8] and Thebes.[9] The type is confined to LB II.

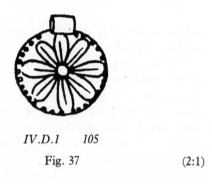

IV.D.1   *105*

Fig. 37   (2:1)

Type IV.D.1–3 Flower or Rosette (*104–107*; pl.9)
The first type (*IV.D.1*) under this heading comprises two sheet gold examples (*104, 105*, pl. 8), which have eight rays or petals in repoussé radiating from a central boss. This design can be interpreted as a flower or a standardized rosette (see *Type VI.G.2*, Chapter 7). *105* has medial lines on each petal ray and punched dots around its periphery. In contrast, *104* lacks punched dots, and straight, overlapping line segments, probably made with a chisel, define the curved edges of the petals or rays. Each pendant has a rolled suspension loop at the top.

The two examples of the eight-rayed variety were found at Lachish:

1. *104* in the deposit of beads and pendants near the west wall of Room E in Fosse Temple III, dated to LB IIB (Tufnell, Inge, and Harding 1940: 42, 74–76, pl. 8:4);
2. *105* from LB IIA Tomb 216 (Tufnell 1958: 232–35).[10]

Although this type is clearly related to the eight-rayed star disc pendant (Type *VI.G.2*), which became especially popular in the Iron Age as an appliqué on garments (Maxwell-Hyslop 1971: 151, 212–13, fig. 156, pl. 179; Oppenheim 1949; Van Buren 1939), no close parallels can be cited. Type *IV.D.1* is possibly limited to LB II Palestine.

The second type (*IV.D.2*) of this group is represented by a single example (*106*; pl. 9), again of sheet gold but with 12 petals or rays worked in repoussé.[11] It has a raised edge, and its central boss is depressed in the middle. The top suspension loop is broken off.

106 was found during the sifting of soil from the Fosse Temple area, and must be dated to the Late Bronze Age generally (Tufnell, Inge, and Harding 1940: 66). Obviously an elaboration of the previous type, the only parallel which could be located was an appliqué from the Level VII temple at Beth Shan (Locus 1068, upper altar room), dated to late LB IIB. Its period of manufacture is again possibly confined to LB II.

Type *IV.D.3* is also represented by only one example (*107*; pl. 9). Twenty-four rays or petals appear to radiate from a central disc; personal examination was not possible, and the published photograph is very dark. It is of blue glazed faience.

107 comes from Pit 176 at Lachish, located east of the Fosse Temple, under Pit 161, and probably belongs to an early phase of LB IIB.[12] The pendant is similar to a mold with 22 rays or petals from el-Amarna,[13] and one with 24 rays or petals from Qantir.[14] A virtually identical pendant was found at Kamid el-Loz.[15] The type was probably manufactured throughout LB II, and possibly continued to be produced at Qantir in the early Iron Age.

Type IV.E Grape Cluster (*108–110*; pl. 9)
Six specimens (*108–109*) of Type *IV.E* are of the same size, style (grape globules unevenly spaced in rows), and color (purple glazed faience), and must have been made in the same mold or affiliated ones (cf. Petrie 1894: pl. 19:443). *110*, which was not personally examined, has more evenly spaced globules, and is reported to be of gray faience (possibly faded from purple). Suspension rings are located at the top and on the flat back near the bottom of all the examples.

108 and *109* from Lachish were recovered from separate rooms of the LB IIB Fosse Temple III: (1) *108* was found with the deposit of beads and pendants near the west wall of Room E (Tufnell, Inge, and Harding 1940: 42, 74–76, pl. 8:4); and (2) *109* comes from the cache of objects in the southeast corner of Shrine 181 of Room D (Tufnell, Inge, and Harding 1940: 76). The remaining example (*110*) is from Tomb 36 B at Megiddo, a locus yielding local and imported LB IIA pottery. El-Amarna[16] provides the best parallels, none of which are exact, and other varieties are to be noted at Qantir,[17] Kamid el-Loz,[18] Gezer,[19] and Tell el-'Ajjul.[20] On the basis of the published parallels, the type belongs to LB II with a probable extension into the early part of Iron I.

IV.F.1   112

Fig. 38

Type IV.F.1–5.b Lotus
The lotus pendant types were extremely popular in
Late Bronze Age Palestine (185 pendants, 17 percent
of the number of floral pendants, and 22 percent of the
total pendants for Late Bronze Age Palestine). As a
popular subject, the various natural forms and motifs
were freely experimented with to produce highly stylized types (note, especially, the palmette varieties at
el-Amarna, Petrie 1894: pl. 18:365–91).

Type IV.F.1 Lotus Bud (*111–117*; pl. 9)
One of the simpler lotus pendant types is the lotus
bud, which is represented by 19 specimens (*111–117*).
The majority of these examples are of variously colored faience: *112*, white; *113* and *114*, blue; and *115*,
yellow (not of gold, as reported by Petrie). *112* (pl. 9)
shows the basic characteristics of a small bud enclosed
by outward-bending leaves (calyx), which sometimes
curve back upon themselves (in particular, *114*; pl. 9).
A unique feature of *112* is the small secondary epi-
calyces below the main calyx. The four specimens of
115 appear to have been made in the same mold, while
the two examples of *113* (pl. 9) derive from a different
mold. Each specimen is flat-backed with a suspension
ring (broken off on *112*). The other examples (*111*,
116, *117*) of this type are all of gold. *111* is an excellent
example of cloissonné workmanship with straight and
curved strips of metal soldered perpendicular to the
base to form compartments that were once filled with
glass or faience, now missing. A suspension loop with
folded-over edges and incised vertical lines is attached,
so that the bud would have hung downward. The ten
virtually identical examples of *116* and *117* show the
tear-shaped bud and two outward-curving leaves
worked in repoussé on an upper sheet, which was then
soldered to a flat base, forming a hollow interior.
Suspension loops are soldered at the bottom for downward suspension.

Type *IV.F.1* is represented at five Palestinian sites.
The Amman Airport Building example (*111*) was from
the 'dedicatory' fill, a very mixed context with material
from most of the Late Bronze Age (Hankey 1974: 135,
Table 3), but which was deposited in LB II. The Beth
Shan example (*112*) comes from Locus 1068, the upper

altar room of the Level VII temple, dated to late LB
IIB. The two examples (*113*) from Lachish were found
in refuse Pit 248 to the east of the Fosse Temple; the
LB IIA pottery types accord with Tufnell's attribution
of the pit to Structure II (Tufnell, Inge, and Harding
1940: 91). The Megiddo example (*114*) was found in
Locus S=2048, Stratum VIII, to the south of the
temple in Area BB (Loud 1948: 159), which probably
belongs to LB IB–IIA in accord with the standard
dating for Stratum VIII.[21] The three entries (*115–117*)
for Tell el-'Ajjul refer to tombs in the '18th Dynasty'
Cemetery:

1. *115* from Tomb 1064, which lacks an adequate
   description or plan (Petrie 1932: 14–15, pl. 52),
   but which yielded LB IIA local and imported
   pottery;
2. *116* from Tomb 1073 (Petrie 1932: 7–8, 14–15,
   pl. 52), which contained LB IIA pottery;
3. *117* from Tomb 1085, which has no published
   pottery evidence, but is dated by Petrie (1932:
   14–15, pl. 62) to the 18th Dynasty.

The faience variety of this type (*112–115*) has good
LB II parallels at el-Amarna,[22] Buhen,[23] Gurob,[24] and
Kahun.[25] An extension of the type into Iron I is poss-
ible.[26]

Of the gold varieties, *116* and *117* appear to be
almost precisely paralleled at Thebes[27]; the period of
manufacture is probably confined to LB I–IIA. The
cloisonné gold variety (*111*) is comparable to the fine
LB IA 'Ajjul goldwork, but may date to a later
period.[28]

IV.F.2   131

Fig. 39

Type IV.F.2 Conventional Lotus (*118–134*; pl. 10)
The conventional lotus pendant is well-named, since it
was extremely common in Late Bronze Palestine
(116+ pendants, 24 percent of the total floral pendants) as well as in Egypt (Petrie 1894: pl. 18:398); it is
one of the least stylized versions of the lotus flower in
bloom. All of the examples are of blue-green glazed

faience (some faded) and thus do not show the color variation typical of true lotus flowers. They are flat-backed with suspension rings at top and bottom (often broken off). The typical calyx of two leaves is shown at one end of the pendant, from which extends 15 to 20 straight or slightly curved petals or sepals. It is very difficult to assign specific examples to the same mold (e.g., a mold with a certain number of petals or sepals), because most of the examples are broken, badly made, or excessively worn. In general, a variety with about 20 petals or sepals (*Nymphaea lotus* – white lotus?) and another with about 15 (*Nymphaea caerulea* – blue lotus?) can be distinguished. The Lachish examples (*133* and *134*) approximate to the 20 petal or sepal variety, and were made from affiliated molds, which had a more broadly spread calyx than the molds used for the Beth Shan examples.

The Beth Shan examples (*118–132*) are concentrated in the temple area, although three examples are from nearby houses:

1. Level IX (Late Bronze Age):
   Below the threshold of Locus 1092 (*118*);
   General area of Locus 1092 (*119*);
   Locus 1233, east side of the courtyard (*120*);
   Locus 1241, south side of the temple courtyard (*121*);
2. Level VIII (early LB IIB):
   Locus 1092, below the area of the Level VII temple steps (*122–123*);
   Below the steps and floor of Locus 1068, the upper altar room of the Level VII temple (*124–125*);
3. Level VII (late LB IIB):
   Near the steps of Locus 1068 (*126*);
   Locus 1072, the temple court (*127*);
   West side of Locus 1072 (*128*);
   Locus 1089, a partially defined room south of the anteroom of the temple (*129*);
   Locus 1262, an entrance to a house on the east side of the temple (*130*);
   Locus 1359, a room in the southwestern residential sector (*131*);
   Locus 1365, another room in the southwestern residential sector (*132*).

Of the Lachish examples (*133–134*), one group (*133*) comes from Room D of Fosse Temple II, dated to LB IIA (Tufnell, Inge, and Harding 1940: 65), whereas the other group (*134*) was found with the deposit of beads and pendants near the west wall of Room E of Fosse Temple III, dated to LB IIB (Tufnell, Inge, and Harding 1940: 42, 74–76, pl. 8:4).

The closest parallel for the Beth Shan examples

occurs at New Kingdom Buhen.[29] El-Amarna[30] has a somewhat different variety with fewer petals or sepals. Varieties with larger calyces and very definite epi-calyces emerge in Iron I.[31] The period of manufacture for Type *IV.F.2* should thus be limited to LB II.

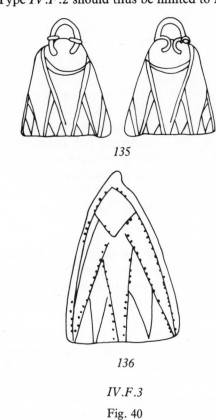

135

136

IV.F.3

Fig. 40

Type IV.F.3 Lotus Flower (*135–136*; pl. 10)
The two sheet gold pendants (*135–136*) of Type *IV.F.3* are a more exact representation of the lotus flower, probably the blue lotus (*Nymphaea caerulea*), which has narrower and more pointed petals/sepals in contrast to the ovoid petals or sepals of the white lotus (Tait 1963). Both examples have petals/sepals and calyx demarcated with incised lines (double in places on *135*). *136* also has punched dots to emphasize the lines of the calyx and petals/sepals. The suspension loop at the base of *135* pierces the calyx and is then bent back upon itself. The suspension loop of *136* is broken off.

The two examples of this type are from Locus 1403 at Beth Shan, located on the west side of the courtyard of the Level IX temple, assigned to the Late Bronze Age generally. Although LB II faience comparisons of inlays and bead spacers are numerous,[32] in view of the popularity of lotus types, a general Late Bronze dating for manufacture is advisable until more evidence is available.

137

139

142

IV.F.4
Fig. 41

Type IV.F.4 Lotus Palmette (137–142; pl. 10)
The examples (*137–142*) of Type *IV.F.4* have little resemblance to natural varieties of the lotus flower and palm. Rather, the various lotus elements have been taken and combined to produce novel, artificial forms (Petrie 1894, pl. 18:365–91).

142, of sheet gold, is perhaps the most ornate of the group. The inward- and outward-swirling calyx encloses a petal or perhaps an elongated bud. The design is worked in repoussé, and the details are emphasized by a chasing of punched dots. A suspension hole at the base is reinforced by a ring of gold wire.

Less fancy are *140* and *141* (pl. 10), which show a similar design of calyces swirling away from each other and then back again toward three slightly splayed petals or palm leaves. They are of approximately the same size, and of sheet gold worked repoussé; the suspension loops are broken off. *139* appears to be a very schematic version of the latter design, having horizontal petals or leaves cut by vertical lines between the calyces (cf. Type *VI.E*, Double Spiral). The eight specimens under this entry may either be incised or worked in repoussé on a gold plate (no first hand examination was possible). Suspension holes were formed by rolling over opposite sides to allow for double stringing of the pendants.

137 and *138* (plate 10) are simpler, less stylized versions of *140* and *141* in blue-green glazed faience (*138*, 'light green' faience). Two petals or leaves are enclosed within a calyx and epicalyx(?). Although *138* could not be examined, its larger dimensions indicate that it must have been made in a different mold than that used for *137*. *137* is flat-backed, and had suspension rings at each end (now broken off).

The two Beth Shan examples (*137–138*) of Type *IV.F.4* come from below the steps and below the floor, respectively, of Locus 1068, the upper altar room of the Level VII temple, and date to early LB IIB. The eight identical examples (*139*) from Beth Shemesh were found in an LB IIB jug buried under the floor of Room 73 of Stratum IV (Grant 1931: 43, plans 4 and 5;

1932: 21; Grant and Wright 1939: 47–48), which probably dates to LB IIB. Of the two examples from Lachish, *140* comes from Room D of Fosse Temple D, a homogeneous LB IIA context, and *141* was found during the sifting of soil from the Fosse Temple area and must be dated to the Late Bronze Age generally. The Tell el-ʿAjjul example (*142*) is from Hoard 1312, found overlying a wall of Town II (Petrie 1934: 8–9, pl. 62) and is to be dated to late LB IA.[33]

The faience variety of the lotus palmette from Beth Shan fits into a larger class of such pendants from el-Amarna[34] (cf., especially, Petrie 1894: pl. 18: 371). The type is generally confined to LB II with a possible extension in Iron I.[35] No close parallels for the gold varieties could be traced; but, given the endless variation of lotus palmette motifs, analogous specimens may eventually be discovered (cf. Petrie 1894: pl. 18: 375, 385). An LB II dating with a possible extension into Iron I fits the presently available data.

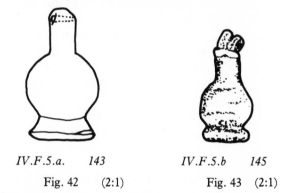

IV.F.5.a.   143   *IV.F.5.b*   145

Fig. 42   (2:1)   Fig. 43   (2:1)

Type IV.F.5.a–b Lotus Seed Vessel (143–159; pl. 11)
The lotus seed vessel pendant occurs in two forms: a thin, flat-backed type (*IV.F.5.a; 143–144*), and a rounded, three-dimensional type (*IV.F.5.b; 145–159*). The current consensus is that a lotus seed vessel rather than a poppy head, lotus bud, pomegranate, or thistle head is being depicted (cf. Rowe 1936: 278; Peet and Woolley 1923: 170). The flat type has a lower height-to-width ratio than the rounded type, and

occurs only in carnelian. The rounded type sometimes was made of faience (blue-green glazed, *145* and *158*; blue glazed, *146*; red glazed, *154*), glass (red, *158*), and once in gold (*159*), although the majority of specimens are of carnelian (*147–152*, *155–157*). Some variation in form exists for each type, because most of the specimens were hand-crafted. Several slight variations should also be noted: (1) a medial, vertical hole drilled from the base and extending two-thirds the length of the pendant (*145*); (2) notches around the edge of the base (*146*); and (3) a long cylindrical base (*159*). The carnelian specimens have horizontal conical perforations drilled from one side of the pendant only, while the faience, glass, and gold examples have suspension rings at the top.

The flat-backed type (*IV.F.5.a*) occurs at Beth Shan and Megiddo. The Beth Shan example (*143*) comes from below the steps of Locus 1068, the upper altar room of the Level VII temple, and is dated to early LB IIB. *144* from Megiddo was found in Tomb 877 C 1 in a disturbed locus with a mixture of LB I and IIA local and imported wares (Guy 1938: 36). More rare than the rounded variety, this type probably first appears in LB II, but possibly continues until Iron II.[36]

The rounded type (*IV.F.5.b*) occurs at five Palestinian sites. At Beth Shan, it is represented in the LB IIB levels:

1. Level VIII (early LB IIB):
   Locus 1292, a 'kitchen' in the southeastern residential sector (*145*);
   Locus 1300, a questionable locus on the south edge of the tell (*146*);
   Below the steps of Locus 1072, the court of the Level VII temple (*147*);
2. Level VII (late LB IIB):
   Locus 1068, the upper altar room of the temple (*148*);
   Locus 1072, the temple court (*149*);
   Locus 1251, a room with a partition wall in the southeastern residential quarter (*150*).

The ten examples (*151*) from Beth Shemesh were found together in an LB IIB jug, which had been buried under the floor of Room 73 of Stratum IV (Grant 1931: 43, plans 4 and 5; 1932: 21; Grant and Wright 1939: 47–48), dated to LB IIB.

The Lachish examples come from the following contexts:

1. *152* from Burial Pit 4013, a homogeneous LB IIB context containing fragmentary, disturbed human skeletal material (Tufnell 1958: 286–87);

2. *153* from Room E of Fosse Temple III, dated to LB IIB (Tufnell, Inge, and Harding 1940: 42, 74–76, pl. 8:4);
3. *154* from Burial Cave 4002, dated to LB II (Tufnell 1958: 89, 280–81).[37]

155 and *156* come from Tombs 877 B 1 and 912 B, respectively, at Megiddo, which are probable LB IIB contexts (Guy 1938: 36, 72).[38]

The four examples (*158*) from Tell Abu Hawam, were found together in a mass of fallen stone and debris above the stone pavement of Building 53 of Stratum V, an LB II context (Hamilton 1934: 74; 1935: 62).[39]

The single Tell el-'Ajjul specimen (*159*) was discovered in Tomb 1080 of the '18th Dynasty' Cemetery, which belongs to LB IIA (Petrie 1932: 7, 14–15, pl. 52).

Numerous parallels for the rounded variety can be cited from Egyptian 18th and 19th Dynasty contexts, including Gurob,[40] Riqqeh,[41] Buhen,[42] and el-Amarna.[43] The type's continuation as late as Iron II is also abundantly attested at Tell el-Far'ah South,[44] Gezer,[45] Megiddo,[46] and Timna.[47]

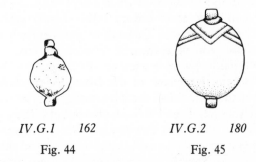

IV.G.1　　162　　　　　IV.G.2　　180

Fig. 44　　　　　　　　　　Fig. 45

Type IV.G.1–2 Mandrake Fruit (*160–188*; pl. 11)
Another extremely popular jewelry pendant in Late Bronze Age Palestine was the mandrake fruit (131 examples, 27 percent of the floral pendants and 16 percent of the total number of pendants), which occurs in small (ca. 15 × 10 × 2 mm) and large (ca. 24 × 15 × 2 mm) types.

Over half of the examples of the small type (*IV.G.1*; *164–166*, *169–170*, pl. 11) portray the true color scheme of the mandrake fruit – yellow fruit and blue calyx – in glazed faience (*169* is reported to be of 'glass'). The remaining examples (*160–163*, *167–168*, pl. 11) are of the standard blue-green glazed faience (some faded) with chevrons (curved for *170*) and hatched lines to show the division between the fruit and calyx (often worn away; cf. a well-preserved example of the large type – *180*, pl. 11). Suspension loops, sometimes broken off, are at both ends, except in the case of the Beth Shan specimens of blue and yellow glazed faience which have the suspension ring attached to the back at the yellow end of the pendant. Because of poor manufacture or the badly worn state of most of the examples, the exact number of molds to account for the different varieties is doubtful. However, a minimum of four molds is probably required to explain the Beth Shan examples (three for the blue-green glazed and one for the yellow and blue glazed faience varieties), in addition to another mold for the Lachish examples (*170*).

The Beth Shan specimens occur in various loci of each Late Bronze level:

1. Level IX (Late Bronze Age generally):
   Locus 1232, the inner sanctuary of the temple, behind the main altar (*160*);
2. Level VIII (early LB IIB):
   Locus 1092, below the area of the Level VII temple steps (*161*);
   Locus 1287, a possible shrine in the southeastern residential sector (*162*);
   Below the steps of Locus 1068, the upper altar room of the Level VII temple (*163* and *165*);
   Below the floor of Locus 1068 (*164*);
3. Level VII (late LB IIB):
   Near the steps of Locus 1068 (*166–168*);
   North of the Locus 1068 steps (*169*).

The 11 Lachish examples (*170*) are from the deposit of beads and pendants near the west wall of Room E of Fosse Temple III, dated to LB IIB (Tufnell, Inge, and Harding 1940: 42, 74–76, pl. 8:4). The yellow and blue glazed faience variety has a close parallel at el-Amarna.[48] The closest parallels for the blue-green glazed variety are found at both el-Amarna[49] and Deir el-Medineh.[50] While the yellow and blue glazed faience variety may be limited to LB IIA, the blue-green glazed faience variety was probably manufactured throughout LB II.

The large mandrake fruit type (*IV.G.2, 171–188*, pl. 11) apparently occurs only in blue-green glazed faience: *171, 175, 177, 180–182, 187–188* (many faded), and possibly *183* ('light blue glass'), *176, 179*, and *184–185* ('light brown and light blue', faded 'light green', 'green' and 'white-green' faience), and *174, 178, 186* (white glazed faience, leached out and faded?). All of the pendants were found at Beth Shan, with the exception of *188* from Lachish. With allowances for manufacturing technique and wear, it is probable that all of the Beth Shan examples were made in the same mold or affiliated molds. Similarly, the 16 identical

specimens from Lachish, which have fewer lines defining the calyx, probably derive from a single mold family. Suspension rings are attached at both ends (often broken off).

The 85 Beth Shan examples are distributed among various loci of the three Late Bronze levels:

1. Level IX (Late Bronze Age generally):
   Below Locus 1092, which is below the area of the Level VII temple steps (*171*);
   Locus 1233, the east side of the temple courtyard (*172*);
   Locus 1234, the inner sanctuary of the temple (*173–175*);
   Locus 1240, a large, undefined area outside the southern wall (*176*).
2. Level VIII (early LB IIB):
   Locus 1092, below the area of the Level VII temple steps (*177*);
   Below the east wall of Locus 1068, the upper altar room of the Level VII temple (*178*);
   Below the floor of Locus 1068 (*179*);
3. Level VII (late LB IIB):
   Near the steps of Locus 1068 (*180*);
   West side of Locus 1072, the temple court (*181–182*);
   Locus 1107, a partially defined room on the north side of the temple outer courtyard (*183*);
   Locus 1359, a room in the southwestern residential sector (*184*);
   Locus 1362, the southwest side of the temple outer courtyard (*185–186*);
   Locus 1366, a room in the southwestern residential sector (*187*).

The 17 Lachish examples (*188*) were found with Type *IV.G.1* in the cache of beads and pendants near the west wall of Room E of Fosse Temple III, dated to LB IIB (Tufnell, Inge, and Harding 1940: 42, 74–76, pl. 8:4). Egyptian parallels occur at el-Amarna[51] and Thebes.[52] Although its main period of manufacture is LB II, the type continues to be made in Iron I.[53]

Type IV.H.1 Bud? (*189*; pl. 12)
The three identical specimens (*189*) are suggestive of buds about to open; Dothan (1979: 73) and Tadmor and Misch-Brandl (1980: 77) describe them as fruit-shaped. Pieces of sheet gold are soldered together to form three elongated swellings below a spheroid. A gold wrapping holds the trilobe form together at the top, above which a gold spheroid is overlaid. A gold cap is soldered to the bottom, and a gold suspension loop protrudes through the top opening. The pendants

IV.H.1   184

Fig. 46

were most likely used on earrings (Dothan 1979: 73–77, figs. 158, 164, 171–173).

The three examples come from Beth Shemesh, where they were found in an LB IIB jug, buried under the floor of a corner of Room 73 of Stratum IV, which is dated to LB IIB (Grant 1931: 43, plans 4 and 5; 1932: 21; Grant and Wright 1939: 47–48). Virtually identical parallels occur at Deir el-Balah,[54] Tell el-Far'ah South,[55] and Ras Shamra.[56] Possibly, the pendants were made at a single southern Palestinian site in LB IIB and Iron I (Dothan 1979: 77).[57]

IV.H.2   190

Fig. 47

Type IV.H.2 Lotus Flower? (190–191; pl. 12)
Apparently related to Type *IV.F.2* is a long-stemmed(?) variety of the conventional lotus pendant (*190*), with suspension rings at both ends. It is probably of blue-green glazed faience (recorded as 'blue' faience). *191* (pl. 12), although badly worn, appears to be a highly naturalistic rendering of a lotus flower in bloom (cf. Type *IV.F.3*, pl. 10). It is of blue glazed faience, and has a suspension ring at each end.

190 comes from Locus 1108, Level VIII, at Beth Shan, which is an area below the court and courtyard of the Level VII temple, dated to an early phase of LB IIB. No close parallels could be traced, but the same dating argument can be applied here as for Type

IV.F.2, viz., it is an Amarna-style pendant that continues to be manufactured in LB IIB.

191 was found with the deposit of beads and pendants near the west wall of Room E of Fosse Temple III, dated to LB IIB (Tufnell, Inge, and Harding 1940: 42, 74–76, pl. 8:4). El-Amarna provides excellent parallels, which may derive from a very similar mold.[58] The variety maintains its popularity into LB IIB.

IV.H.3.a   198

Fig. 48

Type IV.H.3.a–b Petal or Leaf (192–215; pl. 12)
The largest group of uncertain floral pendants (88+ specimens, 18 percent of Class *IV*, 10 percent of the total number of Late Bronze pendants) can be divided into two main types: plain (*IV.H.3.a*) and decorated (*IV.H.3.b*) petals or leaves.

The plain variety usually occurs as glazed faience colored blue-green (*193, 196–201*, some faded; possibly *192* and *202*), yellow (*204*) and blue (*205* and *208*), although single examples were also made of gold (*203*), silver (*207*), and copper or bronze (*206*). All the examples of this type are nondescript (cf. Type *VI.F.2*, elongated drop), and could represent leaves or petals of many different flowers or plants (e.g. willow, lily, lotus, etc.; see Aldred 1971: 207, 211, 231, pls. 65, 71, 125; Pritchard 1954: 73, pl. 259).

The Beth Shan faience specimens (see below) were probably made in at least two molds, a small one ca. 16 × 7 × 2 mm and a large one ca. 25 × 9 × 3 mm. While *204, 205*, and *208* from Lachish may derive from the same or affiliated molds as those used for the Beth Shan examples, they are of different colored glazed faience.

The 23 gold specimens (*203*) conform to the basic leaf or petal form, but are smaller (10 × 4 mm). They are hollow and made of separate sheet gold pieces (flat back and curved front) soldered together; a suspension loop is attached to one end.

The bronze and silver examples (*206–207*, pl. 12) are of somewhat different shape (more elliptical and broader), with a rolled suspension loop at one end.

Type *IV.H.3.a* is best represented at Beth Shan, which has examples from loci of the three Late Bronze levels:

1. Level IX (Late Bronze Age generally):
   Below the general area of Locus 1092, which is below the area of the steps of the Level VII temple (*192*);
   Below the threshold of Locus 1092 (*193*);
   Locus 1234, the inner sanctuary of the temple (*194–196*);
2. Level VIII (early LB IIB):
   Below the steps of Locus 1072, the court of the Level VII temple (*197*);
3. Level VII (late LB IIB):
   Near the steps of Locus 1068, the upper altar room (*198*);
   On the west side of Locus 1072 (*199*);
   Locus 1262, an entrance to a room on the east side of the temple (*200*);
   Locus 1284, a questionable locus east of Fitz-Gerald's deep sounding (*201–202*).

The 23 Dhahrat el-Humraiya examples (*203*) come from Grave 57, a built grave with undisturbed burials (Ory 1948: 13, 87, fig. 2, pl. 31:3), dated to LB II.[59]

The Lachish examples are from the following contexts:

1. *204–205* from the deposit of beads and pendants near the west wall of Room E of Fosse Temple III, dated to LB IIB (Tufnell, Inge, and Harding 1940: 42, 74–76, pl. 8:4);
2. *206* from Pit 172, east of the Fosse Temple and over Pit 199, attributed to Structure III and probably of LB IIB date (Tufnell, Inge, and Harding 1940: 65);
3. *207* from Pit 176, also east of the Fosse Temple and under Pit 161, which is attributed to Structure III and dated to LB IIB (Tufnell, Inge, and Harding 1940: 65);
4. *208* from the sifting of soil from the Fosse Temple area, dated to the Late Bronze Age generally.

Parallels for the variously sized faience varieties can be cited from New Kingdom el-Amarna,[60] Serabit el-Khadem,[61] Deir el-Medineh,[62] and Gurob.[63] The varieties definitely belong to LB II, but may continue into Iron I.[64] The gold variety (*203*) is paralleled at Middle Kingdom Dahshur[65] and Thebes.[66] Type *IV.H.3.a*, therefore, may begin as early as the Middle Kingdom in Egypt and persist throughout the Late Bronze Age. Comparable examples could not be found for the silver and copper-base examples, but they are perhaps later versions of the gold variety.

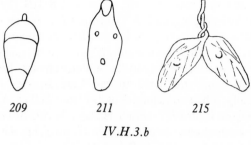

IV.H.3.b

Fig. 49

The decorated leaf or petal type (*IV.H.3.b*) occurs only in gold, apart from *210*, a long narrow white glazed faience pendant with a yellow glazed tip (lily petal?, cf. Pritchard 1954: 259, pl. 73=Aldred 1971: 231, pl. 125). The two specimens of *209* (pl. 13, base only) are unique for their cloisonné workmanship. The standard leaf or petal shape is formed of a gold sheet base with the edges bent up, to which is soldered two thin, perpendicular strips, forming three cloisons of approximately equal area. While the middle cloison is empty, the cloison at one end is filled with brown glass and the one at the other end with white glass. This is very likely an idealized rendering of a petal (cf. Aldred 1971: 208, pl. 65, Treasure of the Three Wives of Thutmose III).

213 (pl. 13) is another gold specimen with a decoration of concentric ellipses entirely filling the area of the petal or leaf (veins of the petal or leaf?). Since the suspension loop is unrolled, it is not clear whether its raised and indented design would have been visible.

The remaining examples of this group are unusual for their decoration in repoussé dots and their occurrence in pairs (except *211*). *212* (pl. 13), *214*, and *215* (pl. 13) are comprised of two petals or leaves with their stems twisted together to form a suspension loop at one end. Single central dots appear on *214* and *215*, which are more ovoid in shape, together with fine hatched lines (a more realistic rendering of veining) worked in repoussé. *212*, in contrast, has two repoussé dots near two apices of the more triangular-shaped plaque (cf. the upper dots on *211* [pl. 13]) and no hatched lines. *211* (pl. 13) has three repoussé dots at the apices of an equilateral triangle at the center of the piriform-shaped pendant, whose design and workmanship is comparable to Type *II.B.2.b* (representational female plaque pendant). It is also the only example of this variety with a rolled suspension loop.

The decorated leaf or petal pendant is found at three Palestinian Late Bronze sites. At Beth Shan, examples occur below the floor of Locus 1068 (*209*) and below the south wall of Locus 1062 (*210*), an area north of the Level VII temple, both of which are assigned to Level

VIII and dated to an early phase of LB IIB. From Level VII proper (late LB IIB) comes *211*, which was found north of the steps of Locus 1068, the upper altar room. The three specimens (*212–213*) from Lachish were found during the sifting of soil from the Fosse Temple, and thus date to the Late Bronze Age generally. The two examples of *214* from Tell el-'Ajjul come from Hoard 277, which had been buried in a partially washed-away room of Town II, probably dating to a later phase of LB IA (Petrie, Mackay, and Murray 1952: 8–10, 28). *215* was found in another hoard (1312) at the same site, which overlay a wall of Town II and which is also to be dated to the end of LB IA (Petrie 1934: 8–10, pl. 62).

The single faience example (*210*) of Type *IV.H.3.b* is paralleled at el-Amarna,[67] and may be confined to LB IIA, which would imply that the Beth Shan example is an heirloom.

The cloisonné variety (*209*) occurs as early as the Middle Kingdom,[68] but it became especially popular during the New Kingdom.[69]

The variety with the punched dots (*211–212, 214–215*), in accord with the dating argument for Type *II.B.2.b*, was manufactured in the Late Bronze Age generally.

IV.H.4   216

Fig. 50

Type IV.H.4 Reeds? (*216–218*; pl. 13)
The final dubious floral type probably represents reeds, but the schematic rendering of rigidly straight, perpendicular elements (stalks?) may be purely geometrical.

The three examples are from three different sites and are of three different varieties:

1. *216* (pl. 13), an example comprised of two elements and of dark blue glazed faience;
2. *217* (pl. 13), 15 specimens with seven elements from the same mold or affiliated molds, and of purple glazed faience;
3. *218*, four specimens with three elements from the same mold family, and of faded blue-green glazed faience.

Suspension rings are attached at top and bottom on all specimens.

The Beth Shan example (*216*) of Type *IV.H.4* is from near the steps of Locus 1068, the upper altar room of the Level VII temple, dated to late LB IIB. The 14 Lachish examples (*217*) come from the deposit of beads and pendants found near the west wall of Room E of Fosse Temple III, which is dated to LB IIB (Tufnell, Inge, and Harding 1940: 42, 74–76, pl. 8:4). The four examples (*218*) from Tell Abu Hawam were found together in a mass of fallen stone and debris above a stone pavement of Building 53, which appears to be a homogeneous LB II context (Hamilton 1934: 74; 1935: 62).

The two-element variety occurs at el-Amarna,[70] but no counterparts for the three- and seven-element varieties could be located. Three- and six-element varieties also occur at Amarna,[71] and a 12-element variety was found at Qantir.[72] The different forms were probably manufactured exclusively in LB II.

B. Summary

Class *IV*, in addition to being represented at more Late Bronze Age Palestinian sites than any other group, is the largest class in absolute numbers (490+ pendants), thus providing the best statistical base from which to draw conclusions. Over half the pendants come from Beth Shan, and belong to 13 of the 20 types comprising the class (Chart 21). Lachish contributes half again this number of pendants (16 types). Other Palestinian sites, including several in the Shephelah (Beth Shemesh, Dhahrat el-Humraiya, and Gezer) and one in Transjordan (Amman), yielded much smaller quantities. The Hill Country, the Huleh and Jordan Valleys (except for Beth Shan), and the Galilee are devoid of Class *IV* pendants.

The class is heavily weighted toward LB IIB faience types from temple contexts at Beth Shan and Lachish, which have close parallels at el-Amarna (Charts 22–25). Since multiple examples of the same type may have gone into making up composite collars,[73] frequency of types rather than the total number of pendants from different loci is stressed here.

Although six types occur at Lachish and not at Beth Shan (*IV.A, IV.B, IV.D.1–3,* and *IV.E*), and, vice versa, two types are found at Beth Shan but not at Lachish (*IV.F.3* and *IV.F.5.a*), ten types are common to both sites: *IV.F.1, IV.F.2, IV.F.4, IV.F.5.b, IV.G.1,2, IV.H.2, IV.H.3.a,b,* and *IV.H.4.* Some types (*IV.F.1* and *IV.F.2*) appear earlier at Lachish in LB IIA temple contexts, and specific types (*IV.D.1,2*) are made in gold. Other types (*IV.F.4* and *IV.H.3.b*) are represented at Beth Shan in gold. Except in these few respects, a southern repertoire of floral pendants is

Chart 21
Site Distribution of Class *IV* Pendants in Late Bronze Age Palestine

Description	Type	Amman	Beth Shan	Beth Shemesh	Dhahrat el-Humraiya	Gezer	Lachish	Megiddo	Tell Abu Hawam	Tell el-'Ajjul	Total	%
Cornflower or cockle	IV.A	–	–	–	–	–	25	–	–	–	25	5
Daisy	IV.B	–	–	–	–	1	3	–	–	–	4	1
Date Fruit	IV.C	–	15	–	–	–	–	–	–	–	15	3
Flower or rosette	IV.D.1	–	–	–	–	–	2	–	–	–	2	0
Flower or rosette	IV.D.2	–	–	–	–	–	1	–	–	–	1	0
Flower or rosette	IV.D.3	–	–	–	–	–	1	–	–	–	1	0
Grape cluster	IV.E	–	–	–	–	–	9	1	–	–	10	2
Lotus bud	IV.F.1	1	1	–	–	–	2	1	–	14	19	4
Conventional lotus	IV.F.2	–	95	–	–	–	21 +	–	–	–	116 +	24
Lotus flower	IV.F.3	–	2	–	–	–	–	–	–	–	2	0
Lotus palmette	IV.F.4	–	3	8	–	–	2	–	–	1	14	3
Lotus seed vessel	IV.F.5.a	–	1	–	–	–	–	1	–	–	2	0
Lotus seed vessel	IV.F.5.b	–	8	10	–	–	5	4	4	1	32	7
Mandrake fruit	IV.G.1	–	18	–	–	–	11	–	–	–	29	6
Mandrake fruit	IV.G.2	–	85	–	–	–	17	–	–	–	102	21
Bud?	IV.H.1	–	–	4	–	–	–	–	–	–	4	1
Lotus flower?	IV.H.2	–	1	–	–	–	3	–	–	–	4	1
Petal or leaf	IV.H.3.a	–	51	–	23	–	3 +	–	–	–	77 +	16
Petal or leaf	IV.H.3.b	–	4	–	–	–	3	–	–	4	11	2
Reeds?	IV.H.4	–	1	–	–	–	15	–	4	–	20	4
Total		1	285	22	23	1	123 +	7	8	20	490 +	100
%		0	58	4	5	0	25	1	2	4		99

* unspecified number of additional specimens

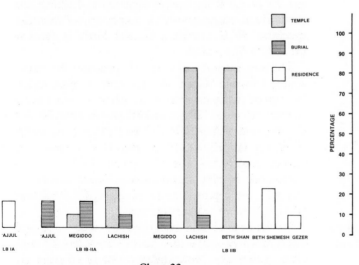

Chart 22
Contextual Distribution of Class *IV* Pendant Types
for Late Bronze Age Palestinian Sites

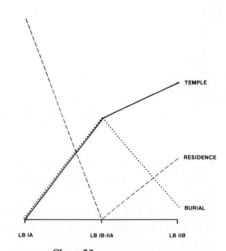

Chart 23
Comparative Importance of Contexts for
Class *IV* Pendant Types

hardly distinguishable from a typical northern collection.

Other Palestinian sites yielded fewer pendants of types that are also represented at Beth Shan or Lachish. The round lotus seed vessel (*IV.F.5.b*) is the most widely dispersed, occurring at Beth Shemesh,

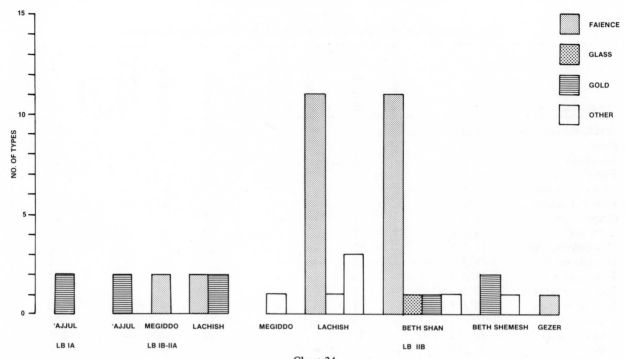

Chart 24

Material Distribution of Class *IV* Pendant Types
for Late Bronze Age Palestinian Sites

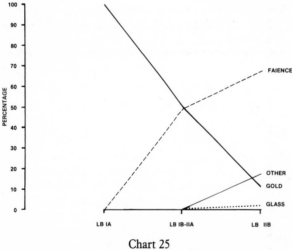

Chart 25

Comparative Importance of Materials for
Class *IV* Pendant Types

Megiddo, Tell Abu Hawam, and Tell el-ʿAjjul, as well as at Beth Shan and Lachish. *IV.H.1* is evidenced only at Beth Shemesh.

Egyptian-related types (*IV.E*, *IV.F.1*, *IV.F.3*, *IV.F.4*, and *IV.F.5.b*) first appear in LB IB–IIA temple and burial contexts (Chart 22), and then dramatically increase in numbers in LB IIB.

By contrast, LB IA is represented exclusively by two Syro-Palestinian gold types (*IV.F.4* [*142*] and

IV.H.3.b) from residential contexts (jewelry hoards) at Tell el-ʿAjjul. LB IIB contributes several additional Syro-Palestinian varieties and types: *IV.F.4* (*139*) and *IV.H.1* from a residence at Beth Shemesh, and *IV.D.1* and *IV.H.3.b* from temple contexts at Lachish and Beth Shan, respectively. A single Syro-Palestinian specimen (*IV.D.1*) from a Lachish burial is dated to the LB IB–IIA period.

The vast majority of Class *IV* pendants are mold-made of faience (Chart 26). In terms of glaze color, blue-green is the favorite, although some types occur in other colors (*IV.H.3.a* and *IV.H.4* in blue; *IV.G.1* in blue and yellow; *IV.F.2* and *IV.G.2* in white; *IV.H.3.a* in yellow). *IV.E* and *IV.F.1* appear in various colors, but not blue-green. *IV.D.3* is evidenced only in blue glazed faience. The several examples that are reported to be of glass (*IV.F.5.b* and *IV.G.1,2*) are very likely faience.

Precious metals and semi precious stones were used much less frequently than faience for Class *IV* pendants (Chart 27). Nevertheless, nine of 20 types are represented in gold: *IV.D.1*, *IV.D.2*, *IV.F.1*, *IV.F.3*, *IV.F.4*, *IV.F.5.b*, *IV.H.1*, and *IV.H.3.a,b*. Examples in silver and copper or bronze are limited to *IV.H.3.a*. Carnelian is the preferred material for *IV.F.5.a,b*, although the type sometimes appears in faience or gold.

Chart 26
Quantitative Analysis of Glass and Faience Used for Class *IV* Pendants in Late Bronze Age Palestine

Description	Type	Faience									Glass and Frit					Total	%
		B	B&Y	B–G	B–G & P	G	P	R	W	Y	Y&W	?	B&Y	R	?		
Cornflower or cockle	*IV.A*	–	–	–	25	–	–	–	–	–	–	–	–	–	–	25	6
Daisy	*IV.B.*	–	–	–	–	–	–	–	–	–	4	–	–	–	–	4	1
Date fruit	*IV.C.*	–	–	14	–	–	–	–	–	–	–	1	–	–	–	15	4
Flower or rosette	*IV.D.3*	1	–	–	–	–	–	–	–	–	–	–	–	–	–	1	0
Grape cluster	*IV.E*	–	–	–	–	1	9	–	–	–	–	–	–	–	–	10	3
Lotus bud	*IV.F.1*	3	–	–	–	–	–	–	1	4	–	–	–	–	–	8	2
Conventional lotus	*IV.F.2*	–	–	109+	–	–	–	–	3	–	–	4	–	–	–	116+	29
Lotus flower	*IV.F.4*	–	–	1	–	–	–	–	–	–	–	2	–	–	–	3	1
Lotus seed vessel	*IV.F.5.b*	1	–	4	–	–	–	3	–	–	–	–	–	1	–	9	2
Mandrake fruit	*IV.G.1*	–	12	14	–	–	–	–	–	–	–	1	2	–	–	29	7
Mandrake fruit	*IV.G.2*	–	–	92	–	–	–	–	3	–	–	6	–	–	1	102	26
Lotus flower?	*IV.H.2*	–	–	3	–	–	–	–	–	–	–	1	–	–	–	4	1
Petal or leaf	*IV.H.3.a*	1+	–	47	–	–	–	–	–	?	–	4	–	–	–	52+	13
Petal or leaf	*IV.H.3.b*	–	–	–	–	–	–	–	–	–	1	–	–	–	–	1	0
Reeds?	*IV.H.4*	1	–	4	–	–	15	–	–	–	–	–	–	–	–	20	5
Total		7+	12	288+	25	1	24	3	7	4+	5	19	2	1	1	399+	100
%		2	3	72	6	0	6	1	2	1	1	5	1	0	0		100

B = blue
B–G = blue-green
G = gray
P = purple
R = red
W = white
Y = yellow
? = unidentified or uncertain
+ = unspecified number of additional specimens

Notes

1 Petrie 1894: pl. 17: 486; Samson 1972: 86, 93, pls. 6 and 8; Frankfort and Pendlebury 1933: pl. 116; cf. Macalister 1912: 332–33, pl. 210:51 (Gezer, Trench 28, between 'Second' and 'Third Semitic' Periods, ca. 1400 B.C.).

2 Locus 2009.1 was the make-up below Surface 2009 and above Surface 2012. This context was assigned to Stratum VB/VA (transitional Late Bronze–Iron Age), but the associated pottery appears to be exclusively LB IIB (see Sauer 1979: 71, who redates the earlier Late Bronze levels at Gezer).

3 Petrie 1894: 29–30, pls. 18:430 (nos. 100–1), 18:407 (no. 99); Frankfort and Pendlebury 1933: pl. 28:6, bottom row, third from left; Petrie Museum Amarna Cabinet, no. 1354.

4 Petrie 1906b: 152, fig. 159, second necklace from top (18th–19th Dynasties).

5 Hamza 1930: 52–53, 64, pl. 4, top (19th–20th Dynasties, molds).

6 Woolley 1955: 271, pl. 68:b3 (Level II, probably later phase of LB IIA).

7 Petrie 1894: pl. 19:450 (red and yellow glazed faience); Samson 1972: pl. 3 (red and yellow glazed faience); cf. late 18th Dynasty, unprovenanced examples in Pritchard 1954: 259, pl. 73, and Aldred 1971: 231, pl. 125.

8 Petrie 1906b: 152, fig. 159, fourth necklace from the top (18th–19th Dynasties).

9 Carter and Mace 1972: pl. 29B (Tomb of Tutankhamun).

10 For dating, see Chapter 2, n. 63.

11 Cf. Petrie 1894: pl. 18:415, 426 (el-Amarna).

12 The presence of only LB IIB pottery corroborates Tufnell's attribution of the pit to Structure III.

Chart 27
Quantitative Analysis of Precious Metals and Semi-Precious Stones Used for
Class *IV* Pendants in Late Bronze Age Palestine

Description	Type	Au	Au & Glass	Ag	Cu	Ca	?	Total	%
Flower or rosette	*IV.D.1*	2	–	–	–	–	–	2	2
Flower or rosette	*IV.D.2*	1	–	–	–	–	–	1	1
Lotus bud	*IV.F.1*	11	–	–	–	–	–	11	12
Lotus flower	*IV.F.3*	2	–	–	–	–	–	2	2
Lotus palmette	*IV.F.4*	11	–	–	–	–	–	11	12
Lotus seed vessel	*IV.F.5.a*	–	–	–	–	2	–	2	2
Lotus seed vessel	*IV.F.5.b*	1	–	–	–	21	1	23	25
Bud?	*IV.H.1*	4	–	–	–	–	–	4	4
Petal or leaf	*IV.H.3.a*	23	–	1	1	–	–	25	27
Petal or leaf	*IV.H.3.b*	8	2	–	–	–	–	10	11
Total		63	2	1	1	23	1	91	98
%		69	2	1	1	25	1	99	

Ag = silver
Au = gold
Ca = carnelian
Cu = copper or bronze
? = unidentified

13 Petrie 1894: pl. 18:435.

14 Hamza 1930: 52–53, 64, pl. 4, second row from the top, second from the left (dated to 19th–20th Dynasties).

15 Hachmann and Kuschke 1966: fig. 20:2 (Area IG13, Level 3, ca. 1500–1200 B.C.).

16 Petrie 1894: pl. 17:443, 445; Frankfort and Pendlebury 1933: pl. 13:2, second row from the bottom, second from the left; Samson 1972: pl. 3.

17 Hamza 1930: pl. 4, third row from the top, middle (dated to 19th–20th Dynasties).

18 Hachmann and Kuschke 1966: fig. 20:5 (from Area IG13, Level 3, ca. 1500–1200 B.C.).

19 Macalister 1912: 109, fig. 289: 9–10 (no stratigraphic details, dated to the 'Third Semitic' Period, ca. 1400–1000 B.C.).

20 Petrie 1932: 3, pls. 25:64, 67 (from MN 1140 and 1162, respectively). These contexts should perhaps be dated to Palace V (i.e. Iron I), although no associated pottery was published (cf. Albright 1938a: 355–56).

21 Although Kenyon (1969: 49–50) has argued that the temple may be dated too early and although some of the walls and floors of this locus had been broken up by robbing, the presence of mostly LB IIA local pottery with some possible LB IB types indicate that the more traditional dating for Stratum VIII (LB IB–IIA) should be followed.

22 Petrie 1894: pl. 19:461–63.

23 Randall-MacIver and Woolley 1911: pl. 55:10235 (Tomb J 43, 18th–19th Dynasties).

24 Brunton and Engelbach 1927: pl. 42:39B, K (uncertain 18th–19th Dynasty context).

25 Petrie 1891a: pl. 26:3 (Tomb of Maket, Coffin 1, probably LB IIA, reported to be green felspar).

26 Guy 1938: pl. 216: 115 (Megiddo, Stratum VIB, heirloom?).

27 Carnarvon and Carter 1912: 85, pl. 73:78 (Tomb 37, LB I).

28 Cf. Tufnell 1958: 82, pl. 25:9 (Lachish, Burial Cave 4004, probably MB III–LB IIA).

29 Randall-MacIver and Woolley 1911: pl. 55:10219 (Tomb H 39, 18th–19th Dynasties).

30 Petrie 1894: pl. 18: 388; Frankfort and Pendlebury 1933: pl. 28:6, second row, third from right; Petrie Museum Amarna Cabinet, no. 1324.

31 Franken 1961: 364, pl. 9 (Deir 'Alla, downhill wash from the sanctuary, transitional Late Bronze–Iron Age); Brunton and Engelbach 1927: pls. 30:13 (Gurob, group 37, 22nd Dynasty), 31:5 (group 36, 22nd Dynasty); cf. Guy 1938: pl. 214:97 (Megiddo, Stratum VIIA, probably an heirloom).

32 E.g., Petrie 1894: pl. 19: 458; Samson 1972: pls. 6 and 8; Frankfort and Pendlebury 1933: pl. 49: type IV.C.22 (el-Amarna); Tufnell, Inge, and Harding 1940: 75, pl. 12 (Lachish, deposit of beads and pendants in Room E, Fosse Temple III, LB IIB); Randall-MacIver and Woolley 1911: pl. 55: 10219 (Buhen, Tomb H 39, 18th–19th Dynasties, glazed pottery?; cf, especially, *136*); Petrie 1914: 50, pl. 45:267c (green glazed faience, assigned to 20th Dynasty?).

33 See stratigraphic discussion, Chapter 3, n.19.

34 See, in particular, Petrie 1894: pl. 18:371.

35 Dothan 1979: 77–80, figs. 174–79 (Deir el-Balah,

Tomb 118, transitional LB–Iron Age, gold and carnelian); Loud 1948: pl. 214:96 (Megiddo, Stratum VIIA, Iron I); also cf. Petrie 1928: 23, pl. 17:58 (Tell Jemmeh, unprovenanced), and earlier Egyptian examples in gold, Aldred 1971: 208–9, pl. 66 (Treasure of the Three Wives, Thutmose III, LB IB).

36 Dothan 1979: 43, figs. 99–102, 107–8 (Deir el-Balah, Tomb 116, transitional LB–Iron Age); Tufnell 1953: 215–17, pl. 67:143 (Lachish, Tomb 224, Iron II); cf. 18 examples, probably from the Gaza Strip, on exhibit in the Israel Museum.

37 Burial Cave 4002 contained LB II local pottery, including a Myceanaean IIIB juglet.

38 Tomb 912 B had some admixture of MB I pottery.

39 The associated finds, including a cylindrical bead and scarabs of Amenhotep III, substantiate the LB II dating.

40 Brunton and Engelbach 1927: pl. 43:45 (18th–19th Dynasties); Petrie 1891a: pls. 17:24 (group of Amenhotep III), 18:24 (group of Ramesses II), 19:24 (group of Seti I).

41 Engelbach 1915: 15, pls. 11:2 (no provenience, 18th Dynasty), 9:4, and frontispiece: 10 (Tomb 296 of the Scribe Bera, Thutmose III).

42 Randall-MacIver and Woolley 1911: pl. 54: 10252 (Tomb H 60, 19th Dynasty).

43 Petrie 1894: pl. 19:470–73; cf. Petrie 1914: pl. 43:271 (ascribed to 18th–19th Dynasties).

44 Starkey and Harding 1932: 23–26, pl. 72:V (Tombs 914, 922, 934, and 960, transitional LB–Iron Age); cf. Starkey 1930: Type V (dated between 19th and 20th Dynasties).

45 Macalister 1912: 207, fig. 289:31 (said to be 'one of the commonest beads of the period,' i.e., 'Third Semitic' Period, ca. 1400–1000 B.C.).

46 Lamon and Shipton 1939: pls. 90:7 (Stratum III), 90:20 (Stratum IV, Iron II).

47 Rothenberg 1972: 172, pl. 12, upper left (transitional LB–Iron Age).

48 Samson 1972: pl. 3; Petrie 1894: pl. 19:453, 455.

49 Frankfort and Pendlebury 1933: pl. 49:IV.C.12b, IV.C.56.

50 Bruyère 1953: 53–54, fig. 11, bottom right (19th–20th Dynasties).

51 Frankfort and Pendlebury 1933: pl. 49:IV.C.12b, IV.C.56.

52 Carter and Mace 1923: pl. 29B (Tomb of Tutankhamun).

53 James 1966: fig. 101:1, 5 (Beth Shan, Level VI); Starkey and Harding 1932: 24–25, pl. 51 (Tell el-Far'ah South, Tomb 934, transitional LB–Iron Age); Franken 1961: 364, pl. 9 (Deir 'Alla, downhill wash from sanctuary, transitional LB–Iron Age).

54 Dothan 1979: 73–77, figs. 158, 164, 171–73 (Tomb 118, transitional LB–Iron Age).

55 Starkey and Harding 1932: 41, pl. 51 (Tomb 934, transitional LB–Iron Age).

56 Schaeffer 1935: 144–45, fig. 6 = 1939, I: 44, fig. 31.

57 Cf. Frankfort and Pendlebury 1933: pl. 49:IV.C.12c (el-Amarna, faience).

58 Petrie 1894: pl. 19:465; Frankfort and Pendlebury 1933: pl. 49: IV.C.22.

59 This is the only built tomb of the 60 graves in the Humraiya cemetery; and, apart from a missing southeast wall, the three burials (husband, wife, and child?) appear to be undisturbed.

60 Petrie 1894: pl. 20:518–20, 548–50; Samson 1972: pl. 3; Frankfort and Pendlebury 1933: 116, pls. 36:1–2, 49:IV.C.8, 28:6, top row, middle.

61 Petrie 1906b: 152, fig. 159, second-fourth and sixth necklaces from the top (18th–19th Dynasties).

62 Bruyère 1953: 53–54, fig. 11, second row, second and third examples from the right (18th–20th Dynasties).

63 Brunton and Engelbach 1927: pl. 43:44N (Tomb 57, possibly LB I; Tomb 228, 18th–19th Dynasties); Petrie 1891a: pl. 17:27 (group of Tutankhamun).

64. Tufnell 1958: 246, pl. 29:31 (Lachish, Burial Pit 557, transitional LB–Iron Age).

65 Aldred 1971: 179, 211, pls. 10 (Princess Ita-weret, Middle Kingdom), 11 (Princess Khnumet, Middle Kingdom).

66 Carter and Mace 1923–33: 146–47 (Tomb of Tutankhamun).

67 Samson 1972: pl. 3; cf. Pritchard 1954: 259, pl. 73 = Aldred 1971: 231, pl. 125 (unprovenanced).

68 Wilkinson 1971: pl. 7 (Princess Neferu-Ptah, Hawara, ca. 1800 B.C.).

69 Aldred 1971: 205–16, 208, pl. 65 (Treasure of the Three Wives of Thutmose III); Wilkinson 1971: pl. 33B (Treasure of the Three Wives of Thutmose III); Carter and Mace 1972: plates on p. 79 and opposite p. 129, gold mask (Tomb of Tutankhamun).

70 Petrie 1894: pl. 17:357–58.

71 Petrie 1894: pl. 18:361; Frankfort and Pendlebury 1933: pl. 49:IV.C.55.

72 Hamza 1930: 53, pl. 4, fourth row from top, fourth from left.

73 The large group of beads and pendants, which were found near the west wall of Room E of Fosse Temple III at Lachish, are convincingly reconstructed in Tufnell, Inge, and Harding 1940: pl. 14. Eight types (*IV.C, IV.F.2, IV.F.4, IV.F.5.a, IV.G.1,2, IV.H.3.a,* and *IV.H.4*) from near the steps of the upper altar room (1068) of the Beth Shan temple may also have been strung together to form a single collar.

Chapter 6

CLASS *V* JEWELRY PENDANTS HIEROGLYPHS

A. Typology and Dating

The third largest class of pendants (116 specimens, 14 percent of the total for Late Bronze Age Palestine) is comprised of six main categories and 17 types of Egyptian hieroglyphic signs. Although the hieroglyphs may have been reinterpreted in a 'Palestinian sense' (see Chapter 8), they are most conveniently described according to their Egyptian equivalents.

V.A.1   219

Fig. 51

Type V.A.1–2 'ankh (219–221; pl. 14)

The examples (*219–220*) of the standard 'ankh pendants (pl. 14), a girdle-tie or sandal-strap signifying 'life' (Gardiner 1957: 508, Sign S 34; Petrie 1914: 14; Vilímková 1969: 34), are of white glazed faience, and have suspension rings at each end (broken off on *219*). Because the upper part of *219* is missing and the specimen is badly worn, it is not possible to determine whether *219* was made in the same mold as *220* (pl. 14).

The Beth Shan example (*219*) comes from Locus 1255, a road in the southeast residential sector of Level VII, which dates to late LB IIB. The three specimens of *220* were found in a mass of fallen stone and debris, including other beads and pendants, above a stone pavement in Building 53, Stratum V, at Tell Abu Hawam, which should probably be dated to LB II (Hamilton 1934: 74; 1935: 21, 62, pl. 11).

Good parallels exist at el-Amarna[1] and Gurob.[2] The form and size of *V.A.1* are probably features specific to LB II.

The single example (*221*, pl. 14) of Type *V.A.2* personifies the 'ankh with slightly curved, outstretched arms holding a *was* scepter to either side, and standing on a plinth. The low relief elliptical plaque of faded blue-green glazed faience was mold-made, and had suspension rings at each end, now broken off.

V.A.2   221

Fig. 52

221 was found in the upper altar room (Locus 1068) of the Level VII temple at Beth Shan, which is dated to a later phase of LB IIB. The only parallel that could be located is a dark blue glass example illustrated in Petrie's corpus,[3] which is a squarish rather than an elliptical plaque and is perforated through one side rather than having top and bottom suspension rings. This dating gains added support from a comparable Amarna example, which shows the 'ankh holding both sides of a *ḥb-sd* booth(?) with its arms.[4] The period of manufacture of Type *V.A.2* is limited to LB II.

V.B.1   223

Fig. 53

Type V.B.1–2 ḏd (222–226; pl. 14)

As for Type *V.A.1,2*, this group is divided between pendants of the standard form (variously interpreted as a bundle of stalks, Osiris' backbone, the four columns of heaven, meaning 'endurance, stability, duration,' see Petrie 1914:15; Aldred 1971: 16; Gardiner

1957: 502, Sign R 11; Budge 1972: 259; Allen 1974: 154–55, Book of the Dead, Spell 155), and those that show the *ḏd* holding two *was* scepters. The 22 examples of the standard type (*222–25*, pl. 14) are virtually identical. However, slight stylistic and dimensional differences between the Beth Shan examples (*222–223*) and the Tell Abu Hawam examples (*224*; pl. 14) indicate that the two groups derive from different molds. The smaller dimensions and the vertical lines on the column of *225* from Tell el-ʿAjjul imply yet another mold, assuming it was made of faience (not examined; material unspecified). Suspension rings are attached at the top and bottom of each example.

Of the Beth Shan examples, *222* comes from Locus 1234, the inner sanctuary of the Level IX temple, dated to the Late Bronze Age generally. *223* was found near the steps of Locus 1068, the upper altar room of the Level VII temple, which dates to late LB IIB. The two examples of *224* are from a deposit of beads and pendants in Building 53, Stratum V, at Tell Abu Hawam, which is dated to LB II. The Tell el-ʿAjjul example (*225*) was recovered from Tomb 1080, a homogeneous LB IIA context (Petrie 1932: 7, 14–15, pl. 52). Parallels occur at New Kingdom Serabit el-Khadem,[5] Deir el-Medineh,[6] and el-Amarna.[7] Since a much more rigid and detailed type develops in the Iron Age,[8] the period of manufacture of Type *V.B.1* is probably limited to LB II with a possible overlap into Iron I.

V.B.2   226

Fig. 54

Type *V.B.2* (*226*, pl. 3:21) portrays the *ḏd* sign on an elliptical plaque with bent arms holding *was* scepters to each side, which is very similar in style and dimensions to Type *V.A.2*. The three examples of *226* were made in the same mold or affiliated molds, are of 'light green' (blue-green?) faience, and have suspension rings at top and bottom.

The three specimens of *226* come from below the floor of Locus 1068, the upper altar room of the Level VII temple at Beth Shan, dated to an early phase of LB IIB. A comparable example, except that it is crowned and much larger, is illustrated in Petrie's corpus.[9] Since the Beth Shan example is similar to Type *V.A.2*, also unique to Beth Shan, an LB II period of manufacture can be suggested for Type *V.B.2*.[10]

V.C.1   230

Fig. 55

Type *V.C.1–3* ḥeḥ (*227–232*; pl. 14)
All the examples (*227–232*) of this hieroglyph, which shows the god supporting a *ḥb-sd* booth (=sky?) with his arms ('million of years', see Gardiner 1957: 449, Sign C 11; Petrie 1914: 19) are of blue-green glazed faience (*228*, white, possibly leached out and faded), and have suspension rings at top and bottom. The examples (*227–230*, pl. 14) of Type *V.C.1* (*ḥeḥ* facing left) appear to derive from the same mold family. The single example (*231*; pl. 14) of Type *V.C.2* (*ḥeḥ* facing right) was made in a mold that had the knee set further away from the pavilion. *232* of Type *V.C.3* (uncertain), which is badly worn and missing most of the body, does not provide sufficient data to determine which way *ḥeḥ* is facing.

All the examples of Type *V.C.1* are from Beth Shan:

1. Level IX (Late Bronze Age generally):
   Locus 1232, the inner sanctuary of the temple behind the brick altar (*227*);
   Locus 1234, the inner sanctuary proper (*228–229*);
2. Level VII (late LB IIB):
   West side of Locus 1072, the temple court (*230*).

No close parallels could be located, but the type differs from examples illustrated in Petrie's corpus[11] and an Iron Age type found below Level V at Beth Shan.[12] The form and stylistic details are comparable to other LB II types (e.g., Types *V.A.2* and *V.B.2*), and thus *V.C.1* was most likely made during this period. The same argument applies to Types *V.C.2* and *V.C.3*, which are represented respectively by one specimen each from Level IX at Beth Shan: (1) *231* from Locus 1235, the southeast side of the outer courtyard; and (2) *232* from Locus 1234, the inner sanctuary of the Level IX 'temple'.

Type *V.D.1–2* ṯit (*233–239*; pl. 15)
The standard *ṯit* (Type *V.D.1*) depicts a woman's girdle-tie or sandal-strap and is interpreted to mean 'life, welfare, etc.' (Gardiner 1957: 508, Sign V 39; Aldred 1971: 16; Petrie 1914: 23; Allen 1974: 155, Book of the Dead, Spell 156; Budge 1972: 256–58). It

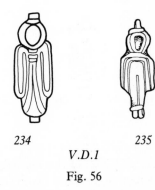

234   *235*

V.D.1

Fig. 56

is represented by 13 blue-green glazed faience pendants. *234* is said to be of 'light green glass,' probably incorrectly, and the glaze color of *236* is unspecified. At least four molds would have been required to produce the examples. *233* (pl. 15) is shorter overall than *235*, but its tie-ends extend lower. The latter in turn is about the same size as *234*, but differs in that it does not have long, elliptical ties. *236* is closest to *233*, but appears to have even longer tie-ends. The ten specimens of *235* derive from the same mold or affiliated molds. Suspension rings are attached at top and bottom (broken on *233* and on some of the *235* specimens).

The three Late Bronze Age levels at Beth Shan are represented by an entry each of Type *V.D.1*:

1. Level IX (Late Bronze Age generally):
   Locus 1234, the inner sanctuary of the temple (*233*);
2. Level VIII (early LB IIB):
   Locus 1092, the area below the steps of the Level VII temple (*234*);
3. Level VII (late LB IIB):
   Near the steps of Locus 1068, the upper altar room of the temple (*235*).

The Tell Abu Hawam example (*236*) was found with a mass of other beads and pendants in Building 53 of Stratum V, dated to LB II (Hamilton 1934: 74; 1935: 21, 62, pl. 11).

234 is very closely paralleled by an el-Amarna example,[13] and the pendants may derive from molds which have a common prototype. The other Late Bronze Palestinian examples, particularly *235*, are similar to an example illustrated in Petrie's corpus.[14] Although the type was manufactured primarily in LB II, it appears to continue into Iron I.[15]

Type *V.D.2* (*237–239*, pl. 15) is a more schematic and simplified form of the standard *tit*. Tie-ends extend to the bottom of the pendant, and there are apparently knots (three parallel horizontal lines) that

border the middle section. All the examples are of blue-green glazed faience (*239*, reported to be of white glazed faience, is probably leached out and faded), have suspension rings at the top, and probably derive from the same mold family.

V.D.2   *238*

Fig. 57

Examples of Type *V.D.2* occur only at Beth Shan: (1) *237* from below Locus 1092, an area below the steps of the Level VII temple (Level IX, Late Bronze Age generally), and (2) *238* from Locus 1092, and *239* from below the steps of Locus 1068, the upper altar room of the Level VII temple (late LB IIB). No parallels could be located for this type, which probably is confined to LB II.

V.E.1.a–2.a wḏ't (*240–250*; pl. 15)

The *wḏ't* eye, which combines a human eye with the cheek feathers of a falcon (='sound, uninjured eye of Horus' conferring protection during the day and night, cf. Gardiner 1957: 451, Sign D 10, Petrie 1914: 32–34, Budge 1972: 263–64, Book of the Dead, Spell 140),[16] most often appears in its simplest form of a standard right (*V.E.1.a*) or left (*V.E.2.a*) eye.

The seven examples (*240–245*, pl. 15) of the right eye (*V.E.1.a*) have similar stylistic features: (1) well-defined iris, (2) mean ratio of length to width of 1.5, (3) faience composition. However, even though all the examples are mold-made, none of the pendants except for the two specimens of *243*, were made in the same mold; note, especially, the flattened iris and chevron-marked eyebrow of *240* (pl. 15), the multiply marked lower eye feather, the spiral feather at the back of the eye, and the hatched eyebrow of *241* (pl. 15), the drooping pointed eye and the broad feather below the eye of *244* (pl. 15), and the larger size of *240* and *243*. Furthermore, there is considerable variation in the glaze colors: blue-green (*240* and *245*), white (*241*, *242*), red (*243*), and yellow (*244*). The examples are all perforated lengthwise.

Three examples of Type *V.E.1.a* come from Beth Shan. *240* and *241* were found below the steps of Locus 1068 (the upper altar room of the Level VII temple), which is dated to an early phase of LB IIB, and *242* comes from Locus 1252, a room in the southeastern residential quarter, dated to late LB IIB.

240 *241* *242* *243*

V.E.1.a

Fig. 58

The two examples of *243* from Lachish are from Burial Cave 4004, which should probably be dated to LB IIB (Tufnell 1958: 281–85).[17] *244*, also from Lachish, was found in Tomb 4011, for which there are no stratigraphic details, but which is definitely an LB IIB context (Tufnell 1958: 286). *245* comes from Tomb 877 B 1 at Megiddo, which dates to LB IIB (Guy 1938: 36). Excellent parallels, none exact, can be cited from New Kingdom el-Amarna[18] and Gurob.[19] Remarkably, Petrie's corpus with two full pages of illustrated examples (1914: pls. 24–25; types 138–42) does not include any examples of this type. Type *V.E.1.a* continues into Iron I.[20] By the start of Iron II, new varieties of the *wḏ't* eye have emerged, which are distinctive for their generally long eye feathers, well-separated eyes and eyebrows, and squared-off outlines.[21] Type *V.E.1.a* was made only during LB II and Iron I.

V.E.1.b *246*

Fig. 59

The single example (*246*, pl. 15) of Type *V.E.1.b*, which has an incised *nfr* sign in a cartouche on the back of a standard *wḏ't* right eye, is unique for the naturalistic rendering of the white of the eye in glazed faience against a blue glazed background, the vertical incisions used to mark the eyebrow, and the intentional aperture below the eye. The flattened upper part of the iris and the in-turned back feather are comparable to *240* and *241*, respectively. The pendant has a lengthwise perforation. *246*, the sole representative of Type *V.E.1.b*, is from an external deposit of Room E, Fosse Temple II, where associated local LB IIA wares are sufficient to date the pendant to this period. The basic form and details of the eye conform to *V.E.1.a*, while the *nfr* sign within a cartouche on the reverse is paralleled by New Kingdom examples from Gurob[22] and el-Amarna.[23] The type is apparently limited to LB II.

V.E.1.c 247

Fig. 60

Type *V.E.1.c* is represented by a single example (*247*) which is most likely a standard right eye *wḏ't* with a disc-crowned uraeus attached at the front (no personal examination was possible). The pendant is of 'light green' (blue-green?) faience, and is pierced lengthwise. *247* comes from below the floor of Locus 1068, the upper altar room of the Level VII temple at Beth Shan, which is dated to early LB IIB. The only possible parallel found for this type is an Iron I example at Megiddo.[24] The overall outline of *247* conforms to Type *V.E.1.a*, and the combination with an uraeus can be compared to Type *I.C.3* (Hathor with flanking uraei), which is dated to LB II–Iron I. A comparable time span can be proposed for Type *V.E.1.c*

The two examples of *248* (Type *V.E.1.d*, simplified right eye) share the characteristic of having virtually no definition of eye features. The slightly larger example does have very faint, schematic lines suggestive of the iris and the lower feathers. Perhaps, the basic outline of an eye was sufficiently representative, especially in the case of hard materials (carnelian). While the perforation of the smaller example runs horizontally through the midline of the pendant, the horizontal perforation of the larger pendant is at the level of the eyebrow.

Both examples of Type *V.E.1.d* come from Tomb 1166 in the Northeast Fosse at Tell el-'Ajjul (Petrie 1932: 7, 15–16, pls. 52–53), which can be assigned to LB II.[25] The simplified, schematic *wḏ't* eye has a long history, beginning in the Old Kingdom,[26] and continuing through Iron I.[27] The period of manufacture of this type is thus nonspecific, extending over at least 1500 years.

The two examples (*249–250*) of *V.E.2.a* are unusual for their large size and the excellent detail of a standard left eye. *249*, with its vertical and horizontal lines on the feathers, hatched eyebrow lines, a well-defined

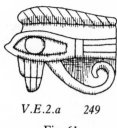

V.E.2.a   249

Fig. 61

iris, and a spiralling back feather is especially note-worthy. While *249* is the only *wd't* pendant in glass (blue), *250* is of faded blue glazed faience. *249* is pierced lengthwise; *250* has suspension holes at each end.

Of the two examples of Type *V.E.2.a*, *249* comes from Pit 555 at Lachish, an uncertain stratigraphic context with pottery covering the entire Late Bronze Age (Tufnell 1958: 244). *250* was found in Square D 5 of Stratum V at Tell Abu Hawam, whose stratigraphic context is also problematical, since no building remains or pottery were published from the area (Hamilton 1935: 63). As for Type *V.E.1.a* (standard right eye), an LB II–Iron I period of manufacture is supported by comparable examples from datable contexts.[28] The type is much less common than Type *V.E.1.a*.

V.F.1   253

Fig. 62

Type V.F.1 ḥst? (*251–255*; pl. 16)
Long narrow (*251–254*) and short broad (*255*) varieties of the *ḥst* vase (a storage jar, meaning 'praise,' see Gardiner 1957: 529, Sign W 14) are to be distinguished under Type *V.F.1*. Either variety can easily be confused with the flat lotus seed vessel pendant (Type *IV.F.5.a*). All examples are of blue-green glazed faience (*252*, which could not be examined, is said to be of 'greenish' faience), and to have suspension rings attached at top and bottom (some are broken off).

The twelve examples of Type *V.F.1* are all from Beth Shan:

1. Level IX (Late Bronze Age generally):
   Locus 1232, the area of the inner sanctuary behind the brick altar (*251*);
   East side of Locus 1234, the inner sanctuary of the 'temple' (*252*);

2. Level VIII (early LB IIB):
   Below the steps of 1068, the upper altar room of the Level VII temple (*253*);
3. Level VII (late LB IIB):
   Near the steps of Locus 1068 (*254–255*).

The long narrow variety occurs at el-Amarna[29] in a form so close to the Palestinian examples that they may all derive from a common mold prototype. No parallels could be located for the broader variety, which is in fact an intermediate form between Type *IV.F.5.a* and the long narrow variety of the *ḥst* pendant. Both varieties are probably limited to LB II.

V.F.2   256

Fig. 63

Type V.F.2 ỉb? (*256–257*; pl. 16)
256 and *257* are most likely heart pendants, which in Egyptian iconography connotes the source of life and thought (Gardiner 1957: 465, Sign F 34; Petrie 1914: 10; Budge 1972: 262–63, Book of the Dead, Spells 26–29). *256* exhibits the features of a physical heart, viz., side vessels, well-marked top edge, and yellow and white curved latitudinal bands on the mottled white glass core, possibly depicting blood vessels on the surface of the heart. Since *257* could not be examined and the photograph is overexposed, its identification with an *ỉb* is uncertain, although the general shape and side projections support this conjecture.

One example (*256*) of the *ỉb* pendant is from Locus 1086, the anteroom of the Level VII temple at Beth Shan, which is dated to late LB IIB. The other example (*257*) was recovered during sifting of soil from the Lachish Fosse Temple area and must be dated to the Late Bronze Age generally. The Beth Shan specimen has a very close parallel at Gurob,[30] and is similar to an example illustrated in Petrie's corpus,[31] as well as to unpublished el-Amarna examples in the Petrie Museum.[32] Thus, this variety appears to be limited to LB II. The broader variety, assuming it to be an *ỉb* pendant, is much less distinctive and may occur as early as the Old Kingdom and persist to the end of the Late Bronze Age.[33]

V.F.3   *258*

Fig. 64

Type V.F.3 nfr? (258–259)
The hieroglyph *nfr* (= 'beauty, excellence, etc.', Gard-iner 1957: 465, Type F 35; Petrie 1914: 14–15; Budge 1972: 264), which probably depicts the heart and windpipe, is represented by *258* and *259*. The six blue-green glazed faience specimens of *258* come from the same mold, and have suspension rings at each end (some broken). Each of 30 specimens (*259*) from the same locus at Dhahrat el-Humraiya is made of a piece of rounded and shaped sheet gold soldered onto a flat base (hollow interior); a small suspension loop is sol-dered to the narrow end of each pendant.

The six examples of *258* were found near the steps leading up to Locus 1068, the upper altar room of the Level VII temple at Beth Shan, which is dated to late LB IIB. The thirty examples of *259* were found

together in Grave 8 at Dhahrat el-Humraiya, which was apparently an undisturbed LB IIA burial.[34]

The Beth Shan examples are virtually identical to an Amarna type.[35] Petrie (1914: 3:31a, 44:31b) also illus-trates two *nfr* pendants in his corpus: the Amarna faience variety, in addition to a gold variety, compar-able to *259*. While the gold variety was manufactured for most of the Late Bronze Age, at least down to LB IIA,[36] the faience variety is confined to LB II.[37]

B. Summary

More than half the Class *V* pendants, representing 14 of the 17 types, come from Beth Shan (Chart 28). Mul-tiple examples of the same type, however, may have been part of a single collar,[38] which certainly would have been the case for the 30 examples of *V.F.3* from a burial at Dhahrat el-Humraiya. Other sites with Class *V* pendants are located in well-traveled areas of nor-thern and southern Palestine. Hieroglyphic pendants have not yet been discovered in the Hill Country, the Galilee, Huleh and Jordan Valleys (except for Beth Shan), or Transjordan.

The types comprising this group are all Egyptian-related with numerous el-Amarna parallels. Examples first appear in the south of Palestine in LB IIA: *V.B.1* and *V.F.3* from burials at Tell el-'Ajjul and Dhahrat

Chart 28
Site Distribution of Class *V* Pendants in Late Bronze Age Palestine

Description	Type	Beth Shan	Dhahrat el-Humraiya	Lachish	Megiddo	Tell Abu Hawam	Tell el-'Ajjul	Total	%
'ankh	*V.A.1*	1	–	–	–	3	–	4	3
'ankh	*V.A.2*	1	–	–	–	–	–	1	1
ḏd	*V.B.1*	19	–	–	–	2	1	22	19
ḏd	*V.B.2*	3	–	–	–	–	–	3	3
ḥeḥ	*V.C.1*	5	–	–	–	–	–	5	4
ḥeḥ	*V.C.2*	1	–	–	–	–	–	1	1
ḥeḥ	*V.C.3*	1	–	–	–	–	–	1	1
tit	*V.D.1*	12	–	–	–	1	–	13	11
tit	*V.D.2*	3	–	–	–	–	–	3	3
wḏ't	*V.E.1.a*	3	–	3	1	–	–	7	6
wḏ't	*V.E.1.b*	–	–	1	–	–	–	1	1
wḏ't	*V.E.1.c*	1	–	–	–	–	–	1	1
wḏ't	*V.E.1.d*	–	–	–	–	–	2	2	2
wḏ't	*V.E.2.a*	–	–	1	–	1	–	2	2
ḥst?	*V.F.1*	12	–	–	–	–	–	12	10
ib?	*V.F.2*	1	–	1	–	–	–	2	2
nfr?	*V.F.3*	6	30	–	–	–	–	36	31
	Total	69	30	6	1	7	3	115	116
	%	59	26	5	1	6	3	100	

el-Humraiya, respectively, and *V.E.1.b* from the
Fosse Temple at Lachish (Charts 29–30). There is a
proliferation of types northward in LB IIB. Except for
V.E.1.a, all the LB IIB types are from the Beth Shan
temple: *V.A.2, V.B.1–2, V.C.1, V.D.1–2, V.E.1.c,*
and *V.F.1–3.*

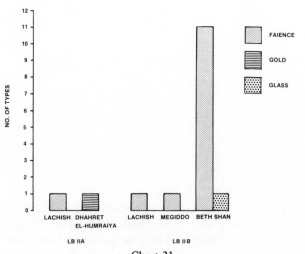

Chart 31
Material Distribution of Class *V* Pendant Types for Late
Bronze Age Palestinian Sites

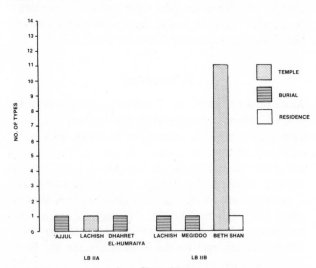

Chart 29
Contextual Distribution of Class *V* Pendant Types for Late
Bronze Age Palestinian Sites

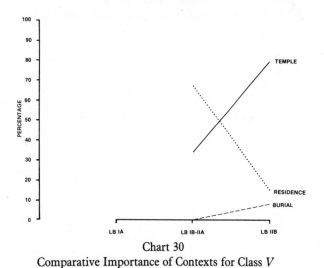

Chart 30
Comparative Importance of Contexts for Class *V*
Pendant Types

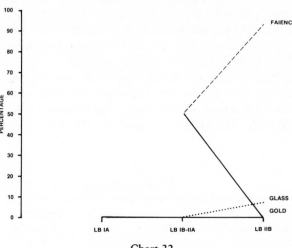

Chart 32
Comparative Importance of Materials for Class *V*
Pendant Types

Faience is the preferred material for Class *V* pendants (Charts 31–33). Of the 12 LB IIB types at Beth
Shan, 11 are mold-made in faience: *V.A.1–2, V.B.1–
2, V.C.1, V.D.1–2, V.E.1.a, V.E.1.c, V.F.1,* and
V.F.3. All of these are glazed blue-green except *V.A.1*
(white). *V.C.1, V.D.2,* and *V.E.1.a* also occur in
white. Possibly, the white examples originally had a
blue-green glaze, which was leached out. The several

LB IIB examples from burials at Lachish and Megiddo
belong to *V.E.1.a*; whereas the latter is blue-green, the
examples from Lachish are of red glazed and yellow
glazed faience. The LB IIA example of *V.E.1.b* from
Lachish combines blue and white glazes.

The relatively large number of gold pendants from
the LB IIA burial at Dhahrat el-Humraiya represents
only a single type (*V.F.3*), which also occurs in blue-
green glazed faience. The one example in glass (*V.F.2*)
from a well-dated context was hand-molded of white
and yellow glass; the type was fabricated in carnelian as
was *V.E.1.d.*

Chart 33
Quantitative Analysis of Materials Used for Class *V* Pendants in Late Bronze Age Palestine

Description	Type	Faience							Glass			Au	Ca	?	Total	%
		B	B–G	B & W	R	W	Y	?	B	W& Y	?					
'ankh	V.A.1	–	–	–	–	1	–	3	–	–	–	–	–	–	4	3
'ankh	V.A.2	–	1	–	–	–	–	–	–	–	–	–	–	–	1	1
ḏd	V.B.1	–	18	–	–	–	–	3	–	–	–	–	–	1	22	19
ḏd	V.B.2	–	–	–	–	–	–	3	–	–	–	–	–	–	3	3
ḥeḥ	V.C.1	–	4	–	–	1	–	–	–	–	–	–	–	–	5	4
ḥeḥ	V.C.2	–	1	–	–	–	–	–	–	–	–	–	–	–	1	1
ḥeḥ	V.C.3	–	1	–	–	–	–	–	–	–	–	–	–	–	1	1
tit	V.D.1	–	11	–	–	–	–	1	–	–	1	–	–	–	13	11
tit	V.D.2	–	2	–	–	1	–	–	–	–	–	–	–	–	3	3
wḏ't	V.E.1.a	1	2	–	2	1	1	–	–	–	–	–	–	–	7	6
wḏ't	V.E.1.b	–	–	1	–	–	–	–	–	–	–	–	–	–	1	1
wḏ't	V.E.1.c	–	–	–	–	–	–	1	–	–	–	–	–	–	1	1
wḏ't	V.E.1.d	–	–	–	–	–	–	–	–	–	–	–	2	–	2	2
wḏ't	V.E.2.a	1	–	–	–	–	–	–	1	–	–	–	–	–	2	2
ḥst?	V.F.1	1	10	–	–	–	–	1	–	–	–	–	–	–	12	10
ib?	V.F.2	–	–	–	–	–	–	–	–	1	–	–	1	–	2	2
nfr?	V.F.3	–	6	–	–	–	–	–	–	–	–	30	–	–	36	30
	Total	3	56	1	2	4	1	12	1	1	1	30	3	1	116	101
	%	3	48	1	2	3	1	10	1	1	1	26	3	1	101	

Au = gold
Ca = carnelian
B = blue
B–G = blue-green
R = red
W = white
Y = yellow
? = unidentified

Notes

1 Petrie 1894: pl. 17:259; Samson 1972: 83, fig. 47(ii), top row, second from right (differs in having four threading holes).

2 Petrie 1891a: pl. 17:27 (group of Tutankhamun); also see Petrie 1914: pl. 3:30b,c (undated).

3 Petrie 1914: pl. 3:30f (undated, but probably 19th Dynasty).

4 Samson 1972: 83, fig. 47(ii), bottom row, first on left.

5 Petrie 1906b: 52, fig. 159 (18th–19th Dynasties).

6 Bruyère 1953: 54, fig. 11 (19th–20th Dynasties)

7 Petrie 1894: pl. 17:264.

8 Petrie 1914: pl. 3:35c (26th Dynasty).

9 1914: pl. 3:35g (undated, but probably 22nd Dynasty or later).

10 However, compare the uncertain photo of a similar pendant of later date in Starkey and Harding 1932: 24–25, pl. 51 (Tell el-Far'ah South, Tomb 934, transitional LB–Iron Age.)

11 1914: 19, pl. 4:59a–d (assigned to either the 11th Dynasty or the Roman period).

12 Rowe 1936: 268, pl. 30:A. 5.

13 Samson 1972: 183, fig. 47(ii), top row, first on left.

14 1914: pl. 7:88g (assigned to the 18th–19th Dynasties); cf. Carnarvon and Carter 1912: 80, pl. 73:53 (Thebes, Tomb 37, LB I, gold).

15 Bruyère 1953: 54, fig. 11 (Deir el-Medineh, 19th–20th Dynasties); Petrie 1891a: pl. 17:27 (Gurob, group of Tutankhamun); Starkey and Harding 1932: 24–25, pl. 51 (Tell el-Far'ah South, Tomb 934, transitional LB–Iron Age).

16 Also see Anthes 1961: 68–90; Borghouts 1973. The intricacy of the symbolism of this hieroglyph goes beyond the scope of this study.

17 For dating, see Chapter 2, n. 53.

18 Samson 1972: fig. 47(ii), bottom row, middle; Petrie 1894: pl. 17:249; Frankfort and Pendlebury 1933: pl. 29:55, bottom row, middle.

19 Petrie 1891a: pls. 18:24 (Ramesses II group), 17:27 (Tutankhamun group).

20 Petrie 1930: pl. 33:370 (Tell el-Far'ah South, Tomb 204); Starkey and Harding 1932: pl. 54 (Tomb 960, transitional Late Bronze–Iron Age).

21 Petrie 1914: 32–33, pls. 24–25:138l and following; Rowe 1936: pl. 31:A. 56–65; Mackenzie 1912–13: 60, pl. 28A (Beth Shemesh, Tomb 1 [11]); James 1966: fig. 113:14–15 (Beth Shan, Upper Level V); Yadin *et al.* 1961: pl. 176:26 (Hazor, Stratum IXB, ca. 900 B.C., upside down).

22 Petrie 1891a: pl. 18:31 (with cartouches of Ramesses II and Nefertari on the reverse: group of Ramesses II); Brunton and Engelbach 1927: pls. 40:27 (cartouche of Thutmose III, Tomb 80, 18th–19th Dynasties), 29:29–32 (Tomb 605, LB IIB).

23 Frankfort and Pendlebury 1933: 116, Type III.B.5 (*nfr*).

24 Schumacher 1908: 88, pl. 28:c (jewelry hoard from Level 4).

25 The mixed context of LB IIA and IIB local wares, Mycenaean IIIB stirrup jars, and Base-Ring II ware demands an LB II dating.

26 Petrie 1914: 32–33, pl. 24:138a–k; Brunton 1937: pl. 57:62.

27 Engelbach 1923: pl. 50:38 (Harageh); Brunton and Engelbach 1927: pl. 42:38G (Gurob, Tomb 276A, 18th–19th Dynasties); Petrie 1906a: pl. 34A (Tell er-Ratabeh, Tomb 20, Iron I); Starkey and Harding 1932: pl. 51 (Tell el-Far'ah South, Tomb 934, transitional Late Bronze–Iron Age), etc.

28 Petrie 1906a: pl. 18:24 (Gurob, Ramesses II group); Starkey and Harding 1932: 24–25, pl. 51 (Tell el-Far'ah South, Tomb 934, transitional Late Bronze–Iron Age).

29 Samson 1972: 82, fig. 47(ii), top row, fourth from left; Petrie 1894: pl. 17:268; Petrie Museum Amarna Cabinet, no. 1377. Also cf. Petrie 1906b: 152, fig. 159 (Serabit el-Khadem, 18th–19th Dynasties).

30 Brunton and Engelbach 1927: pl. 42:26S (Tomb 492, 18th–19th Dynasties, blue and yellow banded glass).

31 1914: 10, pl. 1:7c (assigned to 18th Dynasty, green glass with yellow and white bands).

32 No. 22982iii (yellow, blue, and white banded glass).

33 Petrie 1914: pl. 1:7a–b (undated, without side projections); Brunton 1937: pl. 57:41F$_3$ (Mostagedda, dated to the Old Kingdom, possibly a beetle); Brunton and Engelbach 1927: pl. 42:26N (Gurob, Tomb 225, 18th–19th Dynasties). Also compare Iron Age examples of a different type: Petrie 1891a: pl. 18:26 (Gurob, Ramesses II group); Petrie 1914: pl. 15:129e (Ramesseum, 23rd? Dynasty, bulla pendant, agate).

34 Grave 8 was apparently an undisturbed burial, although the shoulder and skull of the skeleton were missing. Despite the presence of MB I–III button-base juglets that were either heirlooms or intrusions, the tomb contained a homogeneous LB IIA assemblage.

35 Samson 1972: 83, fig. 47(ii), top row, on right: Petrie 1894: pl. 17:266; Petrie Museum Amarna Cabinet, no. 1110; cf. Bruyère 1953: 54, fig. 11 (Deir el-Medineh, 19th–20th Dynasties).

36 Carnarvon and Carter 1912: 85, pl. 73:78 (Thebes, Tomb 37, LB I); Aldred 1971: pls. 66 (Treasure of the Three Wives of Thutmose III) and 71 (collar of Smenkhkare).

37 Compare the somewhat different form and size of an Iron I example from Beth Shan in Rowe 1936: pl. 13:A. 50.

38 In particular, specimens from near the steps of the upper altar room (1068) of the Beth Shan temple may have been combined together into a single jewelry piece, including Types *V.B.1*, *V.D.1*, and *V.F.3*. The same may hold true for *V.A.1*, *V.B.1*, and *V.D.1* which were found together in an LB II jewelry hoard at Tell Abu Hawam.

Chapter 7

CLASS *VI* JEWELRY PENDANTS GEOMETRIC FORMS

A. Typology and Dating

The second largest class of pendants (118 examples, 14 percent of the total for Late Bronze Age Palestine) is comprised of eight main categories and 16 types. Although some of these forms incorporate naturalistic motifs (e.g., Type *VI.C*) and may carry a symbolic import, the geometrical features are stressed here in constructing a generally valid typology.

Type VI.A Circular Crescent with
Granular Clusters (261–266; pl. 17)
Type *VI.A* occurs only at Tell el-'Ajjul, always as a pair (apart from *266*) and exhibiting superb workmanship in gold. Although members of a pair are virtually identical, slight differences exist between pairs, in particular variations on the theme of clusters of granules. Thus, *260* (pl. 17), *264*, and *265* (pl. 17) have variously

sized clusters of granules in two concentric rings; but the number of clusters differ. *261* and *266* (pl. 17) have different numbers of variously sized triangular clusters of granules in two concentric rings. *262* (pl. 17) exhibits a very irregular placement of clusters of granules. Soldered-on gold wires reinforce the inner and outer edges of all examples, but the wire is twisted on *265*; on *266*, two square-sectioned wires are intertwined on the outer edge and a v-shaped strip is applied to the inner edge. Triangular globules sometimes run around the exterior edge (*260*, *261*, and *264*). Twisted wire (*265*) or plain wire accentuated by granulation (*261* and *264*) is used to divide the surface into concentric circles.

Every example is open at the top with the exception of *266* (with a triangular cluster of granules on a gold sheet filling this space); *263* has a knobbed bolt that slides back and forth. The latter example is also unique

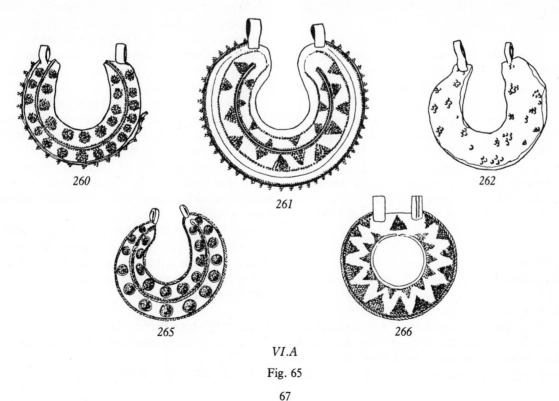

260

261

262

265

266

VI.A

Fig. 65

67

for its granulated clusters in the form of chevrons, which cover the whole surface of the pendant from inner to outer edge.

All the examples are of two curved gold sheets, soldered together and decorated on the external faces. Except for *263*, each example has a pair of suspension loops soldered at the top.

Diameters of individual examples vary from 25 mm (*263*) to 45 mm (*261*), with an average diameter of 34 mm for all the examples.

All the examples of Type *VI.A* are from Tell el-'Ajjul, and date to late LB IA[1]:

1. Six examples (*260–262*) from Hoard 1299, which was in an empty space distant from any structure (Petrie 1934; 6–7; pl. 62; Petrie, Mackay, and Murray 1952: 9–11);
2. Two examples (*263*) from Tomb 1998, located in an empty space in GD 793 (Petrie, Mackay, and Murray 1952: 10–12, 23–24, pls. 2 and 33);
3. Two examples (*264*) from Hoard 277, which had been buried within a partially washed-away room of Town II (Petrie, Mackay, and Murray 1952: 9–11, pl. 34);
4. Two examples (*265*) from Hoard 1312, which was found overlying a wall of Town II (Petrie 1934: 6–8; Petrie, Mackay, and Murray 1952: 10–11);
5. Two examples (*266*) from Hoard 1313, found in a room of Town II (Petrie 1934: 6–7, pl. 62; Petrie, Mackay, and Murray 1952: 10–11).

No close parallels could be located, but the fine granulation is comparable to that of the Dilbat pendants (Maxwell-Hyslop 1971: 89–90, pls. 61, 63, and 64), which have a *terminus ante quem* of ca. 1600 B.C. Pendants of the same type without granulation occur in Early Bronze contexts at Sedment[2] and Kültepe.[3] In light of the other unique jewelry types in gold from LB 'Ajjul (e.g., Types *III.A* and *VI.C*), it is probable that a gold industry had been established here by the beginning of the LBA (*contra* Maxwell-Hyslop 1971: 118). Type *VI.A* was fabricated exclusively in LB IA.

Type VI.B.1–2 Crescent or Horns
(*267–300*; pls. 18–19)
This extremely popular group (36 pendants, 31 percent of Class VI) can be divided into two types: the standard form and the crescent or horns with disc. The combination of the crescent and disc may depict either the moon in a waning phase or the sun and moon together. Some of the examples of Type *VI.B.1* are flattened and have noticeably inturned tips, highly

suggestive of bull's horns,[4] especially *269* (pl. 18), as well as *276*, *278* (pl. 18), *285*, *287* (pl. 18), and *294*.

Other examples have a more circular form with the tips approaching one another and sometimes even touching, in particular *297*; cf. *267*, *270* (pl. 18), *271–273*, *274* (pl. 18), *275* (pl. 18), *277*, *279*, *280–281*, *283*, *286*, *290* (pl. 19), *291* (pl. 19), *292–293*, *295*, and *296* (pl. 19).

The Type *VI.B.1* pendants include 14 examples each of gold and silver, one example (*285*) of electrum, two examples (*275* and *286*) of copper or bronze, and a single example (*291*) of onyx; the material for *283* is unspecified. All the metal pendants are composed of a thick metal open ring to which is soldered a broad suspension loop, so that the crescent or horns hangs downward (opposite to that of bull's horns). Most of the examples are also decorated, although this is sometimes obscured by corrosion on the silver and copper-base specimens: (1) ribbing by incision and beveling on the arms of the shank (*269–271*, *278–279*, *285*, *287–290*, *295*, etc.); (2) incised ribbing and/or folded-over edges on suspension loops (*268–276*, *278–280*, *287*, *293*, *295–297*), (3) incised cross hatching or dots around the periphery of the shank and arms (*268* [dots], *270–271*, *297*). Incised hatching or cross hatching (*279*, *287–288*, and *297*), dots (*270*), and rosettes (*271*), worked in repoussé (center) with surrounding punched dots, sometimes appear on suspension loops.

Even with the limited repertoire of materials and motifs, only several varieties are exactly replicated, viz., the two specimens of *282* and the simple circular crescent or horns with little or no decoration. Other examples exhibit considerable variation in the number of incised ribs on the shank, arms, and suspension loop, size, material, etc.

The largest example is in copper or bronze (*275*), but, in general, the pendants can be divided between a smaller variety (average dimensions: 12 × 15 mm) and a larger variety (average dimensions: 23 × 33 mm).

The one example (*291*, pl. 19) in onyx is beautifully made. The banding of the onyx follows the contours of the crescent or horns and there is a rounded suspension knob at the top.

Type *VI.B.1* occurs at five Late Bronze Palestinian sites with the majority of the examples (23 pendants, 70 percent of the type) coming from Tell el-'Ajjul.

The Beth Shan examples are found in each of the Late Bronze levels:

1. Level IX (Late Bronze Age generally).
   Locus 1234, the inner sanctuary of the temple (*267*);
2. Level VIII (early LB IIB):

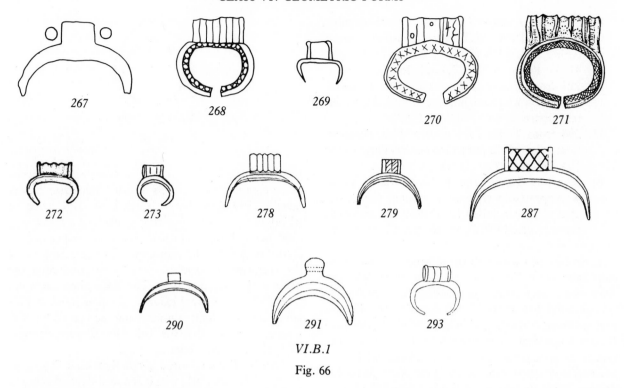

VI.B.1

Fig. 66

Below the floor of Locus 1068, the upper altar room of the Level VII temple (*268*);

3. Level VII (late LB IIB):
   Locus 1085, the room east of the anteroom of the temple (*269*).

Three examples (*271–272*) were found at Beth She-mesh in an LB IIB jug buried in a corner of Room 73 (Stratum IV) under the floor, which is dated to LB IIB (Grant 1931: 43, plans 4 and 5; 1932: 21; Grant and Wright 1939: 47–48). The single Lachish example (*273*) comes from Burial Pit 542 for which there was apparently no stratigraphic separation of the different burials (Tufnell 1958: 242); it contained LB II local and imported pottery.

The Megiddo examples (*274–275*) were found in two contexts: (1) *274* is from Tomb 1145 B, which contained an undisturbed LB I assemblage (Guy 1938: 95), and (2) *275* from Locus 3187 in Stratum VIIB, which was a partially excavated room with an intact plaster floor, assigned to Stratum VIII, and probably dating to LB IIB (Loud 1948: 176, fig. 75).

The Tell el-'Ajjul examples (*276–297*) come from many areas of the tell and several cemeteries:

1. *276* from AN 748, a main street of Town II, which probably dates to LB IA (Petrie 1931: 7–8, pl. 54; 1933: 7–8);
2. *277* from AT 659–760, a pit cut into the debris of Town III, reaching bedrock, dated to LB IA

(Petrie 1931: 7–8, pl. 54);

3. Four examples (*278–281*) from Hoard 1299, found in an empty space distant from any building, dated to late LB IA (Petrie 1934: 5–6, pl. 62);
4. Two examples (*282*) from EAD 877, a large room with ovens to the east, dated to LB IA (Petrie 1934: 3–4, 14–15, pl. 62);
5. *283* from ECE 785 in Town II, probably an LB IA room (Petrie 1934: 3–4, 11, 14–15, pl. 62);[5]
6. *284* from LH[4] 976, a partial room of Palace II with LB IA pottery (Petrie 1933: 3, 7–8, pl. 47);
7. *285* from LK 1002, a room in Palace IIIA, dated to LB IA (Petrie 1933: 3, 7–8, pl. 47);
8. *286* from NB 995, a room of Palace II or IIIA, dated to LB IA (Petrie 1932: 7–9, pl. 46);
9. Four examples (*287–290*) from Hoard 1312, found overlying a wall of Town II, dating to LB IA (Petrie 1934: 8, pl. 62);
10. *291* from Tomb 447, a child's jar burial located west of LA in an open space, dating to LB I (Petrie 1934: 8–9, pl. 61);[6]
11. *292* from Tomb 1502 in the '18th Dynasty' Cemetery, which contained LB I pottery (Petrie 1932: 1–2, pl. 57);
12. *293* from Grave 425 on the west side of the tell in an open space; the small group of published pottery can be dated broadly to LB I–IIA (Petrie 1934: 3–4, 8–9, pl. 60);

13. *294* from a wall of MO 1040, a room of most probably Palace IIIB wth published pottery dating to LB IIA (Petrie 1932: 4, 13–14, pls. 48–49; Petrie 1933: 3, 7–8, pl. 46);

14. *295* from Tomb 1080 of the '18th Dynasty' Cemetery, which is a homogeneous LB IIA context (Petrie 1932: 7, 14–15, pl. 52);

15. *296* from Tomb 1095 of the '18th Dynasty' Cemetery, whose published pottery dates to LB IIB (Petrie 1932: 5, 14–15, pl. 52);

16. *297* from Tomb 1166 in the Northeast Fosse with approximately a dozen burials; the associated pottery included LB II local and imported types (Petrie 1932: 7, 15–16, pls. 52–53).

The different varieties of the crescent or horns pendant have a long history at sites throughout Western Asia and Egypt from as early as ca. 2000 B.C. (Maxwell-Hyslop 1971: 79–80) down to the Roman period (Petrie 1914: 23, pl. 6:85e). None of the Late Bronze Palestinian examples exhibit the fine granulation of the pendant on the Dilbat necklace, which has a *terminus ante quem* date of ca. 1600 B.C. (Maxwell-Hyslop 1971: 91, pls. 61 and 63).[7] The LB IA varieties, all from 'Ajjul, are of both the flattened and circular varieties and have little decorative detail beyond the beveling of the arms of the pendant and incised ribbing, cross hatching, and folded-over edges of some of the suspension loops. Parallels can be cited from Late Bronze and Middle Bronze contexts at Ras Shamra,[8] Alalakh,[9] Mari,[10] Boghazkale,[11] Dinkha Tepe,[12] Assur,[13] and Nuzi.[14] Along with an earlier example from Tell el-'Ajjul,[15] additional parallels occur at Hazor,[16] Gezer,[17] and Nahariyah.[18]

While the same forms and stylistic features continue to appear throughout the rest of the Late Bronze Age and into Iron I, there is a development toward higher-backed suspension rings with well-defined ribbing (sometimes with repoussé and engraved rosettes; cf. *271*) and incised dots or cross hatching on the shank arms (cf. *268, 270–271,* and *297*). Relevant parallels for the latter, as well as the more standard later varieties, occur at Megiddo,[19] Tell el-Far'ah South,[20] Shechem,[21] Deir el-Balah,[22] Beth Shan,[23] and Tel Kittan.[24] The type also is evidenced in New Kingdom Egypt.[25]

Except for the later, more highly developed varieties (*268, 270–271,* and *297*), which were probably manufactured only in LB II and Iron I, the other varieties have hardly any temporal specificity, similar examples having been produced over a period of approximately a millennium.

Type *VI.B.2* (crescent or horns with disc), in con-

VI.B.2   299

Fig. 67

trast to Type *VI.B.1*, occurs in only three contexts, and is composed exclusively of faded blue-green glazed faience (*300* is probably leached out and faded to white) with a suspension ring in place of a metal loop (*300* has a long cylindrical bead for suspension in accord with the metal prototype). The circular form of the crescent or horns is stressed by combining the latter with a circular disc. The Beth Shan examples (*298–299*, pl. 19) were made in the same mold or affiliated molds; slight dimensional and stylistic differences indicate that the Tell Abu Hawam example (*300*) comes from a separate mold.

Type *VI.B.2* was found in two Beth Shan strata: (1) *298* from Locus 1301, which is a well-defined room in the southeastern residential sector (Level IX, Late Bronze Age generally); and (2) *299* from north of the steps of Locus 1068, the upper altar room of the Level VII temple (late LB IIB). *300* comes from a dump outside Building 50 in Stratum V at Tell Abu Hawam, which dates to LB II (Hamilton 1935: 47, 62, pl. 18:1–2).

Egyptian parallels can be cited from New Kingdom el-Amarna[26] and Gurob.[27] In Palestine, comparable examples occur at Gezer[28] and Tell el-Far'ah South.[29] The period of manufacture for Type *VI.B.2* is LB II–Iron I.

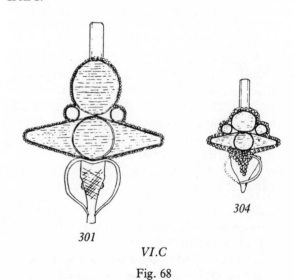

301

304

VI.C

Fig. 68

Type VI.C Cruciform with Stylized Ram's Head
(*301–304*; pl. 20)

Type *VI.C*, represented by seven examples (*301–304*) from Tell el-ʿAjjul, exhibits the same fine gold workmanship that has already been noted for other exclusively ʿAjjul types (*III.A* and *VI.A*). The notable manufacturing characteristic of this type is the cloisonné technique in gold and glass. Circular and triangular compartments are formed of gold strips on a flat base, laid out in a cruciform pattern. Blue glass (faded and discolored in places or disintegrated and missing altogether; cf. *302–304* on pl. 20) was employed to fill the cloissons.

The upper half of all the pendants, including the 'wings,' are virtually identical: fine granulation outlines the borders of the cloissons, which are variously sized and shaped (circular or elliptical), and a large suspension hook is soldered to the back plate.

However, the lower part of the pendant, which depicts a stylized ram's head, varies in design and workmanship. Thus, a triangular cloisson (*303*, pl. 20), granulation (*304*, pl. 20), and incised chevron lines (*302*, pl. 20) can mark the top of the animal's head. Gold globules sometimes represent the eyes (*301–302*), and ears splayed out (*302*) or fitted close to the head (*303*) are portrayed with gold strips (well-formed for *302*) soldered to the side of the head.

All the examples have a gold open ring soldered over the back of the head to represent the ram's horns (more realistically curved inward on *301*; the right horn is missing on *304*). *301–303* occur in identical pairs. The single example of *304* is approximately half the length of the other examples.

Type *VI.C* is only found in tombs at Tell el-ʿAjjul:

1. *301* from Tomb 1203, which was below wall 755 near ECC of Town II; the stratigraphy is unclear because of excessive denudation in this area, but the published pottery points to an early LB IA dating (Petrie 1934: 3–4, 7, 15, pl. 62; Petrie, Mackay, and Murray 1952: 10–11);

2. *302* from Tomb 2070, which was overlying a wall of Town II; the pottery evidence is nonspecific, but the tomb should probably be dated to the beginning of LB IA (Petrie, Mackay, and Murray 1952: 11–12, 23, 24, pls. 2, 4, 33, 35);

3. *303* from Tomb 1998 in an empty space between Towns III and II, and dated to the beginning of LB IA (Petrie, Mackay, and Murray 1952: 11–12, 22, 23, pls. 2, 33);

4. *304* from Tomb 1740, a child's burial in area TDV, which is to be dated to the beginning of LB IA (Petrie 1934: 3, 7–8, 14–15, pl. 63; Petrie,

Mackay, and Murray 1952: 10–11).

The only parallel for this type occurs at Megiddo in Tomb 2117, Area BB, Square N 15 (Loud 1948: 164, fig. 401, pl. 225:12–13), which is ascribed to Stratum IX and possibly dates to LB IA. It differs from the ʿAjjul examples in having a cruciform pattern composed exclusively of large circular cloissons, and inlaid glass *wḏt* eyes on the stylized ram's heads (also cf. Petrie 1914: 44, pl. 38:212n, undated, silver). The juxtaposition of cloisonné and granulation was already familiar to goldsmiths (Hayes 1959: 233, fig. 143; Tufnell and Ward 1966: 189–92; Higgins 1961: 25; Maxwell-Hyslop 1971: 120) when these specimens were more likely fabricated in an atelier of LB IA Tell el-ʿAjjul.

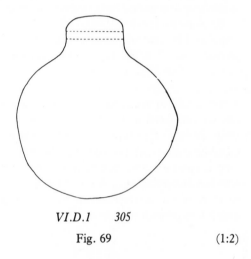

VI.D.1   305

Fig. 69   (1:2)

Type VI.D.1–3 Disc (*305–308*; pl. 21)

The examples (*305–306*) of Type *VI.D.1* (Plain Disc) are among the largest of Late Bronze jewelry pendants, and occur only in glass (primarily blue or blue-green with some admixture of yellow and white, probably from discoloration). A broad projection at one side is horizontally perforated for suspension.

One example (*305*) of Type *VI.D.1* is from Locus 1387, Level IX, at Beth Shan, which is a large room or courtyard in the northwestern residential sector, dated to the Late Bronze Age generally. The other example (*306*) comes from Locus 5029, Area BB, Stratum IX at Megiddo, a probable LB IA context (Loud 1948: 182).[30] Virtually identical pendants were found at Late Bronze Nuzi[31] and Assur.[32] Later examples occur at Megiddo;[33] these may be heirlooms. Although a later date cannot be totally excluded, the type most likely belongs to LB I.

The single example (*307*) of Type *VI.D.2* is distinguished from Type *VI.D.1* in having a central boss.

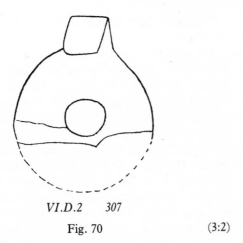

VI.D.2   307

Fig. 70   (3:2)

It is also about a third the size of the latter, and is made of silver with a folded-over suspension loop.

307 is from Tomb 1502 at Tell el-'Ajjul, which belongs to LB I on the basis of the published pottery (Petrie 1932: 7–8, pl. 52). A very close parallel was found at Tell Brak in a hoard of jewelry, probably dating to ca. 2000 B.C. (Mallowan 1947: 177, pl. 35), which is related to a class of circular pendants, usually further decorated with dots or lines (Maxwell-Hyslop 1971: 29–30). This type is a simpler version of Type *VI.G* (star disc), and in fact may belong to the latter type if the rays have been masked by corrosion (no first-hand examination). A much earlier example from Brak does not necessitate an early dating for *307*, which was probably made in LB I.

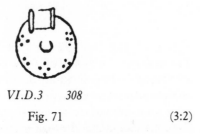

VI.D.3   308

Fig. 71   (3:2)

The single example of Type *VI.D.3* (*308*, pl. 21) has five clusters of four repoussé dots (simulating granulation?) evenly spaced around the periphery of the disc, which has a central boss. This very small gold disc has a rolled suspension loop with folded-over edges.

308 is from Tomb 1037 in the '18th Dynasty' Cemetery at Tell el-'Ajjul, which is dated to LB IIA according to the published pottery (Petrie 1932: 15–16, pl. 56). Other examples of a disc with repoussé dots differently arranged occur at Gezer[34] and Alaca Hüyük.[35] The five clusters of *308* might be related to the dotted lines on the Alaca Hüyük specimen, except that the repoussé technique on sheet gold is commonly employed for other Late Bronze pendant types

(*II.A.1, II.B.2, IV.D, VI.G*). Type *VI.D.3* was most likely produced at Tell el-'Ajjul in LB IIA.

VI.E   309

Fig. 72

Type VI.E Double Spiral (*309*)
The one example (*309*) of this type was not available for personal examination. A strip of copper or bronze had apparently been wound into a double spiral; no soldering joints appear on the line drawing. There is probably a rolled suspension loop at the top, which is hung from a hoop earring.

309 is from Burial Pit 542 at Lachish, a mixed LB II context (Tufnell 1958: 82, 242).[36] This is a rather late example of a form that originated in the Early Dynastic III period and continued until at least as late as the sixth century B.C., being represented at many European and Asian sites.[37] Most of the parallels are of the quadruple spiral form, whereas *309* is a double spiral, which can be compared to specimens at Tell el-'Ajjul,[38] Ur,[39] and Tepe Hissar.[40] *309* was possibly cast in a mold, rather than being wound from wire strands in the usual fashion.[41] Because of the type's wide distribution in time and space, it cannot be resolved whether *309* was manufactured in LB II.

Type VI.F.1–3 Drop (*310–337*; pls. 21–23)
Type *VI.F* is a catch-all category, since the extremely popular drop pendant (32 specimens, 27 percent of the Geometric Forms Class) appears in many varieties differing in material, workmanship, and stylistic features.

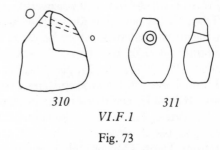

310   311

VI.F.1

Fig. 73

The crude type (*VI.F.1*, *310–311*, pl. 21) exhibits essentially no workmanship beyond the drilling of an

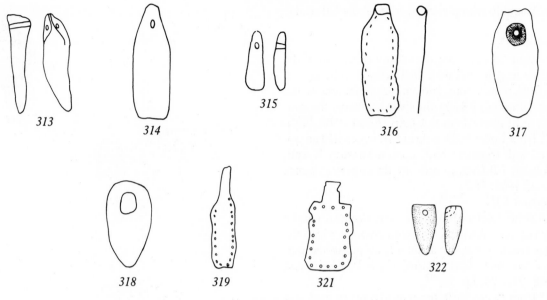

313   314   315   316   317

318   319   321   322

VI.F.2

Fig. 74

off-center perforation. *311*, probably of turquoise, was smoothed off at most; the very irregular shape of *310* suggests that the attractive yellow stone is unworked.

The crude type occurs only in Level IX (Late Bronze Age generally) at Beth Shan: (1) *310* from Locus 1330, a room in the southeastern residential quarter, and (2) *311* from south of the temple in the area of FitzGerald's deep sounding, an uncertain context.

The elongated drop type (*VI.F.2, 312–330*) is the largest group of this category (21 pendants), and it has the widest spectrum of materials of any Late Bronze Age Palestinian pendant type: five blue-green glazed and one 'gray-green' glazed faience, four gold, one green stone, one dark brown stone, one sandstone, two turquoise, one lapis lazuli, one steatite, one hematite, and two bone pendants.

Sizes cluster around a small variety (average length of 15 mm) and a large variety (average length of 27 mm), although examples somewhat larger (*324*) and smaller (*326*) than the standard lengths occur.

The shapes vary from rounded or sharp-pointed tooth-shaped (*312*, pl. 22; *313*, pl. 22; *317, 318*, and *324*) to blunt-ended celt-shaped varieties (*314*, pl. 22; *325, 326, 328* and *330*). There are also more elliptically shaped (*315*, pl. 22), and triangularly shaped varieties (*320* and *322*, pl. 22), and a group of rectangularly shaped gold plaques, which have punched dots in repoussé along their peripheries (*316*, pl. 22; *319*, pl. 22; and *321*) and rolled suspension loops at one end (unrolled for *319*). The remaining gold example (*327*, pl. 22) has similar features, but, instead of peripheral

dots, horizontal and vertical lines are carefully incised on its lower half.

324 (pl. 22) is unusually large (55 × 10 mm), as well as being unique for its material (bone) and the incised markings on its surface. One rectangular plaque in faience (*323*) has no markings.

The elongated drop pendant is found at four Late Bronze Palestinian sites. Beth Shan is the best-represented:

1. Level IX (Late Bronze Age generally):
   East side of Locus 1234, the inner sanctuary of the temple (*312*);
   Locus 1332, an area above rooms 1333–1339 in the southeastern residential sector, a problematical locus (*313*);
   Locus 1339, a partially defined room in the southeastern residential quarter (*314*);
   South of the temple in the area of FitzGerald's deep sounding, an uncertain context (*315*);
2. Level VIII (early LB IIB):
   Locus 1092, the area below the steps of Locus 1068, the upper altar room of the Level VII temple (*316*);
   Below the floor of Locus 1068 (*317–318*);
   Below the steps of Locus 1068 (*319*);
3. Level VII (late LB IIB):
   Near the steps of Locus 1068 (*320*);
   Locus 1087, a partially defined room south of the temple (*321*);
   Locus 1252, a room in the southeastern residential quarter (*322*).

The Megiddo examples come from all the LB strata:

1. Stratum IX:
   324 from Locus 2134, the central courtyard of the palace in Area AA with well-defined walls and an earth or plaster floor, broken to some extent on the east; although it lacks published pottery, the context most likely dates to LB IA (Loud 1948: 165); *325* from Locus 5029 in Area BB, which had an isolated wall fragment built upon a Stratum X wall, probably LB IA in accord with the pottery evidence (Loud 1948: 182);

2. Stratum VIII:
   326 from Locus 3100 in the north-central part of the palace of Area AA, the same room in which the later treasure hoard was found; no published pottery, but most likely dating to LB IB–IIA (Loud 1948: 25, 173, fig. 56);[42] *327* from Locus 5020, the central court of the lesser palace to the east of the gate area in Area AA with a well-preserved lime floor on a crushed stone foundation; no published pottery, but probably belonging to LB IB–IIA (Loud 1948: 113–14, 182, figs. 268, 270–72);

3. Stratum VIIB:
   328 from Locus 1834, a room in Area CC with two floor levels, dated to LB IIB according to the pottery evidence (Loud 1948: 156).

Single examples from Burial Cave A2 on Jebel al-Hawayah (*329*) and Burial Cave B3 on Jebel al-Qesir (*330*) in the Baq'ah Valley on the Transjordanian plateau can be dated to LB I and LB II, respectively (McGovern 1980, 1982, and In press).

Types *VI.F.1–2* have a time span and geographical distribution that almost defy systematization. Aldred (1971: 144) traces the development of Egyptian jewelry in its multifarious forms to a simple drop pendant, often strung as a single element on a necklace.

The crude type and the variously shaped elongated varieties in stone (*310–311, 314–315, 318, 322, 325–326, 328–330*) have parallels from prehistoric times to the Iron Age.[43] Similar forms in faience (*312–313, 320, 323*) begin in the Early Bronze Age, but never become as popular as the varieties in stone and are essentially nonexistent by the Iron Age.[44] The examples in bone (*317 and 324*) also occur in an earlier period,[45] developing into an Iron Age long form, which is often decorated.[46] The gold examples (*316, 319, 321 and 327*) have no close parallels elsewhere, but their form and workmanship conform to other types of gold pendants (e.g., Types *II.A.1* and *II.B.3.a*), and perhaps were manufactured at Beth Shan during LB II.

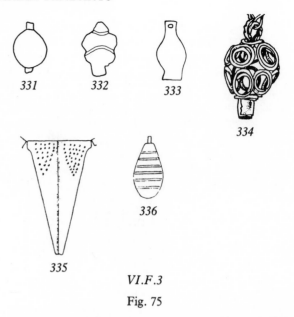

331   *332*   *333*   *334*

336

335

VI.F.3

Fig. 75

Adding to the already complex typology of Type *VI.F*, the miscellaneous type of drop pendant (*VI.F.3*) includes eight more unique varieties, some of which are quite ornamental. In the latter group is a spherical open-worked pendant of gold (*334*) on a chain of linked gold loops. Circlets of two tiers of five circlets are capped by a single circlet at each end. A hollow cylinder is soldered to the bottom, and a twisted double-stranded suspension loop is attached above. A pair of triangular gold sheet pendants (*337*, pl. 23) have triangular-shaped clusters of dots at one end from between which a line extends to the apex, bisecting the triangle, all worked in repoussé. The edges are folded over to form a long suspension loop on the short side of the triangle. The shape and workmanship are comparable to those on the pictorial and female plaque pendants (Types *II.B.1.b* and *II.B.2.b*). Possibly, the two examples of *337* are a further schematization of the pubic triangle region.

Another gold example (*338*, pl. 23) is reminiscent of the leaf or petal type (*IV.H.3*), but diverges from the latter by having horizontal grooved lines that cover most of the surface of an upper gold sheet soldered to a flat base (hollow interior); a suspension ring is soldered to one end. Negby (1970: 44) suggests that the pendant may be an insect pupa, related to the fly pendants (Type *III.C*).

Another gold pendant (*336*) consists of two hemispherical sections soldered together to form a plain globular variety with a suspension loop soldered to one end.

Two other circular varieties (*331* and *333*, cf. *336*) are composed of 'light green' (blue-green?) faience and carnelian, respectively. *335* (pl. 24) is an intermediate form, similar to both Type *V.F.3* (*ḥst*) and Type *IV.F.5* (lotus seed vessel). Finally, *332*, which was not examined, is probably a badly formed circular or rectangular variety; it is flat-backed with suspension rings at each end.

Examples of this type are found at four Palestinian sites. At Beth Shan, two of the LB levels are represented:

1. Level VIII (early LB IIB):
   Locus 1092, the area below the steps of Locus 1068, the upper altar room of the Level VII temple (*331*);
2. Level VII (late LB IIB):
   Locus 1104, a poorly defined room to the north of the temple (*332*),
   Locus 1284, an uncertain context located east of FitzGerald's deep sounding (*333*).

The single example (*334*) from Beth Shemesh comes from the jewelry hoard found in an LB IIB jug under the floor of Room 73, Stratum IV, which should probably be dated to LB IIB (Grant 1931: 43, plans 4 and 5; 1932: 21; Grant and Wright 1939: 47–48).

The Megiddo example (*335*) was found in Locus 2094 of Stratum VIII, a room in Area BB with the floor and walls cut in places (Loud 1948: 163); the published pottery dates to LB IB–IIA in agreement with the excavators' dating of Stratum VIII.

At Tell el-'Ajjul, examples of the miscellaneous drop pendant were found in the following contexts:

1. *336* from Hoard 277, which had been buried in a partially washed-away room of Town II, dated to the end of LB IA (Petrie, Mackay, and Murray 1952: 8–10, 28, pl. 34);
2. *337* from Tomb 1740 in area TDV, which was probably used during the period between Towns III and II, and thus dates to the beginning of LB IA (Petrie 1934: 3, 7–8, 14–15, pl. 63);
3. *338* from Hoard 1313, found in a room of Town II and dated to late LB IA (Petrie 1934: 7, pl. 62).

The gold open-worked spherical pendant (*334*) is similar to two Iron I beads from Megiddo,[47] as well as later Egyptian specimens (Tadmor and Misch-Brandl 1980: 73–75).[48] The period of manufacture of the better made examples is possibly confined to LB IIB–Iron I.

The pair of triangular gold-sheet pendants (*337*) can be compared to a pair of blunt-edged, undecorated earring pendants from Tell el-Far'ah South.[49] However, since the style and advanced workmanship are compar-

able to other LB IA 'Ajjul gold pendants, it is possible that these pendants were produced in early LB at this site.

The circularly shaped pendants (*331, 333*, and *336*) are possibly related to the 'bulla' pendant type, illustrated in Petrie's corpus,[50] which have a long temporal span, particularly in carnelian.[51] While the carnelian example (*333*) cannot be precisely dated, the faience (*331*) and gold (*336*) examples were probably made in the Late Bronze Age, along with the badly formed, rectangularly or circularly shaped example (*332*).

335, an intermediate form between Types *IV.F.5* (lotus seed vessel) and *V.F.1* (*ḥst?*), very likely dates to the same period as the latter, i.e., LB II–Iron I.

No parallels could be located for *338*, but again its excellent workmanship argues for an LB IA 'Ajjul metal-working context.[52]

Type VI.G.1–2.c Star Disc (*339–356*; pls. 23–25)
The rays of the 'star' are very schematically indicated by crossed lines on the three examples (*339–341*, pl. 23) of Type *VI.G.1*. The only example that was available for first-hand examination (*339*) was of white glazed faience with brown decoration. A dot is roughly centered in each quadrant formed by the lines. A rectangular projection, centered on one of the lines, has a horizontal perforation for suspension.

All the examples of Type *VI.G.1* come from Stratum IX at Megiddo:

1. *339* from Locus 5029 in Area BB, which has an isolated wall fragment apparently built upon a Stratum X wall, implying the continuation of the structure into Stratum IX; the published pottery confirms a probable LB IA dating (Loud 1948: 182);
2. *340* from Tomb 2009, a simple burial of a child in an open space of Area CC, which contained pottery dating to LB IA (Loud 1948: 157, fig. 344);
3. *341* from Locus S=2048, south of the temple area in Area BB, a room with fragmentary walls and floors; the pottery evidence includes mixed LB IB and IIA types (Loud 1948: 159).[53]

No parallels in faience were located. However, a comparable example in gold occurs at Ras Shamra in LB IIA,[54] and a four-rayed variety with another four curved rays in place of the dots comes from Shechem.[55] Another variant in yellow glass, which has curved rays encircling each dot, was found at Gurob.[56] Gold, silver, and bronze four-rayed stars worked in repoussé on piriform and violin-shaped plaque pendants may be related.[57] Although the metal variety of Type *VI.G.1* dates to the Late Bronze Age generally, the faience variety was perhaps made only at Megiddo in LB IA.

The plain, eight-rayed type (*VI.G.2.a*) occurs only in precious metals: gold (*342–343*, pl. 24), silver (*344*), and probably electrum (*345*, pl. 24). The smallest example (*342*) has a central boss worked in repoussé and eight roughly incised, pointed rays, which are irregularly spaced around the disc; there is a rolled suspension loop with two incised vertical lines. *343* has rays and central boss worked in repoussé, which are further defined by chasing, which does not extend to the central boss; the rolled suspension loop is not incised. The two larger varieties (*344–345*) of this type have better-defined rays and central bosses worked in repoussé and chased. Both have unincised rolled suspension loops. *344* is unique in having punched repoussé dots around its periphery.

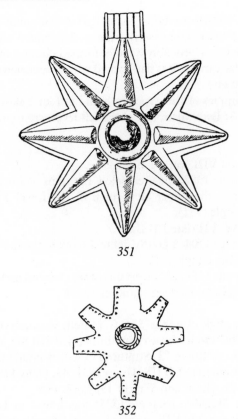

351

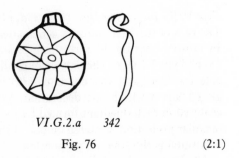

VI.G.2.a   342

Fig. 76   (2:1)

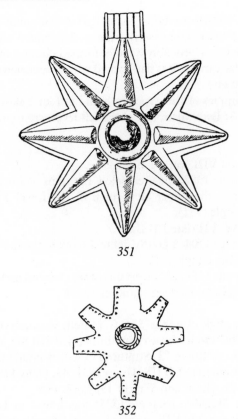

352

VI.G.2.b

Fig. 77

Each of the four examples of Type *VI.G.2.a* comes from a different site. *342* is from below the steps of Locus 1068, the upper altar room of the Level VII temple at Beth Shan, and is dated to early LB IIB. The Lachish example (*343*) was found during sifting of soil from the Fosse Temple, and must be dated to the Late Bronze Age generally (Tufnell, Inge, and Harding 1940: 66). The Tel Kittan example (*344*) is from Stratum III of the temple; stratigraphic details are lacking, but the pottery, which was examined by the writer in Jerusalem, appears to be LB IA (Eisenberg 1977: 80). The example from Shechem (*345*) was found in the cellar under Room G of Field 13, which is a homogeneous LB IIA context (Campbell, Ross, and Toombs 1971: 12).

Comparable examples of somewhat different design can be cited from Late Bronze Alalakh,[58] Tell al-Rimah,[59] and possibly Tel Mevorakh.[60] The type's obvious affinity to the following two types of the star disc group supports an early Late Bronze Age dating for the better-made pendants (*344–345*), and a later LB dating for the smaller pendants with incised rays (*342–343*).

The eight-rayed cut-out star disc (Type *VI.G.2.b*) occurs only in gold, and several varieties are to be dis-

tinguished. The most exquisite examples (*351*, pl. 24; and *353*) have symmetrically placed rays around a central disc, all carefully defined by repoussé work and chasing. Each ray is then cut out to accentuate its form. One of the rays is rolled over to make a suspension loop, which has folded-over edges and incised vertical lines. *347* (pl. 24) is similar to *351* and *353* in design and workmanship, but it is more roughly cut, poorly incised, and lacks a suspension loop. Other examples of this type are even more crudely made. *346*, *348* (pl. 24), *349*, and *350* have very poorly defined rays, which are only partly cut out. *352* (pl. 24) is unusual for its workmanship: slightly ribbed rays worked in repoussé, defined by incised dots and crudely cut out, radiate from a center cloisson(?) to which is soldered a twisted wire.

Type *VI.G.2.b* occurs at only two Late Bronze Palestinian sites. It is found in two contexts at Lachish: (1) *346* is from Room D, the sanctuary of Fosse Temple I, whose pottery substantiates an LB IA dating (Tufnell, Inge, and Harding 1940: 66), and (2) *347–349* from sifting of soil from the Fosse Temple area and therefore dated to the Late Bronze Age generally (Tufnell, Inge, and Harding 1940: 66). The

Tell el-ʿAjjul examples were found in two late LB IA hoards: (1) *350–352* from Hoard 1299, found in an empty space distant from any building (Petrie 1934: 5–7, pl. 62), and (2) *353* from Hoard 277, which had been buried in a partially washed-away room of Town II (Petrie, Mackay, and Murray 1952: 8–10, 28, pl. 34).

This type is apparently unique to Late Bronze Tell el-ʿAjjul and Lachish, since no parallels could be traced elsewhere.[61] All the examples may have been made in LB IA at ʿAjjul, which had a much higher concentration of exquisite goldwork than Lachish.

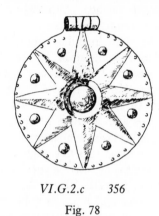

VI.G.2.c   356

Fig. 78

Type *VI.G.2.c* (*354–357*) differs from Type *VI.G.2.b* only in having dots inserted between the rays (cf. Type *VI.G.1*). The two Megiddo specimens in faience (*354*, pl. 25) are made in the same way as *339–341* of Type *VI.G.1*: the eight rays of Type *VI.G.2.c* are schematically indicated by four intersecting lines between which dots are roughly centered. The finer examples in gold (*356*, pl. 25) and silver (*355*, pl. 25) have well-defined bosses and ribbed rays worked in repoussé. *356* has repoussé punched dots around the periphery, chasing to mark the rays, and incised vertical lines on the rolled suspension loop. Since *355* is badly corroded and could not be examined by the writer, any additional decoration could not be confirmed.

The Megiddo examples (*354*) were found in Tomb 2009 in Area CC, Stratum IX, a simple burial of a child in an open space whose pottery dates to LB IA (Loud 1948: 157, fig. 344). Another Megiddo example (*355*) comes from Locus 2064 of Stratum VIII, a large room to the north of the temple in Area BB without floors and with a wall cut by robbing; the pottery from the locus is poorly published, but a LB IIB date is likely (Loud 1948: 160). The single example (*356*) from Tell el-ʿAjjul comes from G 950, which was located somewhere northwest of areas E and F, and probably belongs to LB II.[62]

The eight-rayed star disc with dots has parallels in gold and glass from a fairly wide geographical area in the Late Bronze Age, including Nuzi,[63] Alalakh,[64] and Tepe Giyan.[65] The six-rayed variety with dots, but apparently not the eight-rayed variety, occurs at Ras Shamra in hoards *e*[66] and *f*,[67] both dated to LB IIA. The type was probably manufactured throughout the Late Bronze Age.

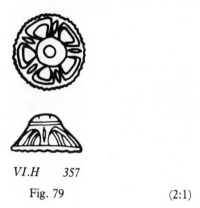

VI.H   357

Fig. 79   (2:1)

Type VI.H. 'Wheel' (*357–359*; pl. 25)
The three examples (*357–359*) of this type appear to represent an open-spoked wheel, an uncertain designation. Even though the specimens are perforated medially and might be classified as beads, their unusual form and their broad geographical distribution (see below) justify classifying them as ornamental pendants.

The two examples from Lachish (*358–359*; pl. 25) probably were made in the same mold, to judge from their identical dimensions and stylistic features – two five-spoked hubs that slant inward to join along a common ring, which is notched around the periphery. Both are probably of faded blue-green glazed faience (*359* could not be examined). By contrast, the Beth Shan example (*357*) has only a single five-spoked slanted hub, which is notched. Although its disposition is unknown and therefore could not be personally examined, it is probably also of blue-green glazed faience ('bluish glass'), and definitely derives from a separate mold.

The Beth Shan example (*357*) comes from Locus 1403 of Level IX, an area on the west side of the temple courtyard, which is dated to the Late Bronze Age generally. Two examples were found at Lachish: (1) *358* is from the deposit of beads and pendants near the west wall of Room E of Fosse Temple III, dated to LB IIB (Tufnell, Inge, and Harding 1940: 42, 74–76, pl. 8:4); and (2) *357* comes from Pit 188, dated to LB IIB (Tufnell, Inge, and Harding 1940: 75).[68]

Parallels for the double-hubbed variety can be cited

from Late Bronze Greece and Cyprus,[69] Egypt,[70] North Syria,[71] and Transcaucasia.[72] All the examples are similar in stylistic features and size. The examples may have been produced at a single site (possibly Alalakh, which has the earliest examples and the largest collection) and disseminated from there. The period of production for Type *VI.H* covered the entire Late Bronze Age.

B. Summary

Class *VI* pendants are distributed among ten Palestinian sites (Chart 34), which is the most for any class. The Hill Country (Shechem), the Jordan Valley (Beth Shan and Tel Kittan), and Transjordan (Umm ad-Dananir) are also better represented, although no examples are yet recorded for the Galilee and the Huleh Valley.

Almost half the pendants come from the major southern littoral site of Tell el-'Ajjul, where eight of the 16 types are represented. Five of these types are from LB IA burial (*VI.A*, *VI.C*, and *VI.F.3*) and residential contexts (*VI.A*, *VI.B.1*, *VI.F.3*, and *VI.G.2.b*), and exhibit superb gold workmanship (Charts 35–39). The concentration of goldwork at 'Ajjul, including several unique types (*VI.A*, *VI.C*,

and *336–338* of *VI.F.3*) argues strongly for a native LB IA industry. The only other LB IA gold pendant type (*VI.G.2.a*) from Tel Kittan is not paralleled at 'Ajjul.

Following LB IA, gold workmanship declines, and less elaborate, more carelessly produced types replace their prototypes (*VI.B.1* and *VI.G.2.a*) or appear for the first time (*VI.D.3*, *VI.F.2* and *VI.F.3* [*334*]).

The only Egyptian-related type, *VI.B.2*, is limited to LB IIB (the Beth Shan temple and a miscellaneous context at Tell Abu Hawam); predictably, it is made of blue-green glazed faience. Otherwise, the Syro-Palestinian types comprising Class *VI* are remarkably nonspecific. The most popular types, *VI.B.1* and *VI.F.2* appear in temple, burial, and residential contexts in various parts of the country throughout the Late Bronze Age. Most of the *VI.B.1* examples are made of gold or silver, although two examples are in copper or bronze and another is in onyx. *VI.F.2* occurs in blue-green glazed faience, gold, bone, and no fewer than seven stone varieties. Egyptian influence may be reflected in the fact that faience becomes as important as gold in LB IIB (Chart 38), although the number of examples and types in gold remains relatively constant from one Late Bronze period to the next. Temple contexts become nearly as common as residential contexts by LB IIB (Chart 36).

Chart 34
Site Distribution of Class *VI* Pendants in Late Bronze Age Palestine

Description	Type	Beth Shan	Beth Shemesh	Gezer	Lachish	Megiddo	Shechem	Tel Kittan	Tell Abu Hawam	Tell el-'Ajjul	Umm ad-Dananir	Total	%
Circular crescent	*VI.A*	–	–	–	–	–	–	–	–	13	–	13	11
Crescent or horns	*VI.B.1*	4	3	–	1	2	–	–	–	23	–	33	28
Crescent or horns	*VI.B.2*	2	–	–	–	–	–	–	1	–	–	3	3
Cruciform	*VI.C*	–	–	–	–	–	–	–	–	7	–	7	6
Disc	*VI.D.1*	1	–	–	–	1	–	–	–	–	–	2	2
Disc	*VI.D.2*	–	–	–	–	–	–	–	–	1	–	1	1
Disc	*VI.D.3*	–	–	–	–	–	–	–	–	1	–	1	1
Double spiral	*VI.E*	–	–	–	1	–	–	–	–	–	–	1	1
Crude drop	*VI.F.1*	2	–	–	–	–	–	–	–	–	–	2	2
Elongated drop	*VI.F.2*	13	–	1	–	5	–	–	–	–	2	21	18
Miscellaneous drop	*VI.F.3*	3	1	–	–	1	–	–	–	4	–	9	8
Star disc	*VI.G.1*	–	–	–	–	3	–	–	–	–	–	3	3
Star disc	*VI.G.2.a*	1	–	–	1	–	1	1	–	–	–	4	3
Star disc	*VI.G.2.b*	–	–	–	4	–	–	–	–	7	–	11	9
Star disc	*VI.G.2.c*	–	–	–	–	3	–	–	–	1	–	4	3
'Wheel'	*VI.H*	1	–	–	2	–	–	–	–	–	–	3	3
Total		27	4	1	9	15	1	1	1	57	2	118	102
%		23	3	1	8	13	1	1	1	48	2	101	

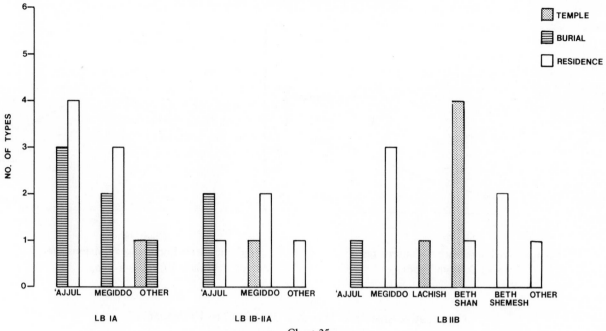

Chart 35
Contextual Distribution of Class *VI* Pendant Types for Late Bronze Age Palestinian Sites

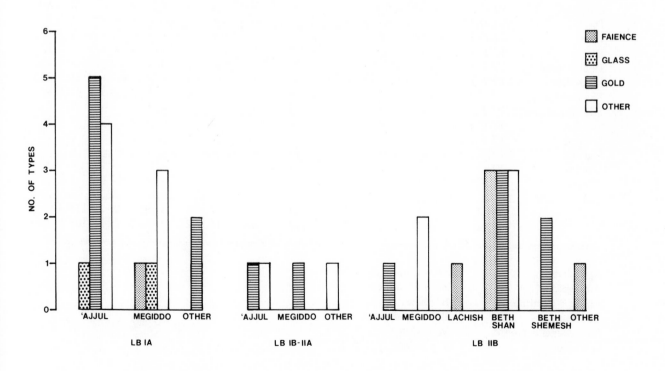

Chart 37
Material Distribution of Class *VI* Pendant Types for Late Bronze Age Palestinian Sites

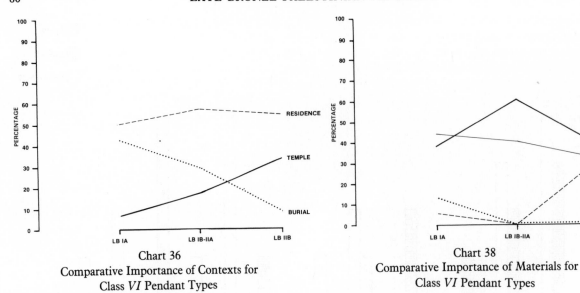

Chart 36
Comparative Importance of Contexts for
Class *VI* Pendant Types

Chart 38
Comparative Importance of Materials for
Class *VI* Pendant Types

Chart 39
Quantitative Analysis of Materials Used for Class *VI* Pendants
in Late Bronze Age Palestine

| Description | Type | Faience | | | | Glass | | | Au | Au & Glass | Ag | Au-Ag | Cu | Stone | | | | Total | % |
		B	B–G	W	?	B–G&W	?							SP	O	B	?		
Circular crescent	*VI.A*	–	–	–	–	–	–	13	–	–	–	–	–	–	–	–	–	13	11
Crescent or horns	*VI.B.1*	–	–	–	–	–	–	14	–	14	1	2	1	–	–	1		33	28
Crescent or horns	*VI.B.2*	–	2	1	–	–	–	–	–	–	–	–	–	–	–	–	–	3	3
Cruciform	*VI.C*	–	–	–	–	–	–	–	7	–	–	–	–	–	–	–	–	7	6
Disc	*VI.D.1*	–	–	–	–	1	1	–	–	–	–	–	–	–	–	–	–	2	2
Disc	*VI.D.2*	–	–	–	–	–	–	–	–	1	–	–	–	–	–	–	–	1	1
Disc	*VI.D.3*	–	–	–	–	–	–	1	–	–	–	–	–	–	–	–	–	1	1
Double spiral	*VI.E*	–	–	–	–	–	–	–	–	–	–	–	1	–	–	–	–	1	1
Crude drop	*VI.F.1*	–	–	–	–	–	–	–	–	–	–	–	2	–	–	–	–	2	2
Elongated drop	*VI.F.2*	–	5	–	1	–	–	4	–	–	–	–	5	3	2	1		21	18
Miscellaneous drop	*VI.F.3*	1	–	–	2	–	–	5	–	–	–	–	1	–	–	–	–	9	8
Star disc	*VI.G.1*	–	–	1	2	–	–	–	–	–	–	–	–	–	–	–	–	3	3
Star disc	*VI.G.2.a*	–	–	–	–	–	–	2	–	1	1	–	–	–	–	–	–	4	3
Star disc	*VI.G.2.b*	–	–	–	–	–	–	11	–	–	–	–	–	–	–	–	–	4	3
Star disc	*VI.G.2.c*	–	–	–	2	–	–	1	–	1	–	–	–	–	–	–	–	4	3
'Wheel'	*VI.H*	2	1	–	–	–	–	–	–	–	–	–	–	–	–	–	–	3	3
	Total	3	8	2	7	1	1	51	7	17	2	3	9	3	2	2		118	102
	%	3	7	2	6	1	1	43	6	14	2	3	8	3	2	2		103	

Ag = silver　　　　　SP = semi-precious
Au = gold　　　　　　? = unidentified
Au-Ag = electrum　　　B = blue
Bo = bone　　　　　　B–G = blue-green
Cu = copper or bronze　W = white
O = other　　　　　　Y = yellow

VI.E (copper or bronze) and *VI.H* (blue and blue-green glazed faience) are unique for their wide geographical distribution in Western Asia and the Mediterranean, which precludes establishing center(s) of production. The one type in glass (*VI.D.1*), which is probably restricted to LB IA northern Palestine, may have been imported from a site further north (Nuzi?).[73]

Notes

1 For the stratigraphic discussion of the 'Ajjul hoards, see Chapter 3, n. 19.

2 Petrie and Brunton 1924: 24, pl. 5:9 (Tomb 310).

3 Maxwell-Hyslop 1971: 47, pl. 37a (grave in Level C, ca. 2000 B.C., earring). An Iron Age variety of the granulated earring type was recovered at Karmir Blur (Maxwell-Hyslop 1971: 203, pl. 158).

4 For a general discussion of the symbolism of the crescent/horns motif, see Maxwell-Hyslop 1971: 150; Yadin 1970: 201–15.

5 The locus is not shown on any plan, but adjacent rooms at approximately this level have LB IA pottery (Petrie 1934: 3–4, 11, 14–15, pl. 62).

6 For dating criteria, see Chapter 2, n. 77.

7 Compare the circular medallion pendant with a crescent outlined in granulation, which was found in the Montet jar (Tufnell and Ward 1966: 189–92, pl. 15, fig. 4:85).

8 Schaeffer 1937: 145, pl. 18 (hoard *e*); 1932: 22, pl. 16:1 (hoard *c*); 1938: 319, fig. 14:14 = 1939a: pl. 32 (hoard *f*), all dated to LB IIA; see stratigraphic discussion, Chapter 3, n. 35.

9 Woolley 1955: 274, pl. 69:t (Level IV, LB IB–IIA).

10 Parrot 1958: fig. 71 (dated ca. 1750 B.C.).

11 Bittel 1938: 21, fig. 10 (dated 14th–13th century B.C.).

12 Dyson 1967: 136 (dated ca. 1550 B.C.).

13 Haller 1954: pls. 34y, 35p (Tomb 45, dated to Tukulti-Ninurta), cf. *290*.

14 Starr 1939: 483, pls. 176:5, 120:TT, UU, VV (Stratum II, LB IB).

15 Petrie 1933: 7–8, pl. 14:30 (Palace I, probably MB III).

16 Appliqués, which were probably sewn onto clothing, were found in the Area H Temple (Yadin *et al.* 1961: pls. 343:32, 35, 270:18–21 (temple 2, LB I), 343:29=278:11–12 (temple 1B, LB IIA), 343:28, 30=278:10, 13 (temple 1A, LB IIB).

17 Macalister 1912: 102–3, fig. 28:11–12 (jewelry hoard in IV 10; 'Fourth Semitic' Period, ca. 1400–1000 B.C.), pl. 31:13, 25 (Cave 28 II, Group A of Chamber 2; mixed Middle Bronze to Late Bronze assemblage); also cf. pl. 136:2, 8.

18 Dothan 1956: 20 (Phase A, unprovenanced; dated to MB I).

19 Loud 1948: 81–83, 159, pl. 214:85 (Temple 2048 jewelry hoard, Area BB, Stratum VII, transitional LB–Iron Age).

20 Starkey and Harding 1932: 23–25, pls. 51 (Tomb 934), 49 and 50:56 (Tomb 925), transitional Late Bronze–Iron Age; Petrie 1930: 10, 13, pls. 36, 39: 456 (Tomb 229, Iron II).

21 Sellin 1926: 231, pl. 3 (five examples from a dump, probably dating to the end of the Late Bronze Age).

22 Dothan 1979: 77, figs. 163, 165 (Tomb 118, transitional LB–Iron Age); cf., especially, *271* and *297* with contiguous arms.

23 Rowe 1940: 75, pl. 30:54 (Level V, dated from ca. 1100–800 B.C.).

24 Eisenberg 1977: 80 (Stratum III temple, unpublished).

25 Petrie 1914: pl. 6:85a–c (assigned to the 18th Dynasty, glass and faience).

26 Petrie 1894: pl. 20:554; cf. Petrie 1914: 23, pl. 6:851 (assigned to the 18th Dynasty).

27 Brunton and Engelbach 1927: pl. 43:44Y (Tomb 237, 18th–19th Dynasties, green glass, disc with rays).

28 Macalister 1912: 109–11, 332, pl. 210:36 (Locus C of Trench 13, dated by Macalister to the period of Amenhotep III, but possibly as late as ca. 1000 B.C. end of the 'Third Semitic' Period).

29 Starkey and Harding 1932: 30, pl. 73:69 (EF 386, probably transitional Late Bronze–Iron Age).

30 For dating, see Chapter 3, n. 5.

31 Starr 1939: 452, pl. 120WW (five complete specimens and fragments of nine others from various loci of Temple A [G 29, G 59, G 53, H 33], dated to LB IB).

32 Andrae 1935: 96, pl. 39:y, aa (Tukulti Ninurta temple to Ishtar, dated to the latter part of the fifteenth century B.C. or perhaps somewhat later).

33 Loud 1948: 145, pls. 214:92 (Square L 16 in Area AA, a large space with remnants of walls and floors, assigned to Stratum VII, transitional LB–Iron Age); 216:119 (uncertain contexts in Stratum VI, Iron I); Schumacher 1908: 147, pl. 48:m (in mixed debris, immediately under the surface).

34 Macalister 1912: 94, 261, fig. 283 (from cistern, undated); 261, pl. 136:12 (Trench 27, 'Second Semitic' Period, ca. 1800–1400 B.C.); both examples have the dots evenly spread over the surface of the disc.

35 Maxwell-Hyslop 1971: 44, pl. C (dots arranged in four or five lines radiating from the center of the disc, perforated base rather than rolled suspension loop, dated ca. 2200–2050 B.C.).

36 For dating criteria, see Chapter 2, n. 75.

37 Maxwell-Hyslop 1971: 11, 23, 78–79, 166, 172, 267; 1953: 76–78; 1960: 108–10, 113; Mallowan 1947: 171–76.

38 Petrie 1933: 5–6, pl. 9:28 (Governor's Tomb, where the example was found under the skull of a burial in the top layer, probably dating to LB IIB).

39 Woolley 1934: pl. 134:U.9656 (P.G. 580, Early Dynastic period).

40 Schmidt 1937: pl. 30:H.2659 (dated to ca. 2000–1500 B.C.).

41 Compare a mold from Nimrud, which was found by Layard and is now in the British Museum (Maxwell-Hyslop 1960: 108, pl. 13:1).

42 An earlier date is argued by Negbi (1970: 35–36) and Epstein (1966: 115, n. 6).

43 E.g., Brunton 1937: pls. 39:89B–F, P (Mostagedda, Tasian, Badarian, and Dynastic periods), 57:56D, 58:89D$_{10}$, M$_3$, R$_8$ (4th–9th Dynasties); Engelbach 1923: pls. 49:44F, L, 51:58J, 44E, H, I, J, K–N (Harageh, Middle Kingdom); Petrie 1914: 13, 28, pls. 2:24d–f, 15:123, 45:123 (dated from the prehistoric period to the 26th Dynasty); Starkey 1930: Types U, W, X (Tell el-Far'ah South, LB IIB and Iron I–II); Brunton and Engelbach 1927: pl. 43:44E, F, J, K (Gurob, New Kingdom); Macalister (1912: 450–51) states that he found examples of these types in every 'Semitic' period at Gezer; Starkey and Harding 1932: 24–25, pl. 51, outer row (seven examples typed to U 32, from Tomb 934, Tell el-Far'ah South, transitional Late Bronze–Iron Age); Tufnell and Ward 1966: 194–96, fig. 4:90–94 (Byblos, late Middle Kingdom).

44 E.g., Engelbach 1923: pl. 51:44A, F, G, X (Harageh, Middle Kingdom); Brunton 1937: pl. 58:89G$_5$ (Mostagedda, 7th and 8th Dynasties); Brunton and Engelbach 1927: pl. 42:32F (Gurob, Tomb 95, probably LB IA); Starkey 1930: Type U 47 (Tell el-Far'ah South, Iron II); Guy 1938: 67, pl. 121–12 (Megiddo, Tomb 911 D, MB III).

45 Brunton 1937: pl. 39:89B$_{12}$ (Mostagedda, prehistoric period, identified as ivory[?]); Engelbach 1923: pl. 51:44Z (Harageh, Middle Kingdom, identified as ivory).

46 James 1966: fig. 113:17 (Beth Shan, Upper Level V, ca. 920–800 B.C.); Tufnell 1953: 381–83, pl. 37 (Lachish); Platt 1978: 24–28.

47 Loud 1948: pl. 215:107 (Locus 3073, Stratum VII A, Iron Age I, without hollow cylinder and suspension loop); also cf. Frankfort and Pendlebury 1933: pl. 28:6, third row, second from left (el-Amarna); Davis et al. 1908: 38–39 (Thebes, 19th Dynasty).

48 Petrie 1927: 3, pl. 1:4 (no provenience, ca. 300 B.C. or later); 12, pl. 9:194 (no provenience, Ptolemaic).

49 Starkey and Harding 1932: 26, pl. 57 (Tomb 983, transitional Late Bronze–Iron Age).

50 1914: 28–29, pls. 15:129f (identified as ivory, undated), 43:129a,b (carnelian, dated to the 6th–12th Dynasties).

51 E.g., Engelbach 1923: pl. 51:44Q (Harageh, Middle Kingdom, carnelian); Karageorghis 1965: 130, fig. 37:52, pl. 10:9 (Akhera, Tomb 3, ca. 1300 B.C., carnelian); Starkey and Harding 1932: 24, pl. 60:80 (Tell el-Far'ah South, Tomb 929, transitional LB–Iron Age, concentric circles of white glazed faience in a matrix of brown/black glazed faience).

52 Compare the rectangular gold pendant with six horizontal lines in repoussé, found at Ras Shamra; Schaeffer 1932: 22–23, pl. 16:2 (Hoard c, dated to LB IIA).

53 For dating, see Chapter 5, n. 21.

54 Schaeffer 1937: 145, pl. 18 (middle)=1939a: pl. 32:1

(Hoard e), and 1938: 319, fig. 48:1, 4, 6, 7 (Hoard f), all dated to LB IIA; see Chapter 3, n. 35.

55 Sellin 1926: 231, pl. 30 (from a dump, probably dating to the end of the Late Bronze Age, gold); cf. Type VI.G.2.a.

56 Brunton and Engelbach 1927: pl. 43:44X (18th–19th Dynasties).

57 Schaeffer 1932: 9, pls. 9:1 (dépôt 213 bis, Minet el-Beida), 16:2 (Ras Shamra, Hoard c); Schaeffer 1938: 318–19, fig. 48:5 (Hoard f), all dated to LB IIA.

58 Woolley 1955: 274, pl. 68:12 (from a cremation burial in Level I, dated to LB IIB).

59 Oates 1966: 125, pl. 25 (Phase I of the temple, 14th–13th century B.C.).

60 Unpublished, probably from the second phase of the courtyard of the temple, dating to LB IIA (Stern 1977: 89–91). Although a photograph of the pendant was kindly furnished by the excavator, it was not possible to determine whether there were bosses/dots between the rays of the heavily corroded and partially damaged pendant.

61 However, an unpublished specimen was possibly found at Ras Shamra (see Maxwell-Hyslop 1971: 141).

62 The locus was somewhere northwest of areas E and F, but is not described or shown on any plan. From its elevation, it should belong to Town I, although the pottery evidence from adjacent loci of approximately this level favors a probable LB II dating.

63 Starr 1939: 451, pl. 120:NN, OO, XX (various loci of Temple A [G 29, G 50, G 53, and H 15], dated to the 15th and beginning of the 14th century B.C., all of glass).

64 Woolley 1955: 274, pl. 69:q (Square L 13, Levels IV–III, dated to LB IB–IIA; gold).

65 Contenau and Ghirshman 1935: 24, 31, pls. 15:8, 24:9 (Tombs 38 and 79, dated to ca. 1500–1300 B.C.).

66 Schaeffer 1937: 145, pl. 18 (top, middle)=1939a: 62, pl. 32:1.

67 Schaeffer 1938: 318–19, figs. 48:3, 50.

68 Pit 188 is south of the Fosse Temple and over Pit 203. The published pottery, including Base-Ring II ware, corroborates Tufnell's attribution of the locus to Structure III, which is dated to LB IIB.

69 Enkomi: British Tomb 88 (Late Cypriot IB–IIC), French Tomb 3^{II} (LC IIB–C); Mycenae: Tomb 527 and Tomb 2 (beginning of 14th century, B.C., gold); Nauplia; Goumenitsa; and Ialyssos. For references, see Åström and Åström 1972: 591, and Wace 1932: 94, 205.

70 Unprovenanced examples from el-Amarna (Leemans and Pleyte 1842: pl. 37:103).

71 Ras Shamra: Schaeffer 1932: 5, pl. 9:2 (LBA); Woolley 1955: 269–70, pl. 68:28 (Levels V–I, covering the entire Late Bronze Age).

72 Schaeffer 1948: 514.

73 Compare the discussion for II.B.1 in Chapter 3.

Chapter 8

PENDANTS AND LATE BRONZE AGE PALESTINIAN CULTURE

A. Pendants as Chronological Indicators

A major objective of this study has been the construction of a chronologically-ordered typology of the major jewelry pendant classes and types for Late Bronze Age Palestine, which can be useful for archaeological dating. The text, catalogue, and graphics are organized with this primary goal in mind. It is hoped that in the future when discoveries of pendants are made at sites in Late Bronze Age Palestine, this study will provide the framework within which to place those pendants in their proper typological context with an accurate assessment of date.

It cannot be claimed that pendants provide a more accurate dating tool than pottery. Certainly, the utilitarian nature of pottery means that it is not hoarded for its own sake, and it undergoes more subtle technological changes over time. However, there was considerable artistic and technological experimentation in the period and area dealt with here, and many of the pendant types were being mass-produced. These factors allow us to construct a fairly tight chronologically-ordered typology.

With several provisos, the corpus of more than eight hundred pendants from Late Bronze Palestine can be considered an adequate sample population. As discussed in Chapter 1, LB IA and IIB are better represented in Palestine than LB IB or IIA. However, even for LB IA and IIB, archaeological investigation has focused on major sites along the coast and in the main inland valleys, largely to the exclusion of other regions of the country. Also, the location of tombs and cemeteries, often distant from the settlement sites, is more difficult and often dependent on the vagaries of discovery.[1] Stratigraphic problems and partial publication are additional considerations, as illustrated by the paucity of data from the numerous temples with LB I phases (Lachish, Shechem, Hazor, Megiddo, Tel Kittan, Tel Mevorakh, and possibly Mount Gerizim).

The data base is skewed to some extent by several loci: near the steps of Locus 1068, the upper altar room of the Level VII temple at Beth Shan (Chart 49), and the deposit of beads and pendants near the west wall of Room E of the Fosse Temple at Lachish (Chart 52). In absolute numbers, these loci yielded more than 379 pendants, 45 percent of the total for Late Bronze Palestine. Many of the types are represented by multiple examples, and were probably combined to form large collars (see Section B.3 below). Yet, in terms of the number of types, the contribution of these loci is not as large as it might seem. Only one of the Beth Shan types (*I.B.2*) and three of the Lachish types (*I.C.1, III.H.2,* and *IV.A*), all Egyptian-related faience types, are unique to these contexts. The statistical effect is negligible, amounting to a maximum 4 percent change in Egyptian-related types in LB IIB temple contexts compared to a total of 48 percent.

B. Patterns of Association

1. *Pendant Classes* (Charts 40–44)

The combined results of the distributional analyses, which are summarized for each class in Chapters 2–7, reveal very clear geographical, contextual, and material patterns.

More than half the pendants come from Beth Shan (Chart 40). Despite the absence of closely dated LB IA–IIA specimens,[2] all classes of pendants are better represented here in the frequency of types than at any other Palestinian site (Chart 41). In absolute terms, only Tell el-'Ajjul has slightly more Class *II* pendants. Tell el-'Ajjul, Lachish, and, to a lesser degree, Megiddo, yielded pendants of all classes, but the collections from these well-excavated sites are much less extensive than that for Beth Shan. Beth Shemesh and Tell Abu Hawam are further removed in type frequency. The remaining Late Bronze sites in inland Palestine contribute only one or two types each.

LB IA pendant types are distributed among Classes *II, III, IV,* and *VI* (Chart 42). Except for *III.H.4,* all the types belong to the Syro-Palestinian cultural sphere (see Section C.1 below). They were generally found in residences, and are made of gold (Charts 43–44).

Chart 40
Site Distribution of Pendants in Late Bronze Age Palestine

Site	I	II	III	Class IV	V	VI	Total	%
Amman	–	–	–	1	–	–	1	0
Beth Shan	35	4	11	285	69	27	431	51
Beth Shemesh	1	–	–	22	–	4	27	3
Dhahrat el-Humraiya	–	–	–	23	30	–	53	6
Gezer	–	–	–	1	–	1	2	0
Lachish	29	3	4	123+	6	9	174+	21
Megiddo	8	2	2	7	1	15	35	4
Shechem	–	–	–	–	–	1	1	0
Tel Kittan	–	–	–	–	–	1	1	0
Tell Abu Hawam	–	1	–	8	7	1	17	2
Tell el-'Ajjul	4	7	10	20	3	57	101	12
Tell Beit Mirsim	1	1	–	–	–	–	2	0
Umm ad-Dananir	–	–	–	–	–	2	2	0
Total	78	18	27	490+	116	118	847+	99
%	9	2	3	58	14	14	100	

+ Unspecified number of additional specimens.

Chart 41
Site Distribution of Pendant Types in Late Bronze Age Palestine

Site	I	II	III	Class IV	V	VI	Total	%
Amman	–	–	–	1	–	–	1	1
Beth Shan	12	4	5	13	14	8	56	34
Beth Shemesh	1	–	–	3	–	2	6	4
Dhahrat el-Humraiya	–	–	–	1	1	–	2	1
Gezer	–	–	–	1	–	1	2	1
Lachish	10	3	3	16	4	5	41	25
Megiddo	4	2	2	4	1	6	19	12
Shechem	–	–	–	–	–	1	1	1
Tell Abu Hawam	–	1	–	2	4	1	8	5
Tell el-'Ajjul	4	2	5	4	2	8	25	15
Tell Beit Mirsim	1	1	–	–	–	–	2	1
Tel Kittan	–	–	–	–	–	1	1	1
Umm ad-Dananir	–	–	–	–	–	1	1	1
Total	32	13	15	45	26	34	165	103
%	19	8	9	27	18	21	102	

By contrast, the LB IIB types cut across all classes of pendants, and are especially weighted towards Classes I, IV, and V, which are comprised almost entirely of Egyptian-related types. The majority of these types are mold-made in blue-green glazed faience, and were discovered in temple contexts. Some of the types also occur in residences and, less frequently, in burials.

In LB IB–IIA, the trend toward Egyptian-related types is evident from the increase in the number of Class I, IV, and V types, which are again mostly mold-made in faience. Burial contexts at southern Palestinian sites predominate.

The total number of Syro-Palestinian types (Classes II, III, IV, and VI) remains fairly constant from one Late Bronze phase to the next. Gold and semiprecious stones are used for specific types throughout the Late Bronze Age. Temple contexts, however, gain in importance, beginning in LB IB–IIA.

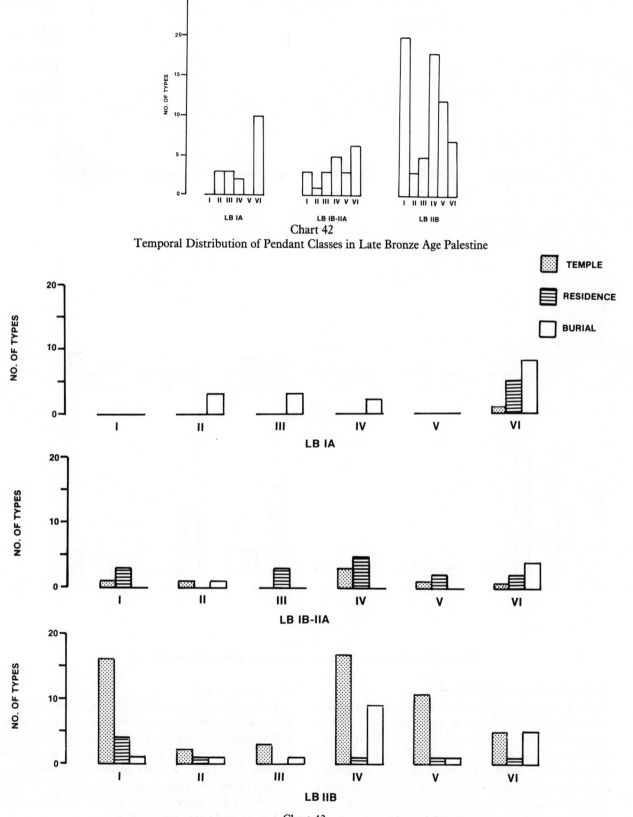

Chart 42
Temporal Distribution of Pendant Classes in Late Bronze Age Palestine

Chart 43
Contextual Distribution of Pendant Classes in Late Bronze Age Palestine

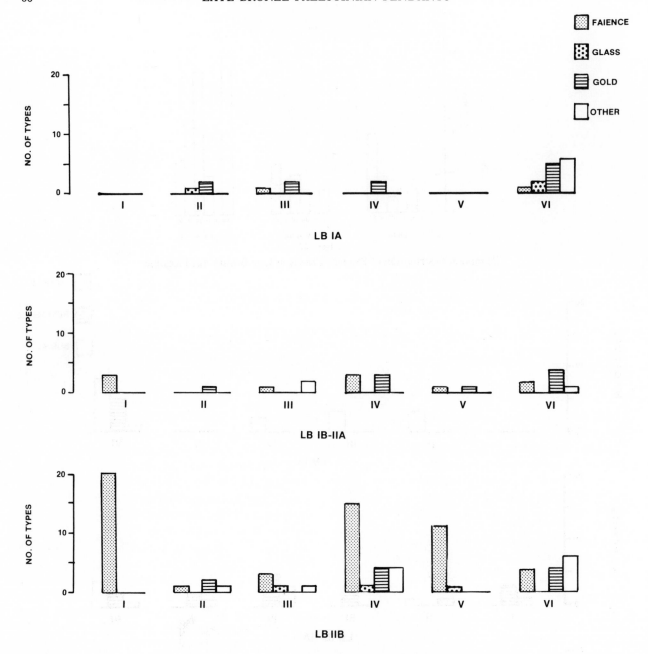

Chart 44
Material Distribution of Pendant Classes in Late Bronze Age Palestine

2. *Pendant Types* (Charts 45–48)

LB IA is dominated by high-quality gold pendant types from Tell el-'Ajjul, the important coastal site in the south (Charts 45–48): *II.B.2.a–b, III.A, III.C, IV.F.4, IV.H.3.b, VI.A, VI.B.1, VI.F.3,* and *VI.G.2.b.* All these types were included in jewelry hoards that had been buried inside houses, except for Type *VI.C,* which was found only in burials. Two types occurred in a material other than gold: *II.B.2.a* in electrum; and *VI.B.1* in silver, electrum, copper or bronze, and onyx.

The northern sites of Megiddo and Tel Kittan produced a different type repertoire from temple, burial, and residential contexts: *II.B.1.a, III.H.4, VI.D.1, VI.F.2, VI.G.1, VI.G.2.a,* and *VI.G.2.c.* In addition to gold (*VI.G.2.a*), a wider spectrum of materials is evidenced in this region, including faience (*III.H.4* and *VI.G.1*), glass (*II.B.1.a* and *VI.D.1*), bone (*VI.B.1*), and hematite (*VI.B.1*).

The evidence for LB IB is unfortunately much more

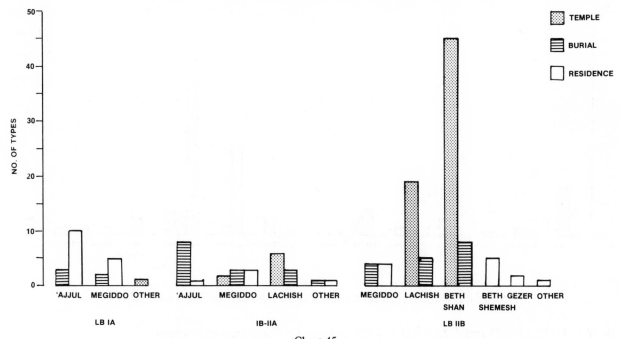

Chart 45
Contextual Distribution of Pendant Types for Late Bronze Age Palestinian Sites

circumscribed than that for LB IA (see Chapter 1). No pendants were found in homogeneous LB IB contexts, and only pendants from LB I and IB–IIA loci at Megiddo and Tell el-'Ajjul, primarily burials, shed light on this problematical period.

The available evidence suggests that Syro-Palestinian types, which were already well-established in the north and south in LB IA, continued into LB IB: *II.B.2.b*, *VI.B.1*, *VI.F.2*, *VI.G.1*, and *VI.G.2.b*. An LB IB dating for four additional types (*III.H.1.a* and *VI.D.1–3*), which occur in LB IB–IIA contexts but are unattested for LB IA, is substantiated by 15th

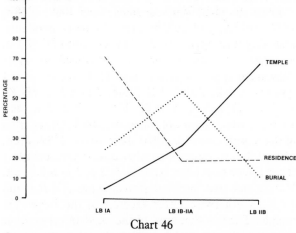

Chart 46
Comparative Importance of Contexts for Late Bronze Age
Pendant Types

century B.C. parallels from north Syrian sites. At the same time, a shift toward Egyptian-related types can already be detected, particularly in the south: *I.G.3*, *III.D*, *III.E*, *IV.F.1* (*114*), and *IV.F.5.a*.

A new repertoire of pendant types has definitely emerged by LB IIA, although the data base is still small. Popular Amarna types in faience first appear at major sites in the south, Lachish and Tell el-'Ajjul, most often in burials: *I.E.2*, *I.G.1.a*, *I.G.5*, *III.B*, *III.D*, *IV.F.1*, *IV.F.2*, *IV.F.4*, *IV.F.5.b*, *V.B.1*, and *V.E.1.b*. Syro-Palestinian types continue to be found in both north (*VI.G.2.a*) and south (*II.B.2.b*, *IV.D.1*, *VI.B.1*, *VI.D.3*, and *VI.F.3*).

A dramatic increase in Egyptian-related types occurs in LB IIB. Generally mold-made of blue-green glazed faience, these types are most prevalent in temple loci at Beth Shan and Lachish: *I.A.1–2*, *I.B.1–2*, *I.C.1–2*, *I.F.1.a*, *I.F.2.a–b*, *I.G.2.a–b*, *I.G.4*, *I.G.5*, *I.G.6.a*, *I.G.6.c*, *I.G.6.b.i–ii*, *III.G*, *III.H.1.c*, *III.H.2*, *IV.A*, *IV.B*, *IV.C*, *IV.D.3*, *IV.E*, *IV.F.1*, *IV.F.2*, *IV.F.4*, *IV.F.5.a–b*, *IV.G.1–2*, *IV.H.2*, *IV.H.3.a*, *IV.H.3.b* (*210*), *IV.H.4*, *V.A.2*, *V.B.1–2*, *V.C.1*, *V.D.1–2*, *V.E.1.a*, *V.E.1.c*, *V.F.1–3*, and *VI.B.2*. Several Egyptian-related types (*I.D.1*, *I.E.1*, *I.G.1.a*, *II.A.3*, and *III.H.3* occur exclusively in burial or residential contexts.

The number of Syro-Palestinian types from various contexts in a variety of materials is comparable to earlier Late Bronze phases: *II.A.1–2*, *II.B.3*, *IV.D.1*,

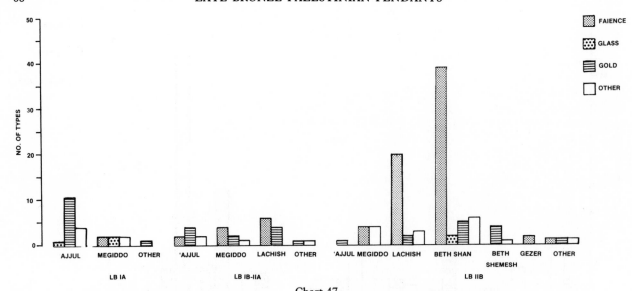

Chart 47

Material Distribution of Pendant Types for Late Bronze Age Palestinian Sites

IV.H.1, *IV.H.3.b* (*209* and *211*), *VI.B.1*, *VI.F.2–3*, *VI.G.2.a*, and *VI.G.2.c*. Egyptian-related types, however, are relatively more important than Syro-Palestinian types in LB IIB (cf. Charts 56–57).

Geographic gaps in the evidence are probably also significant. The Hill Country, the Galilee, the Huleh and central Jordan Valleys, and Transjordan are virtually unrepresented for all of the Late Bronze Age. The several pendants that have been found in this still largely unexplored area are Syro-Palestinian types, which were already well-established in early Late Bronze (*VI.G.2.a* from Shechem, and *VI.F.2* from Umm ad-Dananir). The specimen of *IV.F.1* from the Amman Airport Building may be Egyptian-related. Pending further archaeological work, Egyptian influence appears to have been minimal in these areas.

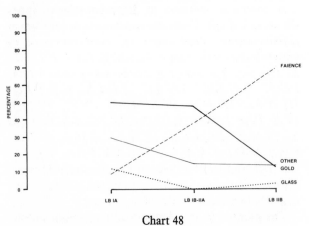

Chart 48

Comparative Importance of Materials for Late Bronze Age Pendant Types

3. *Assemblages of Pendants*

A closer study of the association of pendant types from specific loci reinforces the synthesis outlined above.

a. *Beth Shan* (Charts 49–51)

The highest concentration of pendants at Beth Shan is from near the steps of Locus 1068 (=1068A), the upper altar room of the Level VII temple (Chart 49). More than 30 percent of the Late Bronze Palestinian corpus was found here, representing 12 types: *I.B.2*, *IV.C*, *IV.F.2*, *IV.G.1–2*, *IV.H.3.a*, *IV.H.4*, *V.B.1*, *V.D.1*, *V.F.1*, *V.F.3*, and *VI.F.2*. Multiple examples of the same types, mostly Amarna styles, may have been strung together with other specimens from below the steps (assigned to Level VIII; Chart 50) to form a standard New Kingdom collar (see Section C.3 below).[3] A Syro-Palestinian type (*VI.F.2*) may have been included.

From the vicinity of the steps (Loci 1068, 1068B, 1072, 1072A, and 1072B) came 33 more pendants, matching three types (*IV.F.2*, *IV.G.2*, and *IV.H.3.a*) in 1068A. In addition, these loci produced one Syro-Palestinian type (*IV.H.3.b*) and 13 Egyptian-related types (*I.A.1–2*, *I.B.1*, *I.G.2.a–b*, *I.G.6.b.ii*, *III.G*, *IV.F.1*, *IV.F.5.b*, *V.A.2*, *V.C.1*, *V.E.1.a*, and *VI.B.2*), which were not found in 1068A. Other areas of the temple complex (1070, 1085–1087, 1089, 1104, 1107, 1362) account for another nine types, including three Egyptian-related types (*I.F.2.a*, *I.G.6.b.i*, and *V.F.2*) and two Syro-Palestinian types (*VI.B.1* and *VI.F.3*), otherwise unrepresented in the Level VII temple. The fact that most of the pendant types occur outside of Locus 1068A implies that they were originally not part of a single collar.

Chart 49
Locus Distribution of Late Bronze Age Pendants Beth Shan, Level VII

Description	Type	1068	1068A	1068B	1070	1072	1072A	1072B	1085	1086	1087	1089	1104	1107	1251	1252	1255	1262	1263	1284	1359	1362	1365	1366	1382A
Baboon of Thoth	I.A.1	3	–	–	–	–	–	–	–	–	–	–	–	–	–	–	–	–	–	–	–	–	–	–	–
Baboon of Thoth	I.A.2	1	–	–	–	1	–	–	–	–	–	–	–	–	–	–	–	–	–	–	–	–	–	–	–
Bes	I.B.1	–	–	–	–	1	–	–	–	–	–	–	–	–	–	–	–	–	–	–	–	–	–	–	–
Bes	I.B.2	–	2	–	–	–	–	–	–	–	–	–	–	–	–	–	–	–	–	–	–	–	–	–	–
Uraeus	I.F.2.a	–	–	–	1	–	–	–	–	–	–	–	–	–	–	–	–	–	–	–	–	–	–	–	–
Bes or Ptah-Sokar	I.G.2.a	2	–	–	–	1	1	–	–	1	–	–	–	–	–	–	–	–	–	–	–	–	–	–	–
Bes or Ptah-Sokar	I.G.2.b	1	–	–	–	–	–	–	–	–	–	–	–	–	–	–	–	–	–	–	–	–	–	–	–
Standing figure	I.G.6.b.i	–	–	–	–	–	–	–	–	–	–	–	–	–	–	2	–	–	–	1	–	1	–	–	–
Standing figure	I.G.6.b.ii	–	–	–	–	1	–	–	–	–	–	–	–	–	–	–	–	–	–	–	–	–	–	–	–
Ram's head	III.G	–	–	1	–	–	–	–	–	–	–	1	–	–	–	–	–	–	–	–	–	–	–	–	–
Cat?	III.H.3	–	–	–	–	–	–	–	–	–	–	–	–	–	–	–	–	–	–	–	–	–	–	–	1
Date fruit	IV.C	–	14	–	–	–	–	–	–	–	–	–	–	–	–	–	–	–	–	–	–	–	–	–	–
Lotus bud	IV.F.1	1	–	–	–	–	–	–	–	–	–	–	–	–	–	–	–	–	–	–	–	–	–	–	–
Conventional lotus	IV.F.2	–	77	–	–	1	–	1	1	–	1	–	1	–	–	–	1	–	–	–	–	–	–	–	–
Lotus seed vessel	IV.F.5.b	3	–	–	–	1	–	–	–	–	1	–	–	–	–	–	–	–	–	–	–	–	–	–	–
Mandrake fruit	IV.G.1	–	10	2	–	–	–	–	–	–	–	–	–	–	–	–	–	–	–	–	–	–	–	–	–
Mandrake fruit	IV.G.2	–	67	–	–	–	–	4	–	–	–	–	–	–	–	–	–	–	–	2	1	–	1	1	–
Petal or leaf	IV.H.3.a	–	41	–	–	–	–	1	–	–	–	–	–	–	–	–	–	–	–	2	–	1	–	–	–
Petal or leaf	IV.H.3.b	–	–	1	–	–	–	–	–	–	–	–	–	–	–	–	–	–	–	–	–	–	–	–	–
Reeds?	IV.H.4	–	1	–	–	–	–	–	–	–	–	–	–	–	–	–	–	–	–	–	–	–	–	–	–
'ankh	V.A.1.	–	–	–	–	–	–	–	–	–	–	–	–	–	–	–	–	1	–	–	–	–	–	–	–
'ankh	V.A.2	1	–	–	–	–	–	–	–	–	–	–	–	–	–	–	–	–	–	–	–	–	–	–	–
ḏd	V.B.1	–	18	–	–	–	–	–	–	–	–	–	–	–	–	–	–	–	–	–	–	–	–	–	–
heḥ	V.C.1	–	–	–	–	–	–	2	–	–	–	–	–	–	–	–	–	–	–	–	–	–	–	–	–
tit	V.D.1	–	10	–	–	–	–	–	–	–	–	–	–	–	–	–	–	–	–	–	–	–	–	–	–
wḏ't	V.E.1.a	–	–	–	–	1	–	–	–	–	–	–	–	–	1	–	–	–	–	–	–	–	–	–	–
ḥst?	V.F.1	–	9	–	–	–	–	–	–	–	–	–	–	–	–	–	–	–	–	–	–	–	–	–	–
ib?	V.F.2	–	–	–	–	–	–	–	–	1	–	–	–	–	–	–	–	–	–	–	–	–	–	–	–
nfr?	V.F.3	–	6	–	–	–	–	–	–	–	–	–	–	–	–	–	–	–	–	–	–	–	–	–	–
Crescent or horns	VI.B.1	–	–	–	–	–	–	–	–	1	–	–	–	–	–	–	–	–	–	–	–	–	–	–	–
Crescent or horns	VI.B.2	–	–	1	–	–	–	–	–	–	–	–	–	–	–	–	–	–	–	–	–	–	–	–	–
Elongated drop	VI.F.2	–	3	–	–	–	–	–	–	–	–	–	–	1	–	–	–	1	–	–	–	–	–	–	–
Miscellaneous drop	VI.F.3	–	–	–	–	–	–	–	–	–	–	–	–	–	–	–	–	–	1	–	1	–	–	–	–
Total		12	258	5	1	7	1	8	1	3	2	1	1	1	1	2	1	2	1	5	2	2	1	1	1
%		4	81	2	0	2	0	2	0	1	1	0	0	0	0	1	0	1	0	2	1	1	0	0	0

1068A = near steps
1068B = north of steps
1072A = near steps
1072B = west side
1382A = near wall

There is a very evident decline in the number of pendants and types in areas removed from the temple, namely the southwestern and southeastern residential sectors, including two roads (Loci 1255 and 1263). Among the nine Egyptian-related types, only two (*III.H.3* and *V.A.1*) are not found in the temple (cf. Chart 49). The widespread, seemingly random, distribution suggests that pendants were worn on small necklaces by the general populace (see Section C.3 below).

Chart 50
Locus Distribution of Late Bronze Age Pendants Beth Shan, Level VIII

Description	Type	1062A	1068C	1068D	1068E	1072C	1092	1108	1287	1292	1300	1301
Uraeus	*I.F.1.a*	–	–	6	–	–	–	–	–	–	–	–
Uraeus	*I.F.2.b*	–	–	1	–	–	–	–	–	–	–	–
Bes or Ptah-Sokar	*I.G.2.a*	–	–	1	–	1	–	–	–	–	–	–
Bes or Ptah-Sokar	*I.G.2.b*	–	1	–	–	–	–	–	–	–	–	–
Horus child or Ptah	*I.G.4*	–	–	–	–	–	1	1	–	–	–	–
Standing figure	*I.G.6.a*	–	–	–	–	1	–	–	–	–	–	–
Standing figure	*I.G.6.c*	–	–	–	–	1	–	–	–	–	–	–
Standing figure	*II.B.3*	–	1	–	–	–	–	–	–	–	–	–
Ram's head	*III.G*	–	–	2	–	–	–	–	–	–	–	–
Owl?	*III.H.1.c*	–	–	4	–	–	–	–	–	–	–	–
Date fruit	*IV.C*	–	1	–	–	–	–	–	–	–	–	–
Conventional lotus	*IV.F.2*	–	1	1	–	–	2	–	–	–	–	–
Lotus palmette	*IV.F.4*	–	2	1	–	–	–	–	–	–	–	–
Lotus seed vessel	*IV.F.5.a*	–	–	1	–	–	–	–	–	–	–	–
Lotus seed vessel	*IV.F.5.b*	–	–	–	1	–	–	–	–	1	1	–
Mandrake fruit	*IV.G.1*	–	1	2	–	–	1	–	1	–	–	–
Mandrake fruit	*IV.G.2*	–	–	1	–	1	1	–	–	–	–	–
Lotus flower?	*IV.H.2*	–	–	–	–	–	–	1	–	–	–	–
Petal or leaf	*IV.H.3.a*	–	–	–	–	1	–	–	–	–	–	–
Petal or leaf	*IV.H.3.b*	1	2	–	–	–	–	–	–	–	–	–
ḏ	*V.B.2*	–	3	–	–	–	–	–	–	–	–	–
tỉt	*V.D.1*	–	–	–	–	–	1	–	–	–	–	–
tỉt	*V.D.2*	–	–	1	–	–	1	–	–	–	–	–
wḏ't	*V.E.1.a*	–	–	1	–	–	–	–	–	–	–	–
wḏ't	*V.E.1.c*	–	1	–	–	–	–	–	–	–	–	–
ḥst?	*V.F.1*	–	–	1	–	–	–	–	–	–	–	–
Crescent or horns	*VI.B.1*	–	2	–	–	–	–	–	–	–	–	–
Crescent or horns	*VI.B.2*	–	–	–	–	–	–	–	–	–	–	1
Elongated drop	*VI.F.2*	–	2	1	–	–	1	–	–	–	–	–
Miscellaneous drop	*VI.F.3*	–	–	–	–	–	1	–	–	–	–	–
Star disc	*VI.G.2.a*	–	–	1	–	–	–	–	–	–	–	–
Total		1	17	25	1	5	9	2	1	1	1	1
%		2	27	39	2	8	14	3	2	2	2	2

1062A = below south wall
1068C = below floor
1068D = below steps
1068E = below east wall
1072C = below steps

Level VIII (Chart 50) repeats some of the same types found in Level VII, especially in the area immediately below the steps of the upper altar room (Locus 1068D) and of the courtyard (1072C and 1092): *IV.F.2*, *IV.G.1–2*, *IV.H.3.a*, *V.D.1*, and *V.F.1*. Eleven types from these loci, however, are not evidenced in the Level VII temple, including *I.F.1.a*, *I.F.2.b*, *I.G.4*, *I.G.6.a*, *I.G.6.c*, *II.B.3*, *III.H.1.c*, *IV.F.2*, *V.B.2*, *V.E.1.c*, and *VI.G.2.a*. In general, approximately half of the types in the Level VIII temple complex (Loci 1062A, 1068C–E, 1072C, 1092, and 1108) are matched in the Level VII temple.

A different pendant repertoire is thus documented for the early LB IIB phase of the temple (Level VIII), despite any mixing of materials with Level VII in antiquity or during excavation. With the exception of

Chart 51
Locus Distribution of Late Bronze Age Pendants
Beth Shan, Level IX

Description	Type	1092A	1092B	1232	1233	1234	1234A	1234B	1235	1238	1240	1241	1322	1326	1330	1332	1339	1390	1397	1403
Bes or Ptah-Sokar	*I.G.2.a*	-	-	-	-	-	-	-	-	1	-	-	-	-	-	-	-	-	-	-
Head or face	*II.A.1*	-	-	-	-	-	-	-	-	-	1	-	-	-	-	-	-	-	-	-
Standing figure	*II.B.1.a*	-	-	-	-	-	-	-	-	-	-	-	-	-	-	-	-	1	-	-
Standing figure	*II.B.1.b*	-	-	-	-	-	-	-	-	-	-	-	-	-	-	-	-	-	-	1
Lion fighting bull or dog	*III.F*	-	-	-	-	-	-	1	-	-	-	-	-	-	-	-	-	-	-	-
Mouse?	*III.H.5*	-	-	-	-	-	-	-	-	-	-	-	-	1	-	-	-	-	-	-
Conventional lotus	*IV.F.2*	1	5	-	1	-	-	-	-	-	-	1	-	-	-	-	-	-	-	-
Lotus flower	*IV.F.3*	-	-	-	-	-	-	-	-	-	-	-	-	-	-	-	-	-	-	2
Mandrake fruit	*IV.G.1*	-	1	-	-	-	-	-	-	-	-	-	-	-	-	-	-	-	-	-
Mandrake fruit	*IV.G.2*	-	-	1	1	3	-	-	-	-	-	-	1	-	-	-	-	-	-	-
Petal or leaf	*IV.H.3.a*	1	1	-	-	3	-	-	-	-	-	-	-	-	-	-	-	-	-	-
ḏd	*V.B.1*	-	-	-	-	1	-	-	-	-	-	-	-	-	-	-	-	-	-	-
ḥeḥ	*V.C.1*	-	-	1	-	2	-	-	-	-	-	-	-	-	-	-	-	-	-	-
ḥeḥ	*V.C.2*	-	-	-	-	-	-	1	-	-	-	-	-	-	-	-	-	-	-	-
ḥeḥ	*V.C.3*	-	-	-	-	1	-	-	-	-	-	-	-	-	-	-	-	-	-	-
ṯỉt	*V.D.1*	-	-	-	-	-	1	-	-	-	-	-	-	-	-	-	-	-	-	-
ṯỉt	*V.D.2*	-	1	-	-	-	-	-	-	-	-	-	-	-	-	-	-	-	-	-
ḫst?	*V.F.1*	-	-	-	-	-	1	-	-	-	-	-	-	-	-	-	-	-	-	-
Crescent or horns	*VI.B.1*	-	-	-	-	-	-	-	1	-	-	-	-	-	-	-	-	-	-	-
Plain disc	*VI.D.1*	-	-	-	-	-	-	-	-	-	-	-	-	-	-	-	-	-	1	-
Crude drop	*VI.F.1*	-	-	-	-	-	-	-	1	-	-	-	-	-	1	-	-	-	-	-
Elongated drop	*VI.F.2*	-	-	-	-	1	1	-	-	-	-	-	-	-	-	1	1	-	-	-
'Wheel'	*VI.H*	-	-	-	-	-	-	-	-	-	-	-	-	-	-	-	-	-	-	1
Total		2	8	2	2	11	3	2	2	1	1	1	1	1	1	1	1	1	1	4
%		4	17	4	4	24	7	4	4	2	2	2	2	2	2	2	2	2	2	9

1092A = below threshold
1092B = below 1092
1234A = east side
1234B = south of 'temple'

Types *II.B.3*, *IV.H.3.b* (*209*), *VI.B.1*, *VI.F.2–3*, and *VI.G.2.a*, all the Level VIII pendant types are Egyptian-related. Only three Egyptian-related types (*IV.F.5.b*, *IV.G.1*, and *VI.B.2*) are scattered in residential sectors outside the temple proper.

Although lacking discrete, well-dated loci, the Level IX pendant evidence strongly suggests that a temple dating to LB IB–IIA or even earlier was located in the same general area as the VIII/VII temple. There is a noticeably smaller number of pendants and types (Chart 51), but the majority are Amarna-style types and were found beneath the area of the later temple (Loci 1092A, 1092B, 1232, 1234, and 1234A). Nine of the ten types from these loci occur in Levels VIII and VII: *IV.F.2*, *IV.G.1–2*, *IV.H.3.a*, *V.B.1*, *V.C.1*, *V.D.1–2*, and *V.F.1*; Type *V.C.3* is confined to Level X. The two Syro-Palestinian types, *VI.B.1* and *VI.F.2*, are also represented in the overlying strata.

Moving away from the vicinity of the temple steps, the Syro-Palestinian component of Level IX increases, as might be expected for an earlier LB phase and a different architectural layout. The types include *II.A.1*, *II.B.1.a–b*, *III.F*, *VI.D.1*, *VI.F.1–2*, and *VI.H*. There are five Egyptian-related types: *III.H.5*, *IV.F.2–3*, *IV.G.2*, and *V.C.2*. The dispersal of pendants inside the proposed temple area as well as in outlying areas is analogous to that observed for Levels VIII and VII.

b. *Lachish* (Chart 52)

The temporal distribution of pendant types in assemblages at Lachish is similar to that for Beth Shan, the main distinction being the somewhat different reper-

Chart 52
Temporal Distribution by Locus of Late Bronze Age Pendants at Lachish

Description	Type	I	IIA						IIB											II			LB	
		FT I:D	FT II:D	FT II:E	P. 199	P. 248	P. 4019	T. 216	FT III:D	FT III:E	P. 118	P. 172	P. 176	P. 246	P. 556	P. 4013	C. 4004	T. 502	T. 4011	100 H.	P. 542	C. 4002	FT	P. 555
Bes	*I.B.1*	–	–	–	–	–	–	–	–	1	–	–	–	–	–	–	–	–	–	–	–	–	–	–
Hathor head or face	*I.C.1*	–	–	–	–	–	–	–	–	7	–	–	–	–	–	–	–	–	–	–	–	–	–	–
Hathor head or face	*I.C.2*	–	–	–	–	–	–	–	–	–	–	–	1	–	–	–	–	–	–	–	–	–	–	–
Ptah-Sokar	*I.D.1*	–	–	–	–	–	–	–	–	–	–	–	–	–	–	–	1	–	–	–	–	–	–	–
Ptah-Sokar	*I.D.2*	–	–	–	–	–	–	–	–	–	–	–	–	–	–	–	–	–	–	1	–	–	–	–
Taurt	*I.E.1*	–	–	–	–	–	–	–	–	–	–	–	–	–	–	–	4	–	–	–	–	–	–	–
Bastet or Sekhmet	*I.G.1.a*	–	–	–	–	–	–	3	–	–	–	–	–	–	–	–	–	–	–	–	–	–	–	–
Bes or Ptah-Sokar	*I.G.2.b*	–	–	–	–	–	–	–	–	–	–	–	–	–	–	–	–	–	–	1	–	–	–	–
Taurt?	*I.G.5*	–	–	1	–	–	–	–	–	7	1	–	–	–	–	–	–	–	–	–	–	–	–	–
Uraeus?	*I.G.7*	–	–	–	–	–	–	–	–	–	–	–	–	–	–	–	–	–	–	–	–	–	1	–
Head or face	*II.A.2*	–	–	–	–	–	1	–	–	–	–	–	–	–	–	–	–	–	–	–	1	–	–	–
Head or face	*II.A.3*	–	–	–	–	–	–	–	–	–	–	–	–	–	–	–	1	–	–	–	–	–	–	–
Standing figure	*II.B.2.b*	–	1	–	–	–	–	–	–	–	–	–	–	–	–	–	–	–	–	–	–	–	–	–
Fish	*III.B*	–	–	–	–	1	–	–	–	–	–	–	–	1	–	–	–	–	–	–	–	–	–	–
Goose or duck	*III.H.1.b*	–	–	–	–	–	–	–	–	–	–	–	–	–	–	–	–	–	–	–	–	–	1	–
Bull?	*III.H.2*	–	–	–	–	–	–	–	–	1	–	–	–	–	–	–	–	–	–	–	–	–	–	–
Cornflower or cockle	*IV.A*	–	–	–	–	–	–	–	–	25	–	–	–	–	–	–	–	–	–	–	–	–	–	–
Daisy	*IV.B*	–	–	–	–	–	–	–	1	2	–	–	–	–	–	–	–	–	–	–	–	–	–	–
Flower or rosette	*IV.D.1*	–	–	–	–	–	–	–	–	1	–	–	–	–	–	–	–	–	–	–	–	–	–	–
Flower or rosette	*IV.D.2*	–	–	–	–	–	–	–	–	–	–	–	–	–	–	–	–	–	–	–	–	–	1	–
Flower or rosette	*IV.D.3*	–	–	–	–	–	–	–	–	–	–	–	1	–	–	–	–	–	–	–	–	–	–	–
Grape cluster	*IV.E*	–	–	–	–	–	–	–	1	8	–	–	–	–	–	–	–	–	–	–	–	–	–	–
Lotus bud	*IV.F.1*	–	–	–	2	–	–	–	–	–	–	–	–	–	–	–	–	–	–	–	–	–	–	–
Conventional lotus	*IV.F.2*	–	?	–	–	–	–	–	–	21	–	–	–	–	–	–	–	–	–	–	–	–	–	–
Lotus palmette	*IV.F.4*	–	1	–	–	–	–	–	–	–	–	–	–	–	–	–	–	–	–	–	–	–	1	–
Lotus seed vessel	*IV.F.5.b*	–	–	–	–	–	–	–	–	1	–	–	–	–	–	1	–	–	–	–	3	–	–	–
Mandrake fruit	*IV.G.1*	–	–	–	–	–	–	–	–	11	–	–	–	–	–	–	–	–	–	–	–	–	–	–
Mandrake fruit	*IV.G.2*	–	–	–	–	–	–	–	–	17	–	–	–	–	–	–	–	–	–	–	–	–	–	–
Lotus flower?	*IV.H.2*	–	–	–	–	–	–	–	–	3	–	–	–	–	–	–	–	–	–	–	–	–	–	–
Petal or leaf	*IV.H.3.a*	–	–	–	–	–	–	–	–	?	1	1	–	–	–	–	–	–	–	–	–	–	1	–
Petal or leaf	*IV.H.3.b*	–	–	–	–	–	–	–	–	–	–	–	–	–	–	–	–	–	–	–	–	–	3	–
Reeds?	*IV.H.4*	–	–	–	–	–	–	–	–	15	–	–	–	–	–	–	–	–	–	–	–	–	–	–
wḏ't	*V.E.1.a*	–	–	–	–	–	–	–	–	–	–	–	–	–	–	2	–	1	–	–	–	–	–	–
wḏ't	*V.E.1.b*	–	–	1	–	–	–	–	–	–	–	–	–	–	–	–	–	–	–	–	–	–	–	–
wḏ't	*V.E.2.a*	–	–	–	–	–	–	–	–	–	–	–	–	–	–	–	–	–	–	–	–	–	–	1
ib?	*V.F.2*	–	–	–	–	–	–	–	–	–	–	–	–	–	–	–	–	–	–	–	–	–	1	–
Crescent or horns	*VI.B.1*	–	–	–	–	–	–	–	–	–	–	–	–	–	–	–	–	–	–	1	–	–	–	–
Double spiral	*VI.E*	–	–	–	–	–	–	–	–	–	–	–	–	–	–	–	–	–	–	1	–	–	–	–
Star disc	*VI.G.2.a*	–	–	–	–	–	–	–	–	–	–	–	–	–	–	–	–	–	–	–	–	–	1	–
Star disc	*VI.G.2.b*	1	–	–	–	–	–	–	–	–	–	–	–	–	–	–	–	–	–	–	–	–	3	–
'Wheel'	*VI.H*	–	–	–	–	–	–	–	–	1	1	–	–	–	–	–	–	–	–	–	–	–	–	–
Total		1	2+	1	1	2	1	3	2	121+1	2	2	1	1	2	6	1	1		1	3	3	14	1
%		1	1	1	1	1	1	2	2	69	1	1	1	1	1	3	1	1		1	2	2	8	1

FT = Fosse Temple
FT I:D = Fosse Temple, Structure I, Room D
FT II:D = Fosse Temple, Structure II, Room D
FT II:E = Fosse Temple, Structure II, Room E
FT III:D = Fosse Temple, Structure III, Room D
FT III:E = Fosse Temple, Structure III, Room E

C. = Cave
H. = Houses
P. = Pit
T. = Tomb

+ = unspecified number of additional specimens
? = uncertain number of specimens

Chart 53
Temporal Distribution by Locus of Late Bronze Age Pendants at Tell el-'Ajjul

Description	Type	IA															I			IB–IIA	IIA							IIB	II		
		NB 995	T. 1203	T. 1740	T. 1998	T. 2070	H. 277	H. 1299	H. 1312	H. 1313	AN 748	AT 659–760	EAD 877	ECE 785	LH^4 976	LK 1002	TDK 885	T. 447	T. 1502	T. 425	T. 1037	T. 1064	T. 1073	T. 1080	T. 1085	T. 1663	MO 1040	T. 1095	G 950	T. 1166	T. 1514
Hathor head or face	I.C.3	–	–	–	–	–	–	–	–	–	–	–	–	–	–	–	–	–	–	–	–	–	–	–	–	–	–	–	–	–	1
Taurt	I.E.2	–	–	–	–	–	–	–	–	–	–	–	–	–	–	–	–	–	–	–	–	–	–	–	–	1	–	–	–	–	–
Horus?	I.G.3	–	–	–	–	–	–	–	–	–	–	–	–	–	–	–	1	–	–	–	–	–	–	–	–	–	–	–	–	–	–
Taurt?	I.G.5	–	–	–	–	–	–	–	–	–	–	–	–	–	–	–	–	–	–	–	–	1	–	–	–	–	–	–	–	–	–
Standing figure	II.B.2.a	–	–	–	–	–	1	1	–	–	–	–	–	–	–	–	–	–	–	–	–	–	–	–	–	–	–	–	–	–	–
Standing figure	II.B.2.b	–	–	–	–	–	3	2	–	–	–	–	–	–	–	–	–	–	–	–	–	–	–	–	–	–	–	–	–	–	–
Falcon	III.A	–	–	–	–	–	3	–	–	–	–	–	–	–	–	–	–	–	–	–	–	–	–	–	–	–	–	–	–	–	–
Fly	III.C	–	–	–	–	–	–	–	–	4	–	–	–	–	–	–	–	–	–	–	–	–	–	–	–	–	–	–	–	–	–
Frog or Toad	III.D	–	–	–	–	–	–	–	–	–	–	–	–	–	–	–	–	1	–	–	–	–	–	–	–	–	–	–	–	–	–
Hippopotamus	III.E	–	–	–	–	–	–	–	–	–	–	–	–	–	–	–	–	1	–	–	–	–	–	–	–	–	–	–	–	–	–
Ram?	III.H.6	–	–	–	–	–	–	–	–	–	–	–	–	–	–	–	–	–	–	–	1	–	–	–	–	–	–	–	–	–	–
Lotus bud	IV.F.1	–	–	–	–	–	–	–	–	–	–	–	–	–	–	–	–	–	–	–	–	4	9	–	1	–	–	–	–	–	–
Lotus palmette	IV.F.4	–	–	–	–	–	–	–	1	–	–	–	–	–	–	–	–	–	–	–	–	–	–	–	–	–	–	–	–	–	–
Lotus seed vessel	IV.F.5.b	–	–	–	–	–	–	–	–	–	–	–	–	–	–	–	–	–	–	–	–	–	–	1	–	–	–	–	–	–	–
Petal or leaf	IV.H.3.b	–	–	–	–	–	2	–	2	–	–	–	–	–	–	–	–	–	–	–	–	–	–	–	–	–	–	–	–	–	–
dd	V.B.1.	–	–	–	–	–	–	–	–	–	–	–	–	–	–	–	–	–	–	–	–	–	–	1	–	–	–	–	–	–	–
wd't	V.E.1.d	–	–	–	–	–	–	–	–	–	–	–	–	–	–	–	–	–	–	–	–	–	–	–	–	–	–	–	–	1	–
Circular crescent	VI.A	–	–	–	2	–	2	6	2	1	–	–	–	–	–	–	–	–	–	–	–	–	–	–	–	–	–	–	–	–	–
Crescent or horns	VI.B.1	1	–	–	–	–	–	4	4	–	1	1	2	1	1	1	–	1	1	1	–	–	–	1	–	–	1	1	1	1	–
Cruciform	VI.C	–	2	1	2	2	–	–	–	–	–	–	–	–	–	–	–	–	–	–	–	–	–	–	–	–	–	–	–	–	–
Disc	VI.D.2	–	–	–	–	–	–	–	–	–	–	–	–	–	–	–	–	–	1	–	–	–	–	–	–	–	–	–	–	–	–
Disc	VI.D.3	–	–	–	–	–	–	–	–	–	–	–	–	–	–	–	–	–	–	–	1	–	–	–	–	–	–	–	–	–	–
Miscellaneous drop	VI.F.3	–	–	2	–	–	–	–	1	1	–	–	–	–	–	–	–	–	–	–	–	–	–	–	–	–	–	–	–	–	–
Star disc	VI.G.2.b	–	–	–	–	–	3	4	–	–	–	–	–	–	–	–	–	–	–	–	–	–	–	–	–	–	–	–	–	–	–
Star disc	VI.G.2.c	–	–	–	–	–	–	–	–	–	–	–	–	–	–	–	–	–	–	–	–	–	–	–	–	–	–	–	–	–	–
Total		1	2	3	4	2	14	17	10	6	1	1	2	1	1	1	1	3	2	1	2	5	9	3	1	1	1	1	1	2	1
%		1	2	3	4	2	14	17	10	6	1	1	2	1	1	1	1	3	2	1	2	5	9	3	1	1	1	1	1	2	1

H. = House
T. = Tomb

toire of Egyptian-related types that probably appeared earlier (LB IB–IIA) in southern Palestine.

The majority of the Lachish pendants come from an LB IIB hoard in Room E of Fosse Temple III; they were probably part of a single collar (Tufnell, Inge, and Harding 1940: pl. 14). In addition to two Syro-Palestinian types (*IV.D.1* and *VI.H*), 14 Egyptian-related types are represented: *I.B.1, I.C.1, I.G.5, III.H.2, IV.A, IV.B, IV.E, IV.F.2, IV.F.5.b, IV.G.1–2, IV.H.2, IV.H.3.a,* and *IV.H.4*. Only four of these types (*I.G.5, IV.F.5.b, IV.H.3.a,* and *VI.H*) occur in other LB IIB contexts at Lachish; two types (*IV.D.1* and *IV.F.2*) are matched in LB IIA.

As at Beth Shan, groups comprised of one to three types, Egyptian-related for the most part, are distributed among burials and pits near the temple and on the tell. These assemblages probably constituted small necklaces, which were worn by townspeople and perhaps by itinerants. Syro-Palestinian types are common in such contexts throughout the Late Bronze Age: *IV.D.1–2, IV.H.3.b, VI.B.1, VI.E, VI.G.2.a–b,* and *VI.H.*

c. Tell el-'Ajjul (Chart 53)
A substantial portion of the Tell el-'Ajjul pendant corpus derives from four LB IA jewelry hoards, apparently buried beneath the floors of ordinary residences, possibly by goldsmiths (Petrie 1934: 6–8; Petrie,

Mackay, and Murray 1952: 9–11). Since an LB IA temple was not located and excavated, the evidence from this site may be unduly weighted in favor of residential and burial contexts.

Three of the ten Syro-Palestinian types from the hoards are recorded in other LB IA residential and burial loci at ʿAjjul; these are *VI.A*, *VI.B.1*, and *VI.F.3*. Only Type *VI.C*, usually occurring in pairs, is restricted to tombs. Like Type *VI.A*, which is attested in the hoards and a burial, the pendant pairs may have been worn as earrings, although none are reported to have been found in the vicinity of skulls (Petrie 1934: 7–8; Petrie, Mackay, and Murray 1952: 10–12). Another pair of pendants (Type *VI.F.3*) from Tomb 1740 may have been strung together with five long cylindrical gold beads on a necklace. Only one LB IA pendant type (*VI.B.1*) occurs in both a burial and a residential context other than a jewelry hoard.

Probably beginning in LB IB but certainly by LB IIA, Egyptian-related types (*I.E.2*, *I.G.5*, *III.H.6*, *IV.F.5.b*, and *V.B.1*) appear alongside Syro-Palestinian types (*VI.B.1* and *VI.D.3*), primarily in burials. The one or two, at most three, pendant types from these loci were probably strung together on individual necklaces.

Tell el-ʿAjjul was not as intensively occupied in LB IIB. Indeed, only one Syro-Palestinian type (*VI.B.1*) is documented from a burial.

d. *Megiddo* (Chart 54)

The evidence from Megiddo is probably skewed to some extent by the extensive disturbance and plundering of the temple in Area BB. Otherwise, it is in accord with the general distribution pattern of Late Bronze Age pendants.

LB IA pendants are restricted to Syro-Palestinian types from burials and residential contexts: *II.B.1.a*, *VI.D.1*, *VI.F.2*, *VI.G.1*, and *VI.G.2.c*. One Egyptian-related type (*III.H.4*) may be intrusional. One or two types per context are customary. Locus

Chart 54
Temporal Distribution by Locus of Late Bronze Age Pendants at Megiddo

Description	Type	IA				I	IB–IIA							IIA	IIB						LB			
		2134	4004	5029	T. 2009	T. 1145 B	S=2048	2094	3100	5050	Sq. O.14, BB	T. 877 C 1	T. 3016	T. 36 B	1834	2039	E=2041	2064	3187	T. 877 A 1	T. 877 B 1	T. 912 B	T. 989 C 1	Sq. M 13, BB
Bes	*I.B.1*	–	–	–	–	–	–	–	–	–	–	–	–	–	–	–	–	–	–	1	2	–	–	–
Bastet or Sekhmet	*I.G.1.b*	–	–	–	–	–	–	–	–	–	–	–	–	–	–	2	1	–	–	–	–	–	–	–
Bes or Ptah-Sokar	*I.G.2.a*	–	–	–	–	–	–	–	–	–	–	–	–	–	–	–	–	–	–	–	–	–	–	1
Horus child or Ptah	*I.G.4*	–	–	–	–	–	–	–	–	–	–	–	–	–	–	–	–	–	–	–	1	–	–	–
Standing figure	*II.B.1.a*	–	–	1	–	–	–	–	–	–	–	–	–	–	–	–	–	–	–	–	–	–	–	–
Standing figure	*II.B.2.b*	–	–	–	–	–	–	–	–	1	–	–	–	–	–	–	–	–	–	–	–	–	–	–
Dove?	*III.H.1.a*	–	–	–	–	–	–	–	–	–	–	–	1	–	–	–	–	–	–	–	–	–	–	–
Dog?	*III.H.4*	–	1	–	–	–	–	–	–	–	–	–	–	–	–	–	–	–	–	–	–	–	–	–
Grape cluster	*IV.E*	–	–	–	–	–	–	–	–	–	–	1	–	–	–	–	–	–	–	–	–	–	–	–
Lotus bud	*IV.F.1*	–	–	–	–	–	–	–	1	–	–	–	–	–	–	–	–	–	–	–	–	–	–	–
Lotus seed vessel	*IV.F.5.a*	–	–	–	–	–	–	–	–	–	–	–	–	1	–	–	–	–	–	–	–	–	–	–
Lotus seed vessel	*IV.F.5.b*	–	–	–	–	–	–	–	–	–	–	–	–	–	–	–	–	–	–	–	1	1	2	–
wdʾt	*V.E.1.a*	–	–	–	–	–	–	–	–	–	–	–	–	–	–	–	–	–	–	–	1	–	–	–
Crescent or horns	*VI.B.1*	–	–	–	–	–	1	–	–	–	–	–	–	–	–	–	–	1	–	–	–	–	–	–
Plain disc	*VI.D.1*	–	–	1	–	–	–	–	–	–	–	–	–	–	–	–	–	–	–	–	–	–	–	–
Elongated drop	*VI.F.2*	1	–	1	–	1	–	–	–	–	1	–	–	–	–	–	–	–	1	–	–	–	–	–
Miscellaneous drop	*VI.F.3*	–	–	–	–	–	–	1	–	–	–	–	–	–	–	–	–	–	–	–	–	–	–	–
Star disc	*VI.G.1*	–	–	1	1	–	1	–	–	–	–	–	–	–	–	–	–	–	–	–	–	–	–	–
Star disc	*VI.G.2.c*	–	–	–	2	–	–	–	–	–	–	–	–	–	1	–	–	–	–	–	–	–	–	–
Total		1	1	4	3	1	2	1	1	1	1	1	1	1	1	2	1	1	1	1	5	1	2	1
%		3	3	11	9	3	6	3	3	3	3	3	3	3	3	6	3	3	3	3	14	3	6	3

Sq. = Square
T. = Tomb

5029, a robbed-out room in Area BB, had single examples of four types (*II.B.1.a*, *VI.D.1*, *VI.F.2*, and *VI.G.1*).

Egyptian-related pendants make their appearance in LB IB–IIa temple, burial, and residential contexts, but on a small scale: *IV.E*, *IV.F.1*, and *IV.F.5.a*. Syro-Palestinian types (*II.B.2.b*, *III.H.1.a*, *VI.F.2–3*, and *VI.G.1*) remain popular.

In LB IIB, small numbers of three Syro-Palestinian types (*VI.B.1*, *VI.F.2*, and *VI.G.2.c*) and five Egyptian-related types (*I.B.1*, *I.G.1.b*, *I.G.4*, *IV.F.5.b*, and *V.E.1.a*) from burial and residential contexts reflect the continued practice among the populace of wearing small necklaces.

e. *Other Palestinian Sites*

Loci assemblages from other Palestinian sites do not deviate significantly from the pattern outlined above.

Syro-Palestinian types can occur as single specimens in various contexts: *VI.G.2* in the LB IA 'temple' at Tel Kittan, and in an LB IIA residential context at Shechem; *VI.F.2* in LB I and LB II burials in the Umm ad-Dananir region of Transjordan; and *II.A.1* in an LB II residence at Tell Beit Mirsim. Syro-Palestinian types sometimes occur together with Egyptian-related types, and may have comprised multielement collars. For example a LB IIB hoard at Beth Shemesh included three Syro-Palestinian types (*IV.H.1*, *VI.B.1*, and *VI.F.3*) and two Egyptian-related types (*IV.F.5.b* and *IV.F.4*). Only Egyptian *IV.H.4*, *V.A.1*, *V.B.1*, and related types (*IV.F.5.b*, *IV.H.4*, *V.A.1*, *V.B.1*, and *V.D.1*) were found in a poorly stratified LB II group at Tell Abu Hawam.

C. Cultural and Historical Implications

1. *Foreign Relations and Origins*

The distribution of Syro-Palestinian and Egyptian-related types in Palestine has been a recurring theme in this study. Certain assumptions are built into the assignment of a given pendant type to one of these two cultural spheres. Generally, for the vast majority of pendant types, there is very little doubt about how they should be classified, since the earliest parallels are concentrated at one or more sites in a particular region. Since Egypt more often exported motifs rather than adopting them, the problem actually becomes one of deciding whether a mixed type, which incorporates Egyptian and Levantine or Mesopotamian features, can properly be assigned to the Syro-Palestinian cultural sphere (Maxwell-Hyslop 1971: 106, 164–68; Tufnell and Ward 1966: 226–27; Frankfort 1970: 243–45; Smith 1965b). This writer will generally assign such

types to the Syro-Palestinian group rather than to an uncertain category, e.g., *III.A*, *III.C*, *IV.F.4*, *IV.D.1–2*, *IV.F.4*, *IV.H.3.b* (*209, 211–213*), *VI.F.2* (*316, 319, 321*), and *VI.F.3*. In any case, very few examples fall into this debatable group, and the general conclusions are not affected by this assumption.

Egyptian-related pendants and types greatly overshadow the Syro-Palestinian contribution; 83 percent of the total pendants and 70 percent of the types for Late Bronze Age Palestine are Egyptian-related. This is particularly evident for Classes *I* and *V*, which are exclusively Egyptian-related types, and to a lesser degree for Classes *III* and *IV* (Chart 55). Syro-Palestinian types predominate in Classes *II* and *VI*.

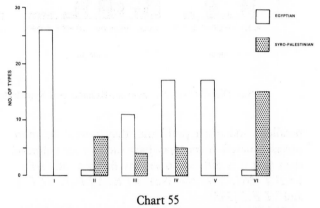

Chart 55

Distribution of Egyptian-Related and Syro-Palestinian Pendant Types by Classes in Late Bronze Age Palestine

The temporal distribution of the two groups reveals another pattern (Charts 56 and 57). Here it can be seen that Syro-Palestinian types are rather evenly apportioned from one Late Bronze phase to the next at sites throughout the country.

Based on the typological analysis in Chapters 2–7, periods of manufacture can be specified for each Syro-Palestinian type (Chart 58). Some types are restricted to LB IA: *III.A*, *IV.F.4* (*142*), *VI.A*, *VI.C*, *VI.F.3* (*336–338*), and *VI.G.2.b*. More often, Syro-Palestinian types are temporally nonspecific. Thus, four types (*II.B.1.a*, *II.B.2.a–b*, and *III.H.1.a*) are carryovers from the Middle Bronze Age, and extend to varying degrees into Late Bronze. Another group is very common in LB II, but continues to be made in Iron I: *IV.H.1*, *VI.B.1* (*268, 270–271, 297*), and *VI.F.3* (*334–335*). A large group occurs throughout most or all of the Late Bronze Age: *IV.H.3.b* (*209, 211–213*), *VI.F.3* (*331–332*), *VI.G.1*, *VI.G.2.a*, *VI.G.2.c*, and *VI.H*. Other types (*II.A.1–2*, *II.B.1.b*, *III.F*, and *VI.D.1–3*) probably belong to Late Bronze; but, because of uncertain contexts, lack of

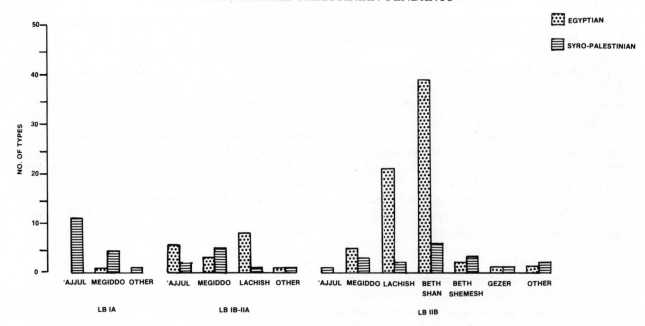

Chart 56
Site Distribution of Egyptian-Related and Syro-Palestinian Pendant Types in Late Bronze Age Palestine

parallels, and other problems, they cannot be more precisely dated. Some types have such a wide temporal span that it is difficult to set any limits at all (*III.C, VI.B.1 (267, 269, 272–296), VI.E, VI.F.1, VI.F.2,* and *VI.F.3 [333]*).

The Egyptian-related types are very heavily weighted towards LB IIB (Charts 56 and 57). While LB IA completely lacks Egyptian-related types, 13 types are found in LB IB–IIA contexts as compared with 31 for LB IIB.

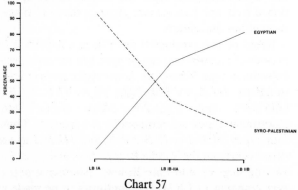

Chart 57
Comparative Importance of Egyptian-Related and Syro-Palestinian Pendant Types in Late Bronze Age Palestine

A very large group of Egyptian-related pendant types, many of which are paralleled at el-Amarna, were manufactured only in LB II (Charts 59, 60): *I.A.1–2, I.B.2, I.C.1, I.E.1–2, I.F.1.a–2.b, I.G.1.a–b, I.G.5,*

I.G.6.b.i, III.B, III.G, III.H.1.b–c, III.H.2, III.H.3, III.H.5, IV.A, IV.B, IV.C, IV.F.2, IV.G.1, IV.H.2, IV.H.3.b (210), IV.H.4, V.A.1–2, V.B.1–2, V.C.1–3, V.D.1–2, V.E.1.b–c, and *V.F.1–3.* Under the assumption that many of the examples from the LB IIB temples at Lachish and Beth Shan were heirlooms, it might even be argued that some LB II types should be limited to LB IIA. The wisest course at present will be to allow for a comfortable margin of error.

Indeed, a sizable LB II group extends into Iron I: *I.B.1, I.C.2–3, I.D.1–2, I.G.2.a–b, I.G.4, I.G.6.a, I.G.6.b.ii, I.G.6.c, II.A.3, IV.D.3, IV.E., IV.F.1 (112–115), IV.F.4, IV.F.5.a–b, IV.G.2, IV.H.3.a (192–202, 204–205, 208), V.E.1.a, V.E.2.a,* and *VI.B.2.*

Several Egyptian-related pendant types (*III.D, IV.F.1 [111, 116–117],* and *IV.H.3.a [203, 206–207]*), were probably produced throughout the Late Bronze Age. Poorly dated types, which are assigned a questionable Late Bronze date, include *I.G.3, I.G.7, IV.F.3,* and *V.E.1.d.*

The contextual and material distributions of the Syro-Palestinian and Egyptian-related types (Charts 61, 62) show that Syro-Palestinian types in gold, primarily from residences, are dominant in LB IA. Egyptian-related faience types from burials appear in LB IB–IIA, and are about equal to the Syro-Palestinian complement for this period. Egyptian-related types from temple contexts greatly exceed the

Chart 58
Manufacturing Periods of Syro-Palestinian Pendant Types in Late Bronze Age Palestine

Description	Type	MB	LB IA	LB IB	LB IIA	LB IIB	Iron Age
Head or face	II.A.1			————————— ? —————————			
Head or face	II.A.2			————————— • ? —————————			
Standing figure	II.B.1.a	– –	—————————				
Standing figure	II.B.1.b		————————— ? —————————				
Standing figure	II.B.2.a	– –	—————————				
Standing figure	II.B.2.b	– –	———————————————————————				
Standing figure	II.B.3		————————— ? —————————				
Falcon	III.A		—————				
Fly	III.C	– –	———————————————————————			– –	
Lion and bull/dog	III.F		————————— ? —————————				
Dove?	III.H.I.a	– –	——————————— – –				
Flower or rosette	IV.D.1		————————— ? —————————				
Flower or rosette	IV.D.2		————————— ? —————————				
Lotus palmette	IV.F.4 (142)		—————				
Bud?	IV.H.1					————— – –	
Petal or leaf	IV.H.3.b		———————————————————————				
Circular crescent	VI.A		—————				
Crescent or horns	VI.B.1	– –	———————————————————————			– –	
Cruciform	VI.C		—————				
Disc	VI.D.1		————————— ? —————————				
Disc	VI.D.2		————————— ? —————————				
Disc	VI.D.3		————————— ? —————————				
Double spiral	VI.E	– –	———————————————————————			– –	
Crude drop	VI.F.1	– –	———————————————————————			– –	
Elongated drop	VI.F.2	– –	———————————————————————			– –	
Miscellaneous drop	VI.F.3	– –	———————————————————————			– –	
Star disc	VI.G.1	– –	———————————————————————			– –	
Star disc	VI.G.2.a		———————————————————————				
Star disc	VI.G.2.b		—————				
Star disc	VI.G.2.c		———————————————————————				
'Wheel'	VI.H		———————————————————————				

more widely dispersed Syro-Palestinian contribution in LB IIB.

2. Interpretation of the Evidence

How is one to account for the distribution pattern of Late Bronze jewelry pendants in Palestine? Before turning to the textual sources, the archaeological evidence should be independently assessed.

Although only one part of the archaeological record is dealt with here, the pendant evidence provides eloquent testimony for virtually no Egyptian influence in Palestinian affairs until LB IB at the earliest. Egyptian iconographic expression was not eschewed in the manufacture of LB IA pendants (cf. II.B.2.b, III.A, III.C, and IV.F.4), but the overall artistic and technological expression is unique to Syria-Palestine. Even allowing for inadequate exploration, mixed contexts, and other limitations, the Egyptian contribution to the

pendant repertoire before LB IIB is approximately the same as the Syro-Palestinian contribution. Only in LB IIB does the Egyptian contribution become predominant. Even then, the numerical increase in the Egyptian-related pendants and types does not detract from the Syro-Palestinian component, which shows a slight increase over LB IIA.

The above reconstruction conforms to a minimalist view of Egyptian control in Palestine preceding LB IIB. Thus, the various campaigns of Ahmose, Thutmose I, and Thutmose II had very little effect on cultural life in Palestine (Gardiner 1961: 169, 178–80; Drioton and Vandier 1962: 397; James 1970–75: 294–96). The adoption of Egyptian artistic motifs was already well-established, and there is no need to invoke a newly established sphere of Egyptian influence in Palestine to account for it. More likely, LB IA Palestinian culture is essentially a continuation of MB

LATE BRONZE PALESTINIAN PENDANTS

Chart 59
Manufacturing Periods of Egyptian-Related Pendant Types (Classes *I–III*)
in Late Bronze Age Palestine

Description	Type	MB	LB IA	LB IB	LB IIA	LB IIB	Iron I	Iron II
Baboon of Thoth	*I.A.1*				———	———		
Baboon of Thoth	*I.A.2*				———	———		
Bes	*I.B.1*				———	———	- - -	
Bes	*I.B.2*				———	———		
Hathor head or face	*I.C.1*				———	———		
Hathor head or face	*I.C.2*					? - - -	———	———
Hathor head or face	*I.C.3*				———	———	———	
Ptah-Sokar	*I.D.1*				———	———	———	———
Ptah-Sokar	*I.D.2*				———	———	———	———
Taurt	*I.E.1*				———	———	———	———
Taurt	*I.E.2*				———	———		
Uraeus	*I.F.1.a*				———	———		
Uraeus	*I.F.2.a*				———	———		
Uraeus	*I.F.2.b*				———	———		
Basket or Sekhmet	*I.G.1.a*				———	———		
Basket or Sekhmet	*I.G.1.b*				———	———		
Bes or Ptah-Sokar	*I.G.2.a*				———	———	———	
Bes or Ptah-Sokar	*I.G.2.b*				———	———	———	
Horus?	*I.G.3*		———	———	? ———	———		
Horus Child or Ptah	*I.G.4*				———	———	———	———
Taurt?	*I.G.5*				———	———		
Standing figure	*I.G.6.a.*				———	———	———	———
Standing figure	*I.G.6.b.i*				———	———		
Standing figure	*I.G.6.b.ii*				———	———	- - -	
Standing figure	*I.G.6.c*				———	———	———	
Uraeus?	*I.G.7*		———	———	? ———	———		
Head or face	*II.A.3*				———	———	———	- - -
Fish	*III.B*				———	———		
Frog or toad	*III.D*		———	———	———	———		
Hippopotamus	*III.E*	———	———	———				
Ram's head	*III.G*				———	———		
Goose or duck	*III.H.1.b*				———	———		
Owl?	*III.H.1.c*				———	———		
Bull?	*III.H.2*				———	———		
Cat?	*III.H.3*				———	———		
Dog?	*III.H.4*					- - -	- - -	- - -
Mouse?	*III.H.5*				———	———		
Ram?	*III.H.6*			- - -	- - -			

traditions (Kenyon 1966: 76; Weinstein 1981: 6–7; Mazar 1968; Kaplan 1971; Dever 1976: 6). The 'Hyksos', recently expelled from Egypt, may never have been fully Egyptianized (Van Seters 1966), but certainly with their reincorporation into Palestinian cultural life came a body of knowledge and skills exhibiting some Egyptian characteristics.

The fourteen campaigns of Thutmose III between regnal years 23 and 42 (1482–1463 B.C., following Wente and van Siclen 1976) were on a much grander scale than previous pharaohs' attempts to bring Palestine under Egyptian dominion (Gardiner 1961: 189–94; Helck 1971: 338, 247). Although the description of the Battle of Megiddo in the temple at Karnak conforms to standard Egyptian rhetoric, the topographical facts have been generally confirmed (Gardiner 1961: 189–90; Aharoni 1979: 152–66; Helck 1971: 12, 126–32). As many as 350 Asiatics are mentioned in the text, reflecting the fragmentation of Palestine into small city–states at the time (Gardiner 1961: 192; Drower 1970–75: 451; Campbell 1976: 39–45). Thutmose is said to have replaced some of the Palestinian

Chart 60
Manufacturing Periods of Egyptian-Related Pendant Types (Classes *IV–VI*) in Late Bronze Age Palestine

Description	Type	MB	LB IA	LB IB	LB IIA	LB IIB	Iron I	Iron II
Cornflower or cockle	*IV.A*				————	————		
Daisy	*IV.B*				————	————		
Date fruit	*IV.C*				————	————		
Flower or rosette	*IV.D.3*				————	————	- - -	
Grape cluster	*IV.E*				————	————	————	
Lotus bud	*IV.F.1*		————	————	————	————	- - -	
Conventional lotus	*IV.F.2*				————	————		
Lotus flower	*IV.F.3*		————	———— ?	————	————		
Lotus palmette	*IV.F.4*				————	————	- - -	
Lotus seed vessel	*IV.F.5.a*				————	————	————	- - -
Lotus seed vessel	*IV.F.5.b*				————	————	————	————
Mandrake fruit	*IV.G.1*				————	————		
Mandrake fruit	*IV.G.2*				————	————	————	
Lotus flower?	*IV.H.2*				————	————		
Petal or leaf	*IV.H.3.a*	- - -	- - -	- - -	————	————	- - -	
Petal or leaf	*IV.H.3.b (210)*				————	————		
Reeds?	*IV.H.4*				————	————		
ʿankh	*V.A.1*				————	————		
ʿankh	*V.A.2*				————	————		
ḏd	*V.B.1*				————	————		
ḏd	*V.B.2*				————	————		
ḥeḥ	*V.C.1*				————	————		
ḥeḥ	*V.C.2*				————	————		
ḥeḥ	*V.C.3*				————	————		
tit	*V.D.1*				————	————		
tit	*V.D.2*				————	————		
wḏʾt	*V.E.1.a*				————	————	————	
wḏʾt	*V.E.1.b*				————	————		
wḏʾt	*V.E.1.c*				————	————		
wḏʾt	*V.E.1.d*	- - -	- - -	- - -	————	————	- - -	
wḏʾt	*V.E.2.a*				————	————	————	
ḫst?	*V.F.1*				————	————		
ib	*V.F.2*				————	————		
nfr?	*V.F.3*				————	————		
Crescent or horns	*VI.B.2*				————	————	————	

princes and to have taken others captive, turned over fields around Megiddo to Egyptians, and rationed supplies to northern Palestinian towns (e.g., Megiddo and Taʿanach), as well as coastal ports such as Ashkelon (Gardiner 1961: 193). However, the fact that he found it necessary to carry out 14 campaigns in Syria-Palestine makes it doubtful that Thutmose III was able to shape a true 'empire' in the region.

Allowing for the inevitable gaps in the historical documentation, it is likely that the seaports were strongly held, and that military governors were stationed at key points in the rest of the country (Helck 1971: 246–53; Mohammad 1959; Klengel 1965–70, 3: 196–202; Malamat 1961; Aḥituv 1978: 94–95; Naʾaman 1981; 177–80). Except for the mention of the receipt of tribute, the last twelve years of Thutmose's reign did not include any campaigns into Palestine, suggesting but not proving that the region remained loyal to the king (Gardiner 1961: 197).

When the historical synthesis is compared with the pendant evidence, claims of Egyptian dominance appear somewhat overstated. There was a gradual infiltration of Egyptian-related types, beginning as early as LB IB. However, this was on a relatively small scale, and can be better explained in terms of small contingents of Egyptian officials and traders in the country rather than in terms of any wholesale Egyptian takeover of major Palestinian sites (Kemp 1978: 43–56; Weinstein 1981: 14–15).

A reassertion of Egyptian military might may have

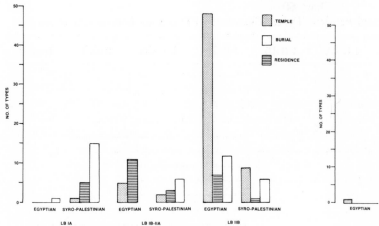

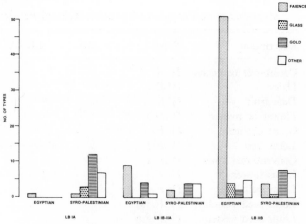

Chart 61
Contextual Distribution of
Egyptian-Related and Syro-Palestinian Pendant Types
in Late Bronze Age Palestine

Chart 62
Material Distribution of
Egyptian-Related and Syro-Palestinian Pendant Types
in Late Bronze Age Palestine

come at the beginning of Amenhotep II's reign (ca. 1450 B.C.), unless his first campaign into Western Asia should be attributed to Thutmose III (Gardiner 1961: 198). In the 'second' campaign in year 7, Amenhotep II was successful at Qatna and Ugarit, and the campaign of year 9 included towns referred to in Thutmose III's lists (Aharoni 1979: 166–68; Aharoni and Avi-Yonah 1968: 34). The end of Amenhotep's reign and the subsequent reign of Thutmose IV was a prosperous period, which reached its peak under Amenhotep III, ca. 1386–1349 B.C. (Gardiner 1961: 202; Giveon 1969; Several 1972; Drower 1970–75: 483–93).

Together with Egyptian alliances with Mitanni, Babylon and probably Hatti, the contemporary political and social situation in Syria-Palestine has been illumined by the Amarna Letters from the last years of Amenhotep III through the early part of Tutankhamun's reign (Knudtzon 1907–1914; Rainey 1970). These invaluable historical sources, in conjunction with the standard inscriptional evidence, show that Syria-Palestine was divided into three administrative districts: Amurru, capital at Sumur (Tell Kazel?); Upi, capital at Kumidi (Kamid el-Loz); and Canaan, capital at Gaza (Gardiner 1961: 205–10; Helck 1971: 246–53; cf. Na'aman 1981: 183–84). Palestine (Lower Retenu) was controlled by local princes, who were theoretically under the supervision of governors called 'overseers of foreign lands' (Helck 1971: 248–49). Gaza and Joppa were the chief Egyptian administrative centers with outposts in the interior, one possibly located at Beth Shan (Helck 1971: 251).

The ineffectiveness of this system is vividly portrayed in the mutual accusations, recriminations,

and excuses found in the Amarna Letters. The more powerful city–states (e.g., Hazor, Shechem, Jerusalem, Gezer, and Megiddo) vied for control of the neighboring lands (Several 1972; Faulkner 1970–75: 218; Albright 1970–75: 104–5). Thus, it is not inconceivable that the supposed Egyptian hegemony during LB IIA was short-lived and actually fell apart under Akhenaten and his successors (Weinstein 1981: 15–16). The pendant evidence, although it cannot discriminate between the reigns of individual pharaohs, is more compatible with the latter position.

Seti I of the 19th Dynasty (ca. 1291–1279 B.C.) was left to rebuild what was more nearly an 'empire' than Egypt had ever achieved in Western Asia (Gardiner 1961: 255). In his first campaign, after slaughtering the Shosu near Gaza ('town of Canaan'), Seti successfully defended Beth Shan, which still appears to have been an Egyptian military base, against attacks from Hamath and Pella (Gardiner 1961: 253–55; Faulkner 1970–75: 221; Aharoni and Avi-Yonah 1968: 37; Pritchard 1955: 253–55). Later pharaohs of the 19th Dynasty, particularly Ramesses II (ca. 1279–1212 B.C.) consolidated Egyptian control at these sites and throughout Palestine, possibly even campaigning into Transjordan (Kitchen 1964).

The pendant evidence is completely in accord with this historical reconstruction. An enormous increase in Egyptian pendant types at major Palestinian sites is superimposed on a Syro-Palestinian repertoire. The increase reflects Egyptian military and economic control as never before in Palestine. Large numbers of Egyptians (administrators, military personnel, merchants, and others) must have taken up residence in the country during the 13th century B.C.

Egyptian activity particularly intensified at Beth Shan and in the southern coastal plain (Gaza, Tell Far'ah South, Tell el-'Ajjul, Tell esh-Shari'a, Tel Mor, Ashdod, Gezer, and Jaffa) to judge from the royal and private statuary and stelae, inscribed architectural elements, and Egyptian-inspired architecture at these sites (Weinstein 1981: 18–19). The distribution of other inscriptional and archaeological evidence (e.g., alabaster and faience vessels, Egyptian pottery types, hieratic ostraca, etc.), which remain to be fully studied, appears to follow the same pattern.

Egyptian presence must have been transitory at best in the Hill Country of Western Palestine, the Galilee, the Huleh and central Jordan Valleys, and Transjordan, where Egyptian-related pendant types are virtually nonexistent.[4] Syro-Palestinian cultural traditions, on the other hand, continued unabated in these areas.

Only the evidence for Egyptian foreign relations has been cited here, because other Late Bronze empires had a minimal impact on Palestine. The real battleground between these powers was further north in Syria, where strong city–states (Alalakh, Ugarit, Qadesh, Qatna, and others) had been established. The latter strategically aligned themselves with the powers (Egypt, Hatti, Mitanni, or Babylon) that happened to be ascendant at any given time. The Egyptian 'control' of Palestine was never really challenged, except by the native rulers.

Nevertheless, Palestinian culture, as a combination of Hurrian, Indo-European, and native Semitic elements (Drower 1970–75: 420–25), is closely related to the city–states farther north in Syria. Palestinian architecture, pottery, and the vast majority of the small objects, particularly in the earlier phases of the Late Bronze Age, belong to a Syro-Palestinian cultural sphere. This is borne out by the pendant evidence: a number of new types appear that are either unique to LB IA (*III.A*, *VI.A*, and *VI.C*) or are first established in Palestine during this period (*II.B.1.a*, *II.B.2.a*, and *III.C*); all of these probably originated in the general area of Syria-Palestine. The fact that many of the early Late Bronze pendant types continue throughout the rest of the Late Bronze Age in the same relative amounts as for LB IA, even in LB IIB when Egyptian pendant types arrive in force, testifies to the strength and resiliency of the Syro-Palestinian culture.

The appearance of Syro-Palestinian pendant types in LB IA and of Egyptian pendant types as early as LB IB comes unexpectedly. Middle Bronze Age settlement sites and burials are largely devoid of pendants except for Types *VI.B.1* and *VI.F.2* (Kenyon 1960: 266); and once the Syro-Palestinian types with their

combination of Egyptian and Mesopotamian motifs had become established, there is no inherent reason to expect wholly Egyptian types to appear.

The only explanation that does justice to all the evidence is that foreigners brought either the pendants or the requisite knowledge and skills to manufacture them while in Palestine. Their introduction *primarily* via trade is ruled out by what appears to be a local gold jewelry industry established at Tell el-'Ajjul in LB IA, and by the occurrence of small numbers of Egyptian-related pendants in LB IB–IIA temples, burials, and residences, which most likely belonged to Egyptians resident in Palestine.

Some of the Syro-Palestinian and Egyptian-related types are unattested outside Late Bronze Palestine, and may have been manufactured locally: *I.C.3*, *I.D.2*, *II.A.1–2*, *II.B.1.b*, *II.B.2.a*, *II.B.3.a*, *III.A*, *III.F*, *III.H.1.c*, *III.H.5*, *IV.D.1–2*, *IV.F.3*, *IV.F.4* (*139–142*), *IV.H.1*, *IV.H.3.b* (*211–215*), *VI.A*, *VI.B.1* (*268*, *270–271*), *VI.C.*, *VI.F.3* (*335–338*), *VI.G.1*, and *VI.G.2.b*. This is very likely the case for most of the Syro-Palestinian types, since some Palestinian sites (Tell el-'Ajjul, Beth Shan, Lachish) were not far behind their northern sister towns, and probably had the technological and cultural ingenuity to devise new types. With regard to the unique Egyptian-related types (*I.C.3*, *I.D.2*, *III.H.1.c*, *III.H.5*, *IV.F.3*, and *IV.F.4* [*139–142*]), Palestinian craftsmen probably could not have imitated Egyptian motifs so closely; New Kingdom parallels may well appear in future exploration or with the fuller publication of excavated Egyptian sites.

Cypriot and Mycenaean pendant types are noticeably absent from the Late Bronze Palestinian repertoire,[5] whereas Syro-Palestinian types are certainly found in Cyprus and Greece (Maxwell-Hyslop 1971: 127–31; Åström and Åström 1972: 617–19; Higgins 1961: 68–89; Karageorghis 1976: 51–52). This is somewhat surprising in view of the amount of Cypriot and Mycenaean pottery that has been found in Palestine (Hankey 1967; Stubbings 1951; Gittlen 1981). One possible explanation is that Levantine traders controlled Mediterranean shipping. They carried native goods to Cyprus (and perhaps to the Aegean), and returned with only a select group of Cypriot and Mycenaean wares (cf. Bass 1973: 34–37; *contra* Muhly 1970). Magical or religious predilections may have militated against the Levantine traders (who were probably accustomed to wearing jewelry pendants) bringing back Cypriot or Mycenaean pendants.

3. Pendants: The Ultimate Attire

Late Bronze Age Palestinian jewelry pendants minimally had an ornamental function as elements of collars, necklaces, and earrings.[6] The evidence from Mesopotamia and Syria[7] and from Egypt,[8] where many of the pendant types were first developed, substantiates this firmly.

The evidence from Palestine itself is more inferential. Although pendants are found with burials, none are described as localized near the ears, necks, or chests of burials.[9] The occurrence of small numbers of pendants in habitational contexts is probably due to accidental loss or intentional deposition of the jewelry by the owners. The large collections of principally Egyptian-related types from LB IIB temple contexts go beyond an ornamental function. The pendants may have been used to adorn a cult statue,[10] or may represent votive offerings or taxes (Oren 1978: 1065). Although a mixed Egyptian–Palestinian cult was probably practiced in the Beth Shan and Lachish temples,[11] jewelry donations to the gods at these sites may have been a subtler form of Egyptian political control.

The magical or religious significance of the pendant types would require a separate study to do adequate justice to the subject. However, several general observations and proposals can be made here, which will serve to put this aspect of pendant study in its proper perspective for Late Bronze Age Palestine.

Brief comments about the magical/religious significance of the Egyptian-related pendant types have been included in the extended typological discussion of Chapters 2–7, since most of these types are unquestionably related to specific deities and hieroglyphs, which had definite meanings in New Kingdom Egypt (Helck and Otto 1975: 232–36). Only native Egyptians in Palestine probably attached the same significance to such pendants. For Palestinians, there may have been some appreciation of the Egyptian meaning, but there would always be the unconscious tendency to recast Egyptian ideas into forms more compatible to the Palestinian mind (e.g., $wḏ't$ = 'evil eye'[12]). While individual city–states or regions of Palestine may have been attached to specific gods, Syria-Palestine as a whole placed primary emphasis on central male and female deities (Negbi 1976: 141). This proclivity is apparent from the pendant evidence.

Thus, Types *II.B.1.a–2.b* probably represent one or more of the female deities for which there is textual attestation in Late Bronze Syria-Palestine: Astarte, Anath, Qadesh, Asherah, etc. (Albright 1939; 1961: 104–7; 1969: 73–75; Pritchard 1967; 83–87). Types *IV.D.1* and *VI.G.1–2* can also be plausibly connected with Ishtar (eight-rayed; plain, cutout, and with dots) and Shamash (four-rayed, six-rayed, and four straight rays with four curved rays), and presumably with their Syro-Palestinian counterparts, Astarte and Baal (Maxwell-Hyslop 1971: 140–49; Van Buren 1945b: 62–64). Type *VI.B.1* may represent Yerah or Nikkal (Maxwell-Hyslop 1971: 149–51; Van Buren 1945b: 60–62; cf. Yadin 1970: 199–231), probably the latter, for whom the Qatna inventories catalogue an incredibly rich collection of jewelry adorning the cult statue (Bottéro 1949).[13]

Other Syro-Palestinian pendant types are of more dubious interpretation. For example, Type *VI.E* (Double Spiral) has been variously explained as a chariot yoke, a headband or wig, scales, a Hittite ideogram meaning 'life,' and a fertility symbol, possibly the swaddling bands of a newborn or the vagina of Ninhursag (Van Buren 1945b: 106–8; Maxwell-Hyslop 1971: 106; Frankfort 1970: 108, n. 7).

The very schematic rendering of Syro-Palestinian pendant types makes identification with a particular deity or magical/religious concept much more difficult than for an Egyptian type, which were more naturalistically rendered. The faunal and floral types, many of which are Egyptian-related and which might be considered purely ornamental today, served important functions in ancient mythologies: in particular, the lotus, mandrake, falcon, fly, frog, lion, ram, bull, and cat. No doubt, they were thought to embody the divine numina (Eliade 1957; Mauss 1975; Otto 1950; Kramer 1961; Frankfort *et al.* 1949; Jacobsen 1976; Frankfort 1961).[14] Thus, one would be hard-pressed to find a Late Bronze Palestinian pendant that did not have some magical or religious significance. Since it has already been determined that the pendants were worn by deities and human beings, their purpose could only have been to enjoin divine favor and protection, also required by the gods themselves (Van Buren 1945b).

Palestinians were content to mix Syro-Palestinian and Egyptian pendant types in their temples, residences, and tombs (e.g., Loci 1068C, 1068D, 1234, and 1403 at Beth Shan; Fosse Temple II:D and III:E, Burial Pit 542 at Lachish; Tomb 1166 at Tell el-'Ajjul; Room 73, Stratum IV at Beth Shemesh). But this is the exception rather than the rule, and such evidence may also be a consequence of Egyptians living, worshipping, and ultimately being buried in Palestine, who were not adverse to their own form of syncretism (Kemp 1978: 12; Helck 1971: 446–73; Albright 1957: 223–24; 1963: 14, 16; Horn 1969).

When the northern and southern Palestinian distributions of Egyptian-related pendant types are examined more closely, certain preferences can be noted. Types *I.C.1–3*, *I.D.1–2*, *I.E.1–2*, *I.G.3*, *II.A.2*, *III.B*, *III.D*, *III.E*, *III.H.1.b*, *III.H.2*, *III.H.6*, *IV.A*, *IV.B*, *V.E.1.b*, and *V.E.1.d* are found only in the south. Types *I.A.1–2*, *I.B.1–2*, *I.F.1.a–2.b*, *I.G.4*, *I.G.6.a–c*, *III.G*, *III.H.1.c*, *III.H.3*, *III.H.5*, *IV.C*, *IV.F.3*, *V.A.2*, *V.B.2*, *V.C.1–3*, *V.E.1.c*, *V.D.2*, and *V.F.1* are restricted to the north. Approximately half of the types from each region are unique to that region, a pattern established by LB IIA and continuing through LB IIB.

Assuming a representative sample, such a pattern could be due to the preferences of either incoming Egyptians or the local Palestinian inhabitants. The former possibility is the more probable. Individuals and communities in Egypt identified themselves with specific deities (Černý 1952), and possibly certain Egyptian communities were transplanted to specific regions in Palestine. Egyptian pendant groups, matching the northern and southern Palestinian repertoires, have not yet been geographically delimited. However, many pendant types occur together at el-Amarna, which was built by workmen from all parts of Egypt. On the basis of the Amarna publications and Petrie's corpus (1914), approximately half to two-thirds of the New Kingdom Egyptian pendant types are documented in Late Bronze Palestine.

4. *Economic Value*

The pendants were inherently valuable and a repository of wealth. This is obvious for the gold, silver, and electrum pendants, which are often found in jewelry hoards buried beneath floors (for Egypt, see Černý 1954). It is less obvious for faience, which at least by LB IIA was being used for pendants, inlays, vessels, etc., and was presumably a cheaper substitute for the more expensive materials, including glass and semiprecious stones (Aldred 1971: 35–45). In Egypt alone, it would not be unreasonable to speak in terms of millions of faience beads and pendants (McKerrell 1972: 292). Palestine was not nearly so well-endowed, but one must be prepared to deal with thousands of faience beads (cf. McGovern forthcoming, which documents about 10,000 beads and more than 400 pendants from LB IIB levels at Beth Shan). Faience as a material may not have been particularly rare, but its use for pendants cannot be considered commonplace and its religious significance would have added to its value.

Since glass and semiprecious stones account for only 2 percent and 4 percent of the LB pendants, respectively, and were used infrequently for other purposes (e.g., only several hundred glass beads were found in the LB IIB levels at Beth Shan), they were probably treasured items.

The few examples of pendants in copper or bronze, bone, and common stones may have been experimental attempts to duplicate pendant types in less expensive materials; however, two of the copper-base pendant types (*III.F* and *VI.E*) are unique.

While temples could afford such luxuries (Peltenberg 1977: 185–88; Maxwell-Hyslop 1971: 32–57; Bottéro 1949), it would be the rare individual who could. This probably accounts for the relatively few burials and residences in Late Bronze Age Palestine that have yielded pendants. In addition to the LB IA hoards and burials at Tell el-'Ajjul, the following exceptions should be noted: Locus 5029, Area BB, Stratum IX, at Megiddo; Room 73 of Stratum IV at Beth Shemesh; and Building 53 of Stratum IV at Tell Abu Hawam. Richer contexts probably belonged to members of the upper class (political and religious leaders), while assemblages with one to three pendants may represent the middle class equivalent of the day. The distribution of pendants in the houses of the 'North Suburb' at el-Amarna (Frankfort and Pendlebury 1933: 78–97) and elsewhere in Egypt suggests that Egyptians had a higher standard of living than Palestinians or could procure faience pendants at less expense.

5. *Industries*

Given the fact that Palestinian Late Bronze Age pendant types generally originated outside Palestine, did Palestinians eventually begin to manufacture these pendants for themselves, did foreigners resident in Palestine produce some of them, or are all the LB Palestinian pendants strictly speaking imports?

The unique LB IA gold pendants found in jewelry hoards and burials at Tell el-'Ajjul have been frequently alluded to in this study. It has been proposed that workshops existed at this site. Since goldsmiths familiar with the same basic techniques and well-versed in combining Egyptian and Mesopotamian motifs produced similar jewelry pieces during the Middle Bronze Age at Levantine sites to the north (Byblos and Ras Shamra), it is very likely that some craftsmen had moved south to 'Ajjul by the mid-16th century B.C. (Maxwell-Hyslop 1971: 106–27; Negbi 1970: 37).

Especially if Tell el-'Ajjul is to be equated with Sharuhen (Kempinski 1974), the constant threat of Egyptian incursions would have predisposed the goldsmiths or their clients to protect their investments. MB III–LB IA hoards with similar pendant types, which were buried under floors, have been found at Ras Shamra, Byblos, and Gezer (see Types *II.B.2.a–b*, Chapter 3), very often in the vicinity of temples or palaces. The pairs of exquisite gold earrings from LB IA tombs at 'Ajjul may have belonged to the wives of local dynasts or priests.

In view of the strained relations between Palestine

and Egypt during the Late Bronze Age, gold may have been obtained through north Syrian sites, which were probably receiving it from farther east or perhaps even from Egypt (Maxwell-Hyslop 1971: lxiv; Drower 1970–75: 480).[15] Unfortunately, geological work has been relatively limited in the Middle East, so that it is very difficult to establish which raw material deposits were exploited in antiquity.[16] This stricture applies equally to the other metals, composite materials, and stones discussed below.

Silver and electrum were probably obtained through the same channels as gold, perhaps having been originally mined in Anatolia (Maxwell-Hyslop 1971: lxv–lxvi; Canby 1965: 54, n. 82; Prag 1978: 36, 40; Mishara and Meyers 1973).

As compared with LB IA, fewer precious metal pendants, which are moreover of a lower quality, are produced in the later Late Bronze Age. They are distributed throughout Palestine, and may have been manufactured in several small-scale workshops (Beth Shan, Lachish, and/or Tell el-'Ajjul?). Alternatively, the jewelry pieces may be the work of itinerant smiths, well-attested for the Early Bronze Age (Canby 1965). Late Bronze Age steatite molds have been found at Beth Shan (Rowe 1940: 93, pl. 71A:5; Locus 1234, inner sanctuary of the Level IX temple, Late Bronze Age), Tell Abu Hawam (Hamilton 1935: 58, no. 359; Locus 67, Stratum V, LB IIB, EB heirloom?), and Hazor (Yadin et al. 1961: pl. 158:31; Locus 366b, Area A, Stratum XIV, LB IIA, including a Cypriot bull's head mold?). Iron I examples occur at Beth Shemesh (Grant 1931: pl. 13; 1932: 30, pl. 47: 7–8; Stratum IV), Megiddo (Stratum VI, J. 36.1991), and Beth Shan (Rowe 1940: 90, pl. 53:8; Early Level VI). A widespread distribution of the several molds might be expected if itinerant smiths were responsible for the pendants.

The Egyptian-related faience pendants, which begin to appear in LB IB and reach a peak in LB IIB, pose a similar problem of manufacturing origin. The greater concentration of such pendants in southern Palestine during LB IB–IIA, although few in absolute numbers, argues for their importation. More accurately, individual Egyptians who wore the pendants probably left them behind during their stays in Palestine.

The much larger number of Egyptian-related types, primarily found in LB IIB temple contexts, points to local production at Lachish and Beth Shan. The increased Egyptian presence would obviously bring more pendants into the country, as well. A faience 'factory' need not be particularly elaborate or complex.[17] A furnace, capable of achieving ca. 900–1000°C, comparable to the temperature-range for well-fired pottery of the period (McGovern, In Press), is required. The necessary raw materials (sand, possibly with an admixture of lime; plant ash and/or a sodium salt) would have been readily available in Palestine. The most important prerequisite would be the know-how to mix the materials in the right proportions (ca. 98 percent silica and 2 percent alkali), possibly add a surface glaze, form the paste by hand or in a mold, and fire it correctly.

A mold can be made by pressing an existing pendant or a specially prepared form into a ball of soft clay and hardening it. One such mold for a fluted bead was found near the steps of Locus 1068, the upper altar room of the Level VII temple at Beth Shan (unpublished), and another example of a Bes mold comes from Tell el-'Ajjul (Petrie 1933: 42, pl. 16:42; unprovenanced, probably an LB II type, cf. Petrie 1894: pl. 17:290).

Faience factories may have been attached to temples in LB IIB Syria-Palestine and Mesopotamia (Peltenberg 1977). Once Egyptian garrisons had been set up at key points in Palestine, it would be expected that full advantage would be taken of any technological skills. Both parties to the arrangement, Palestinians and Egyptians, would benefit from such an arrangement. Thus, although the available evidence is minimal,[18] local faience industries were probably active at Beth Shan and other sites in LB IIB Palestine.

While the full study of the Beth Shan bead and pendant corpus is reserved for the Late Bronze Beth Shan volume (McGovern, forthcoming), several conclusions can be anticipated here. The Beth Shan faience is exclusively made by the efflorescence technique in which the glaze components, which were originally part of the batch mixture, migrate to the surface during drying and form a glaze upon firing (Noble 1969; Kiefer and Allibert 1971). To the extent that Egyptian New Kingdom faience has been studied, the same technique was employed there (Tite et al. 1983), as opposed to the cementation process of the Middle Kingdom (Vandiver 1982b), which entailed roasting the quartz particles in a glazing powder (Wulff, Wulff, and Koch 1968). Colorants derived from the Syro-Palestinian glass industry (see below), such as lead antimonate yellow and manganic purple, were applied as liquid slurries and fired.

Glass was a much rarer material than faience in Late Bronze Palestine, amounting to only 16 pendants, perhaps ten times that many beads, and approximately 15 vessels. Still, apart from two Syro-Palestinian pendant types (*II.B.1.a* and *VI.D.1*), which were probably imported from north Syria (Barag 1970: 140, 185, 187–89), the remaining Egyptian-related pendant types could have been made locally.

The technological step from faience production to glassmaking is not great. Temperature requirements are actually lower (ca. 600–700°C) as a result of the higher alklai content that acts as flux: ca. 65–70 percent silica plus 5–10 percent lime, 10–20 percent alkali, and as much as 10 percent colorant and/or opacifier (Brill 1970: 122; Petrie 1894: 25–27; Lucas 1962: 185; Davison 1972: 13–17).

Pieces of fused glass from the Level VII temple at Beth Shan (unpublished) make local production at this site a realistic possibility. The pendant and bead types appear to have been all formed by hand, using simple tools; swirled designs and overlays of different colored glass is common. Glass cloissons also appear on a unique LB IA type (*VI.C*) at Tell el-'Ajjul, implying that both glass-making and goldsmithing were known here in early LB.

Chemical provenancing of the raw materials in glass production has proved particularly difficult, because it is a complex mixture of several materials (Davison 1972: 8–11).[19] In the Beth Shan study, trace and minor elements associated with colorants have proved to be the most sensitive indicators. For example, copper oxide colorants exhibit higher levels of arsenic and iron, which may characterize the Timna smelting product (Craddock 1980). The copper may have been added to the batch mixture as a bronze refuse, since the tin to copper ratio most often is in the range of 1:10 to 1:20, comparable to Late Bronze tin bronzes. On the other hand, the trace elements associated with lead antimonate yellow (titanium, iron and zinc) are not sufficiently distinctive to delimit specific lead and antimony ore bodies in the Anatolian-Iranian highland region.

Semiprecious stones (primarily carnelian, but also turquoise, lapis lazuli, hematite, and variously colored yellow, green, and dark brown stones) were used for several pendant types. Carnelian and the unidentified stones (mostly quartz varieties) can be found in the desert regions of the Negev and Transjordan (Bender 1974: 167). A major outcropping of turquoise was exploited by the Egyptians at Serabit el-Khadem in the Sinai, and hematite occurs in Egypt (Lucas 1962: 395) and Transjordan (Coughenour 1976). Lapis lazuli had to be imported from Afghanistan or the Lake Baikal region (Lucas 1962: 398; Wilkinson 1971: 200; Aldred 1971: 15).

The stones, whether native or imported, were probably worked locally at various Palestinian sites. Smoothing mortars and unworked stones have been found in Levels VIII and VII at Beth Shan (unpublished), attesting to a stone workshop. A bow drill, which is known from Egypt, was probably also available in Palestine (Wilkinson 1971: 3, fig. 1).

Notes

1 For example, while the Early Bronze, Iron Age, and Roman/Byzantine cemeteries at Beth Shan were located on the north side of the Wâdi Jalud, the main Late Bronze cemetery was never found.

2 It is unfortunate that Level IX at Beth Shan cannot be more precisely dated, since it would undoubtedly contribute valuable evidence for the elucidation of cultural influences during LB IA and LB IB–IIA.

3 Aldred 1971: pl. 125 = Pritchard 1954: pl. 73. Many examples are illustrated in Egyptian tombs, e.g., dancers and an orchestra in the Tomb of Neb-Amun at Thebes (Aldred 1971: pl. 67). Tutankhamun was buried with numerous collars (Carter 1972: 146–57; cf. the listing in Murray and Nuttall 1963).

4 The specimen of Type *IV.F.1* from the 'dedicatory' fill of the LB II Amman Airport Building may be an isolated Egyptian-related type.

5 A Type *IV.F.4* example (*139*) from Beth Shemesh is a possible exception. Compare the palmette motif on a Late Cypriot II frontlet in Pierides 1971: pl. 6:1.

6 The utilitarian and pecuniary value of jewelry tends to be emphasized in modern Western culture, thus misconstruing the deeper significance that such personal possessions had and continue to have among the majority of mankind.

7 Conveniently, Maxwell-Hyslop 1971: figs. 59–60, 62a–c, 63a–b, 64, and 66; Oppenheim 1949; Van Buren 1945b.

8 Aldred 1971: 142–48, pls. 127, 132; Wilkinson 1971: 108, 121–28.

9 However, cf. Dothan 1979: 46, figs. 139 and 158.

10 For examples of cult figures which are shown wearing beads and pendants, see Negbi 1976: pls. 32:1438, 42:1563, 45:1631, 47:1644, 48:1646, 53:1701 and 54:1699, 1700; Yadin 1972: pl. 21.

11 No dedicatory inscriptions have been found in Late Bronze Palestinian temples, such as exist for the Hathor temples at Timna (Rothenberg 1972: 125–207) and Serabit el-Khadem (Petrie 1906b). A foundation deposit plaque suggests that a Ramesside temple to Isis was established at Tel Aphek (Giveon 1978: 26–27).

12 The Egyptian myth of the 'evil eye' (Borghouts 1973) is not evidenced in the contemporary Ugaritic literary corpus. However, it is clear from later Levantine texts (e.g., Iron Age amuletic plaques from Arslan Tash; Gaster 1973), continuing up to the present century (Macalister 1912: 449–50), that a representation of an eye was understood as warding off the 'evil eye' in Syria–Palestine.

13 The excavations at Qatna did not locate the temple, and failed to produce any of the jewelry. Jewelry collections in temples, however, are amply attested in northern Mesopotamia at Assur, Nuzi, Alalakh, and Tell al-Rimah (Peltenberg 1977).

14 Goodenough's *magnum opus* on Jewish symbols (1953–68) is relevant in this context, although his method of discovering the universal value of specific symbols has been questioned (Smith 1967; contrast Meyers 1976; Goff 1963, 1970).

15 For tribute lists, including gold jewelry, from Palestine during the 'Amarna Age,' see Knudtzon 1907–1914: letters 21, 22, and 25; cf. Bottéro 1949: 10–19; Helck 1971: 423–26; Ahituv 1978; Na'aman 1981).

16 Texts and inscriptions sometimes specify mining areas, describe industrial methods, and speak of trade and exchange of various raw materials and finished products (Lucas 1962: *passim*; Helck 1971: 370–434; Harris 1961; Ahituv 1978; Na'aman 1981). However, more detailed investigation is needed to establish the precise referents for the terms. Ideally, the latter should then be correlated with the available archaeological evidence (Maxwell-Hyslop 1971: lxiii, Limet 1960). Paintings and reliefs provide additional information.

17 Such an installation was discovered in the LB II–Iron I strata at Tyre (Bikai 1978: 7–8, 91–92).

18 In addition to the mold, a large piece of Egyptian Blue, a copper calcium silicate frit used as a colorant (Chase 1971), was found in the Level VII temple at Beth Shan (unpublished).

19 Glass also undergoes chemical changes (in particular, the leaching out of alkalies) by reacting with the immediate soil environment and groundwater (Dowman 1970: 26–27; Smith 1970: 622; Aspinall *et al*. 1972). The prospects and pitfalls that attend such studies are well illustrated by the statistical procedures to provenance the segmented faience beads from Europe and the Middle East, all approximately dated to the New Kingdom (Newton and Renfrew 1970; Aspinall *et al*. 1972; McKerrell 1972).

Chapter 9

CATALOGUE OF LATE BRONZE AGE PALESTINIAN PENDANTS

The catalogue of more than 847 pendants is arranged according to the System of Classification, with each major class divided into types. The classes are organized alphabetically as are the types within classes (except in the case of small and large, which are listed in that order). Under each type, the examples are arranged alphabetically by site, and dating within a site goes from the earliest examples to the latest.

LB I follows IB, LB II follows IIB, and specimens dated to the Late Bronze Age generally are listed last. In the case of Beth Shan, Level IX is listed before Levels VIII and VII, because it definitely includes earlier material and certain loci may eventually have to be dated earlier. Within the same Late Bronze phase, the examples are arranged by locus and field number. An asterisk before a catalogue number indicates that this writer has examined the example.

Following site and locus, the information for each specimen includes an assessment of the date, the material, dimensions, field number, museum number, and publication data. Qualifiers ('probably', 'possibly', 'perhaps') are used for dates about which there is some question due to insufficient and/or unpublished stratigraphic details or associated pottery and artifacts. Although the evidence is somewhat stronger in the case of a 'probably,' 'possibles' are still considered dated to the period indicated until new evidence or a reassessment of the available date becomes available.

The first-hand examination by the author of 75 percent of the Late Bronze Age pendants has made it possible to check the identifications of materials in site reports and to make the necessary changes that have been incorporated into the catalogue. This was especially necessary in the case of glass and faience, since a great deal of confusion has been created by terminological inconsistency. 'Faience' is in fact a misnomer, which referred originally to a type of glazed earthenware made in Faenza, Italy. Since the term has become standard in the archaeological literature, it is reluctantly retained here. 'Frit', 'pâté de verre', 'enamel', 'paste', and 'composition' are other loosely used descriptive terms for glass or faience found in the literature. An adequate terminology (faience, glassy faience, frit, and glass) can only be arrived at by using chemical and physical criteria (see Chapter 8). There is no set point at which 'glassy faience' becomes true glass, but this is not a crucial issue for Late Bronze Age glass and faience, which are normally quite distinct. If the glaze completely covers the surface of the pendant, it is sometimes difficult to decide whether the material is glass or faience; but such cases are rare and usually some surface area will show the core.

The colors given for the glass and faience might better have been cited by their Munsell equivalents (Munsell Color Company 1975) except that differential firing, leaching, and chemical changes have usually altered the coloring in such a way that a single pendant may exhibit various color hues, even though it was probably a single color at first. Under these circumstances, the dominant color, or what can be presumed to be the dominant color originally, is listed by its closest primary color or combination of primary colors with the understanding that the actual example may deviate to some extent from the norm.

It has not been possible to include precise definitions of alloys in this study, which would have been highly desirable for the electrum and copper or bronze. Similarly, stones, most of which can be considered semiprecious translucent quartz varieties (carnelian, sardonyx, onyx, etc.) have not been mineralogically identified. Where some doubt exists, only the color of the stone is given.

Quotation marks are used occasionally to query the identification of materials or colors of specimens which could not be personally examined (missing, discarded, disintegrated, etc.). If there appeared to be no reason to question the excavator's identification, it is recorded here without change.

The dimensions of each specimen are listed in the order of maximum length, width, and thickness; some dimensions are lacking when no measurement was available. Reference to the plates should resolve any difficulties. For multiple examples listed under the same catalogue number, the variation in dimensions, if any, is indicated. Where the listing would become excessively long, only the range of variation appears. Much of the variation is because of broken attachments and other imperfections.

Where available, field numbers are listed, and the present provenience by city, museum, and accession number if known. J.= Rockefeller Museum, Jerusalem; P.= University Museum, University of Pennsylvania, Pennsylvania; A.= Jordanian National Museum, Amman.

Only the principal reference(s) for line drawings and/or photographs are included. The line drawings and photographs of the Beth Shan pendants include all of the basic types for Levels IX–VII.

Catalogue of Ornamental
and Amuletic Pendants

I. Egyptian Deities

I.A.1 Baboon of Thoth – in profile
  *1. (Fig. 1, Pl. 1)
    Beth Shan; Level VII; 1068; LB IIB
    White glazed faience
    10×8×4 mm
    Field no. 25.11.132
    P. 29.104.330
    Unpublished
  2. Beth Shan; Level VII; 1068; LB IIB
    2 examples
    White glazed faience
    9×7×4 mm
    Field no. 25.11.127c–d
    J. – missing
    Unpublished

I.A.2 Baboon of Thoth – crowned with crescent and disc
  *3. (Pl. 1)
    Beth Shan; Level VII; 1068; LB IIB
    Blue-green glazed faience, faded
    33×15×11 mm
    Field no. 25.11.127a
    J. J944
    Unpublished
  *4. (Fig. 2)
    Beth Shan; Level VII; 1072; LB IIB
    White glazed faience
    26×14×10 mm
    Field no. 25.11.176
    P. 29.104.176
    Rowe 1940, pl. 33:15

I.B.1 Bes – standard
  *5. (Fig. 3, Pl. 1)
    Beth Shan; Level VII; 1072; LB IIB
    Blue-green glazed faience, faded
    16×9×5 mm
    Field no. 25.11.319
    P. 29.104.179
    Rowe 1940, pl. 33:13

  6. Lachish; Fosse Temple; Structure III; Room
    E; LB IIB
    Blue glazed faience
    16×7 mm
    London
    Tufnell, Inge, and Harding 1940, pl. 21:52
  *7. Megiddo; Sq. W 16; Tomb 877 A 1; LB IIB
    Blue-green glazed faience
    14×7×5 mm
    Field no. M 2607
    J. 34.1557
    Guy 1938, pl. 94:5
  *8. Megiddo; Sq. W 16; Tomb 877 B 1;
    probably LB IIB
    Blue-green glazed faience
    13×7×5 mm
    Field no. M 2461
    J. 34.1634; exhibit no. 1412
    Guy 1938, pl. 95:1
  *9. (Pl. 1)
    Megiddo; Sq. W 16; Tomb 877 B 1;
    probably LB IIB
    Blue-green glazed faience
    13×7×5 mm
    Field no. M 2831
    J. 34.1650; exhibit no. 1412
    Guy 1938, pl. 95:2

I.B.2 Bes – dancing in profile with tambourine
  10. (Fig. 4)
    Beth Shan; Level VII; 1068 (near steps);
    LB IIB
    'Green' glazed faience, faded
    14×8 mm
    Field no. 25.11.487
    P. 29.104.255 – missing
    Rowe 1940, pl. 33:21
  11. Beth Shan; Level VII; 1068 (near steps);
    LB IIB
    Blue-green glazed faience, faded
    Height: 13 mm

Field no. 25.11.489
P. – discarded
Unpublished

I.C.1 Hathor head or face – plain
*12. (Pl. 1)
    Lachish; Fosse Temple; Structure III;
      Room E; LB IIB
    7 examples
    Blue-green glazed faience, faded
    8×11 mm
    J. 34.3007, exhibit no. 1262; London, British
      Museum
    Tufnell, Inge, and Harding 1940, pl. 14 (upper)

I.C.2 Hathor head or face – with collar
*13. (Pl. 1)
    Lachish; Fosse Temple; Pit 246; possibly
      LB IIB
    Blue-green glazed faience, faded
    30×27×9 mm
    Field no. 6440
    London, Institute of Archaeology
    Tufnell, Inge, and Harding 1940, pl. 21:46

I.C.3 Hathor head or face – with flanking uraei
14. (Fig. 5)
    Tell el-ʿAjjul; north of tell; Tomb 1514;
      LB II
    Gold
    26×13 mm
    London
    Petrie 1932, pl. 3:27

I.D.1 Ptah-Sokar – standard
15. (Fig. 6)
    Lachish; Area 500; Sq. D 24; Tomb 502;
      LB IIB
    Green glazed faience
    21×15×9 mm
    Field no. 3423
    Disposition unknown
    Tufnell 1958, pl. 29:62

I.D.2 Ptah-Sokar – with black open disc on head
16. (Pl. 1)
    Lachish; Fosse Temple; 100 Houses; LB
      II
    Black and blue glazed faience
    35×11 mm
    Field no. 3086
    London
    Tufnell, Inge, and Harding 1940, pl. 21:51

I.E.1 Taurt – facing left
*17. (Fig. 7)
    Lachish; Area 4000: Sq. T.1; Cave 4004;
      probably LB IIB
    4 examples
    Blue-green glazed faience, faded
    19×7×4 mm
    Field no. 5819a
    Oxford, Ashmolean Museum
    Tufnell 1958, pl. 29:58

I.E.2 Taurt – facing right
18. (Fig. 8)
    Tell el-ʿAjjul; lower cemetery (northeast
      of tell); Tomb 1663; probably LB IIA
    Violet glazed faience
    26×9 mm
    Disposition unknown
    Petrie 1934, pl. 34:527

I.F.1.a Uraeus – standard; facing right
*19. Beth Shan; Level VIII; 1068 (below
      steps); LB IIB
    Blue-green glazed faience, faded
    21×14×3 mm
    Field no. 26.8.20
    P. 29.104.167
    Unpublished
*20. (Fig. 9, Pl. 1)
    Beth Shan; Level VIII; 1068 (below
      steps); LB IIB
    5 examples
    Blue-green glazed faience, faded
    19×13×3 mm
    Field no. 26.8.40
    P. 29.104.161–65
    Rowe 1940, pl. 34:42

I.F.2.a Uraeus – human-headed; facing left
21. (Fig. 10)
    Beth Shan; Level VII; 1070; LB IIB
    Faience
    24×7 mm
    Field no. 25.11.547
    P. 29.104.224 – missing
    Rowe 1940, pl. 33:7

I.F.2.b Uraeus – human-headed; facing right
*22. (Fig. 11, Pl. 1)
    Beth Shan; Level VIII; 1068 (below
      steps); LB IIB
    Blue-green glazed faience, faded
    21×14×3 mm

Field no. 26.8.20
P. 29.104.166
Rowe 1940, pl. 34:61

I.G.1.a Bastet or Sekhmet – head or face with collar
 *23. (Fig. 12)
       Lachish; Area 200; Sq. A.6; Tomb 216;
         LB IIA
       3 examples
       Blue-green glazed faience, faded
       11×5×2 mm
       Field no. 4679
       London, Institute of Archaeology
       Tufnell 1958, pl. 29:59

I.G.1.b Bastet or Sekhmet – standing figure
  24. Megiddo; Stratum VII B; Area AA; Sq.
         K 8; 2039; probably LB IIB
       Faience
       14×6 mm
       Field no. a 558
       Chicago, Oriental Institute
       Loud 1948, pl. 205:7
  25. Megiddo; Stratum VII B; Area AA; Sq. K 8;
         2039; probably LB IIB
       Faience
       Height: 12 mm; thickness: 5 mm
       Field no. a 557
       Chicago, Oriental Institute
       Loud 1948, pl. 205:8
  26. (Pl. 1)
       Megiddo; Stratum VII B; Area AA; Sq.
         K – L 7 – 8; E=2041; probably LB IIB
       Faience
       14×6 mm
       Field no. a 622
       Chicago, Oriental Institute
       Loud 1948, pl. 205:6

I.G.2.a Standard Bes or Ptah-Sokar – small
 *27. (Pl. 2)
       Beth Shan; Level IX; 1238; LB
       Mottled white glazed faience
       14×9×6 mm
       Field no. 28.11.373
       P. 29.104.232
       Unpublished
  28. Beth Shan; Level VIII; 1092; LB IIB
       White faience
       14×7×5 mm
       Field no. 26.8.153
       P. 29.104.188 – missing
       Unpublished

 *29. Beth Shan; Level VIII; 1068 (below
         steps); LB IIB
       White glazed faience
       13×7×5 mm
       Field no. 26.8.29
       P. 29.104.189
       Unpublished
 *30. (Fig. 13, Pl. 2)
       Beth Shan; Level VIII; 1072 (below
         steps); LB IIB
       White glazed faience
       16×8×5 mm
       P. 29.104.193
       Rowe 1940, pl. 34:55
  31. Beth Shan; Level VII; 1068; LB IIB
       2 examples
       Material unspecified
       Height: 14 mm and 15 mm
       Field no. 25.11.127e – f
       J. – missing
       Unpublished
 *32. (Pl. 2)
       Beth Shan; Level VII; 1072; LB IIB
       White glazed faience
       14×7×6 mm
       Field no. 25.11.177
       P. 29.104.279
       Rowe 1940, pl. 33:11
 *33. (Fig. 13, Pl. 2)
       Beth Shan: Level VII; 1072 (near
         northwestern magazine); LB IIB
       Blue-green glazed faience, faded
       17×9×5 mm
       Field no. 25.11.208
       P. 29.104.213
       Rowe 1940, pl. 33:12
  34. Beth Shan; Level VII; 1086; LB IIB
       'Blue' glazed faience
       14×13 mm
       Field no. 25.11.651
       Discarded
       Unpublished
  35. Megiddo; Stratum IX or later; Area BB;
         Sq. M 13; LB
       Faience
       14×6 mm
       Field no. d 639
       Chicago, Oriental Institute
       Loud 1948, pl. 205:2
  36. Tell Beit Mirsim; Stratum C; SE 23 C;
         possibly LB II
       Faience
       15×8 mm

Disposition unknown
Albright 1938b, pl. 39:2

I.G.2.b Standard Bes or Ptah-Sokar – large
 *37. (Fig. 14, Pl. 2)
      Beth Shan; Level VIII; 1068 (below
          floor); LB IIB
      Blue-green glazed faience, faded
      15×15×7 mm
      Field no. 26.8.63
      P. 29.104.228
      Rowe 1940, pl. 34:60
 *38. (Fig. 14, Pl. 2)
      Beth Shan; Level VII; 1068; LB IIB
      Blue-green glazed faience, faded
      28×15×7 mm
      Field no. 25.11.127b
      J. J945
      Unpublished
 *39. Beth Shemesh; Stratum IV (probably b);
          near V 26; probably LB II
      Blue glazed faience
      33×15 mm
      Field no. 1112
      Disposition unknown
      Grant 1931, pl. 20 (center)
 *40. (Fig. 14)
      Lachish; Area 500; Sq. A.25; Pit 542;
          LB II
      Blue-green glazed faience, faded
      32×15×7 mm
      London, Institute of Archaeology
      Tufnell 1958, pl. 29:63

I.G.3 Horus?
 *41. (Fig. 15)
      Tell el-'Ajjul; near LA; Tomb 447;
          probably LB I
      'Gray lazuli'
      24×12 mm
      J. 35.3783; exhibit no. 1188
      Petrie 1934, pls. 19:152, 20:152

I.G.4 Horus the Child or Ptah
 *42. (Fig. 16, Pl. 2)
      Beth Shan; Level VIII; 1108; LB IIB
      Blue-green glazed faience
      16×11×7 mm
      Field no. 26.11.7
      P. 29.104.225
      Rowe 1940, pl. 34:36
 *43. (Pl. 2)

Megiddo; Sq. W 16; Tomb 877 B 1;
    probably LB IIB
Blue-green glazed faience
28×11×8 mm
Field no. M 2460
J. 34.1633; exhibit no. 1412
Guy 1938, pl. 95:3

I.G.5 Taurt?
 44. Lachish; Fosse Temple; Pit 199;
         probably LB IIA
     Gray 'paste'
     24×9 mm
     London
     Tufnell, Inge, Harding 1940, pl. 35:89
 *45. (Pl. 3)
     Lachish; Fosse Temple; Structure III;
         Room E; LB IIB
     5 examples
     Blue-green glazed faience, faded
     12×6×1 mm
     London, British Museum
     Tufnell, Inge, and Harding 1940, pls.
         35:83, 14 (lower)
 *46. (Pl. 3)
     Lachish; Fosse Temple; Structure III; Room
         E; LB IIB
     Gray 'paste'
     27×9 mm
     Field no. 2635
     J. 34.3007; exhibit no. 1262
     Tufnell, Inge, and Harding 1940, pl.
         35:90
 47. (Pl. 3)
     Lachish; Fosse Temple; Structure III;
         Room E; LB IIB
     Gray 'paste'
     24×9 mm
     Field no. 2635
     London
     Tufnell, Inge, and Harding 1940, pl.
         35:89
 48. Lachish; Fosse Temple; Pit 172;
         probably LB IIB
     Gray 'paste'
     27×9 mm
     London
     Tufnell, Inge, and Harding 1940, pl.
         35:90
 *49 Tell el-'Ajjul; 'Eighteenth Dynasty'
         Cemetery; Tomb 1064; probably LB IIA
     Yellow glazed faience
     16×5×3 mm

London, Institute of Archaeology
Petrie 1932, pl. 8:182

I.G.6.a Standing figure – female
  *50. (Fig. 17, Pl. 3)
      Beth Shan; Level VIII; 1072 (below
        steps); LB IIB
      Blue-green glazed faience, faded
      22×11×8 mm
      Field no. 26.8.5c
      P. 29.104.226
      Rowe 1940, pl. 34:58

*I.G.6.b.i Standing figure holding scepter – missing head
and upper torso; sex uncertain*
  *51. (Fig. 18, Pl. 3)
      Beth Shan; Level VII; 1087; LB IIB
      Blue-green glazed faience, faded
      21×12×8 mm
      Field no. 25.11.304
      P. 29.104.280
      Unpublished
  *52. Beth Shan; Level VII; 1263; LB IIB
      Blue-green glazed faience, faded
      19×11×5 mm
      Field no. 27.11.10
      P. 29.104.219
      Unpublished
  *53. (Fig. 18, Pl. 3)
      Beth Shan; Level VII; 1284; LB IIB
      Blue-green glazed faience, faded
      26×10×13 mm
      Field no. 27.11.173
      P. 29.104.217
      Unpublished
   54. Beth Shan; Level VII; 1284; LB IIB
      White glazed faience
      12×7 mm
      Field no. 27.11.159b
      P. – missing
      Unpublished

I.G.6.b.ii Standing figure holding scepter – ram-headed
  *55. (Fig. 19, Pl. 4)
      Beth Shan; Level VII; 1072; LB IIB
      Blue-green glazed faience, faded
      30×14×10 mm
      Field no. 25.11.231
      P. 29.104.222
      Rowe 1940, pl. 33:17

I.G.6.c Standing figure – sex uncertain
   56. (Fig. 20)

      Beth Shan; Level VIII; 1072 (below
        steps); LB IIB
      Faience
      32×10×10 mm
      Field no. 26.8.5b
      P. 29.104.181 – missing
      Rowe 1940, pl. 34:56

I.G.7 Uraeus?
   57. (Pl. 4)
      Lachish; Fosse Temple area; LB
      Green glazed faience
      21×16×13 mm
      Field no. 2635a
      London
      Tufnell, Inge, and Harding 1940, pl. 21:45

II. Human Forms

II.A.1 Head or face – crude
  *58. (Fig. 21)
      Beth Shan; Level IX; 1322; LB
      Gold
      32×7 mm
      Field no. 27.12.12
      J. J1051
      Unpublished
   59. (Pl. 4)
      Tell Beit Mirsim; Stratum C; SE 22 C–8;
        probably LB IIB
      Dark stone
      35×16 mm
      Field no. 1397
      J. 18994 – missing
      Albright 1938b, pl. 39:1

II.A.2 Head or face – bearded
  *60. (Pl. 4)
      Lachish; Fosse Temple; Room D –
        below altar; LB IIB
      Gold
      27×9 mm
      Field no. 5335
      J. 36.2261
      Tufnell, Inge, and Harding 1940, pl.
        26:5

II.A.3 Head or face – with Egyptian wig
  *61. (Pl. 4)
      Lachish; Area 4000; Sq. T.3; Pit 4013; LB IIB
      Green glazed faience
      22×26 mm
      Field no. 6005

J. 37.826
Tufnell 1958, pl. 29:64

II.B.1.a Standing figure – pictorial female figurine
  62. (Pl. 5)
    Beth Shan; Level IX; 1390; LB
    Green glass
    49×22×17 mm
    Field no. 28.11.1
    J.
    Rowe 1940, pl. 68A:7
  63. (Pl. 5)
    Megiddo; Stratum IX; Area BB; Sq. M.
      13; 5029; probably LB IA
    Glass
    30×22 mm
    Field no. d 100
    Chicago, Oriental Institute
    Loud 1948, pl. 241:4
  64. Unassigned

II.B.1.b Standing figure – pictorial female plaque
  65. (Fig. 23, Pl. 5)
    Beth Shan; Level IX; 1403; LB
    Gold
    47×21 mm
    Field no. 28.11.52
    J. I3810; exhibit no. 1252
    Rowe 1940, pl. 68A:5

II.B.2.a Standing figure – representational female; cut-out figurine plaque
  66. (Pl. 5)
    Tell el-ʿAjjul; EAA?; Hoard 1299; probably
      Town II; probably LB IA
    Gold and electrum
    105×24 mm
    J. 35.3841; exhibit no. 1160
    Petrie 1934, pls. 13:6, 14:6
  67. (Fig. 24)
    Tell el-ʿAjjul; TV (above 910); Hoard
      1312; probably Town II; probably LB IA
    Gold
    80×18 mm
    Oxford, Ashmolean Museum
    Petrie 1934, pls. 19:134, 20:134; Petrie,
      Mackay, and Murray 1952, pl. B:17

II.B.2.b Standing figure – representational female plaque
  68. (Pl. 5)
    Lachish; Fosse Temple; Structure II;
      Room D; LB IIA

Gold
23×9 mm
Field no. 4126
J. 36.1831; exhibit no. 1267
Tufnell, Inge, and Harding 1940, pl.
    26:4
  69. (Pl. 5)
    Megiddo; Stratum VIII; Area BB;
      Sq. 0 14: probably LB IB–IIA
    Gold
    66×25 mm
    Field no. b 11
    Chicago, Oriental Institute
    Loud 1948, pl. 213:68
  70. (Fig. 25, Pl. 5)
    Tell el-ʿAjjul; EAA?; Hoard 1299;
      probably Town II; probably LB IA
    Gold
    97×60 mm
    J. 35.3842; exhibit no. 1157
    Petrie 1934, pls. 13:8, 14:8
  71. (Pl. 6)
    Tell el-ʿAjjul; EAA?; Hoard 1299,
      probably Town II; probably LB IA
    Gold
    71×14 mm
    J. 35.3843; exhibit no. 1158
    Petrie 1934, pls. 13:9, 14:9
  72. (Pl. 6)
    Tell el-ʿAjjul; GDF 921; Hoard 277;
      probably Town II; probably LB IA
    Gold
    79×43 mm
    Oxford, Ashmolean Museum
    Petrie, Mackay, and Murray 1952, pls. B:17,
      6:12
  73. Tell el-ʿAjjul; GDF 921; Hoard 277;
      probably Town II; probably LB IA
    Gold
    46×23 mm
    Disposition unknown
    Petrie, Mackay, and Murray 1952, pl.
      6:14
  74. (Pl. 6)
    Tell el-ʿAjjul; GDF 921; Hoard 277;
      probably Town II; probably LB IA
    Gold
    91×53 mm
    London, British Museum
    Petrie, Mackay, and Murray 1952, pls.
      B:17, 6:13, 8:1

II.B.3 Pictorial figure plaque – sex uncertain

*75. (Fig. 26)
   Beth Shan; Level VIII; 1068 (below
      floor); LB IIB
   Gold
   43×16 mm
   Field no. 26.8.67
   P. 29.105.57
   Rowe 1940, pl. 34:57
*76. (Pl. 6)
   Tell Abu Hawam; Stratum V; Sq. D 6;
      probably LB IIB
   Gold
   36×12 mm
   J. 34.239; exhibit no. 1291
   Hamilton 1935, pl. 39:1, fig. 416 (p. 64)

III. Fauna

III.A Falcon
*78. Tell el-'Ajjul; GDF 921; Hoard 277;
      probably Town II; probably LB IA
   2 examples
   Gold
   Diameter: 33 mm
   London, British Museum; Cambridge,
      Fitzwilliam Museum
   Petrie, Mackay, and Murray 1952,
      pls. B:20, 6:1, 3
*79. (Fig. 27, Pl. 6)
   Tell el-'Ajjul: GDF 921; Hoard 277;
      probably Town II; probably LB IA
   Gold
   43×45 mm
   J. 38.535
   Petrie, Mackay, and Murray 1952, pls.
      6:2, 8:4

III.B Fish
80. (Fig. 28)
   Lachish; Area 4000; Sq. T.2; Pit 4019;
      LB IIA
   Faience
   13×6×2 mm
   Disposition unknown
   Tufnell 1958, pl. 29:60
81. (Fig. 28)
   Lachish; Area 500; Sq. A.24; Pit 556;
      LB IIB
   Faience
   17×11×4 mm
   Field no. 3867a
   Disposition unknown
   Tufnell 1958, pl. 29:61

III.C Fly
*82. (Fig. 29, Pl. 6)
   Tell el-'Ajjul; TV; Hoard 1313;
      probably Town II; probably LB IA
   4 examples
   Gold
   12×8 mm
   J. 35.3906–7; exhibit no. 1185
   Petrie 1934, pls. 15:63–66, 16:63–66;
      Petrie, Mackay, and Murray 1952,
      pls. B:26, 8:2

III.D Frog or toad
*83. (Pl. 6)
   Tell el-'Ajjul; TDK 885; Town II;
      probably LB I
   Carnelian
   26×16×13 mm
   J. 35.4280; exhibit no. 1415
   Petrie 1934, pl. 8 (middle, right)

III.E Hippopotamus
*84. (Fig. 30)
   Tell el-'Ajjul; near LA; Tomb 447;
      probably LB I
   Amethyst
   20×8 mm
   J. 35.3783; exhibit no. 1188
   Petrie 1934, pls. 19:153, 20:153

III.F Lion fighting bull or dog
*85. (Fig. 31, Pl. 7)
   Beth Shan; Level IX; 1235; LB
   Copper or bronze
   125×111×42 mm
   Field no. 27.10.328
   J. M1056
   Rowe 1940, pl. 71A:1

III.G Ram's head
86. Beth Shan; Level VIII; 1068 (below
      steps); LB IIB
   Glass, mottled
   22×13×8 mm
   Field no. 25.11.443
   P. 29.104.191 – missing
   Rowe 1940, pl. 33:1
*87. (Fig. 32, Pl. 7)
   Beth Shan; Level VIII; 1068 (below
      steps); LB IIB
   Brown, white, and blue glass, mottled
   19×15×12 mm

Field no. 25.11.393
P. 29.104.190
Rowe 1940, pl. 33:2

88. Beth Shan; Level VII; 1068 (north of
      steps); LB IIB
Blue and brown glass, mottled
18×17 mm
Field no. 25.11.422
J. – missing
Unpublished

★89. (Fig. 32, Pl. 7)
Beth Shan; Level VII; 1086; LB IIB
White and brown glass, mottled
20×16×11 mm
Field no. 25.11.394
P. 29.104.192
Unpublished

III.H.1.a Bird – dove?
90. (Pl. 8)
Megiddo; Stratum VIII; Area BB; Sq. 0 15;
      Tomb 3016; probably LB IB–IIA
White stone
18×12 mm
Field no. b 135
Chicago, Oriental Institute
Loud 1948, pl. 205:5

III.H.1.b Bird – goose or duck
91. (Pl. 8)
Lachish; Fosse Temple area; LB
Blue glazed faience
23×20 mm
Field no. 3081
London
Tufnell, Inge, and Harding 1940, pl. 21:44

III.H.1.c Bird – owl?
★92. (Fig. 33, Pl. 8)
Beth Shan; Level VIII, 1068 (below
      steps); LB IIB
4 examples
Blue-green glazed faience, faded
23×13×2 mm
Field no. 26.8.41
P. 29.104.184–86, 227
Rowe 1940, pl. 34:41

III.H.2 Bull?
★93. (Pl. 8)
Lachish; Fosse Temple; Structure III;
      Room E; LB IIB
Yellow glazed faience

11×9 mm
J. 34.7744; exhibit no. 1266
Tufnell, Inge, and Harding 1940, pl. 21:53

III.H.3 Cat?
★94. (Fig. 34, Pl. 8)
Beth Shan; Level VII; 1382 (near wall);
      LB IIB
Green stone
25×19×9 mm
Field no. 28.10.381
J. I3908; exhibit no. 1374
Rowe 1929a: fig. on p. 65

III.H.4 Dog?
95. (Pl. 8)
Megiddo; Stratum IX; Area AA; Sq.
      L 7; 4004; probably LB IA
Faience
21×20 mm
Field no. a 1060
Chicago, Oriental Institute
Loud 1948, pl. 205:4

III.H.5 Mouse?
★96. (Fig. 35, Pl. 8)
Beth Shan; Level IX; 1326; LB
Blue-green glazed faience, faded
14×6×9 mm
Field no. 27.12.175
P. 29.104.171
Unpublished

III.H.6 Ram?
★97. (Pl. 8)
Tell el-'Ajjul; '18th Dynasty' Cemetery;
      Tomb 1037; probably LB IIA
Silver
20×21 mm
J. 32.1873; exhibit no. 1414
Petrie 1932, pl. 8:176

IV. Flora

IV.A Cornflower or corn cockle
★98. (Pl. 9)
Lachish; Fosse Temple; Structure III;
      Room E; LB IIB
25 examples
Blue-green and purple glazed faience, faded
28×12×5 mm
Field no. 2635
J. 34.3006, exhibit no. 1262; London,

British Museum
Tufnell, Inge, and Harding 1940, pls.
14, 36:93

IV.B Daisy

99. Gezer; Stratum 5B/5A; Field I; Area 2;
Locus 2009.1; probably LB IIB
White and yellow 'frit'
Diameter: 14 mm; thickness: 2 mm
Disposition unknown
Dever, Lance, and Wright 1970, pl. 36:9

*100. Lachish; Fosse Temple; Structure III;
Room D; Shrine 181; LB IIB
White and yellow glazed faience
19×16×5 mm
J. 34.7694
Tufnell, Inge, and Harding 1940, pl. 36:92

*101. (Pl. 9)
Lachish; Fosse Temple; Structure III;
Room E; LB IIB
2 examples
White and yellow glazed faience
19×16×5 mm
Field no. 2635
London, British Museum
Tufnell, Inge, and Harding 1940, pls. 14
(upper), 36:92

IV.C Date fruit

102. Beth Shan; Level VIII; 1068 (below
floor); LB IIB
'Light green' faience
18×6 mm
Field no. 26.8.130o
J. – missing
Unpublished

*103. (Fig. 36, Pl. 9)
Beth Shan; Level VII; 1068 (near steps);
LB IIB
14 examples
Blue-green glazed faience
22×9×2 mm; 23×8×3 mm
Field no. 25.11.495
P. 29.104.288 and J. 36.1647
Unpublished

IV.D.1 Flower or rosette – eight-rayed

*104. (Pl. 9)
Lachish; Fosse Temple; Structure III;
Room E; LB IIB
Gold
17×15 mm
Field no. 2968
J. 34.7732

Tufnell, Inge, and Harding 1940, pl. 26:9

*105. (Fig. 37)
Lachish; Area 200; Sq. A.6; Tomb 216;
LB IIA
Gold
14×13 mm
Field no. 4661
London, Institute of Archaeology
Tufnell 1958, pls. 25:24, 54:27

IV.D.2 Flower or rosette – 12-rayed

*106. (Pl. 9)
Lachish; Fosse Temple area; LB
Gold
23×21 mm
Field no. 3044
London, Institute of Archaeology
Tufnell, Inge, and Harding 1940, pl. 26:13

IV.D.3 Flower or rosette – 24-rayed

*107. (Pl. 9)
Lachish; Fosse Temple; Pit 176; LB IIB
Blue glazed faience
Diameter: 12 mm
Field no. 2635
J. 34.3007; exhibit no. 1262
Tufnell, Inge, and Harding 1940, pl. 36:101

IV.E Grape cluster

*108. Lachish; Fosse Temple; Structure III;
Room E; LB IIB
8 examples
Purple glazed faience
19×11×6 mm
Field no. 2635
J. 34.3007, exhibit no. 1262; London,
British Museum
Tufnell, Inge, and Harding 1940, pls. 14
(upper), 36:94

*109. Lachish; Fosse Temple; Structure III;
Room D; Shrine 181; LB IIB
Purple glazed faience
19×11×6 mm
J. 34.7693
Tufnell, Inge, and Harding 1940, pl. 36:94

110. (Pl. 9)
Megiddo; Sqs. U–V 19; Tomb 36 B;
probably LB IIA
Gray faience
17×9×4 mm
Field no. x 525 a
Chicago, Oriental Institute
Guy 1938, pl. 156:7

IV.F.1 Lotus bud

*111. Amman Airport Building; dedicatory
      fill; probably LB II
      Gold
      18×12 mm
      A. 5879
      Jordanian Department of Antiquities 1975: fig.
      28 (bottom row, second from left)

*112. (Fig. 38, Pl. 9)
      Beth Shan; Level VII; 1068; LB IIB
      White glazed faience
      20×15×4 mm
      Field no. 25.11.125
      J. J943
      Rowe 1940, pl. 33:28

113. (Pl. 9)
      Lachish; Fosse Temple; Pit 248; LB IIA
      2 examples
      Probably blue glazed faience
      12×9 mm
      London
      Tufnell, Inge, and Harding 1940, pls.
      35:88, 36:103

114. (Pl. 9)
      Megiddo; Stratum VIII; Area BB;
      Sq. 0 13–14; S=2048; probably LB IB–IIA
      Dark blue faience
      14×10 mm
      Field no. a 314
      Chicago, Oriental Institute
      Loud 1948, pl. 213:72

*115. Tell el-'Ajjul; '18th Dynasty' Cemetery;
      Tomb 1064; probably LB II
      4 examples
      Yellow glazed faience
      13×9×3 mm
      London, Institute of Archaeology
      Petrie 1932, pl. 8:181

*116. Tell el-'Ajjul; '18th Dynasty' Cemetery;
      Tomb 1073; probably LB IIA
      9 examples
      Gold
      9×7 mm
      J. 32.1919; exhibit no. 1202
      Petrie 1932, pls. 1 (bottom, right), 3:35

117. Tell el-'Ajjul; '18th Dynasty' Cemetery;
      Tomb 1085; possibly LB IIA
      Probably gold
      9×7 mm
      Belfast
      Petrie 1932, pl. 3:35

IV.F.2 Lotus – conventional

*118. Beth Shan; Level IX; 1092 (below threshold);
      LB
      Blue-green glazed faience, faded
      23×20×3 mm
      Field no. 27.9.416
      P. 29.104.266
      Unpublished

*119. Beth Shan; Level IX; below 1092; LB
      5 examples
      Blue-green glazed faience, faded; 1 white
      glazed
      E.g., 25×16×4 mm, 25×19×5 mm,
      28×16×4 mm
      Field no. 27.9.444–48
      P. 29.104.203–205, 265, 325
      Unpublished

120. Beth Shan; Level IX; 1233; LB
      Faience
      Field no. 27.10.37
      P. – missing
      Unpublished

*121. Beth Shan; Level IX; 1241; LB
      Blue-green glazed faience, faded
      22×16×3 mm
      Field no. 27.10.434
      P. 29.104.273
      Unpublished

*122. Beth Shan; Level VIII; 1092; LB IIB
      White glazed faience
      20×10×3 mm
      Field no. 27.9.408
      P. 29.104.267
      Unpublished

*123. Beth Shan; Level VIII; 1092; LB IIB
      Blue-green glazed faience, faded
      24×16×3 mm
      Field no. 27.9.467
      P. 29.104.269
      Unpublished

*124. Beth Shan; Level VIII; 1068 (below
      steps); LB IIB
      Blue-green glazed faience, faded
      22×17×3 mm
      Field no. 26.8.22b
      P. 29.104.258
      Rowe 1940, pl. 34:44

125. Beth Shan; Level VIII; 1068 (below
      floor); LB IIB
      'Light green' faience
      23×17×2 mm
      Field no. 26.8.82g
      J. – missing
      Unpublished

*126. Beth Shan; Level VII; 1068 (near steps);
LB IIB
77 examples
Blue-green glazed faience, some faded
E.g., 22×14×3 mm, 29×19×4 mm,
31×23×4 mm
Field no. 25.11.483
J. 36.1645
Unpublished

*127. Beth Shan; Level VII; 1072; LB IIB
Blue-green glazed faience, mottled and faded
22×15×3 mm
Field no. 25.11.341
P. 29.104.259
Rowe 1940, pl. 33:40

*128. Beth Shan; Level VII; 1072 (west side);
LB IIB
White glazed faience
20×17×4 mm
Field no. 26.8.135h
P. 29.104.263
Unpublished

129. Beth Shan; Level VII; 1089; LB IIB
Blue-green glazed faience, faded
18×16 mm
Field no. 25.11.442
P. – discarded
Unpublished

130. Beth Shan; Level VII; 1262; LB IIB
Faience
31×20 mm
Field no. 27.10.841a
P. – missing
Unpublished

*131. (Fig. 39, Pl. 10)
Beth Shan; Level VII; 1359; LB IIB
Blue-green glazed faience, faded
32×19×3 mm
Field no. 28.9.312
P. 29.104.327
Unpublished

132. Beth Shan; Level VII; 1365; LB IIB
Faience
25×18×5 mm
Field no. 28.9.311
P. – discarded
Unpublished

133. Lachish; Fosse Temple; Structure II;
Room D; LB IIA
Blue-green glazed faience
Number of examples unspecified
37×23×6 mm
Disposition unknown

Tufnell, Inge, and Harding 1940, pl. 36:91

*134. Lachish; Fosse Temple; Structure III;
Room E; LB IIB
21 examples
Blue-green glazed faience, faded
37×23×6 mm
Field no. 2635
J. 34.3007, exhibit no. 1262; London,
British Museum
Tufnell, Inge, and Harding 1940, pls. 14
(lower), 36:91

IV.F.3 Lotus flower
*135. (Fig. 40, Pl. 10)
Beth Shan; Level IX; 1403; LB
Gold
31×24 mm
Field no. 28.11.37
P. 29.105.30
Rowe 1929c, pl. 8:6

*136. (Fig 40, Pl. 10)
Beth Shan; Level IX; 1403; LB
Gold
47×31 mm
Field no. 28.11.52
J. I3811
Rowe 1929c, pl. 8:7

IV.F.4 Lotus palmette
*137. (Fig. 41, Pl. 10)
Beth Shan; Level VIII; 1068 (below
steps); LB IIB
Blue-green glazed faience, faded
19×13×2 mm
Field no. 26.8.22c
P. 29.104.328
Rowe 1940, pl. 34:45

138. Beth Shan; Level VIII; 1068 (below
floor); LB IIB
2 examples
'Light green' faience
24×15 mm
Field no. 26.8.130l
J. – missing
Unpublished

139. (Fig. 41)
Beth Shemesh; Stratum IV; Sq. W 27;
Room 73; probably LB IIB
8 examples
Gold
23×21 mm
Disposition unknown
Grant 1931, pl. 18 (second row, center); Grant

1932, pl. 49:19; Tadmor and Misch – Brandl
1980: fig. 9

*140. Lachish; Fosse Temple; Structure II;
       Room D; LB IIA
       Gold
       24×17 mm
       Field no. 4128
       London, Institute of Archaeology
       Tufnell, Inge, and Harding 1940, pl. 26:6

 141. (Pl. 10)
       Lachish; Fosse Temple area; LB
       Gold
       22×20 mm
       London
       Tufnell, Inge, and Harding 1940, pl. 26:7

*142. (Fig. 41, Pl. 10)
       Tell el-'Ajjul; TV (above 910); Hoard 1312;
         probably Town II; probably LB IA
       Gold
       37×35 mm
       J. 35.3880; exhibit no. 1331
       Petrie 1934, pls. 19:141, 20:141

IV.F.5.a Lotus seed vessel – flat

*143. (Fig. 42, Pl. 11)
       Beth Shan; Level VIII; 1068 (below
         steps); LB IIB
       Carnelian
       17×9×3 mm
       Field no. 26.8.22f
       P. 29.104.211
       Unpublished

 144. Megiddo; Tomb 877 C 1; probably LB
       IB–IIA
       Carnelian
       14×8×4 mm
       Field no. M 2949
       Chicago, Oriental Institute
       Guy 1938, pl. 96:14

IV.F.5.b Lotus seed vessel – round

*145. (Fig. 43, Pl. 11)
       Beth Shan; Level VIII; 1292; LB IIB
       Blue-green glazed faience
       15×6 mm
       Field no. 27.11.265
       P. 29.104.335
       Unpublished

*146. Beth Shan; Level VIII; 1300; LB IIB
       Blue glazed faience
       19×7 mm
       Field no. 27.11.261b
       P. 29.104.337

Unpublished

*147. Beth Shan; Level VIII; 1072 (below
         steps); LB IIB
       Carnelian
       13×5 mm
       Field no. 26.8.13
       P. 29.104.340
       Unpublished

*148. Beth Shan; Level VII; 1068; LB IIB
       3 examples
       Carnelian
       13×4 mm; 15×7 mm; 16×5 mm
       Field no. 25.11.124a
       P. 29.104.341
       Unpublished

*149. Beth Shan; Level VII; 1072; LB IIB
       Carnelian
       15×6 mm
       Field no. 25.11.189a
       J. 36.1634
       Unpublished

*150. (Pl. 11)
       Beth Shan; Level VII; 1251; LB IIB
       Carnelian
       15×5 mm
       Field no. 27.10.577
       P. 29.104.336
       Unpublished

*151. Beth Shemesh; Stratum IV; W 27; Room
         73; probably LB IIB
       10 examples
       Carnelian
       15×7 mm
       J. I5914
       Grant 1932, pl. 49:45

 152. Lachish; Area 4000; Sq. T.3; Pit 4013;
       LB IIB
       Carnelian
       13×2 mm
       Disposition unknown
       Tufnell 1958: pl. 29:43

*153. Lachish; Structure III; Fosse Temple;
         Room E; LB IIB
       Material and size unspecified
       J. 34.3007
       Unpublished

 154. Lachish; Area 4000; Sq. S.1; Cave 4002; LB II
       3 examples
       Red glazed faience
       13×7 mm
       Field no. 6949
       Disposition unknown
       Tufnell 1958, pl. 29:43

*155. (Pl. 11)
Megiddo; Sq. W 16; Tomb 877 B 1;
    probably LB IIB
Carnelian
13×5 mm
Field no. M 2464
J. 34.1637
Guy 1938, pl. 95:27

*156. Megiddo; Tomb 912 B; probably LB IIB
Carnelian
18×7 mm
Field no. M 2997
J. 34.1890
Guy 1938, pl. 132:10

*157. Megiddo; Tomb 989 C 1; LB IIB
2 examples
Carnelian
19×8 mm
Field no. M 2840
J. 34.2104–5; exhibition no. 1086
Guy 1938, pl. 100:18a–b

*158. Tell Abu Hawam; Stratum V; Sq. D 4;
    Building 53; probably LB II
4 examples
3 blue-green glazed faience, faded; 1 red glass
12×5 mm; 13×7 mm
J. 34.329
Hamilton 1935, pl. 25:h (group 399)

159. Tell el-'Ajjul; '18th Dynasty' Cemetery;
    Tomb 1080; LB IIA
Gold
6×2 mm
London
Petrie 1932, pl. 8:177

IV.G.1 Mandrake fruit – small
*160. Beth Shan; Level IX; 1232; LB
Blue-green glazed faience
13×14×3 mm
Field no. 27.10.88
P. 29.104.271
Unpublished

*161. Beth Shan; Level VIII; 1092; LB IIB
Blue-green glazed faience, faded
12×14×3 mm
Field no. 27.9.468
P. 29.104.270
Unpublished

*162. (Fig. 44, Pl. 11)
Beth Shan; Level VIII; 1287; LB IIB
Blue-green glazed faience, faded
18×11×3 mm
Field no. 27.12.15

P. 29.104.251
Unpublished

*163. Beth Shan; Level VIII; 1068 (below
    steps); LB IIB
Blue-green glazed faience, faded
13×12×2 mm
Field no. 26.8.35b
J. J976b
Unpublished

164. Beth Shan; Level VIII; 1068 (below
    floor); LB IIB
Yellow and blue faience
13×10 mm
Field no. 26.8.130v
J. – missing
Rowe 1940, pl. 34:50

*165. Beth Shan; Level VIII; 1068 (below
    steps); LB IIB
Yellow and blue glazed faience
13×10×2 mm
Field no. 26.8.35a
J. J976a
Unpublished

*166. Beth Shan; Level VII; 1068 (near steps);
    LB IIB
Yellow and blue glazed faience
13×11×2 mm
Field no. 25.11.453
J.
Unpublished

*167. Beth Shan; Level VII; 1068 (near steps);
    LB IIB
4 examples
Blue-green glazed faience
16×11×2 mm
Field no. 25.11.484
P. 29.104.285
Unpublished

*168. Beth Shan; Level VII; 1068 (near steps);
    LB IIB
5 examples
Blue-green glazed faience
17×10 mm; 20×12 mm
Field no. 25.11.488
P. 29.104.286–87; J. 36.1646
Unpublished

169. Beth Shan; Level VII; 1068 (north of
    steps); LB IIB
2 examples
Yellow frit and blue glaze
14×11×2 mm; 15×11×2 mm
Field no. 25.11.423
P. 29.104.311

Unpublished
*170. (Pl. 11)
     Lachish; Fosse Temple; Structure III;
        Room E; LB IIB
     11 examples
     Yellow and blue glazed faience
     18×14×6 mm
     J. 34.3007, exhibit no. 1262; London,
        British Museum
     Tufnell, Inge, and Harding 1940, pls. 14 (top),
        36:96

IV.G.2 Mandrake fruit – large
*171. Beth Shan; Level IX; below 1092; LB
     Blue-green glazed faience, faded
     25×19×5 mm
     Field no. 27.9.447
     P. 29.104.325
     Unpublished
 172. Beth Shan; Level IX; 1233; LB
     Faience
     21×17×4 mm
     Field no. 27.10.137
     P. – missing
     Unpublished
 173. Beth Shan; Level IX; 1234; LB
     Faience
     23×21×4 mm
     Field no. 27.10.140
     P. 29.104.683 – missing
     Unpublished
*174. Beth Shan; Level IX; 1234; LB
     White glazed faience
     19×18×4 mm
     Field no. 27.10.128
     P. 29.104.272
     Unpublished
*175. Beth Shan; Level IX; 1234; LB
     Blue-green glazed faience
     21×16 mm
     Field no. 27.10.173
     J. 36.1682
     Unpublished
 176. Beth Shan; Level IX; 1240; LB
     'Light brown and light blue' faience
     14×12 mm
     Field no. 27.10.384
     J. J1026 – missing
     Unpublished
*177. Beth Shan; Level VIII; 1092; LB IIB
     Blue-green glazed faience
     26×21×4 mm
     Field no. 27.9.404

P. 29.104.326
Unpublished
178. Beth Shan; Level VIII; 1068 (below east
        wall); LB IIB
     White faience
     16×14×4 mm
     Field no. 27.9.464
     P. 29.104.268 – missing
     Unpublished
179. Beth Shan; Level VIII; 1068 (below
        floor); LB IIB
     'Light green' faience, faded
     26×16×2 mm
     Field no. 26.8.130n
     J. – missing
     Unpublished
*180. (Fig. 45, Pl. 11)
     Beth Shan; Level VII; 1068 (near steps);
        LB IIB
     67 examples
     Blue-green glazed faience, many faded
     E.g., 20×15×2 mm, 25×21×4 mm,
        28×21×5 mm
     Field no. 25.11.484
     P. 29.104.285
     Unpublished
*181. Beth Shan; Level VII; 1072 (west side);
        LB IIB
     3 examples
     Blue-green glazed faience, faded
     19×17×3 mm; 22×17×2 mm;
        24×16×1 mm
     Field no. 26.8.135a
     P. 29.104.260–62
     Rowe 1940, pl. 34:52
*182. Beth Shan; Level VII; 1072 (west side);
        LB IIB
     Blue-green glazed faience, faded
     18×17×2 mm
     Field no. 26.8.135g
     P. 29.104.264
     Rowe 1940, pl. 34:51
183. Beth Shan; Level VII; 1107; LB IIB
     'Light blue glass'
     20×20×2 mm
     Field no. 26.9.158b
     P. – discarded
     Unpublished
184. Beth Shan; Level VII 1359; LB IIB
     'Green' faience, faded
     19×18 mm
     Field no. 28.9.294
     P. – discarded

Unpublished
185. Beth Shan; Level VII; 1362; LB IIB
'White-green' faience
14×13 mm
Field no. 28.10.3c
Disposition unknown
Unpublished
186. Beth Shan; Level VII; 1362; LB IIB
White faience
23×21 mm
Field no. 28.9.331
P. – discarded
Unpublished
*187. Beth Shan; Level VII; 1366; LB IIB
Blue-green glazed faience
24×18 mm
Field no. 28.9.340a
P. 29.104.323
Unpublished
*188. Lachish; Fosse Temple; Structure III;
Room E; LB IIB
17 examples
Blue-green glazed faience, faded
24×20×6 mm
Field no. 2635
J. 34.3007, exhibit no. 1262; London,
British Museum
Tufnell, Inge, and Harding 1940, pls. 14
(lower), 36:95

IV.H.1 Bud?
*189. (Fig. 46, Pl. 12)
Beth Shemesh; Stratum IV; Sq. W 27;
Room 73; probably LB IIB
4 examples
Gold
39×14 mm
Field no. 1064
P. 61.14.707; J. I5937
Grant 1931, pl. 18 (top, center); Grant 1932,
pl. 49:22; Tadmor and Misch-Brandl 1980:
fig. 6

IV.H.2 Lotus flower?
190. (Fig. 47)
Beth Shan; Level VIII; 1108; LB IIB
'Blue' glazed faience
49×19×14 mm
Field no. 26.10.504
Disposition unknown
Unpublished
*191. (Pl. 12)
Lachish; Fosse Temple; Structure III;

Room E; LB IIB
3 examples
Blue-green glazed faience, faded
19×16×2 mm
Field no. 2635
J. 34.3007; exhibit no. 1262
Tufnell, Inge, and Harding 1940, pls.
14, 36:100

IV.H.3.a Petal or leaf – plain
192. Beth Shan; Level IX; below 1092; LB
'White faience with green edge'
17×7×3 mm
Field no. 27.9.443
P. 29.104.310 – missing
Unpublished
193. Beth Shan; Level IX; 1092 (below
threshold); LB
Blue-green glazed faience, faded
16×6×3 mm
Field no. 27.9.417
P. 29.10.310 – missing
Unpublished
*194. Beth Shan; Level IX; 1234; LB
Faience
17×6×3 mm
Field no. 27.10.141
Disposition unknown
Unpublished
195. Beth Shan; Level IX; 1234; LB
Faience
14×7×3 mm
Field no. 27.10.151
Disposition unknown
Unpublished
*196. (Pl. 12)
Beth Shan; Level IX; 1234; LB
Blue-green glazed faience, faded
16×8×2 mm
Field no. 27.10.338a
P. 29.104.247
Unpublished
*197. Beth Shan; Level VIII; 1072 (below
steps); LB IIB
Blue-green glazed faience
19×7×2 mm
Field no. 26.8.8c
P.—missing
Unpublished
198. (Fig. 48, Pl. 12)
Beth Shan; Level VII; 1068 (near steps);
LB IIB
41 examples

Blue-green glazed faience, some faded
28×9×3 mm
Field no. 25.11.496
P. 29.104.322; J. – missing
Rowe 1940, pl. 33:32

*199. Beth Shan; Level VII; 1072 (west side);
    LB IIB
    Blue-green glazed faience
    15×7×2 mm
    Field no. 26.8.135f
    P. 29.104.250
    Unpublished

*200. Beth Shan; Level VII; 1262; LB IIB
    Blue-green glazed faience, faded
    25×9×3 mm
    Field no. 27.10.841b
    P. 29.104.248
    Unpublished

*201. Beth Shan; Level VII; 1284; LB IIB
    Blue-green glazed faience, faded
    16×6×3 mm
    Field no. 27.11.159a
    P. 29.104.249
    Unpublished

202. Beth Shan; Level VII; 1284; LB IIB
    'Green' glazed faience
    19×6×2 mm
    Field no. 27.11.186
    P. – missing
    Unpublished

*203. Dhahrat el-Humraiya; Sq. c/6; Grave 57;
    LB II
    23 examples
    Gold
    10×4 mm
    J. 44.311
    Ory 1948, pl. 33.16

*204. Lachish; Fosse Temple; Structure III; Room
    E; LB IIB
    Number of examples unspecified
    Yellow glazed faience
    13×7×5 mm
    Field no. 2635
    J. 34.3007; exhibit no. 1262
    Tufnell, Inge, and Harding 1940, pl. 36:98

*205. Lachish; Fosse Temple; Structure III;
    Room E; LB IIB
    Number of examples unspecified
    Blue glazed faience
    26×8×4 mm
    Field no. 2635
    J. 34.3007; exhibit no. 1262
    Tufnell, Inge, and Harding 1940, pl. 36:99

206. Lachish; Fosse Temple; Pit 172;
    probably LB IIB
    Bronze
    16×9 mm
    London
    Tufnell, Inge, and Harding 1940, pl. 26:1

207. (Pl. 12)
    Lachish; Fosse Temple; Pit 176;
    probably LB IIB
    Silver
    24×12 mm
    London
    Tufnell, Inge, and Harding 1940, pl. 26.2

208. Lachish; Fosse Temple area; LB
    Blue glazed faience
    18×11 mm
    London
    Tufness, Inge, and Harding 1940, pl. 35:86

IV.H.3.b Petal or leaf – decorated

*209. (Fig. 49, Pl. 13)
    Beth Shan; Level VIII; 1068 (below
        floor); LB IIB
    2 examples
    Gold with brown and white glass
    20×9×2 mm
    Field no. 26.8.97
    J. J935a–b; exhibit no. 1254
    Rowe 1940, pl. 34:16

210. Beth Shan; Level VIII; 1062 (below
        south wall); LB IIB
    White and yellow glazed faience
    30×8×3 mm
    Field no. 26.9.171
    P. 29.104.334
    Unpublished

*211. (Fig. 49, Pl. 13)
    Beth Shan; Level VII; 1068 (north of
        steps); LB IIB
    Gold
    23×9 mm
    Field no. 25.11.433
    P. 29.105.43
    Unpublished

*212. (Pl. 13)
    Lachish; Fosse Temple area; LB
    2 examples
    Gold
    15×5 mm
    London, Institute of Archaeology
    Tufnell, Inge, and Harding 1940, pl. 26:8

*213. (Pl. 13)
    Lachish; Fosse Temple area; LB

Gold
29×8 mm
London, Institute of Archaeology
Tufnell, Inge, and Harding 1940, pl. 26:3

*214. Tell el-'Ajjul; GDF 321; Hoard 277; probably
    Town II; probably LB IA
    2 examples
    Gold
    34×5 mm
    Cambridge, Fitzwilliam Museum;
       London, British Museum
    Petrie, Mackay, and Murray 1952,
       pls. B:15, 6:19-20

*215. (Fig. 49, Pl. 13)
    Tell el-'Ajjul; TV (above 910); Hoard 1312;
       probably Town II; probably LB IA
    2 examples
    Gold
    26×8 mm
    J. 35.3888; exhibit no. 1126
    Petrie 1934, pl. 20:144

IV.H.4 Reeds?

*216. (Fig. 50, Pl. 13)
    Beth Shan; Level VII; 1068 (near steps);
       LB IIB
    Dark blue glazed faience
    21×7×3 mm
    Field no. 25.11.475
    P.29.104.311
    Rowe 1940, pl. 33:44

*217. Lachish; Fosse Temple; Structure III;
       Room E; LB IIB
    15 examples
    Purple glazed faience
    23×13×4 mm
    Field no. 2635
    J. 34.3007, exhibit no. 1262; London,
       British Museum
    Tufnell, Inge, and Harding 1940, pls. 14
       (upper), 36:97

*218. Tell Abu Hawam: Stratum V; Sq. D 4;
       Building 53; probably LB II
    4 examples
    Blue-green glazed faience, faded
    25×8 mm
    J. 34.329
    Hamilton 1935, pl. 25:e (group 399)

V. Egyptian Hieroglyphs

V.A.1 'ankh – standard
*219. (Fig. 51)

Beth Shan; Level VII; 1255; LB IIB
White glazed faience
15×10×2 mm
Field no. 27.11.92
P. 29.104.246
Unpublished

*220. (Pl. 14)
    Tell Abu Hawam; Stratum V; Sq. D 4;
       Building 53; probably LB II
    3 examples
    Faience
    23×10 mm
    J. 34.329
    Hamilton 1935, pl. 25:g (group 399)

V.A.2 'ankh – holding two was scepters
*221. (Fig. 52, Pl. 14)
    Beth Shan; Level VII; 1068; LB IIB
    Blue-green glazed faience, faded
    20×10×3 mm
    Field no. 25.11.126
    P. 29.104.210
    Rowe 1940, pl. 33:26

V.B.1 ḏd – standard
222. Beth Shan; Level IX; 1234; LB
    'Green' faience
    26×11×4 mm
    Field no. 27.12.247
    P. 29.104.239 – missing
    Unpublished

*223. (Fig. 53, Pl. 14)
    Beth Shan; Level VII; 1068 (near steps); LB
       IIB
    18 examples
    Blue-green glazed faience, some faded
    E.g., 20×9×4 mm, 24×10×3 mm
       26×10×4 mm
    Field no. 25.11.486
    P. 29.104.194, 196–202; J. J940
    Rowe 1940, pl. 33:27

*224. (Pl. 14)
    Tell Abu Hawam; Stratum V; Sq. D 4;
       Building 53; probably LB II
    2 examples
    Faience
    22×8 mm
    J. 34.329
    Hamilton 1935, pl. 25:g (group 399)

225. Tell el-'Ajjul; '18th Dynasty' Cemetery;
       Tomb 1080; LB IIA
    Material unspecified
    14×6 mm

London
Petrie 1932, pl. 8:179

V.B.2 ḏd – holding two was scepters
226. (Fig. 54)
Beth Shan; Level VIII; 1068 (below
    floor); probably LB IIB
3 examples
'Light green' faience
20×12 mm
Field no. 26.8.130p
J. 36.1645 – missing
Rowe 1940, pl. 34:63

V.C.1 ḥeḥ – facing left
227. Beth Shan; Level IX; 1232; LB
White faience
12×8 mm
Field no. 27.10.41
P. – discarded
Unpublished
*228. (Pl. 14)
Beth Shan; Level IX; 1234; LB
Blue-green glazed faience, faded
15×9×2 mm
Field no. 27.10.147
P. 29.104.235
Unpublished
*229. Beth Shan; Level IX; 1234; LB
Blue-green glazed faience, faded
15×9×2 mm
Field no. 27.10.339
P. 29.104.234
Unpublished
*230. (Fig. 55)
Beth Shan; Level VII; 1072 (west side);
    LB IIB
2 examples
Blue-green glazed faience, faded
18×10×1 mm
Field no. 26.8.135
P. 26.104.168
Rowe 1940, pl. 34:59

V.C.2 ḥeḥ – facing right
*231. (Pl. 14)
Beth Shan; Level IX; 1235; LB
Blue-green glazed faience, mottled
13×10×1 mm
Field no. 27.10.293
P. 29.104.237
Unpublished

V.C.3 ḥeḥ – direction uncertain
*232. Beth Shan; Level IX; 1234; LB
Blue-green glazed faience, faded
9×7×1 mm
Field no. 27.10.340
P. 29.104.236
Unpublished

V.D.1 tit – standard
*233. (Pl. 15)
Beth Shan; Level IX; 1234 (east of
    room); LB
Blue-green glazed faience, faded
19×10×3 mm
Field no. 27.12.271
P. 29.104.243
Unpublished
234. (Fig. 56)
Beth Shan; Level VIII; 1092; LB IIB
'Light green glass'
28×10×2 mm
Field no. 26.8.143b
J. 36.1645 – missing
Rowe 1940, pl. 34:37
*235. (Fig. 56, Pl. 15)
Beth Shan; Level VII; 1068 (near steps);
    LB IIB
10 examples
Blue-green glazed faience
E.g., 20×11×3 mm, 25×10×4 mm,
    26×9×3 mm
Field no. 25.11.493
P. 29.104.278; J. J941
Rowe 1936, no. A. 51

*236. Tell Abu Hawam; Stratum V; Sq. D 4;
    Building 53; probably LB II
Faience
22×7 mm
J. 34.329
Hamilton 1935, pl. 25:g (group 399)

V.D.2 tit – simplified
237. Beth Shan; Level IX; below 1092; LB
White faience
15×9×2 mm
Field no. 27.9.441
P. – discarded
Unpublished
*238. (Fig. 57, Pl. 15)
Beth Shan; Level VIII; 1092; LB IIB
Blue-green glazed faience, faded
19×8×1 mm

Field no. 27.9.469
P. 29.104.310
Unpublished

*239. Beth Shan; Level VIII; 1068 (below
     steps); LB IIB
Blue-green glazed faience, faded
17×9×2 mm
Field no. 26.8.22d
P. 29.104.245
Rowe 1940, pl. 34:46

V.E.1.a wḏ't – right eye; standard
*240. (Fig. 58, Pl. 15)
Beth Shan; Level VIII; 1068 (below
     steps); LB IIB
Blue-green glazed faience, faded
24×15×5 mm
Field no. 25.11.377
P. 29.104.187
Rowe 1940, pl. 33:22
*241. (Fig. 58, Pl. 15)
Beth Shan; Level VII; 1072; LB IIB
White glazed faience
15×11×4 mm
Field no. 25.11.340
P. 29.104.183
Rowe 1940, pl. 33:23
*242. (Fig. 58, Pl. 15)
Beth Shan; Level VII; 1252; LB IIB
White glazed faience, mottled
13×10×3 mm
Field no. 27.10.544
P. 29.104.170
Unpublished
*243. Lachish; Area 4000; Sq. T.1; Cave 4004;
     probably LB IIB
2 examples
Red glazed faience
26×11 mm
Field no. 5826
Oxford, Ashmolean Museum
Tufnell 1958, pl. 29:57
*244. (Pl. 15)
Lachish; Area 4000; Sq. U.3; Tomb
    4011; LB IIB
Yellow glazed faience
13×10×4 mm
J. 37.752
Unpublished
*245. Megiddo; Sq. W 16; Tomb B 1;
     probably LB IIB
Blue-green glazed faience
14×10 mm

Field no. M 2462
J. 34.1635
Guy 1938, pl. 95:4

V.E.1.b wḏ't – right eye; with nfr on back
*246. (Fig. 59, Pl. 15)
Lachish; Fosse Temple; Structure II; Room E;
    LB IIA
Blue and white glazed faience
13×11 mm
Field no. 3256
J. 36.1810; exhibit no. 1273
Tufnell, Inge, and Harding 1940, pl. 32A–B: 18

*V.E.1.c wḏ't – right eye; with probable disc-crowned
uraeus*
247. (Fig. 60)
Beth Shan; Level VIII; 1068 (below floor); LB
    IIB
'Light green' faience
15×10 mm
Field no. 26.8.130q
J. 36.1645 – missing
Rowe 1940, pl. 34:64

V.E.1.d wḏ't – right eye; simplified
248. Tell el-'Ajjul; Northeast Fosse; Tomb
    1166; LB II
2 examples
Carnelian
10×6 mm; 14×9 mm
Disposition unknown
Petrie 1932, pls. 25:109, 125

V.E.2.a wḏ't – left eye; standard
*249. (Fig. 61, Pl. 15)
Lachish; Area 500; Sq. A.25–26; Pit
    555; LB
Blue glass
31×23 mm
J. 36.1824
Tufnell 1958, pl. 29:56
*250. (Pl. 15)
Tell Abu Hawam; Stratum V; Sq. D 5;
    LB II
Blue glazed faience, faded
51×32 mm
J. 34.233; exhibit no. 1292
Hamilton 1935, pl. 35:404

V.F.1 ḥst?
*251. Beth Shan; Level IX; 1232; LB
Blue glazed faience
21×10×4 mm

Field no. 27.10.88
P. 29.104.271 – missing
Unpublished

252. Beth Shan; Level IX; 1234 (east side of room);
     LB
     'Greenish' faience
     22×8×3 mm
     Field no. 27.12.270
     P. 29.104.318 – missing
     Unpublished

*253. (Fig. 62)
     Beth Shan; Level VIII; 1068 (below
        steps); LB IIB
     Blue-green glazed faience, faded
     20×8×3 mm
     Field no. 26.8.22a
     P. 29.104.247
     Rowe 1940, pl. 34:43

*254. (Pl. 16)
     Beth Shan; Level VII; 1068 (near steps);
        LB IIB
     4 examples
     Blue-green glazed faience
     29×7×3 mm
     Field no. 25.11.488
     P. 29.104. 286–87; J. 36.1646
     Unpublished

*255. (Pl. 16)
     Beth Shan; Level VII; 1068 (near steps);
        LB IIB
     5 examples
     Blue-green glazed faience
     20×10×3 mm
     Field no. 25.11.492
     P. 29.104.381
     Unpublished

V.F.2 ib?
*256. (Fig. 63, Pl. 16)
     Beth Shan; Level VII; 1086; LB IIB
     White glass with yellow and white
        latitudinal bands
     24×18×11 mm
     Field no. 25.11.343
     P. 29.105.744
     Unpublished

257. (Pl. 16)
     Lachish; Fosse Temple area; LB
     Carnelian
     17×11 mm
     London
     Tufnell, Inge, and Harding 1940, pl. 35:87

V.F.3 nfr?
*258. (Fig. 64, Pl. 16)
     Beth Shan; Level VII; 1068 (near steps);
        LB IIB
     6 examples
     Blue-green glazed faience
     E.g., 23×9×3 mm, 27×8×3 mm
     Field no. 25.11.494
     J. 38.1185
     Unpublished

*259. Dhahrat el-Humraiya; Sq. e/4; Grave 8;
     LB IIA
     30 examples
     Gold
     18×4 mm
     J. 44.303
     Ory 1948, pl. 13:17

VI. Geometric Forms

VI.A Circular crescent with granular clusters
*260. (Fig. 65, Pl. 17)
     Tell el-'Ajjul; EAA?: Hoard 1299;
        probably Town II; probably LB IA
     2 examples
     Gold
     Diameter: 35 mm
     J. 35.3849; exhibit no. 1153
     Petrie 1934, pls. 13:30–31, 14:30–31

*261. (Fig. 65, Pl. 17)
     Tell el-'Ajjul; EAA?; Hoard 1299;
        probably Town II; probably LB IA
     2 examples
     Gold
     Diameter: 45 mm
     J. 35.3847; exhibit no. 1154
     Petrie 1934, pls. 13:28–29, 14:28–29; Petrie,
        Mackay, and Murray 1952, pl. B:23

*262. (Fig. 65, Pl. 17)
     Tell el-'Ajjul; EAA?; Hoard 1299;
        probably Town II; probably LB IA
     2 examples
     Gold
     Diameter: 33 mm
     J. 35.3848; exhibit no. 1155
     Petrie 1934, pl. 13:26–27, 14:26–27

*263. Tell el-'Ajjul; GD 793; Tomb 1998;
     probably Town II; probably LB IA
     2 examples
     Gold
     Diameter: 25 mm
     J. 38.493
     Petrie, Mackay, and Murray 1952,

pl. 7:23–24

*264. Tell el-'Ajjul; GDF 921; Hoard 277;
probably Town II; probably LB IA
2 examples
Gold
Diameter: 39 mm
Cambridge, Fitzwilliam Museum;
Oxford, Ashmolean Museum
Petrie, Mackay, and Murray 1952, pls. B:23,
6:4–5

*265. (Fig. 65, Pl. 17)
Tell el-'Ajjul; TV (above 910); Hoard 1312;
probably Town II: probably LB IA
2 examples
Gold
Diameter: 30 mm
J. 35.3882
Petrie 1934, pls. 19:132–33, 20:132–33

*266. (Fig. 65, Pl. 17)
Tell el-'Ajjul; TV; Hoard 1313;
probably Town II; probably LB IA
Gold
Diameter: 32 mm
J. 35.3910; exhibit no. 1182
Petrie 1934, pls. 15:67, 16:67

VI.B.1 Crescent or horns – standard

267. (Fig. 66)
Beth Shan; Level IX; 1234; LB
Silver
15×30 mm
Field no. 27.10.124
P. 29.105.149 – missing
Unpublished

268. (Fig. 66)
Beth Shan; Level VIII; 1068 (below
floor); LB IIB
Gold
21×20 mm
Field no. 26.8.58
P. 29.105.46 – missing
Rowe 1940, pl. 34:12

*269. (Fig. 66, Pl. 18)
Beth Shan; Level VIII; 1068 (below
floor); LB IIB
Gold
11×10×1 mm
Field no. 26.8.59
P. 29.105.55
Rowe 1940, pl. 34:13

*270. (Fig. 66, Pl. 18)
Beth Shan; Level VII; 1085; LB IIB
Gold

25×23 mm
Field no. 25.11.311
Probably J. J933
Rowe 1940: pl. 30:53

*271. (Fig. 66)
Beth Shemesh; Stratum IV; Sq. W 27;
Room 73; probably LB IIB
2 examples
Gold
24×27 mm
J. I5933; P.
Grant 1931, pl. 18 (second row, left and right;
Grant 1932, pl. 49:20; Tadmor and Misch-
Brandl 1980: fig. 8a

*272. (Fig. 66)
Beth Shemesh; Stratum IV; Sq. W 27;
Room 73; probably LB IIB
Probably gold
12×15 mm
J. I5934
Grant 1931, pl. 18 (fourth row, second from
left); Tadmor and Misch-Brandl 1980: fig. 8b

*273. (Fig. 66)
Lachish; Area 500; Sq. A.25; Pit 542;
LB II
Gold
10×10 mm
Field no. 3737
J. 36.1819; exhibit no. 1268
Tufnell 1958, pl. 25:65

*274. (Pl. 18)
Megiddo; Sq. U 17; Tomb 1145 B; LB I
Silver
16×15 mm
Field no. M 3573
Guy 1938, pl. 152:11

275. (Pl. 18)
Megiddo; Stratum VII B; Area AA; Sq.
K 6; 3187; probably LB IIB
Bronze
79×90 mm
Field no. b 561
Chicago, Oriental Institute
Loud 1948, pl. 213:80

*276. Tell el-'Ajjul; AN 748; Town II;
probably LB IA
Gold
22×39 mm
London, British Museum
Petrie 1933, pls. 14:29, 15:29

277. Tell el-'Ajjul; AT 659–760; probably
Town II; probably LB IA
Silver

28×38 mm
London
Petrie 1931, pls. 13:43, 15:1

*278. (Fig. 66, Pl. 18)
Tell el-ʿAjjul; EAA?; Hoard 1299;
    probably Town II; probably LB IA
Silver
14×22 mm
J. 35.3858; exhibit no. 1167
Petrie 1934, pls. 13:12, 14:12

279. (Fig. 66)
Tell el.ʿAjjul; EAA?; Hoard 1299;
    probably Town II; probably LB IA
Silver
13×18 mm
Disposition unknown
Petrie 1934, pl. 14:11

280. Tell el-ʿAjjul; EAA?; Hoard 1299;
    probably Town II; probably LB IA
Silver
25×43 mm
Disposition unknown
Petrie 1934, pl. 12 (top, center)

281. Tell el-ʿAjjul; EAA?; Hoard 1299;
    probably Town II; probably LB IA
Silver
17×33 mm
Disposition unknown
Petrie 1934, pl. 11:4 (bottom)

*282. Tell el-ʿAjjul; EAD 877; probably
    Town II; probably LB IA
2 examples
Silver
Width: 30 mm and 29 mm
J. 47.413/1–2
Unpublished

283. Tell el-ʿAjjul; ECE 785; probably
    Town II; probably LB IA
Material unspecified
30×36 mm
Disposition unknown
Petrie 1934, pl. 34:524

284. Tell el-ʿAjjul; LH⁴ 976; Palace II;
    probably LB IA
Silver
14×27 mm
Disposition unknown
Petrie 1933, pl. 14:33

285. Tell el-ʿAjjul; LK 1002; Palace IIIA; probably
    LB IA
Electrum
12×23 mm
Disposition unknown

Petrie 1933, pls. 14:31, 15:31

286. Tell el-ʿAjjul; NB 995; Palace II or IIIA;
    probably LB IA
Probably bronze
24×21 mm
Disposition unknown
Petrie 1932, pl. 18:241

*287. (Fig. 66, Pl. 18)
Tell el-ʿAjjul; TV (above 910); Hoard 1312;
    probably Town II; probably LB IA
Silver
33×64×10 mm
J. 35.3902; exhibit no. 1137
Unpublished

*288. Tell elʿAjjul; TV (above 910); Hoard 1312;
    probably Town II; probably LB IA
Silver
10×19 mm
J. 35.3902; exhibit no. 1137
Unpublished

*289. Tell el-ʿAjjul; TV (above 910); Hoard 1312;
    probably Town II; probably LB IA
Gold
21×34 mm
J. 35.3878; exhibit no. 1129
Petrie 1934, pls. 19:128, 20:128

*290. (Fig. 66, Pl. 19)
Tell el-ʿAjjul; TV (above 910); Hoard 1312;
    probably Town II; probably LB IA
Gold
10×14 mm
J. 35.3879; exhibit no. 1130
Petrie 1934, pls. 19:154, 20:154

*291. (Fig. 66, Pl. 19)
Tell el-ʿAjjul; west of LA; Grave 447; probably
    LB IA
Onyx
18×22 mm
J. 35.3789; exhibit no. 1190
Petrie 1934, pls. 19:154, 20:154

292. Tell el-ʿAjjul; '18th Dynasty' Cemetery; Tomb
    1502; probably LB I
Silver
21×30 mm
Ipswich
Petrie 1932, pl. 3:29

293. (Fig. 66)
Tell el-ʿAjjul; west end of tell; Grave 425;
    probably LB IB–IIA
Gold
13×14 mm
Disposition unknown
Petrie 1934, pl. 20:174

*294. Tell el-'Ajjul; MO 1040; probably Palace IIIB;
       probably LB IIA
   Silver
   30×72×5 mm
   London, British Museum
   Petrie 1933, pl. 14:32

295. Tell el-'Ajjul; '18th Dynasty' Cemetery; Tomb
       1080; probably LB IIA
   Gold
   11×11 mm
   Disposition unknown
   Petrie 1932, pl. 3:22

*296. (Pl. 19)
   Tell el-'Ajjul; '18th Dynasty' Cemetery; Tomb
       1095; probably LB IIB
   Gold
   13×12 mm
   J. 32.1941; exhibit no. 1213
   Petrie 1932, pls. 3:22, 5 (third row, left)

297. Tell el-'Ajjul; Northeast Fosse; Tomb 1166;
       LB II
   Probably gold
   14×16 mm
   Newcastle
   Petrie 1932, pl. 3:23

VI.B.2 Crescent or horns – with disc
*298. (Fig. 67, Pl. 19)
   Beth Shan; Level VIII; 1301; LB IIB
   Blue-green glazed faience, faded
   20×19×4 mm
   Field no. 27.11.268
   P. 29.104.274
   Unpublished

*299. Beth Shan; Level VII; 1068 (north of steps); LB
       IIB
   Blue-green glazed faience, faded
   22×19×4 mm
   Field no. 25.11.425
   P. 29.104.242
   Rowe 1940, pl. 33:29

*300. Tell Abu Hawam; Stratum V; Sq. C 6; probably
       LB IIB
   White glazed faience
   17×18×4 mm
   J. 34.148
   Hamilton 1935, pl. 24:a (group 394)

VI.C Cruciform with stylized ram's head
301. (Fig. 68, Pl. 20)
   Tell el-'Ajjul; near ECC; Tomb 1203; Town
       II; probably LB IA
   2 examples
   Gold and blue glass

52×38 mm
J. 35.3805; exhibit no. 1180
Petrie 1934, pls. 15:51–52, 16:51–52

302. (Pl. 20)
   Tell el-'Ajjul; GAN 852; Tomb 2070; Town
       II; probably LB IA
   2 examples
   Gold and blue glass
   52×38 mm
   J. 38.599
   Petrie, Mackay, and Murray 1952, pls. A:2,
       7:28

303. (Pl. 20)
   Tell el-'Ajjul; GD 793; Tomb 1998; Town
       II; probably LB IA
   2 examples
   Gold and blue glass
   62×35 mm
   J. 38.495
   Petrie, Mackay, and Murray 1952, pls. A:2,
       7:27

304. (Fig. 67, Pl. 20)
   Tell el-'Ajjul; TDV; Tomb 1740; Town II;
       probably LB IA
   Gold and blue glass
   30×20 mm
   J. 35.4136; exhibit no. 1282
   Petrie 1934, pls. 17:90, 18:90

VI.D.1 Disc – plain
*305. (Fig. 69, Pl. 21)
   Beth Shan; Level IX; 1397; LB
   White and blue-green variegated glass
   96×86×7 mm
   Field no. 28.10.403
   J. I3858; exhibit no. 996
   Unpublished

*306. Megiddo; Stratum IX; Area BB; Sq. M 13;
       5029; probably LB IA
   Blue and yellow mottled glass
   82×68×9 mm
   Field no. d 105
   J. 39.513
   Loud 1948, pl. 210:41

VI.D.2 Disc – with central boss
307. (Fig. 70, Pl. 21)
   Tell el-'Ajjul; '18th Dynasty' Cemetery; Tomb
       1502; probably LB I
   Silver
   31×25 mm
   Disposition unknown
   Petrie 1932, pl. 3:41

VI.D.3 Disc – with central boss and groups of dots
*308. (Fig. 71, Pl. 21)
      Tell el-'Ajjul; '18th Dynasty' Cemetery; Tomb
         1037; probably LB IIA
      Gold
      12×10×4 mm
      J. 32.1874
      Petrie 1932, pl. 3:32

VI.E Double spiral
 309. (Fig. 72)
      Lachish; Area 500; Sq. A.25; Pit 542; LB II
      Copper or bronze
      10×14 mm
      Field no. 3732a
      Disposition unknown
      Tufnell 1958, pl. 25:44

VI.F.1 Drop – crude
*310. (Fig. 73, Pl. 21)
      Beth Shan; Level IX; 1330; LB
      Yellow stone
      21×16×17 mm
      Field no. 27.12.314
      P. 29.104.663
      Unpublished
*311. (Fig. 73, Pl. 21)
      Beth Shan; Level IX; south of temple; LB
      Probably turquoise
      16×11×8 mm
      Field no. 31.11.341
      P. 31.11.341
      Unpublished

VI.F.2 Drop – elongated
*312. (Pl. 22)
      Beth Shan; Level IX; 1234 (east side); LB
      Blue-green glazed faience, faded
      26×7×6 mm
      Field no. 27.12.293
      P. 29.104.209
      Unpublished
*313. (Fig. 74, Pl. 22)
      Beth Shan; Level IX; 1332; LB
      Blue-green glazed faience, faded
      28×7×6 mm
      Field no. 28.8.18
      P. 29.104.346
      Unpublished
*314. (Fig. 74, Pl. 22)
      Beth Shan; Level IX; 1339; LB
      Dark brown stone
      29×11×5 mm
      Field no. 28.9.25

P. 29.104.782
Unpublished
*315. (Fig. 74, Pl. 22)
      Beth Shan; Level IX; south of temple; LB
      Probably turquoise
      15×4×2 mm
      Field no. 31.11.341
      P. 31.11.341
      Unpublished
*316. (Fig. 74, Pl. 22)
      Beth Shan; Level VIII; 1092; LB IIB
      Gold
      28×9 mm
      Field no. 27.9.373b
      P. 29.105.58
      Unpublished
 317. (Fig. 74)
      Beth Shan; Level VIII; 1068 (below floor); LB
         IIB
      Bone
      29×12×8 mm
      Field no. 26.8.130u
      J. – missing
      Rowe 1940, pl. 34:69
*318. (Fig. 74)
      Beth Shan; Level VIII; 1068 (below floor); LB
         IIB
      Lapis lazuli
      23×12 mm
      Field no. 25.11.424
      J. J973
      Rowe 1940, pl. 33:83
*319. (Fig. 74, Pl. 22)
      Beth Shan; Level VIII; 1068 (below steps); LB
         IIB
      Gold
      26×5 mm
      Field no. 25.11.385
      P. 29.105.64
      Unpublished
*320. Beth Shan; Level VII; 1068 (near steps); LB
         IIB
      3 examples
      Blue-green glazed faience
      E.g., 16×12×3 mm, 21×10×4 mm
      Field no. 25.11.488
      P. 29.104.286–87; J. 36.1646
      Unpublished
*321. (Fig. 74)
      Beth Shan; Level VII; 1087; LB IIb
      Gold
      25×17 mm
      Field no. 25.11.513

P. 29.105.66
Unpublished
*322. (Fig. 74, Pl. 22)
Beth Shan; Level VII; 1252; LB IIB
Probably steatite
14×7 mm
Field no. 27.10.667
P. 29.104.347
Unpublished
323. Gezer; Stratum VB/VA; Field I; Area 3; Locus
3012.1; probably LB IIB
'Gray-green' faience
23×9×2 mm
Disposition unknown
Dever, Lance, and Wright 1970, pl. 36:6
324. (Pl. 22)
Megiddo; Stratum IX; Area AA; Sq. K 8; 2134;
probably LB IA
Bone
55×10 mm
Field no. a 1168
Chicago, Oriental Institute
Loud 1948, pl. 211:49
325. Megiddo; Stratum IX; Area BB; Sq. M 13;
5029; probably LB IA
Hematite
31×12 mm
Field no. d 103
Chicago, Oriental Institute
Loud 1948, pl. 210:40
326. Megiddo; Stratum VIII; Area AA; Sq. K 7;
3100; probably LB IB–IIA
Material unspecified
9×3 mm
Field no. b 1002
Chicago, Oriental Institute
Loud 1948, pl. 213:61
327. (Pl. 22)
Megiddo; Stratum VIII; Area DD; Sq. K 11;
5020; probably LB IB–IIA
Gold
32×7 mm
Field no. d 131
Chicago, Oriental Institute
Loud 1948, pl. 213:69
328. Megiddo; Stratum VII B; Area CC; Sq. S 9;
1834; probably LB IIB
Sandstone
28×9 mm
Field no. M 6067
Chicago, Oriental Institute
Loud 1948, pl. 213:78
*329. Umm ad-Dananir; Jebel al-Hawayah; Cave A2;

Layer 2a; Locus 3; probably LB I
Green Stone
25×10×5 mm
A.
McGovern, In Press
*330. Umm ad-Dananir; Jebel al-Qesir; Cave B3;
Locus 3; probably LB II
Probably turquoise
35×21×7 mm
A.
McGovern, In Press

VI.F.3 Drop – miscellaneous, including fancy types
331. (Fig. 75)
Beth Shan; Level VIII; 1092; LB IIB
'Light green' faience
13×8×2 mm
Field no. 26.8.143e
J. – missing
Rowe 1940, pl. 34:38
332. (Fig. 75)
Beth Shan; Level VII; 1104; LB IIB
Faience
13×10×5 mm
Field no. 26.9.177b
Disposition unknown
Unpublished
333. (Fig. 75)
Beth Shan; Level VII; 1284; LB IIB
Carnelian
15×8×3 mm
Field no. 27.11.189b
P. – missing
Unpublished
*334. (Fig. 75)
Beth Shemesh; Stratum IV; Sq. W 27; Room
73; probably LB IIB
Gold
27×13 mm
J. I5931
Grant 1931, pl. 18 (center); Grant 1932,
pl. 49:17; Tadmor and Misch-Brandl 1980:
fig. 3
335. (Pl. 23)
Megiddo; Stratum VIII; Area BB; Sq. N–O 14;
2094; probably LB IB–IIA
Blue faience
14×7 mm
Field no. a 1053
Chicago, Oriental Institute
Loud 1948, pl. 213:70
*336. (Pl. 23)
Tell el-'Ajjul; GDF 921; Hoard 277; probably

Town II; probably LB IA
Gold
19×12 mm
London, British Museum
Petrie, Mackay, and Murray 1952, pls. B:14, 6:9

*337. (Fig. 75, Pl. 23)
Tell el-'Ajjul; TDV; Tomb 1740; Town II;
probably LB IA
2 examples
Gold
30×18 mm
J. 35.4134; exhibit no. 1281
Petrie 1934, pls. 17:88, 18:88

*338. (Fig. 75, Pl. 23)
Tell el-'Ajjul; TV; Hoard 1313; probably Town
II; probably LB IA
Gold
16×8 mm
J. 35.3908; exhibit no. 1185
Petrie 1934, pls. 15:61, 16:61

VI.G.1   Star disc – four-rayed with dots
*339. Megiddo; Stratum IX; Area BB; Sq. M 13;
5029; probably LB IA
White glazed faience with brown decoration
Diameter: 23 mm
Field no. d 101
J. 39.511
Loud 1948, pl. 210:44

340. (Pl. 23)
Megiddo; Area CC; Sq. R 10; Tomb 2009;
probably LB IA
Faience
Diameter: 24 mm
Field no. a 68
Chicago, Oriental Institute
Loud 1948, pl. 212:55

341. Megiddo; Stratum VIII; Area BB; Sq. 0 13–14;
S=2048; probably LB IB–IIA
Faience
30×27 mm
Field no. a 334
Chicago, Oriental Institute
Loud 1948, pl. 213:66

VI.G.2.a   Star disc – eight-rayed; plain
*342. (Fig. 76, Pl. 24)
Beth Shan; Level VIII; 1068 (below steps): LB
IIB
Gold
Diameter: 9 mm
Field no. 25.11.387
P. 29.105.93

Rowe 1940, pl. 30:60

*343. Lachish; Fosse Temple area: LB
Gold
13×10 mm
J. 36.2260
Tufnell, Inge, and Harding 1940, pl. 26:10

*344. Tel Kittan; Stratum 3 'temple'; probably LB IA
Silver
Size unspecified
J.
Eisenberg 1977, p. 81 (bottom, right)

345. (Pl. 24)
Shechem; Stratum 14; Field 13; cellar under
Room G; LB IIA
Probably electrum
30×24 mm
Disposition unknown
Campbell, Ross, and Toombs 1971, fig. 7:c

VI.G.2.b   Star disc – eight-rayed; cut-out
*346. Lachish; Fosse Temple; Structure I; Room D;
LB I
Gold
24×22×4 mm
Field no. 5325
J. 36.2252
Tufnell, Inge, and Harding 1940, pl. 26:15

*347. (Pl. 24)
Lachish; Fosse Temple area; LB
Gold
24×22×1 mm
Field no. 5336
London, Institute of Archaeology
Tufnell, Inge, and Harding 1940, pl. 26:14

*348. (Pl. 24)
Lachish; Fosse Temple area; LB
Gold
27×16 mm
London, Institute of Archaeology
Tufnell, Inge, and Harding 1940, pl. 26:11

*349. Lachish; Fosse Temple area; LB
Gold
20×10×1 mm
London, Institute of Archaeology
Tufnell, Inge, and Harding 1940, pl. 26:12

*350. Tell el-'Ajjul; EAA?; Hoard 1299; probably
Town II; probably LB IA
Gold
Diameter: 45 mm
J. 35.3845; exhibit no. 1162
Petrie 1934, pl. 14:13

*351. (Fig. 77, Pl. 24)
Tell el-'Ajjul; EAA?; Hoard 1299; probably

Town II; probably LB IA
2 examples
Gold
63×54 mm; 59×57 mm
J. 35.3846; exhibit no. 1156
Petrie 1934, pls. 13:14–15, 14:14–15; Petrie,
Mackay, and Murray 1952, pl. A:10

*352. (Fig. 77, Pl. 24)
Tell el-'Ajjul; EAA?; Hoard 1299; probably
Town II; probably LB IA
Gold
Diameter: 30 mm
J. 35.3866; exhibit no. 1168
Petrie 1934, pls. 13:36, 14:36

*353. Tell el-'Ajjul; GDF 921; Hoard 277; probably
Town II; probably LB IA
3 examples
Gold
47×43 mm; 64×54 mm; 46×42 mm
Cambridge, Fitzwilliam Museum; Oxford,
Ashmolean Museum; London, British
Museum
Petrie, Mackay, and Murray 1952, pls. A:10,
6:6–8, 8:3, 5

VI.G.2.c Star disc – eight-rayed; with dots
354. (Pl. 25)
Megiddo; Stratum IX; Area CC; Sq. R 10;
Tomb 2009; probably LB IA
2 examples
Material uncertain
Diameter: 24 mm and 23 mm
Field no. a 68
Chicago, Oriental Institute
Loud 1948, pl. 212:55

355. (Pl. 25)
Megiddo; Stratum VIIB; Area BB; Sq. M 13;

2064; probably LB IIB
Silver
62×48 mm
Field no. a 669
Chicago, Oriental Institute
Loud 1948, pl. 213:79

*356. (Fig. 78, Pl. 25)
Tell el-'Ajjul; G 950; probably Town I;
probably LB II
Gold
41×38 mm
J. 35.4239; exhibit no. 1215
Petrie 1934, pls. 17:112, 18:112

VI.H 'Wheel'
357. (Fig. 79)
Beth Shan; Level IX; 1403; LB
'Bluish glass'
10×20 mm
Field no. 28.11.32e
Disposition unknown
Unpublished

*358. Lachish; Fosse Temple; Structure III; Room
E; LB IIB
Blue-green glazed faience, faded
16×23 mm
Field no. 2635
London, British Museum
Tufnell, Inge, and Harding 1940, pls. 14
(lower), 35:81

359. Lachish; Fosse Temple; Pit 188; probably LB
IIB
Blue glazed faience
16×23 mm
Field no. 2842
Disposition unknown
Tufnell, Inge, and Harding 1940, pl. 35:80

Abbreviations

AAAS *Les Annales Archéologiques de Syrie*

AASOR Annual of the American Schools of Oriental Research

ADAJ *Annual of the Department of Antiquities of Jordan*

AfO *Archiv für Orientforschung*

AJA *American Journal of Archaeology*

AJSLL *American Journal of Semitic Languages and Literatures*

APEF *Annual of the Palestine Exploration Fund*

ASOR American Schools of Oriental Research

AUSS *Andrews University Seminary Studies*

BA *Biblical Archaeologist*

BAH Bibliothèque Archéologique et Historique

BASOR *Bulletin of the American Schools or Oriental Research*

BMB *Bulletin du Musée de Beyrouth*

BMMA *Bulletin of the Metropolitan Museum of Art*

BSA *Annual of the British School of Archaeology in Athens*

BSAE British School of Archaeology in Egypt

CAH³ *Cambridge Ancient History.* Eds. I. E. S. Edwards, C. J. Gadd, and N. G. L. Hammond. 3d ed., rev. 2 vols. Cambridge: Cambridge University Press, 1970–75

CCG *Catalogue général des antiquités égyptiennes du Musée du Caire*

EEF Egypt Exploration Fund

EI *Eretz-Israel*

ERA Egyptian Research Account

IEJ *Israel Exploration Journal*

IES Israel Exploration Society

IFAO Institut Français d'Archéologie Orientale

JAOS *Journal of the American Oriental Society*

JBL *Journal of Biblical Literature*

JCS *Journal of Cuneiform Studies*

JEA *Journal of Egyptian Archaeology*

JESHO *Journal of the Economic and Social History of the Orient*

JGS *Journal of Glass Studies*

JNES *Journal of Near Eastern Studies*

JPOS *Journal of the Palestine Oriental Society*

LAAA *Liverpool Annals of Archaeology and Anthropology*

MDOG *Mitteilungen der Deutschen Orient-Gesellschaft*

MIOF *Mitteilungen des Instituts für Orientforschung*

MMA Metropolitan Museum of Art

MRS Mission de Ras Shamra

OIP Oriental Institute Publications

QDAP *Quarterly of the Department of Antiquities of Palestine*

PEF Palestine Exploration Fund

PEFQS *Palestine Exploration Fund Quarterly Statement*

PEQ *Palestine Exploration Quarterly*

PPS *Proceedings of the Prehistoric Society*

RA *Revue d'Assyriologie*

RB *Revue Biblique*

SAOC Studies in Ancient Oriental Civilizations

SMA Studies in Mediterranean Archaeology

VT *Vetus Testamentum*

ZA *Zeitschrift für Assyriologie und Vorderasiatische Archäologie*

ZAW *Zeitschrift für alttestamentliche Wissenschaft*

ZDPV *Zeitschrift der Deutschen Palästina-Vereins*

SELECTED BIBLIOGRAPHY

Aharoni, Y. 1979 *The Land of the Bible: A Historical Geography*. 2d ed., rev. and enlarged. Trans. A. F. Rainey. Philadelphia: Westminster.

Aharoni, Y., and Avi-Yonah, M. 1968 *The Macmillan Bible Atlas*. New York: Macmillan.

Aḥituv, S. 1972 Did Ramesses II Conquer Dibon? *IEJ* 22: 141–42.

1978 Economic Factors in the Egyptian Conquest of Canaan. *IEJ* 28: 93–105.

Albright, W. F. 1932 *The Excavation of Tell Beit Mirsim. Vol. 1: The Pottery of the First Three Campaigns*. AASOR, 12. New Haven: ASOR.

1933 *The Excavation of Tell Beit Mirsim. Vol. 1A: The Bronze Age Pottery of the Fourth Campaign*. AASOR 13: 55–127. New Haven: ASOR.

1938a The Chronology of a South Palestinian City, Tell el-ʿAjjûl. *AJSLL* 55: 337–59.

1938b *The Excavation of Tell Beit Mirsim. Vol. 2: The Bronze Age*. AASOR, 17. New Haven: ASOR.

1939 Astarte Plaques and Figurines from Tell Beit Mirsim. Pp. 107–20 in Vol. 1 of *Mélanges syriens offerts à Monsieur René Dussaud*. BAH, vol. 30. Paris: Geuthner.

1941 The Egypto-Canaanite Deity Ḥaurôn. *BASOR* 84: 7–12.

1952 The Smaller Beth-Shan Stele of Sethos I (1309–1290 B.C.). *BASOR* 125: 24–32.

1957 *From the Stone Age to Christianity*. 2d ed., rev. Garden City, N.Y.: Doubleday, Anchor.

1961 *The Archaeology of Palestine*. Harmondsworth, England: Penguin; Pelican.

1963 *The Biblical Period from Abraham to Ezra*. New York: Harper and Row; Harper Torchbook.

1965 The Role of the Canaanites in the History of Civilization. Pp. 438–87 in *The Bible and the Ancient Near East*, ed. G. E. Wright. Garden City, N.Y.: Doubleday, Anchor.

1968 *Yahweh and the Gods of Canaan: An Historical Analysis of Two Contrasting Faiths*. Jordan Lectures, School of Oriental and African Languages, University of London, 1965. Garden City, N.Y.: Doubleday.

1969 *Archaeology and the Religion of Israel*. 5th ed., rev. Garden City, N.Y.: Doubleday, Anchor.

1970–75 The Amarna Letters from Palestine. Pp. 98–116 in Vol. II/2 of *CAH*³.

Albright, W. F., and Rowe, A. 1928 A Royal Stele of the New Kingdom from Galilee. *JEA* 14: 281–87.

Aldred, C. 1968 *Akhenaten: Pharaoh of Egypt – A New Study*. New Aspects of Antiquity, ed. M. Wheeler. London: Sphere Books; Abacus.

1971 *Jewels of the Pharaohs: Egyptian Jewelry of the Dynastic Period*. New York: Praeger.

Allen, T. G., trans. 1974 *The Book of the Dead or Going Forth by Day; Ideas of the Ancient Egyptians Concerning the Hereafter as Expressed in Their Own Terms*. SAOC, no. 37. Chicago: University of Chicago.

Amiran, R. 1960 A Late Bronze Age II Pottery Group from a Tomb in Jerusalem. *EI* 6: 25–37 (Hebrew).

Amiran, R., and Eitan, A. 1964 A Canaanite-Hyksos City at Tell Nagila. *Archaeology* 18: 219–31.

Andrae, W. 1935 *Die jüngeren Ischtar-tempel in Assur*. Wissenschaftliche Veröffentlichungen der Deutschen Orient-gesellschaft, no. 58. Leipzig: J. C. Hinrichs.

Anthes, R. 1961 Mythology in Ancient Egypt. Pp. 1–92 in *Mythologies of the Ancient World*, ed. S. N. Kramer. Garden City, NY: Doubleday; Anchor.

Aspinall, A. *et al.* 1972 Neutron Activation Analysis of Faience Beads. *Archaeometry* 14: 27–40.

Astour, M. 1970 Ma'hadu, the Harbor of Ugarit. *JESHO* 13: 113–27.

Åström, L., and Åström, P. 1972 *The Late Cypriote Bronze Age: Other Arts and Crafts, (and) Relative and Absolute Chronology, Foreign Relations, Historical Conclusions*. Vol. 4, pt. 1D: *Swedish Cyprus Expedition*. Lund: Swedish Cyprus Expedition.

Avi-Yonah, M., and Stern, E., eds. 1975–78 *Encyclopedia of Archaeological Excavations in the Holy Land*. 4 vols. Englewood Cliffs, N.J.: Prentice-Hall.

Ayrton, E. R., Currelly, C. T., and Weigall, A. E. P. 1904 *Abydos III*. EEF, mem. 25. London: EEF.

Barag, D. 1962 Mesopotamian Glass Vessels of the Second Millennium B.C. *JGS* 4: 9–27.

1970 Mesopotamian Core-Formed Glass Vessels (1500–500 B.C.). Pp. 131–200 in *Glass and Glassmaking in Ancient Mesopotamia* by A. L. Oppenheim, R. H. Brill, D. Barag, and A. von Saldern. Corning, N.Y.: Corning Museum of Glass.

Bass, G. F. 1967 *Cape Gelidonya: A Bronze Age Shipwreck. Transactions of the American Philosophical*

Society, n.s., vol. 5, pt. 8. Philadelphia: American Philosophical Society.

1973   Cape Gelidonya and Bronze Age Maritime Trade. Pp. 29–37 in *Orient and Occident: Essays Presented to Cyrus A. Gordon on the Occasion of His Sixty-fifth Birthday*, ed. H. A. Hoffner, Jr. Alter Orient and Altes Testament. Kevelaer: Butzon and Bercker.

Beck, H.   1964   Glass before 1500 B.C. *Ancient Egypt and the East*, 7–21.

1973   Classification and Nomenclature of Beads and Pendants. *Archaeologia* 77: 1–76; reprint ed., York, Pa.: Liberty Cap.

Beck, H., and Stone, J. F. S.   1935   Faience Beads of the British Bronze Age. *Archaeologia* 85: 203–52.

Bender, F.   1974   *Geology of Jordan*. Trans. M. K. Khdeir. Contributions to the Regional Geology of the Earth, ed. H. J. Martini. Berlin: Bornträger.

Ben-Arieh, S., and Edelstein, G.   1977   *Akko: Tombs Near the Persian Garden*. 'Atiqot (English Series), vol. 12. Jerusalem: Department of Antiquities and Museums.

Ben-Dor, I.   1950   A Middle Bronze-Age Temple at Nahariyah. *QDAP* 14: 1–41.

Bikai, P.   1978   *The Pottery of Tyre*. Warminster: Aris and Phillips.

Bittel, K.   1938   Vorläufiger Bericht über die Ergebnisse der Ausgrabungen in Boğazköy im Jahre 1937. *MDOG* 72: 13–47.

Bleeker, C. J.   1973   *Hathor and Thoth: Two Key Figures of the Ancient Egyptian Religion*. Studies in the History of Religion (Supplement to *Numen*), no. 26. Leiden: E. J. Brill.

Bliss, F. J.   1894   *A Mound of Many Cities or Tell el Hesy Excavated*. London: PEF.

Bliss, F. J., and Macalister, R. A. S.   1902   *Excavations in Palestine during the Years 1898–1900*. London: Committee of PEF.

Boling, R. G.   1969   Bronze Age Buildings at the Shechem High Place: ASOR Excavations at Tananir. *BA* 32: 81–103.

Bonner, C.   1950   *Studies in Magical Amulets, Chiefly Graeco-Egyptian*. Ann Arbor: University of Michigan.

Bonnet, H.   1952   *Reallexikon der ägyptischen Religionsgeschichte*. Berlin: de Gruyter.

Borghouts, J. F.   1973   The Evil Eye of Apopis. *JEA* 59: 114–50.

Bottéro, J.   1949   Les Inventaires de Qatna. *RA* 43: 138–215.

Branigan, K.   1970   Minoan Foot Amulets and Their Near Eastern Counterparts. *Studi Micenei ed Egeo-Anatolica* 11: 7–23.

Breasted, J. H.   1933   *A History of Egypt from the Earliest Times to the Persian Conquest*. New York: Bantam.

1972   *The Development of Religion and Thought in Ancient Egypt*. New York: Scribner's; reprint ed., Philadelphia: University of Pennsylvania.

Brill, R. H.   1970   The Chemical Interpretation of the Texts. Pp. 103–28 in *Glass and Glassmaking in Ancient Mesopotamia* by A. L. Oppenheim, R. H. Brill, D. Barag, and A. von Saldern. Corning, NY: Corning Museum of Glass.

Brothwell, D., and Higgs, E.   1970   *Science in Archaeology: A Survey of Progress and Research*. 2d ed., rev. and enlarged. New York: Praeger.

Brunton, G.   1927–30   *Qua and Badari*. 3 vols. BSAE and ERA, vols. 44, 45, and 50. London: BSAE.

1937   *Mostagedda and the Tasian Culture*. London: B. Quaritch.

Brunton, G., and Engelbach, R.   1927   *Gurob*. BSAE and ERA, vol. 41. London: BSAE and B. Quaritch.

Bruyère, B.   1953   Rapport sur les fouilles de Deir el-Médineh. Fouilles de l'IFAO. 10 vols. Cairo: IFAO.

Budge, E. A. W.   1970   *Amulets and Talismans*. Oxford and Cambridge: Masters and Fellows of Oxford and Cambridge Universities, 1930; reprint ed., New York: Collier.

1971   *Egyptian Magic*. London: Kegan Paul, Trench, Trübner, 1901; reprint ed., New York: Dover.

1972   *The Mummy*. 2d ed. Cambridge University, 1925; reprint ed., New York: Collier.

Campbell, E. F.   1976   Two Amarna Notes: The Shechem City–State and Amarna Administrative Terminology. Pp. 39–54 in *Magnalia Dei: The Mighty Acts of God; Essays on the Bible and Archaeology in Memory of G. Ernest Wright*, eds. F. M. Cross, W. E. Lemke, and P. D. Miller, Jr. Garden City, NY: Doubleday.

Campbell, E. F., Ross, J. F., and Toombs, L. E.   1971   The Eighth Campaign at Balâṭah (Shechem). *BASOR* 204: 2–17.

Canby, J. V.   1965   Early Bronze Age 'Trinket' Moulds. *Iraq* 27: 42–61.

Carnarvon, Earl of, and Carter, H.   1912   *Five Years' Explorations at Thebes: A Record of Work Done 1907–1911*. London: Oxford University.

Carter, H.   1972   *The Tomb of Tutankhamen*. Abridged ed. London: Sphere.

Carter, H., and Mace, A.C.   1923–33   *The Tomb of Tut·ankh·amen: Discovered by the Late Earl of Carnarvon and Howard Carter*. 3 vols. London: Cassel.

Černý, J.   1952   *Ancient Egyptian Religion*. London: Hutchinson.

1954   Prices and Wages in Egypt in the Rameside Period. *Cahiers d'Histoire Mondiale* 1: 903–21.

1958   Stela of Ramesses from Beisan. *EI* 5: 72*–82*.

Chase, W. T.   1971   Egyptian Blue as a Pigment and Ceramic Material. Pp. 80–90 in *Science and Archaeology*, ed. R. H. Brill. Cambridge: Massachusetts Institute of Technology.

Chéhab, M.   1937   Un trésor d'orfèvrerie Syro-Egyptien. *BMB* 1: 7–21.

Cintas, P.   1946   *Amulettes puniques*. Publications d'Institut des Hautes Etudes de Tunis, vol. 1. Tunis: Institut des Hautes Etudes.

Clamer, C., and Ussishkin, D.   1977   A Canaanite Temple at Tell Lachish. *BA* 40: 71–76.

Clark, R. T. 1959 *Myth and Symbol in Ancient Egypt.* London: Thames and Hudson.

Coche de la Ferté, E. 1956 *Les Bijoux antiques.* Paris: Presses Universitaires.

Contenau, G., and Ghirschman, R. 1935 *Fouilles du Tépé Giyan près de Néhavand, 1931 et 1932.* Paris: Geuthner.

Cook, S. A. 1930 *The Religion of Ancient Palestine in the Light of Archaeology.* Schweich Lectures, 1925. London: British Academy.

Coughenour, R. A. 1976 Preliminary Report on the Exploration and Excavation of Mughâret el Wardeh and Abu Thawab. *ADAJ* 21: 71–78.

Courtois, J. C. 1974 Ugarit Grid, Strata, and Find-Localizations: A Re-assessment. *ZDPV* 90: 97–114.

Craddock, P. T. 1980 The Composition of Copper Produced at the Ancient Smelting Camps in the Wadi Timna, Israel. Pp. 165–73 in *Scientific Studies in Early Mining and Extractive Metallurgy*, ed. P. T. Craddock. British Museum Occasional Paper, 20. London: British Museum.

Cross, F. M., Jr. 1971 *Canaanite Myth and Hebrew Epic: Essays in the History of the Religion of Israel.* Cambridge: Harvard University.

Crowfoot, J. W., Crowfoot, G. M., and Kenyon, K. M. 1957 *The Objects from Samaria.* Samaria-Sebaste: Reports of the Work of the Joint Expedition in 1931–1933 and of the British Expedition in 1935, no. 3. London: PEF.

Culican, W. 1964 Spiral-end Beads in Western Asia. *Iraq* 26: 36–43.

Dajani, R. W. 1964 Iron Age Tombs from Irbed. *ADAJ* 8–9: 99–101.

1966a Four Iron Age Tombs from Irbed. *ADAJ* 11: 88–101.

1966b Jebel Nuzha Tomb at Amman. *ADAJ* 11: 48–49.

1970 A Late Bronze-Iron Age Tomb Excavated at Sahab. *ADAJ* 15: 29–36.

Dales, G. F. 1963 Necklaces, Bands and Belts of Mesopotamian Figurines. *RA* 57: 21–40.

Davico, A. *et al.* 1967 *Missione archaeologica italiana in Siria: Rapporto preliminare della campagna 1966 (Tell Mardikh).* Rome: Istituto di Studi del Vicino Oriente.

Davies, N. de G. 1908–1918 *The Rock Tombs of El Amarna.* Archaeological Survey of Egypt, vols. 13–18. 6 vols. London: Paul.

1913 *Five Theban Tombs: Being Those of Mentuherkhepeshef, User, Daga, Nehemawäy and Tati.* Archaeological Survey of Egypt, vol. 21. London: EEF.

1925 *The Tomb of Two Sculptors at Thebes.* MMA Egyptian Expedition. Robb de Peyster Tytus Memorial Series, vol. 4, ed. A. M. Lythgoe. New York: MMA.

1933 *The Tomb of Nefer-hotep at Thebes.* 2 vols. MMA Egyptian Expedition, vol. 9. New York: MMA Egyptian Expedition.

1941 *The Tomb of Vizier Ramose.* Mond Excavations at Thebes, 1. London: EES.

1943 *The Tomb of Rekh-mi-Re' at Thebes.* 2 vols. MMA

Egyptian Expedition, vol. 11, ed. L. Bull. New York: Plantin.

Davis, T. M. 1910 *The Tomb of Queen Tîyi.* Theodore M. Davis' Excavations: Bibân el-Molûk, vol. 6. London: Constable.

Davis, T. M. *et al.* 1908 *The Tomb of Siphtah: The Monkey Tomb and the Gold Tomb.* T. M. Davis' Excavations: Bibân el-Molûk, vol. 5. London: Constable.

Davis, T. M., Naville, E., and Carter, H. 1906 *The Tomb of Hatshopsîtû.* T. M. Davis' Excavations: Bibân el-Molûk, vol. 2. London: Constable.

Davison, C. C. 1972 Glass Beads in African Archaeology: Results of Neutron Activation Analysis, Supplemented by Results of X-Ray Fluorescence Analysis. Ph.D. dissertation, University of California, Berkeley.

Deroches-Noblecourt, C. 1963 *Tutankhamun: Life and Death of a Pharaoh.* Boston: New York Graphic Society.

Dever, W. G. 1976 The Beginning of the Middle Bronze Age in Syria-Palestine. Pp. 3–38 in *Magnalia Dei: The Mighty Acts of God; Essays on the Bible and Archaeology in Memory of G. Ernest Wright*, eds. F. M. Cross, W. E. Lemke, and P. D. Miller, Jr. Garden City, NY: Doubleday.

Dever, W. G. *et al.* 1971 Further Excavations at Gezer, 1967–1971. *BA* 34: 94–132.

1974 *Gezer II: Report of the 1967–70 Seasons in Fields I and II.* Annual of the Hebrew Union College/Nelson Glueck School of Biblical Archaeology. Jerusalem: Hebrew Union College/Nelson Glueck School of Biblical Archaeology.

Dever, W. G., Lance, H. D., and Wright, G. E. 1970 *Gezer I: Preliminary Report of the 1964–66 Seasons.* Annual of the Hebrew Union College and Archaeological School in Jerusalem. Jerusalem: Hebrew Union College.

Dikaios, P. 1969–71 *Enkomi: Excavations 1948–1958.* 3 vols. Mainz: Philipp von Zalbern.

Dornemann, R. H. 1970 The Cultural and Archaeological History of the Transjordan in the Bronze and Iron Ages. 2 vols. Ph.D. dissertation, University of Chicago.

Dothan, M. 1956 The Excavation at Nahariyah: Preliminary Report (Seasons 1954/55). *IEJ* 6: 14–25.

1957 Some Aspects of the Religious Life in Palestine during the Hyksos Rule. *Antiquity and Survival* 2: 121–30.

1971 *Ashdod II–III: The Second and Third Seasons of Excavations 1963, 1965; Soundings in 1967.* 2 vols. 'Atiqot (English Series), vols. 9–10. Jerusalem: Department of Antiquities and Museums, Department of Hebrew University, and IES.

1973 The Foundation of Tel Mor and of Ashdod. *IEJ* 23: 1–17.

Dothan, T. 1972 Anthropoid Clay Coffins from a Late Bronze Age Cemetery near Deir el-Balaḥ (Preliminary Report). *IEJ* 22: 65–72.

1973 Anthropoid Clay Coffins from a Late Bronze Age

Cemetery near Deir el-Balaḥ (Preliminary Report II). *IEJ* 23: 129–46.

1979 *Excavations at the Cemetery of Deir el-Balaḥ. Qedem* 10. Jerusalem: Institute of Archaeology, Hebrew University.

1982 *The Philistines and Their Material Culture.* New Haven: Yale University.

Dowman, E. A. 1970 *Conservation in Field Archaeology.* London: Methuen.

Drioton, E., and Vandier, J. 1962 *L'Egypt.* 'Clio': Introduction aux études historiques. Les Peuples de l'Orient méditerranéen 2. 4th ed., rev. and enlarged. Paris: Presses Universitaires de France.

Driver, G. R. 1956 *Canaanite Myths and Legends.* Old Testament Studies, no. 3. Edinburgh: T. & T. Clark.

Drower, M. S. 1970–75 Syria, c. 1550–1400 B.C. Pp. 417–525 in *CAH³* II/1.

Dunand, M. 1937–73 *Fouilles de Byblos.* Etudes et documents d'archéologie, vols. 1, 3, and 5. Paris: Geuthner.

Dunand, M., Bounni, A., and Saliby, N. 1964 Fouilles de Tell Kazel. *AAAS* 14: 1–14.

Duncan, J. G. 1930 *Corpus of Dated Palestinian Pottery.* BSAE and ERA, vol. 49. London: BSAE.

Dussaud, R. 1949 *L'Art phénicien du IIᵉ millénaire.* Paris: Geuthner.

Dyson, R. H. 1967 Survey of Excavations in Iran during 1965–66: Dinkha Tepe. *Iran* 5: 136–37.

Edelstein, G. 1973 Tombs de marchands guerriers au nord d'Acre. *Archéologia (Trésors des Ages)* 60: 57–63.

Edgerton, W. F. 1947 The Government and the Governed in the Egyptian Empire. *JNES* 6: 152–60.

Ehrich, R. W., ed. 1965 *Chronologies in Old World Archaeology.* Chicago: University of Chicago.

Eisenberg, E. 1977 The Temples at Tel Kittan. *BA* 40: 77–81.

Eliade, M. 1957 *The Sacred and the Profane.* New York: Harcourt, Brace, and World.

Engelbach, R. 1915 *Riqqeh and Memphis VI.* BSAE and ERA, vol. 25. London: BSAE and B. Quaritch.

1923 *Harageh.* BSAE and ERA, vol. 28. London: BSAE and B. Quaritch.

Epstein, C. 1966 *Palestinian Bichrome Ware.* Leiden: E. J. Brill.

Erickson, J. M. 1969 *The Universal Bead.* New York: W. W. Norton.

Evans-Pritchard, E. E. 1965 *Theories of Primitive Religion.* Oxford: Oxford University; pb.

Farbridge, M. B. 1970 *Studies in Biblical and Semitic Symbolism.* Prolegomenon by H. G. May. Originally published in 1923; reprint ed., New York: Ktav.

Faulkner, R. O. 1947 A Syrian Trading Venture to Egypt. *JEA* 33: 34–39.

1975 Egypt: From the Inception of the Nineteenth Dynasty to the Death of Ramesses III. Pp. 217–51 in *CAH³* II/2.

Feucht, E. 1967 *Die königlichen Pektorale: Motive, Sinngehalt und Zweck.* Bamberg: K. Urlaub.

1971 *Pektorale nichtköniglicher Personen.* Ägyptologische Abhandlungen, vol. 22. Wiesbaden: Harrassowitz.

FitzGerald, G. M. 1930 *The Four Canaanite Temples of Beth-Shan.* Part 2: *The Pottery.* Publications of the Palestine Section of the University Museum, vol. 2. Philadelphia: University Museum.

1935 The Earliest Pottery of Beth-Shan. *The Museum Journal* 24: 5–22.

Fohrer, G. 1968 *Introduction to the Old Testament.* Trans. D. E. Green. Nashville: Abingdon.

Foster, K. P. 1979 *Aegean Faience of the Bronze Age.* New Haven: Yale University.

Foster, K. P. and Kaczmarczyk, A. 1982 X-Ray Fluorescence Analysis of Some Minoan Faience. *Archaeometry* 24: 143–57.

Franken, H. J. 1960 The Excavations at Deir 'Alla in Jordan. *VT* 10: 86–93.

1961 The Excavations at Deir 'Alla in Jordan: 2nd Season. *VT* 11: 361–72.

1962 The Excavations at Deir 'Alla in Jordan: 3rd Season. *VT* 12: 378–82.

1964 Excavations at Deir 'Alla, Season 1964: Preliminary Report. *VT* 14: 417–22.

1969 *Excavation at Tell Deir 'Alla, I.* Leiden: Brill.

1970 The Other Side of Jordan. *ADAJ* 15: 5–10.

1970–75 Palestine in the Time of the Nineteenth Dynasty: (b) Archaeological Evidence. Pp. 331–37 in *CAH³*, II:2.

Frankfort, H. 1961 *Ancient Egyptian Religion: An Interpretation.* New York: Columbia University, 1948; reprint ed., New York: Harper and Row.

1965 *Cylinder Seals: A Documentary Essay on the Art and Religion of the Ancient Near East.* London: Macmillan, 1939; reprint ed., London: Gregg.

1970 *The Art and Architecture of the Ancient Orient.* The Pelican History of Art, ed. N. Pevsner. Harmondsworth, England: Penguin.

Frankfort, H. *et al.* 1949 *Before Philosophy: The Intellectual Adventure of Ancient Man.* Harmondsworth, England: Penguin.

Frankfort, H., and Pendlebury, J. D. S. 1933 *The City of Akhenaten.* Part 2: *The North Suburb and the Desert Altars.* EEF, mem. 40. London: EEF.

Frazer, J. G. 1975 *Folklore in the Old Testament: Studies in Comparative Religion, Legend and Law.* London: Macmillan, 1918; reprint ed., New York: Hart.

Free, J. P. 1962 The Seventh Season of Excavation at Dothan. *ADAJ* 6–7: 117–20.

Fugmann, E. 1958 *Hama: Fouilles et recherches de la Fondation Carlberg, 1931–1938.* Vol. 2: *L'Architecture des périodes pré-Hellénistiques.* Nationalmuseets skrifter, Større beretninger, 4. Copenhagen: National Museum.

Gardiner, A. 1957 *Egyptian Grammar: Being an Introduction to the Study of Hieroglyphs.* 3rd ed., rev. Oxford: Griffith Institute.

1961 *Egypt of the Pharaohs: An Introduction.* New York: Oxford University.

Garstang, J. 1933 Jericho: City and Necropolis. *LAAA* 20: 3–42.

1934 Jericho: City and Necropolis; Fourth Report. *LAAA* 21: 99–136.

Garstang, J., and Garstang, J. B. E. 1948 *The Story of Jericho*. 2nd ed. London: Marshall, Morgan, and Scott.

Gaster, T. H. 1969 *Myth, Legend, and Custom in the Old Testament*. New York: Harper and Row.

1973 A Hang-Up for Hang-Ups: The Second Amuletic Plaque from Arslan Tash. *BASOR* 109: 18–26.

Gelb, I. J. et al., eds. 1964– *Assyrian Dictionary*. Chicago: Oriental Institute.

Gittlen, B. 1981 The Cultural and Chronological Implications of the Cypro-Palestinian Trade During the Late Bronze Age. *BASOR* 241: 49–59.

Giveon, R. 1969 Tuthmosis IV and Asia. *JNES* 28: 54–59.

1978 *The Impact of Egypt on Canaan*. Orbis Biblicus et Orientalis 20. Fribourg: Universitätsverlag.

Glueck, N. 1934 *Explorations in Eastern Palestine, I*. AASOR 14, eds. M. Burrows and E. A. Speiser. Philadelphia: ASOR.

1939 *Explorations in Eastern Palestine, III*. AASOR 18–19, eds. M. Burrows and E. A. Speiser. New Haven: ASOR.

1951 *Explorations in Eastern Palestine, IV*. AASOR 25–28. New Haven: ASOR.

1968 *The River Jordan*. New York: McGraw-Hill.

1970 *The Other Side of Jordan*. 2nd ed. Cambridge, Mass. ASOR.

Görg, M. 1979 Tuthmosis III. und die Š'św-Region. *JNES* 38: 199–202.

Goetze, A. 1957 On the Chronology of the Second Millennium B.C. *JCS* 11: 53–61.

1964 The Kassites and Near Eastern Chronology. *JCS* 18: 97–101.

Goff, B. L. 1963 *Symbols of Prehistoric Mesopotamia*. New Haven: Yale University.

1970 The Significance of Symbols: A Hypothesis Tested with Relation to Egyptian Symbols. Pp. 476–505 in *Religions in Antiquity: Essays in Memory of Erwin Ramsdell Goodenough*, ed. J. Neusner. Studies in the History of Religions, Supplements to *Numen*, 14. Leiden: E. J. Brill.

Goldin, J. 1976 The Magic of Magic and Superstition. Pp. 115–47 in *Aspects of Religious Propaganda in Judaism and Early Christianity*, ed. E. S. Fiorenza. Notre Dame: University of Notre Dame.

Goldman, H., ed. 1950–63 *Excavations at Gözlü Kule, Tarsus*. 3 vols. Publication of the Institute for Advanced Study. Princeton: Princeton University.

Goodenough, E. R. 1937 Symbolism in Hellenistic Jewish Art; The Problem of Method. *JBL* 56: 103–14.

1953–68 *Jewish Symbols in the Greco-Roman Period*. 13 vols. Bollingen Series. New York: Pantheon Books.

Gorelick, L., and Gwinnett, A. J. 1978 Ancient Seals and Modern Science. *Expedition* 20: 38–47.

Grant, E. 1929 *Beth Shemesh*. Biblical and Kindred Studies, no. 2. Haverford, Pa.: Haverford College.

1931–32 *Ain Shems Excavations, 1928, 1929, 1930, 1931, 1932*. Biblical and Kindred Studies, nos. 3 and 4. 2 pts. Haverford: Haverford College.

1934 *Rumeileh: Being Ain Shem Excavations*. Biblical and Kindred Studies, no. 5. Haverford: Haverford College.

Grant, E., and Wright, G. E. 1938–39 *Ain Shems Excavations*. Biblical and Kindred Studies, no. 8. 2 pts. Haverford: Haverford College.

Guiges, P. E. 1939 Lébé'a, Kafer-Ǧarra, Qrayé, nécropoles de la région sidonienne. *BMB* 3: 53–63.

Guy, P. L. O. 1938 *Megiddo Tombs*. OIP, 33. Chicago: University of Chicago.

Hachmann, R. 1970 *Bericht über die Ergebnisse der Ausgrabungen in Kāmid el-Lōz (Libanon) in den Jahren 1966 und 1967*. Saarbrücker Beiträge zur Altertumskunde, vol. 4, eds. R. Hachmann and W. Schmitthenner. Bonn: R. Habelt.

Hachmann, R., and Kuschke, A. 1966 *Bericht über die Ergebnisse der Ausgrabungen in Kāmid-el-Lōz, Libanon in den Jahren 1963 und 1964*. Saarbrücker Beiträge zur Altertumskunde, vol. 3. Bonn: R. Habelt.

Hachmann, R., and Metzger, M. 1973 Arbeiten auf dem Tell Kāmid el-Lōz (Libanon) 1970 und 1971. *AfO* 24: 176–79.

Haller, A. 1954 *Die Gräber und Grufte von Assur*. Wissenschaftliche Veröffentlichungen der Deutschen Orient-Gesellschaft in Assur, 65. Berlin: Deutsche Orient-Gesellschaft.

Hamilton, R. W. 1934 Tall Abū Hawam. *QDAP* 3: 74–80.

1935 Excavations at Tell Abu Hawām. *QDAP* 4: 1–69.

Hamza, M. 1930 Excavation of the Department of Antiquities at Qantîr (Faqûs District). *Annales du Service des Antiquités de l'Egypte* 30: 31–68.

Hankey, V. 1966 Late Mycenaean Pottery at Beth-Shan. *AJA* 70: 169–71.

1967 Mycenaean Pottery in the Middle East. *BSA* 62: 104–47.

1974 A Late Bronze Age Temple at Amman. *Levant* 6: 131–78.

Hankey, V., and Warren, P. 1974 The Absolute Chronology of the Aegean Bronze Age. *Bulletin of the Institute of Classical Studies of the University of London* 21: 142–52.

Harding, G. L. 1953 Four Tomb Groups from Jordan. *APEF* 6: 27–47.

Harif, A. 1974 A Mycenaean Building at Tell Abu-Hawam in Palestine. *PEQ*, pp. 83–90.

Harris, J. R. 1961 *Lexicographical Studies in Ancient Egyptian Minerals*. Deutsche Akademie der Wissenschaften zu Berlin, Institut für Orientforschung, vol. 54. Berlin: Akademie-Verlag.

Harrison, M. 1947 Toilet Articles, Jewelry, and Other Artistic Products. Pp. 267–68 in *Tell en-Naṣbeh*, vol. 1:

Archaeological and Historical Results by C. C. McCown and H. C. Wampler. Berkeley: Palestine Institute of the Pacific School of Religion and ASOR.

Hartner, W.   1965   The Earliest History of the Constellations in the Near East and the Motif of the Lion-Bull Combat. *JNES* 24: 1–16.

Hayes, W. C.   1953–59   *The Scepter of Egypt: A Background for the Study of the Egyptian Antiquities in the Metropolitan Museum of Art.* 2 pts. New York: MMA.

1970–75   Chronology: I. Egypt—To the End of the Twentieth Dynasty. pp. 173–93 in *CAH*[3] I/1.

Hedges, R. E. M.

1976   Pre-Islamic Glazes in Mesopotamia—Nippur. *Archaeometry* 18: 209–38.

1982   Early Glazed Pottery and Faience in Mesopotamia. Pp. 93–103 in *Early Pyrotechnology: The Evolution of the First Fire-Using Industries*, eds. T. A. Wertime and S. F. Wertime. Washington, D.C.: Smithsonian Institution.

Hedges, R. E. M., and Moorey, P. R. S. Pre-Islamic Ceramic Glazes at Kish and Nineveh in Iraq. *Archaeometry* 17: 25–43.

Helck, W.   1960   Die ägyptische Verwaltung in den syrischen Besitzungen. *MDOG* 92: 1–13.

1968–69   Zur staatlichen Organization Syriens im Beginn der 18. Dynastie. *AfO* 22: 27–29.

1971   *Die Beziehungen Ägyptens zu Vorderasien im 3. und 2. Jahrtausends vor Chr.* Ägyptologische Abhandlungen, vol. 5. 2d ed., rev. Wiesbaden: Harrassowitz.

Helck, W., and Otto, E., eds.   1972   *Lexikon der Ägyptologie.* Wiesbaden: Harrassowitz.

Hennessy, J. B.   1966   Excavations of a Late Bronze Age Temple. *PEQ*, pp. 155–62.

Higgins, R. A.   1961   *Greek and Roman Jewellery.* Metheun's Handbooks of Archaeology. London: Methuen.

Hoffmann, H., and Davidson, P. F.

1967   *Greek Gold: Jewelry from the Age of Alexander.* Ed. A. von Saldern. Brooklyn: Brooklyn Museum.

Horn, S. H.   1962   Scarabs from Shechem. *JNES* 21: 1–14.

1969   Foreign Gods in Ancient Egypt. Pp. 37–42 in *Studies in Honor of John A. Wilson.* SAOC, no. 35. Chicago: University of Chicago.

Hornung, E.   1964   *Untersuchungen zur Chronologie und Geschichte der Neuen Reiches.* Ägyptologische Abhandlungen, vol. 2. Wiesbaden: Harrassowitz.

Ibrahim, M.   1978   The Collared-Rim Jar of the Early Iron Age. Pp. 117–26 in *Archaeology in the Levant: Essays for Kathleen Kenyon*, eds. R. Moorey and P. Parr. Warminster: Aris and Phillips.

Ibrahim, M., Sauer, J. A., and Yassine, K.   1976   The East Jordan Valley Survey, 1975. *BASOR* 222: 41–66.

Ingholt, H.   1940   *Rapport préliminaire sur sept campagnes de fouilles à Hama en Syrie (1932–1938).* Det Kgl. Danske Videnskabernes Selskak, Archaeologiskkunsthistoriske Meddelelser, vol. 3, no. 1. Copenhagen: Munksgaar.

Jacobsen, T.   1976   *The Treasures of Darkness: A History of Mesopotamian Religion.* New Haven: Yale University.

James, F. W.   1966   *The Iron Age at Beth Shan: A Study of Levels VI–IV.* University Monograph. Philadelphia: University Museum.

James, T. G. H.   1971   Egypt: From the Expulsion of the Hyksos to Amenophis I. Pp. 289–312 in *CAH*[3] II/1.

Johns, C. N.   1932   Excavations at ʿAtlīt (1930–1). *QDAP* 2: 41–104.

Jordanian Department of Antiquities   1973   *The Archaeological Heritage of Jordan.* Part 1: *The Archaeological Periods and Sites (East Bank).* Amman: Department of Antiquities.

1975   *The Archaeology of Amman, 2000 B.C.–750 A.D.* Amman: Department of Antiquities.

Kafafi, Z. el-K.   1977   Late Bronze Age Pottery in Jordan (East Bank): 1575–1225 B.C. M.A. dissertation, University of Jordan.

Kantor, H. J.   1947   The Aegean and the Orient in the Second Millennium B.C. *AJA* 51: 1–103.

1956   Syro-Palestinian Ivories. *JNES* 15: 153–74.

Kaplan, J.   1955   A Cemetery of the Bronze Age Discovered near Tel Aviv Harbour. *ʿAtiqot* (English Series) 1: 1–12.

1971   Mesopotamian Elements in the Middle Bronze II Culture of Palestine. *JNES* 30: 293–307.

1972   The Archaeology and History of Tel Aviv–Jaffa. *BA* 35: 66–95.

Karageorghis, V.   1965   *Nouvaux documents pour l'étude du Bronze Récent à Chypre.* Trans. R.–P. Charles and Mme. V. Karageorghis. Etudes chypriotes, 3. Paris: E. de Boccard.

1969   Contribution to the Religion of Cyprus in the 13th and 12th Centuries B.C. Pp. 105–9 in *Mycenaeans in the Eastern Mediterranean.* Acts of the International Archaeological Symposium, 22 March–2 April, 1972. Nicosia: Department of Antiquities.

1976   *Kition: Mycenaean and Phoenician Discoveries in Cyprus.* New Aspects of Antiquity, ed. M. Wheeler. London: Thames and Hudson.

Kees, H.   1961   *Ancient Egypt: A Cultural Topography.* Ed. T. G. H. James. Trans. F. D. Morrow. London: Faber and Faber.

Keimer, L.   1967   *Die Gartenpflanzen im alter Ägypten.* Ägyptologische Studien. Berlin: 1924; reprint ed., Hildesheim: G. Olms.

Kemp, B. J.   1978   Imperialism and Empire in New Kingdom Egypt. Pp. 7–57 in *Imperialism in the Ancient World*, eds. P. D. A. Garnsey and C. R. Whittaker. The Cambridge University Research Seminar in Ancient History. Cambridge: Cambridge University.

Kempinski, A.   1974   Tell el-ʿAjjûl—Beth-Eglayim or Sharuḥen? *IEJ* 24: 145–52.

Kenyon, K. M.   1958   Some Notes on the Early and Middle Bronze Age Strata of Megiddo. *EI* 5: 51*–60*.

1960–65   *Excavations at Jericho.* Vol. 1: *The Tombs Exca-*

vated in 1952–4. Vol. 2: *The Tombs Excavated in 1955–8*. London: British School of Archeology in Jerusalem.

1966 *Amorites and Canaanites*. Schweich Lectures. London: Oxford University.

1969 The Middle and Late Bronze Age Strata at Megiddo. *Levant* 1: 25–60.

1971 Palestine in the Time of the Eighteenth Dynasty. Pp. 526–56 in *CAH*[3] II/1.

1979 *Archaeology in the Holy Land*. 4th ed. London: E. Benn.

Kiefer, C., and Allibert, A. 1971 Pharaonic Blue Ceramics: The Process of Self-Glazing. *Archaeology* 24: 107–17.

Kitchen, K. A. 1962 *Suppliluliuma and the Amarna Pharaohs: A Study in Relative Chronology*. Liverpool Monographs in Archaeology and Oriental Studies. Liverpool: Liverpool University.

1964 Some New Light on the Asiatic Wars of Ramesses II. *JEA* 50: 47–50.

1969 Interrelations of Egypt and Syria. Pp. 77ff in *Siria nel Tardo Bronzo*, ed. M. Liverani. Orientis Antiqui Collectio, no. 9. Rome.

Klengel, H. 1959 Neue Lamaštu-Amulette aus dem Vorderasiatischen Museum zu Berlin und dem British Museum. *MIOF* 7: 334–55.

1961–63 Weitere Amulette gegen Lamaštu. *MIOF* 8: 24–29.

1965–70 *Geschichte Syriens im 2. Jahrtausend vor unserer Zeitalter*. Deutsche Akademie der Wissenschaften zu Berlin, Institut für Orientforschung, nos. 40 and 70. 3 pts. Berlin: Akademie-Verlag.

Knudtzon, J. A., ed. 1907–14 *Die el-Amarna Tafeln*. 3 vols. Vorderasiatische Bibliothek. Leipzig: J. C. Hinrichs.

Kramer, S. N., ed. 1961 *Mythologies of the Ancient World*. Garden City, NY: Doubleday; Anchor.

Kühne, C. 1963 Zum Status der Syro-Palästinischen Vassalen des Neuen Reiches. *AUSS* 1: 73ff.

Kühne, K. 1969 *Zur Kenntnis silikatischer Werkstoffe und der Technologie ihrer Herstellung im 2. Jahrtausend vor unserer Zeitrechnung*. Abhandlung der Deutschen Akademie der Wissenschaften zu Berlin. Berlin: Akademie Verlag.

Lacau, P. 1904–06 *Sarcophages antérieures au nouvel empire*. *CCG*, nos. 28001–126. 2 vols. Cairo: IFAO.

Lamon, R. S., and Shipton, G. M. 1939 *Megiddo I: Seasons of 1925–1934*. OIP, 42. Chicago: University of Chicago.

Landsberger, B. 1954 Assyrische Königsliste und 'Dunkles Zeitalter'. *JCS* 8: 31–73, 106–33.

Lange, K., and Hirmer, M. 1968 *Egypt: Architecture, Sculpture, and Painting in Three Thousand Years*. Trans. R. H. Boothroyd. J. Filson, and B. Taylor. 2d ed., rev. London: Phaidon.

Lapp, P. 1967a The Conquest of Palestine in the Light of Archaeology. *Concordia Theological Monthly* 38: 283–300.

1967b Taanach by the Waters of Megiddo. *BA* 30: 1–27.

1967c The 1966 Excavations at Tell Ta'annek. *BASOR* 185; 2–39.

1969 The 1968 Excavations at Ta'annek. *BASOR* 195: 2–49.

Leemans, C., and Pleyte, W. 1842 *Monuments égyptiens du Musée d'antiquités de Pays Bas à Leyde*. 2 pts. Leiden.

Liebowitz, H. A. 1977 Bone and Ivory Inlay from Syria and Palestine, *IEJ* 27: 89–97.

Limet, H. 1960 *Le Travail du métal au pays de Sumer au temps de la IIIe dynastie d'Ur*. Bibliothèque de la Faculté de philosophie et lettres de l'Université de Liège, no. 155. Paris: Société d'Édition Les Belles Lettres.

Loud, G. 1948 *Megiddo II: Seasons of 1935–1939*. OIP, 62. Chicago: University of Chicago.

Lucas, A. 1962 *Ancient Egyptian Materials and Industries*. 4th ed, rev. and enlarged by J. R. Harris. London: E. Arnold.

Lurker, M. 1964 *Symbole der alten Ägypter: Einführung und kleines Wörterbuch*. Zeichen und Symbole. Weilheim: O. W. Barth.

1974 *Götter und Symbole der alter Ägypter*. Bern: O. W. Barth.

Ma'ayeh, F. S. 1960 Recent Archeological Discoveries in Jordan: Quailba (Irbid District). *ADAJ* 4–5: 116.

Macalister, R. A. S. 1912 *The Excavation of Gezer, 1902–1905 and 1907–1909*. 3 vols. London: J. Murray for the PEF.

McClellan, T. L. 1979 Chronology of the 'Philistine' Burials at Tell el-Far'ah (South). *Journal of Field Archaeology* 6: 57–73.

Macdonald, E., Starkey, J. L., and Harding, L. 1932 *Beth-Pelet II*. BSAE and ERA, vol. 52. London: British School of Archaeology in Jerusalem.

McGovern, P. E. 1979 The Baq'ah Valley, Jordan: A Cesium Magnetometer Survey. *MASCA Journal* 1: 39–41.

1980 Explorations in the Umm ad-Danānīr Region of the Baq'ah Valley, 1977–1978. *ADAJ* 24: 55–67.

1981 The Baq'ah Valley, Jordan: Test Soundings of Cesium Magnetometer Anomalies. *MASCA Journal* 1: 214–17.

1982 Exploring the Burial Caves of the Baq'ah Valley of Jordan. *Archaeology* 35: 46–57.

In Press *The Late Bronze/Early Iron Age of Central Transjordan: The Baq'ah Valley Project 1977–1981*. Philadelphia: University Museum.

Forthcoming The Pendants and Beads. In the Late Bronze Beth Shan volume. Philadelphia: University Museum.

Mackenzie, D. 1912–13 Excavations at Ain Shems (Beth-Shemesh). *PEFA* 2: 1–100.

McKerrell, H. 1972 On the Origins of British Faience Beads and Some Aspects of the Wessex-Mycenae Relationship. *PPS* 38: 286–301.

Mace, A. C., and Winlock, H. E. 1916 *The Tomb of Senebtisi at Lisht*. Publications of MMA Egyptian Expedition, vol. 1. New York: Gilliss.

Malamat, A. 1961 Campaigns of Amenhotep II and Thutmose IV to Canaan. *Scripta Hierosolymitana* 8: 218–31.

Mallowan, M. E. L. 1947 Excavations at Brak and Chagar Bazar. *Iraq* 9: 1–259.

Marshall, F. H. 1911 *Catalogue of the Jewellery, Greek, Etruscan, and Roman in the Departments of Antiquities, British Museum*. London: Trustees of the British Museum.

Martin, G. T. 1971 *Egyptian Administrative and Private-Name Seals: Principally of the Middle Kingdom and Second Intermediate Period*. Oxford: Griffith Institute.

1972 Introduction to *Amulets* by W. M. F. Petrie. Reprint of 1914 ed., Warminster: Aris & Philipps.

Mauss, M. 1975 *A General Theory of Magic*. Trans. R. Brain. New York: W. W. Norton; Norton Library.

Maxwell-Hyslop, R. 1953 Bronze Lugged Axe- or Adze Blades from Asia. *Iraq* 15: 69–87.

1960 The Ur Jewellery. *Iraq* 22: 105–15.

1971 *Western Asiatic Jewellery, c. 3000–612 B.C.* Methuen's Handbooks of Archaeology. London: Methuen.

May, H. G. 1935 *Material Remains of the Megiddo Cult*. OIP, 26. Chicago: University of Chicago.

Mazar [Maisler], B. 1932–33 Cypriote Pottery at a Tomb-cave in the Vicinity of Jerusalem. *AJSL* 49: 248–53.

1954 The Stratification of Tell Abu Hawam on the Bay of Acre. *BASOR* 134: 21–25.

1968 The Middle Bronze Age in Palestine. *IEJ* 18: 65–97.

Mendenhall, G. E. 1973 *The Tenth Generation: The Origins of the Biblical Tradition*. Baltimore: Johns Hopkins University.

Du Mesnil du Buisson, R. 1932 Une campagne de fouilles à Khan Sheikhoun. *Syria* 13: 171–88.

Merrillees, R. S. 1968 *The Cypriote Bronze Age Pottery Found in Egypt*. SMA, vol. 18. Lund: P. Åström.

1971 The Early History of the Late Cypriote I. *Levant* 3: 56–79.

Meyers, C. L. 1976 *The Tabernacle Menorah: A Synthetic Study of a Symbol from the Biblical Cult*. ASOR Dissertation Series, ed. D. N. Freedman, no. 2. Missoula, Mont. ASOR.

Mishara, J., and Meyers, P. 1973 Ancient Egyptian Silver: A Review. Pp. 29–45 in *Recent Advances in Science and Technology of Materials*, vol. 3, ed. A. Bishay. New York: Plenum.

Mohammad, M.A.-K. 1959 The Administration of Syro-Palestine during the New Kingdom. *ASAE* 56: 105–37.

Mond, R., and Myers, O. H. 1940 *Temples of Armant: A Preliminary Survey*. EES, mem. 43. pts. 1–2. London: EES.

Montet, P. 1929 *Byblos et l'Egypt: Quatre campagnes de fouilles à Gebeil, 1921–1924*. 2 vols. BAH, vol. 11.

Paris: Geuthner.

1959 *L'Egypt et la Bible*. Cahiers d'archéologie biblique, no. 11. Neuchâtel: Delachaux et Niestle,

Moortgat, A. 1969 *The Art of Ancient Mesopotamia: The Classical Art of the Near East*. Trans. J. Filson. London: Phaidon.

Morenz, S. 1973 *Egyptian Religion*. Trans. A. E. Keep. Ithaca, NY: Cornell University.

Müller, K. 1909 Alt-Pylos, II. Die Funde aus den Kuppelgräbern von Kakovatos. *Mitteilungen des Deutschen Archäologischen Instituts, Athenische Abteilung* 34:229–328.

Müller, U. 1970 Kritische Bemerkungen zu den Straten XIII bis IX in Megiddo. *ZDPV* 86: 50–86.

Muhly, J. D. 1970 Homer and the Phoenicians: The Relations between Greece and the Near East in the Late Bronze and Early Iron Ages. *Berytus* 19: 19–64.

Munn-Rankin, J. M. 1956 Diplomacy in Western Asia in the Early Second Millennium B.C. *Iraq* 18: 68–110.

Munsell Color Company 1975 *Munsell Soil Color Charts*. Baltimore: Munsell Color Company

Murray, H., and Nuttal, M., compilers 1963 *A Handlist to Howard Carter's Catalogue of Objects in Tut'ankhamun's Tomb*. Tut'ankhamun's Tomb Series, 1. Oxford: Oxford University.

Murray, M. A. 1953 Faience Amulets. Pp. 378–81 in *Lachish III. The Iron Age* by O. Tufnell. London: Oxford University for the Trustees of the late Sir Henry Wellcome.

Na'aman, N. 1981 Economic Aspects of the Egyptian Occupation of Canaan. *IEJ* 31: 172–85.

Naville, E., and Griffith, F. L. 1890 *Mound of the Jews and the City of Onias*, (and) *The Antiquities of Tell el-Yahudiyeh*. EEF, mem. 7. London: Kegan Paul, Trench, Trübner.

Negbi, O. 1970 *The Hoards of Goldwork from Tell el-'Ajjul*. SMA, vol. 25, ed. Paul Åström. Göteborg: SMA.

1976 *Canaanite Gods in Metal: An Archaeological Study of Ancient Syro-Palestinian Figurines*. Publications of the Institute of Archaeology, no. 5. Tel Aviv: Institute of Archaeology, Tel Aviv University.

Neusner, J., ed., 1970 *Religions in Antiquity: Essays in Memory of Erwin Ramsdell Goodenough*. Studies in the History of Religion, Supplements to *Numen*, 14. Leiden: Brill.

Newton, R. G., and Renfrew, C. 1970 British Faience Beads Reconsidered. *Antiquity* 44: 199–206.

Noble, J. V. 1969 The Technique of Egyptian Faience. *AJA* 73: 435–39.

North, R. 1973 Ugarit Grid, Strata, and Find-Localizations. *ZDPV* 89: 113–60.

Oates, D. 1965 The Excavations of Tell el Rimah, 1964. *Iraq* 27: 62–80.

1966 The Excavations at Tell al Rimah, 1965. *Iraq* 28: 122–39.

Ohata, K., ed. 1966–70 *Tel Zeror I–III*. Tokyo: Society

for Near Eastern Studies in Japan.

Oppenheim, A. L. 1949 The Golden Garments of the Gods. *JNES* 8: 172–93.

1974 A Note on Research in Mesopotamian Glass. *JGS* 15: 9–11.

Oppenheim, A. L., Brill, R. H., Barag, D., and von Saldern, A. 1970 *Glass and Glassmaking in Ancient Mesopotamia*. Corning, N.Y.: Corning Museum of Glass.

Oren, E. 1969 Cypriote Imports in the Palestinian Late Bronze I Context. *Opuscula Atheniensis* 9: 127–50.

1973 *The Northern Cemetery at Beth Shan*. Museum Monograph of the University Museum of the University of Pennsylvania. Leiden: E. J. Brill.

1978 Tell esh-Shari'a (Tel Sera'). Pp. 1059–69 in vol. 4 of *Encyclopedia of Archaeological Excavations in the Holy Land*, ed. M. Avi-Yonah and E. Stern. Englewood Cliffs: Prentice Hall.

Ory, J. 1944 A Late Bronze Tomb at Tell Jerishe. *QDAP* 10: 55–57.

1948 A Bronze-Age Cemetery at Dhahrat el Humraiya, *QDAP* 13: 75–89.

Otto, R. 1950 *The Idea of the Holy: An Inquiry into the Non-Rational Factor in the Idea of the Divine and Its Relation to the Rational*. Trans. J. W. Harvey. 2d ed. London: Oxford University; Galaxy pb.

Parker, B. 1949 Cylinder Seals from Palestine. *Iraq* 11: 1–43.

Parrot, A. 1956–68 *Mission archéologique de Mari*. 6 vols. BAH, vols. 65, 68, 70, 86, 87. Paris: Geuthner.

1969 De la Méditerranée à l'Iran: Masques énigmatiques. Pp. 409–418 in *Ugaritica VI*. Mission de Ras Shamra, vol. 17, ed. C. F. A. Schaeffer. BAH, vol. 81. Paris: Mission Archéologique de Ras Shamra.

Peet, T. E., and Woolley, C. L. 1923 *The City of Akhenaten*. Part 1: Excavations of 1921 and 1922 at El-'Amarnah. EES, mem. 38. London: EES.

Peltenberg, E. J. 1971 Some Early Developments of Vitreous Materials. *World Archaeology* 3: 6–12.

1974 The Glazed Vases. Appendix 1, pp. 107–143 in *Excavations at Kition, I: The Tombs* by V. Karageorghis. Nicosia: Department of Antiquities.

1977 A Faience from Hala Sultan Tekke and Second Millennium B.C. Western Asiatic Pendants Depicting Females. Pp. 177–92 in *Hala Sultan Tekke 3: Excavations 1972* by P. Åström, G. Hult, and M. S. Olofsson. SMA, vol. 45:3. Göteborg: P. Åström.

Pendlebury, J. D. S. 1951 *The City of Akhenaten*. Part 3: *Central City and the Official Quarters*. 2 vols. EES, mem. 44. London: EES.

Petrie, W. M. F. 1890 *Kahun, Gurob, and Hawara*. London: Kegan Paul, Trench, Trübner.

1891a *Illahun, Kahun, and Gurob, 1889–1890*. London: D. Nutt.

1891b *Tell el Hesy (Lachish)*. London: A. P. Watt for PEF.

1894 *Tell el Amarna*. London: Methuen; reprint ed.,

1974, Warminster: Aris & Philipps.

1897 *Six Temples at Thebes, 1896*. London: B. Quaritch.

1902–06 *Abydos I–II*. 2 vols. EEF, mems. 22 and 24. London: EEF.

1904 *Ehnasya*. EEF, mem. 26. London: EEF.

1906a *Hyksos and Israelite Cities*. Double vol. BSAE and ERA, vol. 12. London: BSAE and B. Quaritch.

1906b *Researches in Sinai*. London: J. Murray.

1914 *Amulets*. London: Constable; reprint ed., 1972, Warminster: Aris & Philipps.

1923 *The Arts and Crafts of Ancient Egypt*. 2d ed., rev. London: T. N. Foulis.

1927 *Objects of Daily Use*. BSAE and ERA, vol. 42. London: BSAE and B. Quaritch.

1928 *Gerar*. BSAE and ERA, vol. 43. London: B. Quaritch.

1930 *Beth-Pelet I*. BSAE and ERA, vol. 48. London: BSAE and B. Quaritch.

1931–34 *Ancient Gaza, I–IV*. BSAE and ERA, vols. 53–56. London: BSAE and B. Quaritch.

Petrie, W. M. F., and Brunton, G. 1924 *Sedment I–II*. BSAE and ERA, vols. 34–35. London: BSAE and B. Quaritch.

Petrie, W. M. F., Brunton, G., and Murray, M. A. 1923 *Lahun II*. BSAE and ERA, vol. 33. London: BSAE and B. Quaritch.

Petrie, W. M. F., and Griffith, F. L. 1886 *Tanis II: Nebeshah and Defenneh*. EEF, mem. 4. London: EEF.

Petrie, W. M. F., Mackay, E. J. H., and Murray, M. A. 1952 *City of Shepherd Kings and Ancient Gaza V*. BSAE and ERA, vol. 64. London: BSAE and B. Quaritch.

Petrie, W. M. F., Mackay, E. J. H., and Wainwright, G. 1910 *Meydum and Memphis (III)*. BSAE and ERA, vol. 18. London: BSAE and B. Quaritch.

Petrie, W. M. F., Wainwright, G. A., and Mackay, E. J. H. 1912 *The Labyrinth, Gerzeh, and Mazghuneh*. BSAE and ERA, vol. 21. London: BSAE and B. Quaritch.

Pézard, M. 1922 Mission archéologique à Tell Nebi Mend (1921): Rapport sommaire. *Syria* 3: 89–115.

1931 *Qadesh: Mission archéologique à Tell Nebi Mend 1921–1922*. BAH, vol. 15. Paris: Geuthner.

Pierides, A. 1971 *Jewellery In the Cyprus Museum*. Picture Book No. 5. Nicosia: Department of Antiquities.

Platt, E. E. 1973 Palestinian Iron Age Jewelry from Fourteen Excavations. Ph.D. dissertation, Harvard University.

1976 Triangular Jewelry Plaques, *BASOR* 221: 103–111.

1978 Bone Pendants. *BA* 41: 23–28.

1979 Jewelry of Bible Times and the Catalog of Isaiah 3:18–23. 2 pts. *AUSS*.

Pollard, A. M., and Moorey, P. R. S. 1982 Some Analyses of Middle Assyrian Faience and Related Materials from Tell al-Rimah in Iraq. *Archaeometry* 24: 45–50.

Pope, M. H., and Tigay, J. H. 1971 A Description of Baal. *Ugarit-Forschungen* 3: 117–30.

Porada, E. 1947 *Seal Impressions of Nuzi*. AASOR 24. New Haven: ASOR.

Porter, B., and Moss, R. 1960 *Topographical Bibliography of Ancient Egyptian Hieroglyphic Texts, Reliefs, and Paintings*. 7 vols. 2d ed. Oxford: Oxford University.

Prag, K. 1978 Silver in the Levant in the Fourth Millennium B.C. Pp. 36–45 in *Archaeology in the Levant: Essays for Kathleen Kenyon*, eds. R. Moorey and P. Parr. Warminster: Aris & Phillips.

Pritchard, J. B. 1951 Syrians as Pictured in the Paintings of Theban Tombs. *BASOR* 122: 36–41.

1954 *The Ancient Near East in Pictures Relating to the Old Testament*. Princeton: Princeton University.

1955 *Ancient Near Eastern Texts Relating to the Old Testament*. Princeton: Princeton University.

1963 *The Bronze Age Cemetery at Gibeon*. Museum Monograph. Philadelphia: University Museum.

1964 Two Tombs and a Tunnel in the Jordan Valley: Discoveries at Biblical Zarethan. *Expedition* 6: 2–9.

1965 A Cosmopolitan Culture of the Late Bronze Age. *Expedition* 7: 26–33.

1967 *Palestinian Figurines in Relation to Certain Goddesses Known through Literature*. American Oriental Series, vol. 24, ed. Z. S. Harris. New Haven: American Oriental Society, 1943; reprint ed., New York: Kraus.

1968 New Evidence on the Role of the Sea Peoples in Canaan at the Beginning of the Iron Age. Pp. 99–112 in *The Role of the Phoenicians in the Interaction of Mediterranean Civilizations*. Beirut: American University of Beirut.

1969 *The Ancient Near East: Supplementary Texts and Pictures Relating to the Old Testament*. Princeton: Princeton University.

1975 *Sarepta: A Preliminary Report on the Iron Age*. University Monograph. Philadelphia: University Museum.

1980 *The Cemetery at Tell es-Sa'idiyeh, Jordan*. University Museum Monograph 41. Philadelphia: University Museum.

Quibell, J. E. 1898 *El Kab*. ERA, vol. 3. London: B. Quaritch.

Quillard, B. 1973 Les Etuis porte-amulettes carthaginois. *Karthago* 16: 1–32.

Rahmani, L. Y. 1959 A Lion-Faced Figurine from Beth-She'an. *'Atiqot* (English Series) 2: 184–85.

Rainey, A. F. 1970 *El Amarna Tablets 359–379*. Alter Orient und Altes Testament. Kevelaer: Butzon and Bercker.

Randall-MacIver, D., and Woolley, C. L. 1911 *Buhen*. Eckley B. Coxe Expedition to Nubia, vol. 7. 2 vols. Philadelphia: University Museum.

Read, J. G. 1970 Early Eighteenth Dynasty Chronology. *JNES* 29: 1–11.

Redford, D. B. 1967 *History and Chronology of the Eighteenth Dynasty of Egypt: Seven Studies*. Toronto: University of Toronto.

1973 New Light on the Asiatic Campaigning of Horemheb. *BASOR* 211: 36–49.

1979 A Gate Inscription from Karnak and Egyptian Involvement in Western Asia During the Early 18th Dynasty. *JAOS* 99: 270–87.

Reisner, G. A. 1907 *Amulets*. CCG, nos. 5218–6000 and 12001–13595. 2 vols. Cairo: IFAO.

1923 *Excavations at Kerma*. Harvard African Studies, vols. 5–6. 2 vols. Cambridge: Peabody Museum of Harvard University.

Reviv, H. 1966 The Government of Shechem in the El-Amarna Period and in the Days of Abimelech. *IEJ* 16: 252–57.

1967 On the Urban Representative Institution and Self-Government in Syria-Palestine in the Second Half of the Second Millennium B.C. *JESHO* 12: 283–97.

Riefstahl, E. 1968 *Ancient Egyptian Glass and Glazes in the Brooklyn Museum*. Wilbour Monographs, 1. Brooklyn: Brooklyn Museum.

Roeder, G. 1916 *Zauberei and Jenseitsglauben im alten Ägypten*. Zurich.

Rosenthal, R. 1973 *Jewellery in Ancient Times*. Cassell's Introducing Archaeology Series. London: Cassell.

Rothenberg, B. 1972 *Were These King Solomon's Mines?: Excavations in Timna Valley*. New Aspects of Archaeology, ed. M. Wheeler. New York: Stein and Day.

Rowe, A. 1927a The Discoveries at Beth-shan during the 1926 Season. *Museum Journal* 19: 9–45.

1927b The Expedition at Beisan. *Museum Journal* 18: 411–41.

1928 The 1927 Excavations at Beisan. *Museum Journal* 19: 145–68.

1929a The Palestine Expedition: Report of the 1928 Season. *Museum Journal* 20: 37–87.

1929b The Two Royal Stelae of Beth-shan. *Museum Journal* 20: 89–98.

1929c Palestine Expedition of the Museum of the University of Pennsylvania, Third Report – 1928 Season. *PEFQS*, pp. 78–94.

1930 *Topography and History of Beth-shan*. Publications of the Palestine Section of the University Museum, University of Pennsylvania, vol. 1. Philadelphia: University of Pennsylvania for the University Museum.

1936 *A Catalogue of Egyptian Scarabs, Scaraboids, Seals and Amulets in the Palestine Archaeological Museum*. Cairo: IFAO.

1940 *The Four Canaanite Temples of Beth-shan: The Temples and Cult Objects*. Publications of the Palestine Section of the University Museum, vol. 1, pt. 1. Philadelphia: University Museum.

Rowton, M. B. 1966 The Material from Western Asia and the Chronology of the Nineteenth Dynasty. *JNES* 25: 240–58.

Saller, S. J. 1964 *The Jebusite Burial Place*. The Excavation at Dominus Flevit (Mount Olivet, Jerusalem), pt. 2. Publications of the Studium Biblicum Franciscanum, no. 13. Jerusalem: Franciscan Press.

Samson, J. 1972 *Amarna, City of Akhenaten and Nefertiti: Key Pieces from the Petrie Collection*. London: Department of Egyptology.

Sanders, J. A., ed. 1970 *Near Eastern Archaeology in the Twentieth Century: Essays in Honor of Nelson Glueck*. Garden City, N.Y.: Doubleday.

Sasson, J. 1966 Canaanite Maritime Involvement in the Second Millennium B.C. *JAOS* 86: 126–38.

Sauer, J. A. 1979 A review of *Gezer II* (HUC). *BASOR* 233: 70–74.

Sayre, E. V. 1963 The Intentional Use of Antimony and Manganese in Ancient Glasses. Pp. 263–82 in *Advances in Glass Technology*, Part 2, eds. F. R. Matson and G. E. Rindone. New York: Plenum.

Schaeffer, C. F. A. 1929 Les fouilles de Minet-el Beida et de Ras Shamra: Campagne de printemps 1929. *Syria* 10: 285–97.

1932 Les Fouilles de Minet-et-Beida et de Ras-Shamra: Troisième campagne (printemps 1931). *Syria* 13: 1–27.

1935 Les Fouilles de Ras Shamra-Ugarit: Sixième campagne (printemps 1934). *Syria* 16: 141–76.

1937 Les Fouilles de Ras Shamra-Ugarit: Huitième campagne (printemps 1936). *Syria* 18: 125–54.

1938 Les Fouilles de Ras Shamra-Ugarit: Neuvième campagne (printemps 1937). *Syria* 19: 193–255, 313–27.

1939a *The Cuneiform Texts of Ras Shamra-Ugarit*. Schweich Lectures, 1936. London: British Academy.

1939b *Ugaritica*. 6 vols. BAH, vols. 31, 47, 64, 74, 80, 81. MRS, vols. 3, 5, 8, 15–17. Paris: Geuthner.

1948 *Stratigraphie comparée et chronologie de l'Asie occidentale (IIIe et IIe millenaires): Syrie, Palestine, Asie Mineure, Chypre, Perse et Caucase*. Oxford: Griffith Institute, Ashmolean Museum.

1952 *Enkomi-Alasia: Nouvelles missions en Chypre, 1946–1950*. Mission archéologique française et de la Mission du Gouvernement de Chypre à Enkomi, vol. 1. Paris: Klincksieck.

1957–65 *Le Palais royal d'Ugarit*. 4 vols. MRS, vols 6–7, 9–10. Paris: Imprimerie Nationale.

1971 *Alasia*. Mission archéologiques d'Alasia, vol. 4. Paris: Mission archéologique d'Alasia.

Schmidt, E. F. 1937 *Excavations at Tepe Hissar, Damghan*. Publication of the Iranian Section of the University Museum, University of Pennsylvania. Philadelphia: University Museum.

Schumacher, G. 1908 *Tell et-Mutesellim*. Vol. 1: *Fundbericht*, ed. C. Steuernagel. Leipzig: R. Haupt.

Scott, N. E. 1964 Egyptian Jewelry. *BMMA*, n.s., 22: 223–34.

Seefried, M. 1976 Les Pendentifs en verre faconnes sur noyau du Musée National du Bardo et du Musée National de Carthage. *Karthago* 17: 37–66.

Seger, J. D. 1972a Shechem Field XIII, 1969. *BASOR* 205: 20–35.

1972b *Tomb Offerings from Gezer*. Catalogue no. 94 for Summer 1972 exhibit. Jerusalem: Rockfeller Museum.

1974 The Middle Bronze IIC Date of the East Gate at Shechem. *Levant* 5: 117–30.

1975 The MB II Fortifications at Shechem and Gezer—A Hyksos Retrospective. *EI* 12: 34*–45*.

1976 Reflections on the Gold Hoard from Gezer. *BASOR 221*: 133–40.

Sellin, E. 1904 *Tell Ta'annek*. Denkschriften der Kaiserlichen Akademie der Wissenschaften in Wien, Philosophisch-historische Klasse, vol. 50, no. 4. Vienna: C. Gerold for Kaiserliche Akademie der Wissenschaften in Wien.

1926 Die Ausgrabung von Sichem. *ZDPV* 49: 230–37.

Sellin, E., and Watzinger, C. 1913 *Jericho: Die Ergebnisse der Ausgrabungen*. Veröffentlichungen der Deutschen Orient-Gesellschaft, vol. 22. Leipzig: J. C. Hinrichs.

Several, M. 1972 Reconsidering the Egyptian Empire in Palestine during the Amarna Period. *PEQ*, pp. 123–33.

Shea, W. H. 1979 The Conquests of Sharuhen and Megiddo Reconsidered. *IEJ* 29: 1–5.

Simons, J. J. 1937 *Handbook for the Study of Egyptian Topographical Lists Relating to Western Asia*. Leiden: E. J. Brill.

Simpson, W. K. 1960 Reshep in Egypt. *Orientalia*, n.s., 29: 63–74.

Sjöqvist, E. 1940 *Problems of the Late Cypriote Bronze Age*. Stockholm: Swedish Cyprus Expedition.

Smith, G. A. 1901 Notes of a Journey through Hauran. PEFQS, pp. 340–61.

Smith, M. 1967 Goodenough's Jewish Symbols in Retrospect. *JBL* 86: 53–68.

Smith, R. H. 1973 *Pella of the Decapolis*. Wooster, Ohio: College of Wooster.

Smith, R. W. 1970 The Analytical Study of Glass in Archaeology. Pp, 614–23 in *Science in Archaeology: A Survey of Progress and Research*, eds. D. Brothwell and E. Higgs. 2d ed., rev. and enlarged. New York: Praeger.

Smith, W. S. 1965a *The Art and Architecture of Ancient Egypt*. Pelican History of Art. Baltimore: Penguin.

1965b *Interconnections in the Ancient Near East: A Study of the Relationships between the Arts of Egypt, the Aegean, and Western Asia*. New Haven: Yale University.

Starkey, J. L. 1930 Beth-Pelet Beads. In *Corpus of Dated Palestinian Pottery* by J. G. Duncan. BSAE and ERA, vol. 49. London: BSAE.

Starkey, J. L., and Harding, L. 1932 Beth-Pelet Cemetery. In *Beth-pelet II* by W. M. F. Petrie, J. L. Starkey, and L. Harding. BSAE and ERA, vol. 52. London: B. Quaritch.

Starr, R. F. S. 1939 *Nuzi: Report on the Excavation at Yorgan Tepe near Kirkuk, Iraq*. 2 vols. Cambridge: Harvard University.

Stern, E. 1977 A Late Bronze Temple at Tell Mevorakh. *BA* 40: 80–91.

Stewart, J. R. 1974 *Tell el-'Ajjul: The Middle Bronze Age*

Remains. SMA, vol. 38. Göteborg: SMA.

Stone, J. F. S., and Thomas, L. C. 1956 The Use and Distribution of Faience in the Ancient East and Prehistoric Europe. *PPS* 22: 37-84.

Stubbings, F. H. 1951 *Mycenaean Pottery from the Levant.* Cambridge: Cambridge University.

Sukenik, E. L. 1948 Archaeological Investigations at 'Affula. *JPOS* 21: 1-78.

Swift, G. F. 1958 The Pottery of the 'Amuq Phases K to O, and Its Historical Significance. Ph.D. dissertation, University of Chicago.

Tadmor, M., and Misch-Brandl, O. 1980 The Beth Shemesh Hoard of Jewellery. *The Israel Museum News* 16: 71-82.

Tait, G. A. D. 1963 The Egyptian Relief Chalice. *JEA* 49: 93-139.

Thompson, H. O. 1970 *Mekal: The God of Beth-shan.* Leiden: E. J. Brill.

Tite, M. S. 1972 *Methods of Physical Examination in Archaeology.* Studies in Archaeological Science, ed. G. W. Dimbleby. London: Seminar Press.

Tite M. S., Freestone, I. C., Meeks, N. D., and Bimson, M. 1982 The Use of Scanning Electron Microscopy in the Technological Examination of Ancient Ceramics. Pp. 109-120 in *Archaeological Ceramics*, eds. J. S. Olin and A. D. Franklin. Washington, D.C.: Smithsonian Institution.

Tite, M. S., Freestone, I. C., and Bimson, M. 1983 Egyptian Faience: An Investigation of the Methods of Production. *Archaeometry* 25: 17-27.

Toombs, L. E. 1976 The Stratification of Tell Balâṭah (Shechem). *BASOR* 223: 57-59.

Tsountas, C., and Monatt, J. I. 1887 *The Mycenaean Age: A Study of the Monuments and Culture of Pre-Homeric Greece.* Boston: Houghton, Mifflin.

Tufnell, O. 1953 *Lachish III: The Iron Age.* London: Oxford University for the Trustees of the late Sir Henry Wellcome.

1958 *Lachish IV (Tell ed-Duweir): The Bronze Age.* London: Oxford University for the Trustees of the late Sir Henry Wellcome.

1962 The Courtyard Cemetery at Tell el-'Ajjul, Palestine, Excavations of 1931-34: A Type Site Reconsidered. *Bulletin of the Institute of Archaeology, University of London* 3: 1-37.

1975 Tell el-'Ajjul. Pp. 52-61 in vol. 1 of *Encyclopedia of Archaeological Excavations in the Holy Land*, ed. M. Avi-Yonah. Englewood Cliffs: Prentice-Hall.

1978 Graves at Tell el-Yehudiyeh: Reviewed after a Lifetime. Pp. 76-101 in *Archaeology in the Levant: Essays for Kathleen Kenyon*, eds. R. Moorey and P. Parr. Warminster: Aris & Phillips.

Tufnell, O., Inge, C. H., and Harding, L. 1940 *Lachish II: The Fosse Temple.* London: Oxford University for the Trustees of the late Sir Henry Wellcome.

Tufnell, O., and Ward, W. A.
1966 Relations between Byblos, Egypt and Mesopotamia at the End of the Third Millennium B.C.: A Study of the Montet Jar. *Syria* 43: 165-241.

Unger, E. 1940 S.v. 'Göttersymbol'. In *Reallexikon der Assyriologie*, eds. E. Ebeling and B. Meissner. Berlin: de Gruyter.

Ussishkin, D. 1978 Excavations at Lachish - 1973-1977, Preliminary Report. *Tel Aviv* 5: 1-97.

Van Buren, E. D. 1936 Sheep and Corn. *Orientalia* 5: 127-37.

1939 The Rosette in Mesopotamian Art. *ZA* 45: 99-107.

1945a Amulets in Ancient Mesopotamia. *Orientalia* 14: 18-23.

1945b *Symbols of the Gods in Mesopotamian Art.* Analecta Orientalia, 23. Rome: Pontifical Biblical Institute.

1950 Amulets, Symbols, or Idols? *Iraq* 12: 193-96.

Vandiver, P. 1982a Mid-Second Millennium B.C. Soda-Lime-Silicate Technology at Nuzi (Iraq). Pp. 73-92 in *Early Pyrotechnology of the First Fire-Using Industries*, eds. T. A. Wertime and S. F. Wertime. Washington, D. C.: Smithsonian Institution.

1982b Technological Change in Egyptian Faience. Pp. 167-79 in *Archaeological Ceramics*, eds. J. S. Olin and A. D. Franklin. Washington, D. C.: Smithsonian Institution.

Van Seters, J. 1966 *The Hyksos: A New Investigation.* New Haven: Yale University.

de Vaux, R. 1951 La Troisième Campagne de fouilles à Tell el-Far'ah, près Naplouse. *RB* 58: 391-430.

1952 La Quatrième Campagne de fouilles à Tell el-Far'ah, près Naplouse. *RB* 59: 551-83.

1957 Les Fouilles de Tell el-Far'ah, près Naplouse. *RB* 64: 552-80.

1965 *Ancient Israel.* 2 vols. New York: McGraw-Hill.

de Vaux, R., and Stève, A. M. 1947 La Première Campagne de fouilles à Tell el-Far'ah, près Naplouse. *RB* 54: 394-433.

1948 La Seconde Campagne de fouilles à Tell el-Far'ah, près Naplouse. *RB* 55: 544-80.

Vercoutter, J. 1945 *Les Objets égyptiens et égyptisant du mobilier funeraire carthaginois.* BAH, vol. 40. Paris: Geuthner.

Vernier, E. S. 1907 *Bijouterie et la joaillerie égyptiennes.* Mémoires publiés par les membres de l'IFAO, vol. 2. Cairo: IFAO.

1927 *Bijoux et orfèvreries.* 2 vols. *CCG*, nos. 52001-53855. Cairo: IFAO.

Vilímková, M. 1969 *Egyptian Jewellery.* Trans. I. Urwin. London: P. Hamlyn.

Wace, A. J. B. 1932 *Chamber Tombs at Mycenae.* Archaeologia 82.

Wainwright, G. 1920 *Balabish.* EES, mem. 37. London: G. Allen & Urwin.

Ward, W. A. 1973 A Possible New Link between Egypt and Jordan during the Reign of Amenhotep III. *ADAJ* 18: 45-46.

Watzinger, C. 1929 *Tell el-Mutesellim.* Vol. 2. Leipzig: R. Haupt.

Weippert, M.   1971   *The Settlement of the Israelite Tribes in Palestine; A Critical Survey of Recent Scholarly Debate.* Trans. J. D. Martin. Studies in Biblical Theology (2d series), 21. Naperville, Ill. A. R. Allenson.

Weinstein, J. M.   1981 The Egyptian Empire in Palestine: A Reassessment. *BASOR* 241: 1–28.

Wente, E. F., and Van Siclen, C. C.   1976   A Chronology of the New Kingdom. Pp. 217–61 in *Studies in Honor of George R. Hughes.* SAOC, no. 39. Chicago: Oriental Institute.

Wheeler, M.   1954   *Archaeology from the Earth.* Baltimore: Penguin.

Wiedemann, A.   1910   *Die Amulette der alter Aegypter.* Der Alte Orient, vol. 12, no. 1. Leipzig: J. C. Hinrichs.

Wilkinson, A.   1971   *Ancient Egyptian Jewellery.* Methuen's Handbooks of Archaeology. London: Methuen.

Wilson, V.   1975   The Iconography of Bes with Particular Reference to the Cypriote Evidence. *Levant* 7: 77–102.

Woolley, C. L.   1934   *Excavations at Ur.* Vol. 2: *The Royal Cemetery.* Publications of the Joint Expedition of the British Museum and the Museum of the University of Pennsylvania to Mesopotamia. Oxford: Trustees of the Two Museums.

   1955   *Alalakh: An Account of the Excavations at Tell Atchana in the Hatay, 1937–1949.* Reports of the Research Committee of the Society of Antiquaries of London, 18. Oxford: Society of Antiquaries of London.

Wright, G. E.   1961   The Archaeology of Palestine. Pp. 85–139 in *The Bible and the Ancient Near East*, ed. G. E. Wright. Garden City N.Y.: Doubleday; Anchor.

   1965   *Shechem: The Biography of a Biblical City.* New York: McGraw-Hill.

Wright, G. R. H.   1966   The Bronze Age Temple at Amman. *ZAW* 78: 350–57.

Wulff, H. E., Wulff, H. S., and Koch, L.   1968   Egyptian Faience: A Possible Survival in Iran. *Archaeology* 21: 98–107.

Yadin, Y.   1967   Hazor. Pp. 245–63 in *Archaeology and Old Testament Study*, ed. D. W. Thomas. Oxford: Oxford University.

   1970   Symbols of Deities at Zinjirli, Carthage, and Hazor. Pp. 199–231 in *Near Eastern Archaeology in the Twentieth Century*, ed. J. A. Sanders. Garden City, N.Y.: Doubleday.

   1972   *Hazor.* Schweich Lectures, 1970. London: British Academy.

Yadin, Y. *et al.*   1958, 1960, 1961   *Hazor I–III/IV.* Jerusalem: Magnes Press.

Yeivin, S.   1950   Canaanite and Hittite Strategy in the Second Half of the Second Millennium B.C. *JNES* 9: 101–7.

PLATES

PLATE 1   151

I.A.1 1
(3.3:1)

I.A.2 3
(1.6:1)

I.B.1 5
(3.3:1)

I.B.1 9
(1.9:1)

I.C.1 12
(2.0:1)

I.C.2 13
(1.2:1)

I.D.2 16
(1.7:1)

I.F.1.a 20
(3.5:1)

I.F.2.b 22
(3.5:1)

I.G.1.b 26
(1.6:1)

I.G.2.a 27
(3.3:1)

I.G.2.a 30
(3.3:1)

I.G.2.a 32
(3.5:1)

I.G.2.a 33
(3.3:1)

I.G.2.b 37
(3.3:1)

I.G.2.b 38
(1.5:1)

I.G.4 43
(1.0:1)

I.G.4 42
(3.3:1)

PLATE 3

153

I.G.5 45
(1.7:1)

I.G.5 46
(1.6:1)

I.G.5 47
(1.7:1)

I.G.6.a 50
(3.0:1)

I.G.6.b.i 51
(3.5:1)

I.G.6.b.i 53
(3.1:1)

PLATE 4

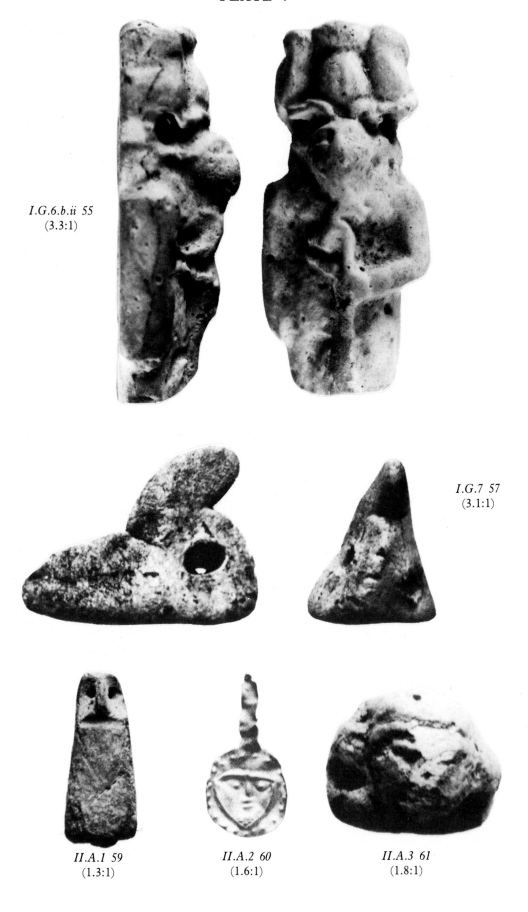

I.G.6.b.ii 55
(3.3:1)

I.G.7 57
(3.1:1)

II.A.1 59
(1.3:1)

II.A.2 60
(1.6:1)

II.A.3 61
(1.8:1)

PLATE 5   155

II.B.1.a 62
(2.0:1)

II:B.1.a 63
(1.5:1)

II.B.1.b 65
(1.1:1)

II.B.2.b 68
(1.6:1)

II.B.2.a 66
(1.0:1)

II.B.2.b 69
(1.7:1)

II.B.2.b 70
(0.9:1)

II.B.2.b 71
(1.4:1)

II.B.2.b 72
(0.9:1)

II.B.2.b 74
(0.7:1)

II.B.3.a 76
(1.3:1)

III.A. 79
(1.0:1)

III.C 82
(2.2:1)

III.D. 83
(2.1:1)

PLATE 7

157

III.F. 85
(0.6:1)

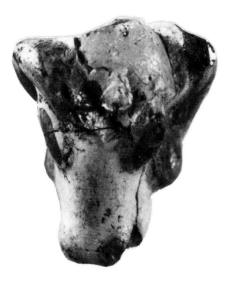

III.G 87
(3.2:1)

III.G 89
(3.3:1)

PLATE 8

III.H.1.a 90
(1.5:1)

III.H.1.b 91
(2.2:1)

III.H.1.c 92
(3.3:1)

III.H.2 93
(1.5:1)

III.H.3 94
(1.5:1)

III.H.4 95
(1.6:1)

III.H.5 96
(3.0:1)

III.H.6 97
(1.9:1)

PLATE 7   157

III.F. 85
(0.6:1)

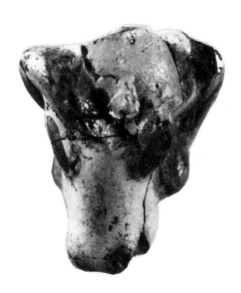

III.G 87
(3.2:1)

III.G 89
(3.3:1)

PLATE 8

III.H.1.a 90
(1.5:1)

III.H.1.b 91
(2.2:1)

III.H.1.c 92
(3.3:1)

III.H.2 93
(1.5:1)

III.H.3 94
(1.5:1)

III.H.4 95
(1.6:1)

III.H.5 96
(3.0:1)

III.H.6 97
(1.9:1)

PLATE 9   159

IV.A. 98
(1.8:1)

IV.B 101
(1.8:1)

IV.C 103
(3.4:1)

IV.D.1 104
(1.0:1)

IV.D.2 106
(1.4:1)

IV.D.3 107
(2.0:1)

IV.E 109
(1.8:1)

IV.F.1 112
(1.6:1)

IV.F.1 113
(2.0:1)

IV.F.1 114
(2.0:1)

IV.F.3 135
(2.0:1)

IV.F.3 136
(1.0:1)

IV.F.2 131
(3.3:1)

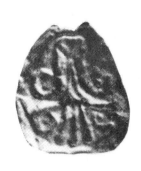

IV.F.4 137
(3.3:1)

IV.F.4 141
(1.6:1)

IV.F.4 142
(1.3:1)

PLATE 11

161

IV.F.5.a 143
(3.5:1)

IV.F.5.b 145
(3.3:1)

IV.F.5.b 150
(3.5:1)

IV.F.5.b 155
(1.9:1)

IV.G.1 162
(3.1:1)

IV.G.1 170
(1.8:1)

IV.G.2 180
(3.1:1)

IV.H.1 189
(2.1:1)

IV.H.2 191
(1.9:1)

IV.H.3.a 196
(3.3:1)

IV.H.3.a 207
(1.7:1)

IV.H.3.a 198
(3.3:1)

PLATE 13

IV.H.3.b 212
(1.7:1)

IV.H3.b 213
(1.9:1)

IV.H.3.b 209
(1.6:1)

IV.H.3.b 211
(3.4:1)

IV.H.3.b 215
(1.4:1)

IV.H.4 216
(3.2:1)

IV.H.4 217
(1.6:1)

V.B.1 224
(2.0:1)

V.A.1 220
(2.0:1)

V.A.2 221
(3.0:1)

V.B.1 223
(3.4:1)

V.C.1 228
(2.9:1)

V.C.2 231
(3.4:1)

PLATE 15

165

V.D.1 233
(3.1:1)

V.D.2 238
(3.0:1)

V.D.1 235
(3.4:1)

V.E.1.a 240
(3.2:1)

V.E.1.a 241
(3.3:1)

V.E.1.a 242
(3.2:1)

V.E.1.a 244
(3.5:1)

V.E.1.b 246
(2.2:1)

V.E.2.a 249
(0.9:1)

V.E.2.a 250
(0.9:1)

V.F.1 255
(3.4:1)

V.F.1 254
(3.3:1)

V.F.2 257
(1.6:1)

V.F.2 256
(3.4:1)

PLATE 17

167

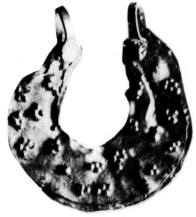

VI.A 260
(1.3:1)

VI.A 261
(1.0:1)

VI.A 262
(1.6:1)

VI.A 265
(1.3:1)

VI.A 266
(1.2:1)

VI.B.1 269
(3.3:1)

VI.B.1 270
(1.6:1)

VI.B.1 274
(1.3:1)

VI.B.1 275
(0.9:1)

VI.B.1 278
(1.6:1)

VI.B.1 287
(1.1:1)

PLATE 19

169

VI.B.1 290
(3.5:1)

VI.B.1 291
(2.0:1)

VI.B.1 296
(1.8:1)

VI.B.2 299
(3.2:1)

PLATE 20

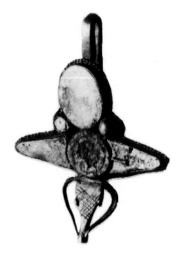

VI.C 301
(1.2:1)

VI.C 302
(1.1:1)

VI.C 303
(1.1:1)

VI.C 304
(1.8:1)

PLATE 21

171

VI.D.1 305
(0.7:1)

VI.D.1 306
(1.0:1)

VI.D.3 308
(1.5:1)

VI.F.1 310
(2.9:1)

VI.F.1 311
(2.5:1)

VI.F.2 312
(2.7:1)

VI.F.2 313
(2.5:1)

VI.F.2 314
(2.7:1)

VI.F.2 315
(2.6:1)

VI.F.2 316
(2.9:1)

VI.F.2 319
(3.4:1)

VI.F.2 322
(3.4:1)

VI.F.2 324
(1.7:1)

VI.F.2 327
(1.7:1)

PLATE 23

VI.F.3 335
(1.6:1)

VI.F.3 337
(2.2:1)

VI.F.3 338
(2.1:1)

VI.G.1 340
(1.7:1)

VI.G.2.a 342
(3.0:1)

VI.G.2.a 345
(0.7:1)

VI.G.2.b 347
(1.8:1)

VI.G.2.b 348
(1.8:1)

VI.G.2.b 351
(0.8:1)

VI.G.2.b 352
(1.5:1)

PLATE 25   175

VI.G.2.c 355
(0.9:1)

VI.G.2.c 356
(1.1:1)

INDEX OF AUTHORS AND INDIVIDUALS

INDEX OF SITES

GENERAL INDEX